2014 YEARBOOK

OF THE GENERAL ASSEMBLY

CUMBERLAND PRESBYTERIAN CHURCH

Office of the General Assembly

Cumberland Presbyterian Church

May 2014

8207 Traditional Place
Cordova (Memphis), Tennessee 38016

Published and distributed exclusively by The Discipleship Ministry Team, CPC, Memphis, Tennessee. Additional copies may be acquired through Cumberland Presbyterian Resources.

The Discipleship Ministry Team of the Ministry Council of the Cumberland Presbyterian Church is the successor organization to the Board of Christian Education of the Cumberland Presbyterian Church.

Funded, in part, by your contributions to Our United Outreach.

First Edition 2014

ISBN-13: 978-0692214145
ISBN-10: 0692214143

OUR UNITED OUTREACH
Made Possible In Part By Your Tithe To Our United Outreach

2014 YEARBOOK

General Assembly
Cumberland Presbyterian Church

Vision of Ministry

Biblically-based and Christ-centered
   born out of a specific sense of mission,
   the Cumberland Presbyterian Church strives to be true to its heritage:
   to be open to God's reforming spirit,
   to work cooperatively with the larger Body of Christ,
   and to nurture the connectional bonds that make us one.
The Cumberland Presbyterian Church seeks—to be the hands and feet of Christ in
witness and service to the world and, above all, the Cumberland Presbyterian Church
lives out the love of God to the glory of Jesus Christ.

Containing Statistics for the Year 2013

Changes Made to Other Data Through Print Time

(The Yearbook is updated periodically on our website www.cumberland.org/gao)

Cover Artwork (Women in Ministry 125th Anniversary Logo) by Joanna Bellis

Edited by Elizabeth Vaughn

TABLE OF CONTENTS

GENERAL ASSEMBLY OFFICERS

MODERATOR
THE REVEREND FOREST PROSSER
1157 MOUNTAIN CREEK ROAD
CHATTANOOGA, TN 37405
(423)877-4114
forestprosser@comcast.net

VICE MODERATOR
THE REVEREND JAMES (JAMIE) W. LIVELY
906 LYLE CIRCLE
GREENEVILLE, TN 37745
(423)798-1959
jlively@gcpchurch.org

STATED CLERK AND TREASURER
THE REVEREND MICHAEL SHARPE
8207 Traditional Place
Cordova, TN 38016
(901)276-4572
FAX (901)272-3913
msharpe@cumberland.org

ENGROSSING CLERK
THE REVEREND VERNON SANSOM
7810 Shiloh Road
Midlothian, TX 76065
(972)825-6887
vernon@sansom.us

THE BOARD OF DIRECTORS OF THE GENERAL ASSEMBLY CORPORATION

(Members whose terms expire in 2014)
(3)REV. TERRY HUNLEY, 48 Charleston Square, Jackson, TN 38305
thunley1@charter.net
(3)MS. GRACE WHITFIELD, 245 Monterey Circle, Gadsden, AL 35901
gracenaomi@aol.com
(Members whose terms expire in 2015)
(3)REV. MELISSA MALINOSKI, 9087 Fenmore Cove, Cordova, TN 38016
bobby.coleman@gmail.com
(3)MR. JERRY WEATHERSBY, 119 County Road 743, Cullman, AL 35055
jerryw@cullmanelectric.com
(Members whose terms expire in 2016)
(1)MR. TIM GARRETT, 150 Third Avenue South, Suite 2800, Nashville, TN 37201
tgarrett@bassberry.com
(1)REV. BOBBY COLEMAN, 704 E Webb Street, Mountain View, AR 72560
bobby.coleman@gmail.com

*Ecumenical Partners
+Cumberland Presbyterians in America
Numbers in parenthesis denote number of terms.

MINISTRY COUNCIL

(Members whose terms expire in 2014)
(1)REV. DONNY ACTON, 1413 Oakridge Drive, Birmingham, AL 35242
(2)REV. MICHELE GENTRY DE CORREAL, Calle 3 Norte #12-87, Armenia, Quinido,
    COLOMBIA, SOUTH AMERICA
(1)REV. LANNY JOHNSON, 120 S Mill Street, Morrison, TN 37357
(1)REV. TOM SANDERS, 4201 W Kent Street, Broken Arrow, OK 74012
(3)MR. ROY SHANKS, 3997 N 100th Street, Casey, IL 62420
(Members whose terms expire in 2015)
(2)MS. SALLY ALLEN, 3190 Gray Hawk Court, Clarksville, TN 37043
(1)MS. MARY ANN COLE, 620 Plum Springs Road, Bowling Green, KY 42101
(3)REV. CARLTON HARPER, 8764 Cody Dan Court, Ooltewah, TN 37363
(1)REV. RON MCMILLAN, 675 Kimberly Drive, Atoka, TN 38004
(2)REV. LISA SCOTT (address on file)
(Members whose terms expire in 2016)
(3)MS. JILL CARR, PO Box 1547, Lebanon, MO 65536
(2)REV. TROY GREEN, 105 Cobb Hollow Lane, Petersburg, TN 37144
(3)MS. ELIZABETH HORSLEY, 1200 Imperial Drive, Denton, TX 76201
(3)MS. GWEN RODDYE, 3728 Wittenham Drive, Knoxville, TN 37921
(3)REV. SAM ROMINES, PO Box 127, Lewisburg, KY 42256

YOUTH ADVISORY MEMBERS
MR. ETHAN MORGAN, 119 Mountain Top Lane, Cookeville, TN 38506 (Term expires in 2014)
MR. EDDIE MONTOYA, JR, 270 Windsor Drive, Roselle, IL 60172 (Term expires in 2015)
MS. CAROLINA GILLIS, 6243 Sioux Lane, Birmingham, AL 35242 (Term expires in 2016)

ADVISORY MEMBERS
REV. FOREST PROSSER, 1157 Mountain Creek Road, Chattanooga, TN 37405
REV. ROBERT D. RUSH, 17822 Deep Brook Drive, Spring, TX 77379
REV. MICHAEL SHARPE, 8207 Traditional Place, Cordova, TN 38016

COMMUNICATIONS MINISTRY TEAM

(Members whose terms expire in 2014)
(2)MS. B. DENISE ADAMS, 126 Ray, Monticello, AR 71655
(1)MRS. DUSTY SHULL, 938B North 37th Street, Paducah, KY 42001
(Members whose terms expire in 2015)
(2)REV. MICHAEL CLARK, 134 Overlook Court, Winchester, TN 37398
(2)REV. JAMES D. MCGUIRE, 220-2 Southwind Circle, Greeneville, TN 37743
(Members whose terms expire in 2016)
(1)REV. NICHOLAS CHAMBERS, 11300 Road 101, Union, MS 39365
(1)REV. STEVEN SHELTON, 7886 Farmhill Cove, Bartlett, TN 38135

*Ecumenical Partners
+Cumberland Presbyterians in America
Numbers in parenthesis denote number of terms.

DISCIPLESHIP MINISTRY TEAM

(Members whose terms expire in 2014)
(1)MS. LE ILA DIXON, 4406 John Reagan Street, Marshall, TX 75672
(1)REV. AARON FERRY, 122 Crimson Drive, Winchester, TN 37398
(2)MS. SAMANTHA HASSELL, 510 N Main Street, Sturgis, KY 42459
(Members whose terms expire in 2015)
(2)MS. JOANNA D. BELLIS, 334 Village Green Drive, Nashville, TN 37217
(1)MS. RACHEL COOK, 210 Bynum Street, Scottsboro, AL 35768
(1)REV. CHRISTIAN SMITH, 7401 Bonny Oaks Drive, Chattanooga, TN 37421
(Members whose terms expire in 2016)
(3)REV. MINDY ACTON, 1413 Oak Ridge Drive, Birmingham, AL 35242
(1)REV. NANCY MCSPADDEN, 2011 Woodridge Drive, St Peters, MO 63376
(1)REV. JOSEFINA SANCHEZ, 7 Hancock Street, Melrose, MA 02176

MISSIONS MINISTRY TEAM

(Members whose terms expire in 2014)
(1)REV. JAMES BUTTRAM, 103 Golfcrest Lane, Oak Ridge, TN 37830
(2)REV. JIMMY BYRD, 176 E Valley Road, Whitwell, TN 37397
(2)REV. RICARDO FRANCO, 7 Hancock Street, Melrose, MA 02176
(1)MRS. NANCY GORDON, 1193 Madison 522, Fredericktown, MO 63645
(3)MRS. BEVERLY STOTT, 200 East Main Street, Dresden, TN 38225
(Members whose terms expire in 2015)
(2)REV. JIM BARRY, 1405 Anna Street, Hixson, TN 37343
(1)REV. CARDELIA HOWELL-DIAMOND, 1580 Jeff Road NW, Huntsville, AL 35806
(2)MS. SHERRY POTEET, P.O. Box 313, Gilmer, TX 75644
(1)MS. MELINDA REAMS, 10 W Azalea Lane, Russellville, AR 72802
(Members whose terms expire in 2016)
(2)REV. MAKIHIKO ARASE, 3-355-4 Kamikitadai Higashiyamato-Shi, Tokyo, 207-0023 JAPAN
(1)REV. VICTOR HASSELL, 510 N Main Street, Sturgis, KY 42459
(1)MR. DOMINIC LAU, 3820 Anza Street, San Francisco, CA
(1)MS. BRITTANY MEEKS, 2664 Morning Sun Road, Cordova, TN 38016
(1)REV. CHRIS WARREN, 906 Prince Lane, Murfreesboro, TN 37129

PASTORAL DEVELOPMENT MINISTRY TEAM

(Members whose terms expire in 2014)
(1)REV. AMBER CLARK, 338 Royal Oak Drive, Winchester, TN 37398
(1)REV. DREW HAYES, 629 High Street, Union City, TN 38261
(Members whose terms expire in 2015)
(1)REV.DUAWN MEARNS, 107 Westoak Place, Hot Springs, AR 71913
(2)REV. LINDA SNELLING, 15791 State Highway W, Ada, OK 74820
(Members whose terms expire in 2016)
(2)MS. MICAIAH THOMAS, PO Box 5204 SBN 499, Princeton, NJ 08543
(1)REV. PATRICK WILKERSON, 3419 Jaydens Nest Way Apt 202, Powell, TN 37849

*Ecumenical Partners
+Cumberland Presbyterians in America
Numbers in parenthesis denote number of terms.

GENERAL ASSEMBLY BOARD OF:

I. TRUSTEES OF BETHEL UNIVERSITY

(Members whose terms expire in 2014)

(1)*DR. JANET AYERS, 314 Whitworth Way, Nashville, TN 37205
(1)*MS. LISA COLE, PO Box 198615, Nashville, TN 37219
(3)*DR. PAUL COWELL, c/o Whitestone Country Inn, 1200 Paint Rock Road, Kingston, TN 37763
(1)MR. CHESTER (CHET) DICKSON, 24 W Rivercrest Drive, Houston, TX 77042
(3)REV. LINDA H. GLENN, 49 Mason Road, Three Way, TN 38343
(1)*MR. ARTHUR (ART) LAFFER, JR., 410 Wilsonia Avenue, Nashville, TN 37205
(3)*DR. RAY MORRIS, PO Box 924528, Norcross, GA 30010
(2)MR. BOBBY OWEN, 1625 Cabot Drive, Franklin, TN 37064
(1)DR. ED PERKINS, 721 Paris Street, McKenzie, TN 38201
(2)REV. ROBERT (ROB) TRUITT, 1238 Old East Side Road, Burns, TN 37029

(Members whose terms expire in 2015)

(3)*MR. MICHAEL (MIKE) CARY, 181 Angel Cove, Huntingdon, TN 38344
(2)*MR. ANDY CREIGHTON, PO Box 1467, Smyrna, TN 37167
(2)MR. CHARLIE GARRETT, 107 Willow Green Drive, Jackson, TN 38305
(1)+REV. ELTON C. HALL, SR., 305 Tiffton Circle, Hewitt, TX 76643
(1)REV. MARK S. HESTER, 763 Finn Long Road, Friendsville, TN 37737
(3)*MS. CHARLENE P. JONES, 137 Moore Avenue W, McKenzie, TN 38201
(1)MS. DEWANNA LATIMER, 1077 Jr. Jones Road, Humboldt, TN 38343
(2)REV. EUGENE LESLIE, 13155 Center Hill Road, Olive Branch, MS 38654
(1)*MS. VIOLA MILLER, 1614 5th Avenue N., Nashville, TN 37208

(Members whose terms expire in 2016)

(1)MR. JEFF AMREIN, 11711 Paramont Way, Prospect, KY 40059
(3)DR. LARRY A. BLAKEBURN, 230 Heathridge Drive, Dyersburg, TN 38024
(2)*JUDGE BEN CANTRELL, 415 Church Street #2513, Nashville, TN 37219
(2)+DR. AMY DANIEL, 3125 Searcy Drive, Huntsville, AL 35810
(3)MR. LAWRENCE (LADD) DANIEL, 13023 Taylorcrest, Houston, TX 77079
(1)MR. BILL DOBBINS 5716 Quest Ridge Road, Franklin, TN 37064
(3)DR. JAMES (JIMMY) M. LATIMER, 3381 Moss Rose Drive, Memphis, TN 38115
(2)DR. ROBERT LOW, c/o New Prime, Inc., 2740 W Mayfair Avenue, Springfield, MO 65803
(3)MR. BEN T. SURBER, 1145 Hico Road, McKenzie, TN 38201

Trustee Emeritus – Dr. Vera Low, 3653 Prestwick Court, Springfield, MO 65809 (deceased)

II. TRUSTEES OF CUMBERLAND PRESBYTERIAN CHILDREN'S HOME

(Members whose terms expire in 2014)

(2)+MS. MAMIE HALL, 305 Tiffton Circle, Hewitt, TX 76643
(2)REV. YOONG KIM, 8601 Dogwood Road, Germantown, TN 38139
(3)REV. NORLAN SCRUDDER, 29688 South 534 Road, Park Hill, OK 74451
(1)MS. TIFFANY SMITH, 2901 Corporate Circle, Flower Mound, TX 75028
(2)REV. DON TABOR, 9611 Mitchell Place, Brentwood, TN 37027

(Members whose terms expire in 2015)

(2)*MS. KAY GOODMAN, 1042 Bobcat Road, Sanger, TX 76266
(3)MS. PAT HUFF, 249 Rancho Drive, Saginaw, TX 76179
(2)REV. MELISSA KNIGHT, 5730 Haley Road, Meridian, MS 39305
(3)MS. RUBY LETSON, 2921 Alexander, Florence, AL 35633
(2)*MR. BARON H. SMITH, 3401 Hasland Drive, Flower Mound, TX 75022

*Ecumenical Partners
+Cumberland Presbyterians in America
Numbers in parenthesis denote number of terms.

(Members whose terms expire in 2016)
(1)MR. RICHARD DEAN, 2140 Cove Circle North, Gadsden, AL 35903
(2)MS. PATRICIA LONG, 525 E Oak Street, Aledo, TX 76008
(3)REV. ALFONSO MARQUEZ, 389 Bethel Drive, Lenoir City, TN 37772
(3)MR. MICKEY SHELL, 2143 Griderfield-Ladd Road, Pine Bluff, AR 71601

III. TRUSTEES OF HISTORICAL FOUNDATION

(Members whose terms expire in 2014)
(2)+MS. EDNA BARNETT, 7 Breezewood Cove, Jackson, TN 38305
(1)MR. MICHAEL FARE, 401 E Deanna Lane, Nixa, MO 65714
(1)*MS. DOROTHY HAYDEN, 3103 Carolina Avenue, Bessemer, AL 35020
(2)+REV. RICK WHITE, 124 Towne West, Lorena, TX 76655
(Members whose terms expire in 2015)
(3)REV. TOMMY JOBE, 807 Rockwood Drive, Nolensville, TN 37135
(2)DR. SIDNEY L. SWINDLE, 4407 Swann Avenue, Tampa, FL 33609
(Members whose terms expire in 2016)
(3)+MS. VANESSA BARNHILL, 819 King Street, Sturgis, KY 42459
(3)MS. PAMELA DAVIS, 5111 County Road 7545, Lubbock, TX 79424
(3)+MS. NAOMI KING, 3850 Millsfield Highway, Dyersburg, TN 38024 (resigned)
(2)MS. MARY KATHRYN KIRKPATRICK, 401 1/2 Henley-Perry Drive, Marshall, TX 75670
(3)MS. SIDNEY MILTON, 27 Kalee Lane, Calvert City, KY 42029

IV. TRUSTEES OF MEMPHIS THEOLOGICAL SEMINARY OF THE CUMBERLAND PRESBYTERIAN CHURCH

(Members whose terms expire in 2014)
(3)*REV. D. TOM BELL Jr., PO Box 4286, Huntsville, AL 35815
(2)REV. DOY DANIELS Jr., 6083 S First Street, Milan, TN 38358
(1)*REV. ROBERT MARBLE, 515 Shamrock Drive, Little Rock, AR 72205
(2)MS. PAT MEEKS, 8540 Edney Ridge Drive, Cordova, TN 38016
(1)REV. JENNIFER NEWELL, 2322 Marco Circle, Chattanooga, TN 37421
(2)REV. ROBERT M. SHELTON, 7128 Lakehurst Avenue, Dallas, TX 75230
(2)+DR. JOE WARD, 2620 Rabbit Lane, Madison, AL 35758
(2)*MS. RUBY WHARTON, 1183 E Parkway South, Memphis, TN 38114
(Members whose terms expire in 2015)
(2)REV. KEVIN BRANTLEY, 729 Old Hodgenville Road, Greensburg, KY 42743
(3)REV. JODY HILL, 4030 St Andrew Circle, Corinth, MS 38834
(3)MS. JAN HOLMES, 5209 87th Street, Lubbock, TX 79424
(2)MR. MARK MADDOX, 225 Oak Drive, Dresden, TN 38225
(1)MS. SONDRA RODDY, 2583 Hedgerow Lane, Clarksville, TN 37043
(2)MR. TAKAYOSHI SHIRAI, 25 Minami Kibogaoka Asahi-ku, Yokohama, Kanagawa-ken 241-0824 JAPAN
(1)*REV. MELVIN CHARLES SMITH, 1263 Haynes Street, Memphis, TN 38114
(1)*MS. LATISHA TOWNS, The Med, 877 Jefferson Avenue, Memphis, TN 38103
(Members whose terms expire in 2016)
(2)MR. MICHAEL R. ALLEN, 149 Windwood Circle, Alabaster, AL 35007
(1)*MR. JOHNNIE COOMBS, PO Box 127, Blue Mountain, MS 38610
(2)MS. DIANE DICKSON, 24 West Rivercrest, Houston, TX 77042
(2)*MR. HARVEY G. FERGUSON, 630 Gaines Road, Hernando, MS 38682
(3)*MR. DAN HATZENBUEHLER, 1544 Carr Avenue, Memphis, TN 38104
(1)*DR. RICK KIRCHOFF, 2044 Thorncroft Drive, Germantown, TN 38138
(3)MR. TIM ORR, 1591 Laura Lane, Dyersburg, TN 38024

*Ecumenical Partners
+Cumberland Presbyterians in America
Numbers in parenthesis denote number of terms.

(2)*DR. INETTA RODGERS, 1824 S Parkway E, Memphis, TN 38114
(3)*MRS. K.C. WARREN, 215 Buena Vista Place, Memphis, TN 38112

V. STEWARDSHIP, FOUNDATION AND BENEFITS

(Members whose terms expire in 2014)
(2)MR. CHARLES DAY, 9312 Owensboro Road, Falls of Rough, KY 40119
(2)MS. SYLVIA HALL, 930 Sherry Circle, Hixson, TN 37343
(2)MR. JACKIE SATTERFIELD, 2303 County Road 730, Cullman, AL 35055
(3)MRS. DEBRA SHANKS, 3997 North 100th Street, Casey, IL 62420
(Members whose terms expire in 2015)
(2)MR. ANDREW B. FRAZIER, JR., 107 Doris Street, Camden, TN 38320
(3)MR. ROBERT LATIMER, RR 1 Box 123, Miami, MO 65344
(1)MR. MICHAEL ST. JOHN, 324 Carriage Place, Lebanon, MO 65536
(Members whose terms expire in 2016)
(3)MR. CHARLES G. FLOYD, 1617 Championship Drive, Franklin, TN 37064
(1)REV. CHARLES (BUDDY) POPE, 2391 Fairfield Pike, Shelbyville, TN 37160
(2)MS. SUE RICE, 1301 Brooker Road, Brandon, FL 33511
(2)MS. DEBBIE SHELTON, 1255 MG England Road, Manchester, TN 37355

GENERAL ASSEMBLY COMMISSIONS:

I. MILITARY CHAPLAINS AND PERSONNEL

(1) Term Expires in 2014–REV. MARY MCCASKEY BENEDICT, 69 Lennox Court, Richmond Hill, GA 31324
(2) Term Expires in 2015–REV. LOWELL RODDY, 2583 Hedgerow Lane, Clarksville, TN 37043
(1) Term Expires in 2016–REV. CASSANDRA THOMAS, 1920 Dancy Street, Fayetteville, NC 28301

These three persons and the Stated Clerk represent the denomination as members of the Presbyterian Council for Chaplains and Military Personnel, 4125 Nebraska Avenue NW, Washington, DC 20016

GENERAL ASSEMBLY COMMITTEES

I. JUDICIARY

(Members whose terms expire in 2014)
(1)REV. PERRYN RICE, 537 Edgerowe Court, Cookeville, TN 38506
    perryn@cookevillecpchurch.org
(1)REV. ROBERT D. RUSH, 17822 Deep Brook Drive, Spring, TX 77379
    rushrd74@comcast.net
(2)MR. WENDELL THOMAS, JR., 1200 Paradise Drive, Powell, TN 37849
    volbaby@comcast.net
(Members whose terms expire in 2015)
(1)REV. ANNETTA CAMP, 2263 Mill Creek Road, Halls, TN 38040
    anetta@cumberlandchurch.com

(3)MR. CHARLES DAWSON, PO Box 904, Scottsboro, AL 35768
   rdpfcd@scottsboro.org
(2)MS. KIMBERLY SILVUS, 1128 Madison Street, Clarksville, TN 37040
   kgsilvus@gmail.com
(Members whose terms expire in 2016)
(3)REV. SHERRY LADD, 4521 Turkey Creek Road, Williamsport, TN 38487
   revsherryladd@gmail.com
(2)REV. ANDY MCCLUNG, 919 Dickinson Street, Memphis, TN 38107
   scubarev@att.net
(3)MS. FELICIA WALKUP, 179 Mary Anne Lane, Manchester, TN 37355
   fbwalkup@gmail.com

II. JOINT COMMITTEE ON AMENDMENTS

The committee consists of five members of the Judiciary Committee of the Cumberland Presbyterian Church in America and the Cumberland Presbyterian Church.

III. NOMINATING

(Members whose terms expire in 2014)
(1)MRS. FRANCES DAWSON, PO Box 904, Scottsboro, AL 35768
   rdpfcd@scottsboro.org
(1)REV. DON NUNN, 203 Bridgers Hill Road, Longview, TX 75604
   dwnunn@earthlink.net
(1)MR. KEN SMITH, 6197 34th Street, Lubbock, TX 79407
   knsmth@earthlink.net
(1)REV. JESSE THORNTON, 122 E Cherry Street, Chandler, IN 47610
   jessthornton@msn.com
(Members whose terms expire in 2015)
(1)MR. RICK GAMBLE, 2430 Mount View Road, Manchester, TN 37355
   gamble-ra@charter.net
(1)REV. ISAAC GRAY, 1211 AR 223 Highway, Pineville, AR 72566
   revgray08@gmail.com
(Members whose terms expire in 2016)
(1)MS. NANCY BEAN, 3510 Clubhouse Road, Somerset, KY 42503
   beann@bethelu.edu
(1)REV. CHARLES MCCASKEY, 679 Canter Lane, Cookeville, TN 38501
   charles@cookevillecpchurch.org
(1)REV. JIMMY PEYTON, 1455 County Road 643, Cullman, AL 35055
   jakjpeyton@att.net
(1)MS. MARJORIE SHANNON, 2307 Littlemore Drive, Cordova, TN 38016
   margieshannon@att.net

IV. OUR UNITED OUTREACH COMMITTEE

(Members whose terms expire in 2014)
(2)MS. SHARON RESCH, PO Box 383, Dongola, IL 62926
(2)REV. WILLIAM RUSTENHAVEN III, PO Box 1303, Marshall, TX 75671
(Members whose terms expire in 2015)
(1)MR. RANDY WEATHERSBY, 1502 Pinecrest Street NW, Cullman, AL 35055
(1)MS. ROBIN WILLS, 4607 E Richmond Shop Road, Lebanon, TN 37090
(Members whose terms expire in 2016)
(3)MR. RON D. GARDNER, 8668 Wood Mills Drive W, Cordova, TN 38016

*Ecumenical Partners
+Cumberland Presbyterians in America
Numbers in parenthesis denote number of terms.

V. PLACE OF MEETING

THE STATED CLERK OF THE GENERAL ASSEMBLY
THE MODERATOR OF THE GENERAL ASSEMBLY
A REPRESENTATIVE OF WOMEN'S MINISTRIES OF THE MISSIONS MINISTRY TEAM

VI. UNIFIED COMMITTEE ON THEOLOGY AND SOCIAL CONCERNS

(Members whose terms expire in 2014)
(1)+DR. NANCY FUQUA, 1963 County Road 406, Towncreek, AL 35672
    fug23@bellsouth.net
(1)REV. RANDY JACOB, PO Box 158, Broken Bow, OK 74728
    chocpres@pine-net.com
(3)+REV. JACKIE LANG, 904 35th Avenue, Tuscaloosa, AL 35401
(2)+REV. NOVALENE SITGRAVES, 3345 Grand Avenue, Louisville, KY 40211
(Members whose terms expire in 2015)
(1)DR. STEVE PARRISH, 4610 Dunn Avenue, Memphis, TN 38117
    sparrish@memphisseminary.edu
(1)MR. DAVID PHILLIPS-BURK, 1065 Legacy Lake Circle 104, Collierville, TN 38017
    dlphillipsburk@aol.com
(1)REV. SHELIA O'MARA, 533 Loughton Lane, Arnold, MD 21012
    chaplainshelia@aol.com
(Members whose terms expire in 2016)
(3)MS. LEZLIE P. DANIEL, 13023 Taylorcrest Road, Houston, TX 77079
    lululoop@me.com
(2)+MRS. JIMMIE DODD, c/o Hopewell CPCA, 4100 Millsfield Highway, Dyersburg, TN 38024
    dodd125@gmail.com
(2)REV. BYRON FORESTER, 2376 Eastwood Place, Memphis, TN 38112
    bforester@bellsouth.net
(2)+DR. CHARLES E. REESE, 2903 Grand Avenue, Dallas, TX 79215
    creese213@yahoo.com
(1)REV. JOHN A. SMITH, 916 Allen Road, Nashville, TN 37214
    john.a.smith.81@gmail.com
(2)+ELDER JOY WALLACE, 6940 Marvin D Love Freeway, Dallas, TX 75237
    jwallace@wlgllc.net
President of Memphis Theological Seminary - Ex-officio Member

OTHER DENOMINATIONAL PERSONNEL

REPRESENTATIVES TO:

American Bible Society: REV. MICHAEL SHARPE, 8207 Traditional Place, Cordova, TN 38016

Caribbean and North American Area Council, World Communion of Reformed Churches:
STATED CLERK MICHAEL SHARPE, 8207 Traditional Place, Cordova, TN 38016

(Member whose terms expire in 2014)
(2)MS. LAURIE SHARPE, 3423 Summerdale Drive, Bartlett, TN 38133

LIVING GENERAL ASSEMBLY MODERATORS

2013—REV. FOREST PROSSER, 1157 Mountain Creek Road, Chattanooga, TN 37405
2012—REV. ROBERT D. RUSH, 17822 Deep Brook Drive, Spring, TX 77379
2011—REV. DON M. TABOR, 9611 Mitchell Place, Brentwood, TN 37027
2010—REV. BOYCE WALLACE, Cra 101 No 15-93, Cali, Colombia, South America
2009—ELDER SAM SUDDARTH, 206 Ha Le Koa Court, Smyrna, TN 37167
2008—REV. JONATHAN CLARK, 88 Woodcrest Drive, Winchester, TN 37398
2007—REV. FRANK WARD, 8207 Traditional Place, Cordova, TN 38016
2006—REV. DONALD HUBBARD, 2128 Campbell Station Road, Knoxville, TN 37932
2005—REV. LINDA H. GLENN, 49 Mason Road, Threeway, TN 38343
2004—REV. EDWARD G. SIMS, 2161 N. Meadows Drive, Clarksville, TN 37043
2003—REV. CHARLES MCCASKEY, 679 Canter Lane, Cookeville, TN 38501
2001—REV. RANDOLPH JACOB, 610 W. Adams Street, Broken Bow, OK 74728
1999—ELDER GWENDOLYN G. RODDYE, 3728 Wittenham Drive, Knoxville, TN 37921
1998—REV. MASAHARU ASAYAMA, 3-15-9 Higashi, Kunitachi-shi, Tokyo, JAPAN
1996—REV. MERLYN A. ALEXANDER, 80 N. Hampton Lane, Jackson, TN 38305
1995—REV. CLINTON O. BUCK, 4986 Warwick, Memphis, TN 38117
1993—REV. ROBERT M. SHELTON, 7128 Lakehurst Avenue, Dallas, TX 75230
1992—REV. JOHN DAVID HALL, 109 Oddo Lane SE, Huntsville, AL 35802
1990—REV. THOMAS D. CAMPBELL, PO Box 315, Calico Rock, AR 72519
1989—REV. WILLIAM RUSTENHAVEN, Jr., 703 W. Burleson, Marshall, TX 75670
1988—ELDER BEVERLY ST. JOHN, 806 Evansdale Drive, Nashville, TN 37220
1987—ELDER WILBUR S. WOOD, Box 122, Palestine, AR 72372
1985—REV. VIRGIL H. TODD, 3095 Glengarry Road, Memphis, TN 38128
1982—REV. WILLIAM A. RAWLINS, 3100 Cook Lane, Longview, TX 75604
1981—REV. W. JEAN RICHARDSON, 7533 Lancashire, Powell, TN 37849
1978—REV. JOSE FAJARDO, 101 Vanderbilt, Waxahachie, TX 75165
1975—REV. ROY E. BLAKEBURN, 111 Park Place, Greeneville, TN 37743
1969—REV. J. DAVID HESTER, 1212 Woodbury Court, Knoxville, TN 37922-6000

*Ecumenical Partners
+Cumberland Presbyterians in America
Numbers in parenthesis denote number of terms.

SYNOD AND PRESBYTERY CLERKS

SYNOD OF GREAT RIVERS

The Reverend Andy McClung
919 Dickinson Street
Memphis, TN 38107
(901)606-6615
scubarev@att.net

Arkansas Presbytery (GRAR)

Janie Stamps
4008 Logan Lane
Fort Smith, AR 72903
(479)478-0161 (Home)
(479)883-5633 (Cell)
(479)782-0454 FAX
bjstamps@msn.com (Home)

Missouri Presbytery (GRMI)

Larry Nottingham
PO Box 281
Stockton, MO 65785
(417)276-3792
mopresbyterycpc@yahoo.com

West Tennessee Presbytery (GRWT)

The Reverend C. William Jones, Jr.
109 Lakewood Drive
Lexington, TN 38351
(731)967-7618 (Home)
(731)968-7176 (Church)
patfreelandjones@yahoo.com

**SYNOD OF MIDWEST
(MI)**

The Reverend Carroll Richards
210 Allison Drive
Lincoln, IL 62656
(217)732-7894
(217)732-7894 (FAX)
midwestsynod@comcast.net

Covenant Presbytery (MICO)

Reese Baker
1175 Rowland Cemetery Road
Fredonia, KY 42411
(270)545-3483
rbaker@kynet.biz

Cumberland Presbytery (MICU)

The Reverend Darrell Pickett
113 Woods Drive
Glasgow, KY 42141
(270)834-6102
dpickett@glasgow-ky.com

North Central Presbytery (MINC)

The Reverend Ralph Blevins
1623 County Road 2375 E
Geff, IL 62842
(618)854-2494
statedclerk@ncpwebsite.com

SYNOD AND PRESBYTERY CLERKS

MISSION SYNOD
(MS)

Joseph Owen Smith
119 Pine Island Drive
Marshall, TX 75672
(903)928-9887
otsmith@gmx.com

Andes Presbytery (MSAN)

The Reverend Diana Valdez
Calle 65 #98-45, interior 174
Altos de la Macarena
(Robledo-LaCampina)
Medellin, Antioquia
Colombia, South America
(57)313-826-3153
dianamariavaldezduque@gmail.com

Cauca Valley Presbytery (MSCA)

Jairo Lopez
Paraiso la Morada
5ta Etapa, Casa 36, Jamundi
Colombia, South America
011-5726-615410

Choctaw Presbytery (MSCH)

The Reverend Virginia Espinoza
PO Box 132
Boswell, OK 74727
(580)434-7971
vespinoza@choctawnation.com

Presbytery del Cristo (MSDC)

Karen Avery
9420 Layton Court NE
Albuquerque, NM 87111
(505)821-7668
kavery5@comcast.com

Hong Kong Presbytery (MSHK)

Eliza Yl Chui
2/F Welland Plaza
188 Nam Chong Street
Sham Shui Po, Hong Kong
(011)852-2783-8923
(011)852-2771-2726 FAX
elizaylyau@yahoo.com.hk

Japan Presbytery (MSJA)

Takoyoshi Shirai
25 Minami Kobogaoka
Asahi-ku Yokohama
Kanagawa-ken
241-0824 JAPAN
(011)81-45-361-0059
cpc_japan@ybb.ne.jp

Red River Presbytery (MSRR)

The Reverend Vernon Sansom
7810 Shiloh Road
Midlothian, TX 76065
(972)825-6887
vernon@sansom.us

SYNOD AND PRESBYTERY CLERKS

Trinity Presbytery (MSTR)

Paula Hayes
PO Box 5449
Longview, TX 75608
(903)759-1896 (Home)
(903)759-0092 (Work)
phayes7442@aol.com

SYNOD OF SOUTHEAST
(SE)

The Reverend Forest Prosser
1157 Mountain Creek Road
Chattanooga, TN 37405
(423)877-4114
forestprosser@comcast.net

Cumberland East Coast Presbytery (SEEC)

The Reverend Forest Prosser
1157 Mountain Creek Road
Chattanooga, TN 37405
(423)877-4114
forestprosser@comcast.net

Presbytery of East Tennessee (SEET)

The Reverend Ronald L. Longmire
2041 Eckles Drive
Maryville, TN 37804
(865)984-1647
ronaldlongmire@charter.net

Grace Presbytery (SEGR)   INTERIM

The Reverend J. Don Clark
1601 Lake Ridge Circle
Birmingham, AL 35216
(205)942-4054
jdsjcl@charter.net

Hope Presbytery (SEHO)

Mr. Gerald McGee
9491 Highway 101
Lexington, AL 35648
(256)229-5613
nebo9491@gmail.com

Robert Donnell Presbytery (SERD)

Frances Dawson
PO Box 904, 221 S Market St.
Scottsboro, AL 35768
(256)244-0554 (Cell)
(256)259-0904 (Business)(FAX)
rdpfcd@scottsboro.org

Tennessee-Georgia Presbytery (SETG)

Tracey Gann
475 Sequachee Drive
Whitwell, TN 37397
(423)309-1497
tngastatedclerk@gmail.com

SYNOD AND PRESBYTERY CLERKS

TENNESSEE SYNOD
(TN)

The Reverend Charles McCaskey
565 East Tenth Street
Cookeville, TN 38501
(931)526-6585 (Office)
(931)372-2620 FAX
charles@cookevillecpchurch.org

Columbia Presbytery (TNCO)

The Reverend Charles (Buddy) Pope
2391 Fiarfield Pike
Shelbyville, TN 37160
(931)680-4334
pope6897@yahoo.com

Murfreesboro Presbytery (TNMU)

The Reverend Charles McCaskey
565 East Tenth Street
Cookeville, TN 38501
(931)526-6585 (Office)
(931)528-2273 FAX
charles@cookevillecpchurch.org

Nashville Presbytery (TNNA)

The Reverend Fred Polacek
907 Graham Drive
Old Hickory, TN 37138
(615)754-5328 (Home)
nashvillepresb.sc.treasurer@gmail.com

MINISTERS GAINED AND LOST IN 2013

MINISTERS RECEIVED BY ORDINATION

NAME	PRESBYTERY	DATE
Buchanan, Larry	Covenant	12/15/13
Chen, Steven	del Cristo	09/29/13
Jones, Victor	Arkansas	10/13/13
Mata, Isaac	del Cristo	10/20/13
Ricketts, Roger	Cumberland	09/14/13
Rincon, Lyvia	del Cristo	10/20/13
Smith, James	Robert Donnell	10/06/13

MINISTERS REINSTATED OR RECEIVED FROM OTHER DENOMINATIONS

NAME	PRESBYTERY	CHURCH	DATE
Lee, Timothy Daniel	Grace	Southern Baptist	10/18/13

MINISTERS WHO HAVE MOVED TO OTHER DENOMINATIONS

NAME	DENOMINATION	DATE
Allison, Mark	Baptist	10/05/13

MINISTERS DROPPED FROM MINISTRY BY PRESBYTERY

NAME	PRESBYTERY	DATE

MILITARY CHAPLAINS

Acuff, David (M8)
4969 Quail Lane
Columbia, SC 29206
david.acuff@us.army.mil
(803)790-9151   TNNA#7300

Headrick, Anthony (M8)
3327 N Eagle Road Ste 110-132
Meridian, ID 83646
chaps2a@yahoo.com
(619)435-0825   SEGR#0100

LeFavor, David E (M8)
4100 W 3rd Street
Dayton, OH 45428
david.lefavor@med.va.gov
(813)613-4133   SEGR#0100

Logan, Jason B (M8)
4895 Diggins Drive
Fort Meade, ND 20755
jason.b.logan@us.army.mil
(410)305-8494   TNMU#7200

McBeth, David L (M8)
PSC Box 20085
Camp LeJeune, NC 28542-0085
david.mcbeth@usmc.mil
(910)451-2375   SEET#2200

Nash, Zachary (M8)
11585 Alamo Ranch Parkway
San Antonio, TX 78253
pastorzac@yahoo.com
(580)213-7211   GRWT#9100

O'Mara, Shelia (M8)
533 Loughton Lane
Arnold, MD 21012
chaplainshelia@aol.com
(410)757-5713   MSDC#8700

Prewitt, Curtis (M8)
3712 Carmel Lane
Paducah, KY 42003
prewitt@apex.net
(270)554-9779   MICO#3400

Santillano, Ray Paul (M8)
12313 Olga Mapula
El Paso, TX 79936
ramon.santillano@us.army.mil
(915)500-4928   MSTR#8704

Sumrall, Phil (M9)
107 Barnhardt Circle
Fort Oglethorpe, GA 30742
phil.sumrall@gmail.com
(423)903-1938   SETG#2100

NON-MILITARY CHAPLAINS

Aden, Marty (M9)
202 Bennington Place
Wilmington, NC 28412
maden@ec.rr.com
(910)274-8465   MSRR#8400

Anderson, Lisa (M9)
1790 Faxon Avenue
Memphis, TN 38112
anderli@aol.com
(901)725-0924   GRWT#9305

Bone, Leslie (M9)
16504 George Franklyn Drive
Independence, MO 64055
lesliebone@comcast.net
(816)373-6625   GRMI#4100

Bowers, Sharon G (M9)
1800 Post Road Apt 612
San Marcos, TX 78666
sharon.bowers@gmail.com
(512)230-7078   MSTR#8100

Brown, Mark (M9)
752 Hawthorne Street
Memphis, TN 38107
dmbrown@utmem.edu
(901)274-1474   GRWT#9100

Carter, Patricia (M9)
2509 Decatur Stratton Road
Decatur, MS 39327
revtree@yahoo.com
(601)635-4120   SEGR#0100

Cook, Lisa (M9)
4101 Dalemere Court
Nashville, TN 37207
tgoose@comcast.net
(615)868-4118   TNNA#7300

Diamond, James (M9)
PO Box 1220
Smyrna, TN 37167
FAX: (615)220-1077
jameswdiamond@yahoo.com
(615)220-2341   TNMU#7229

Drylie, James (M9)
512 JE Blaydes Parkway
Atoka, TN 38004
(901)837-1627   GRWT#9100

Ferrol, Ruben (M9)
1823 Straford Court
Allentown, PA 18103
rubeferrol@msn.com
(610)966-7289   MSRR#8400

Gentry, Michele (M9)
Calle 3 Norte #12-87
Armenia
Quindio, Colombia
South America
gentry.andes@yahoo.com
(576)745-1614   MSAN#8900

Hames, Anne (M9)
118 Paris Street
Mc Kenzie, TN 38201
FAX: (731)352-4069
hamesa@bethel-college.edu
(731)352-4066   GRWT#9100

Hartung, J Thomas (M9)
2291 Americus Boulevard W Apt 1
Clearwater, FL 33763
revtom6@aol.com
(727)797-2882   SEGR#0100

Jackson, Terry (M9)
1461 Mt Pleasant Road
Hernando, MS 38632
tjackson48@comcast.net
(662)429-9741   GRWT#9100

Kelly, Patrick L (M9)
1449 Rainbow Road
Mountain City, TN 37683-2110
(423)727-4067   SEET#2200

Kennemer, Darren (M9)
8828 Highway 119
Alabaster, AL 35007
(205)663-3152
darren.kennemer@va.gov   SERD#0107

Knight, Melissa (M9)
5730 Haley Road
Meridian, MS 39305
(530)632-6472
revlissa@gmail.com   MSDC#8700

Lain, Judy (M9)
1928 Pine Ridge Drive
Bedford, TX 76021-4650
(817)660-8020   MSRR#8400

Lounsbury-Lombard, Kristi (M9)
902 Clearview
Krum, TX 76249
kristilounsbury@gmail.com
(940)435-5077   MSRR#8400

McCarty, John (M9)
305 W Martindale Drive
Marshall, TX 75672
(423)827-6060   SETG#2100

McClung, Tiffany (M9)
919 Dickinson Street
Memphis, TN 38107
tmcclung@memphisseminary.edu
(901)606-6604   GRWT#9100

McKee, Margaret (M9)
774 Beasley Street
Memphis, TN 38111
(901)323-2339   GRWT#9100

McSpadden, Nancy (M9)
2011 Woodridge Drive
St Peters, MO 63376
revnancy77@gmail.com
(870)612-0067   GRAR#1100

Melson, Glenda (M9)
634 W Fremont Road
Lebanon, MO 65536
glendamelson@fidnet.com
(417)588-2758   GRMI#4309

Messer, James C (M9)
3653 Old Madisonville Road
Henderson, KY 42420
jcmess@hotmail.com
(270)827-0711   MINC#5304

Mills, David M (M9)
528 County Road 322
Bertram, TX 78605
(512)355-3511   MSTR#8100

Oliver, Lisa (M9)
110 Allen Drive
Hendersonville, TN 37075
( )   TNMU#7200

Pickett, Pat (M9)
1460 Cheatham Dam Road
Ashland City, TN 37015
(615)792-4973   TNNA#7300

Rice, Keith (M9)
PO Box 100
Itasca, TX 76055
rsvkeith@yahoo.com
(254)087-2418   MSRR#8400

Richards, Carroll (M9)
210 Allison Drive
Lincoln, IL 62656
FAX: (217)732-7894
dr_cr@comcast.net
(217)732-7894   MINC#5200

Ruggia, Mario (Bud) (M9)
603 Rumsey Street
Kiowa, KS 67070
ruggia@aol.com
(620)825-4509   MSRR#8400

Scott, Lisa (M9)
lascott1979@att.net
(816)332-0604   GRMI#4100

Scott, Jerry (M9)
2310 Sentell Drive
Maryville, TN 37803
dmjlscott@yahoo.com
(865)809-2621   SEET#2200

Travis, Kermit (M9)
3220 Sharon Highway
Dresden, TN 38225
(731)364-2315   GRWT#9415

Truax, Robert Lee, Jr (M9)
2989 Champions Drive Apt 204
Lakeland, TN 38002
revtruax@yahoo.com
(901)266-5927   GRWT#9100

Varner, Susan (M9)
2766 N Rockcreek Parkway
Cordova, TN 38016
smvarner76@yahoo.com
(901)371-1249   TNNA#7300

West, David (M9)
2027 Lucille Street
Lebanon, TN 37087
(217)732-7568   MINC#5405

Winslett, Don (M9)
Baptist Hospital Pastoral Care
1000 W Moreno Street
Pensacola, FL 32521
(217)732-7568   MINC#5405

MEMORIAL ROLL OF MINISTERS

IN MEMORY OF
MINISTERS LOST BY DEATH

NAME	PRESBYTERY	AGE	DATE
Andrews, Leonard	Nashville	93	05/16/13
Berry, Ephraim A	Cumberland	91	05/07/13
Brown, Richard C	Grace	86	11/16/13
Broyles, Lon B	East Tennessee	68	09/30/13
Butler, George A	West Tennessee	73	08/10/13
Dixon, Robert W	Covenant	78	10/10/13
Hensley, Howard L	Missouri	69	07/23/13
McGregor, David	Columbia	86	01/23/14
Rodriguez, Paul	Cauca Valley		03/10/14
Tant, Robert H	Grace	76	02/19/13
Warren, George H	Hope	92	12/09/13
Watson, David E	Murfreesboro	81	11/04/13
Wilkins, Marvin E	Columbia	65	04/01/14

SURVIVING SPOUSES OF MINISTERS BY PRESBYTERY
(Deceased spouse in parenthesis.)

ARKANSAS

Batholomew, Maudline
(Harold Bartholomew)
  13395 Highway 265
  Prairie Grove, AR 72753
  (479)846-2850

DuBose, Sandra
(Paul DuBose)
  207 7th Street
  Cotter, AR 72626
  (870) 373-1021

Elkins, Patsy
(Robert Harold Elkins)
  525 Elkins Road
  Magazine, AR 72943
  (479)637-3723
  robtelkins@cej.net

Faith, Jeannine
(Charles Faith)
  4710 Mount Olive Road
  Melbourne, AR 72556
  (870)368-4069

Hollenbeck, Linda
(Edward B. Hollenbeck)
  409 Carson Drive
  Benton, AR 72015
  (501)315-9737

Kinslow, Jean
(Alfred Kinslow)
  29209 Perdido Beach Blvd
  Vista Bella #701
  Orange Beach, AL 36561
  (251)981-8385

Wynne, Glenna
(W. J. Wynne)
  1501 W Block
  El Dorado, AR 71730
  (870)863-9444

CAUCA VALLEY

Munoz, Aliria Correal de
(Gerardo Munoz)
  5405 Robelene Drive
  Metaire, LA 70003
  gwilson54@cox.net

Yepez, Mrs. (??)
(Juan Yepez)
  Colombia, South America

COLUMBIA

Bates, Betty Ruth
(Harold Bates)
  204 Apache Trail
  Columbia, TN 38401
  (931)381-6737

Burns, Angela C.
(Bobby G. Burns)
  328 Dunnaway Road
  Shelbyville, TN 37160
  (931)294-5105

Gibson, Ernestine
(Charles Gibson)
  33 Hilldale Church Road
  Fayetteville, TN 37334
  (931)433-2666

Green, Marie
(Odis Green)
  18 Oakwood Street NW
  Rome, GA 30165
  (706)291-1738

Nugent, Sue
(Samuel Ellis Nugent)
  2124 Carrie Court
  Columbia, TN 38401
  (931)490-7571
  sue@cadprodinc.com

Sain, Sally
(Edwin Sain)
  27 Hilltop Road
  Fayetteville, TN 37334
  (931)433-8708
  ssain@fayelectric.com

Seaton, Whitney
(Charlie Seaton)
  111 W Hardin Drive
  Columbia, TN 38401
  (931)388-0319

Smith, Patricia
(Cordell Smith)
  5808 Robertson Avenue
  Nashville, TN 37209
  (615)731-0938

Walker, Lilly Mae
(James Finis Walker)
  704 Woods Drive
  Columbia, TN 38401

Wilkins, Dianne S
(Marvin Edward Wilkins)
  209 Mackey Street
  Rogersville, AL 35652
  (256)247-5557
  marvinwilkins@msn.com

COVENANT

Atchison, Cheryl
(Dean Atchison)
  206 Marsha Drive
  Ledbetter, KY 42058

Cannon, Joyce
(Chester Cannon)
  1026 W Center Street
  Madisonville, KY 42431

Clark, Eileen
(Morris Clark)
  8720 State Route 132 W
  Clay, KY 42404

Dixon, Sonja
(Robert Dixon)
  8550 Lafayette Road
  Hopkinsville, KY 42240
  (270)886-7647
  sonjadixon@earthlink.net

Lindsey, Pearl
(Eugene Lindsey)
  311 Oak Hurst Circle
  Cadiz, KY 42211
  (270)522-3398

Lively, Louella
(James Lively)
  196 Vicksburg Estate Road
  Benton, KY 42025
  (270)527-3776

Marsiglio, June
(Roger Marsiglio)
  505 Logan
  Providence, KY 42450)

Moreland, Eva
(James Moreland)
  9158 Tom Counce Road
  South Fulton, TN 38257

Murphy, Robbie
(Vernon Murphy)
  128 New Liberty Church Road
  Kevil, KY 42053
  (270)522-3398

Owen, Pat
(Bert Owen)
  7906 Manner Pointe Drive
  Louisville, KY 40220
  (502)749-1940
  bertorpatowen@insightbb.com

Pettit, Jennie
(William H. Pettit)
  248 Skyline Drive
  Princeton, KY 42245
  (270)365-9076

Wiman, Louise
(Wayne Wiman)
  1205 S Feagal Street
  Harrisburg, IL 62946
  (270)442-7474
  1wiman@vci.net

SURVIVING SPOUSES OF MINISTERS BY PRESBYTERY CONTINUED
(Deceased spouse in parenthesis.)

CULLMAN

Kimbrell, Glenda
(Bobby Kimbrell)
  9479 Cumberland Oaks Drive
  Pinson, AL 35126
  (205)680-1743

Weathersby, Dorothy
(E.W. Weathersby)
  1203 2nd Avenue NE
  Cullman, AL 35055
  (256)734-2886

CUMBERLAND

Graham, Mary
(Harold Graham)
  103 Freeman Green Drive
  Elizabethtown, KY 42701
  (270)360-1191

Johnson, Genevie
(Robert Johnson)
  351 Bacon Court
  Harrodsburg, KY 40330
  (859)734-3789

Milam, Dona
(Robert Milam)
  9294 Owensboro Road
  Falls of Rough, KY 40119
  (270)879-8985

Mouser, Wynemia Despain
(Calvin Mouser)
  204 Sunrise Drive
  Greensburg, KY 42743
  (270)932-7377

Phelps, Diann
(John Phelps)
  4743 Happy Hollow Road
  Hawesville, KY 42348
  (270)927-9835
  haor@juno.com

Renner, Wallace
(Patricia Renner)
  1648 Griffith Avenue
  Owensboro, KY 42301
  (270)685-4359
  pwrenner@adelphia.com

Sprague, Rose
(George Sprague)
  101 Clyde Morris Hall #242
  Ormond Beach, FL 32174

DEL CRISTO

Appleby, Judy
(Bob Appleby)
  3265 16th Street
  San Francisco, CA 94103
  (415)703-6090
  gfcc@gum.org

Ellis, Ernestine
(John Ellis)
  1432 Cape Verde Place
  Tucson, AZ 85748
  (520)296-9027

Freeman, ??
(Jack Freeman)
  3559 Cody Way
  Sacramento, CA 95864
  (916)489-2567

Kennedy, Louise
(John F Kennedy)
  4916 44th Street
  Lubbock, TX 79414
  (806)796-0738

Moss, Beth
(Greg Moss)

EAST TENNESSEE

Alexander, Carolyn Roberts
(Don Charles Alexander)
  2520 107 Cutoff
  Greeneville, TN 37743
  (423)638-8453
  alexandercda@msn.com

Broyles, Elizabeth
(Lon Broyles)
  753 Snapp Bridge Road
  Limestone, TN 37681
  (865)483-8433

Broyles, Minnie
(Raymond Broyles)
  4944 Kilaminajaro
  Old Hickory, TN 37138-4102
  (615)428-8640

Johnson, Rebecca
(Scott Johnson)
  512 Rolling Creek Circle
  Knoxville, TN 37922
  (865)966-3699

Scott, Betty
(Lee Scott)
  319 Lavista Drive
  Maryville, TN 37804
  (731)415-2936

GRACE

Baker, Ola
(L. G. Baker)
  7208 12th Street
  Tampa, FL 33604
  (813)5239-3356

Brown, Marye
(Richard C Brown)
  2100 NE 140th Street Apt 510E
  Edmond, OK 73013
  (205)663-5486

Buerhaus, Charity
(Chuck Buerhaus)
  313 S Main Street
  Piedmont, AL 36272
  (256)447-6195

Hegwood, Clara
(James "Pete" Hegwood)
  125 Pinewood Lane
  Montevallo, AL 35115
  (205)665-2134

Mims, Martha Jo
(Howell "Gay" Mims)
  3011 Wolfe Road
  Columbus, MS 39705
  (662)328-3778
  mmims@muw.edu

Phillips, Edna
(Troy Phillips)
  2024 Hilltop Road
  Rock Hill, SC 29732
  (803)325-1416

Tant, Becky
(Robert H Tant)
  516 Davis Drive
  Glencoe, AL 35905
  (256)494-9450
  rtant82091@aol.com

HOPE

Bright, Mildred
(J. P. Bright)
  1716 Broadway Boulevard
  Florence, AL 35630
  (256)766-8361

Copeland, Frances S.
(Bill Copeland)
  142 Thornton Terrace Drive
  Rogersville, AL 35652
  (256)247-1688

Hyden, Mae
(Lee Hyden)
  2195 Allsboro Road
  Cherokee, AL 35616
  (256)360-2896

MISSOURI

Bornert, Paughnee
(Robert D. Bornert)
  932 E Snider Street
  Springfield, MO 65803
  (417)833-2627

SURVIVING SPOUSES OF MINISTERS BY PRESBYTERY CONTINUED

(Deceased spouse in parenthesis.)

Campbell, Margaret
(Thomas H. Campbell)
8 Oak Ridge Road
Buffalo, MO 65622
(417)345-0262

Cantrell, Mary
(Ernest Cantrell)
7047 N Garnet Lane
Strafford, MO 65757
(417)736-9017

Cravens, Hallie
(Ellis Cravens)
9566 Highway Z
Hartville, MO 65667
(417)668-5954

Cravens, Thelma
(Wilbur Cravens)
2144 Wilbur Road
Mansfield, MO 65704
417-924-8553

Dailey, Sarah
(Larry Dailey)
656 Grand Point Boulevard
Sunrise Beach, MO 65079
(573)374-9537

Fleming, Betty
(Ronald Fleming)
657 S Main Avenue Apt 1
Springfield, MO 65806
(417)873-2222

Gardner, Dossie
(Don Gardner)
26 W Pearl
Aurora, MO 65605
(417)678-3278

Gould, Marjorie
(Robert Gould)
204 W Pleasant
Aurora, MO 65605
(417)678-5422

Hensley, Jean Ann
(Howard Hensley)
537 Piperpoint
Rogersville, Mo 65742
(414)753-1108

McCloud, Johnnie
(Theron McCloud)
419 Magnolia Court
Lebanon, MO 65536
(417)532-3388
jmccloud@advertisenet.com

Scobey, Darlis
(James Scobey)
105 Oak Hill Downs Street
Farmington, MO 63640
(578)756-1683

MURFREESBORO

Basham, Earline
(Willard Basham)
335 Myers Road
Winchester, TN 37398

Breeding, Karen
(Gordon Breeding)
1907 Susan Drive
Murfreesboro, TN 37129
(615)867-3660
zanylady1000@yahoo.com

Dickerson, Helen
(Andrew Mizel Dickerson, Jr.)
914 Dogwood Drive
Murfreesboro, TN 37129

Martindale, Dana
(J. Craig Martindale)
2913 Pellas Place
Murfreesboro, TN 37127
(615)653-0858
w5bu@hotmail.com

Salisbury, Helen Margaret
(A.D. Salisbury)
1927 Memorial Boulevard
Murfreesboro, TN 37129

Salisbury, Rebecca
(Loyce Estes)
1033 Twin Oaks Drive
Murfreesboro, TN 37130
(615)410-7801
rebsalisbury@yahoo.com

Watson, Mary Leota
(David E Watson)
804 W Main Street
McMinnville, TN 37110
(931)473-7561
leotaw@blomand.net

NASHVILLE

Allen, Hester
(Paul Allen)
300 Bantam Court
LaVerne, TN 37086

Burnett, Mary Lee
(Cecil Burnett)
321 Raindrop Lane
Hendersonville, TN 37075

Maxedon, Chris
(Julian Maxedon)
2260 Highway 31
White House, TN 37188

Stiles, Peggy
(John Stiles)
300 Bantam Court
Clarksville, TN 37043

Wilkins, Connie
(Tom Wilkins)
109 Annalise Drive
Clarksville, TN 37043
(931)358-2892

NORTH CENTRAL

McCain, Violet
(Terence McCain)
15804 Camden Avenue
Eastpointe, MI 48021
(586)774-4861

Springer, Eileen
(Robert Springer)
403 Prairie Ridge Court
Eureka, IL 61530
(309)467-5030

RED RIVER

Brown, Beth
(LaRoyce Brown)
311 S 8th Street
Marlow, OK 73055
(580)658-3989

Gilbert, Freda M
(James C. Gilbert)
c/o Elizabeth G. Horsley
1200 Imperial Drive
Denton, TX 76209
(940)387-2272

ROBERT DONNELL

Hunter, Jean
(James E. Hunter)
1905 Delynn
Hazel Green, AL 35750
(256)838-3902

TENNESSEE-GEORGIA

Galloway, Katherine
(Cliff Galloway)
7127 White Oak Valley Road
McDonald, TN 37353

Kapperman, Linda
(Glenn Kapperman)
2719 Rio Grande Road
Chattanooga, TN 37421
(423)894-7924

SURVIVING SPOUSES OF MINISTERS BY PRESBYTERY CONTINUED

(Deceased spouse in parenthesis.)

Naugher, Catherine
(Doyce Naugher)
  985 Mt Pleasant Road
  Rydal, GA 30171
  (770)382-1982

TRINITY

Allen, Ann M
(Paul Allen)
  1814 Swan
  Longview, TX 75604
  (903)759-5508

Johnson, Clyde
(Dave Johnson)
  2801 E Travis Apt 108
  Marshall, TX 75672
  (903)938-9953

Leslie, Jenann
(Marvin E. Leslie)
  300 Henley Perry Drive
  Marshall, TX 75670
  (903)938-6642

Ward, Suzie
(Kevin Ward)
  216 E Caroline
  Marshall, TX 75672

WEST TENNESSEE

Brown, Beverly
(Paul B. Brown)
  406 N McNeil Street
  Memphis, TN 38112
  (901)278-6909

Brown, Phyllis
(David Brown)
  1930 Mignon
  Memphis, TN 38107
  (901)274-1513

Cook, Marcine
(Paul V. Cook)
  144 Big John Drive
  Martin, TN 38237
  (731)587-0787
  marcine175@aol.com

Davis, Willene
(Harold Davis)
  7820 Walking Horse Circle #311
  Germantown, TN 38138
  (901)757-1394

Forester, Edna Jean
(Robert Forester)
  200 Blackburn Avenue
  McKenzie, TN 38201
  (731)352-7608

Forester, Willie Mae
(J. C. Forester)
  833 Main Street
  McKenzie, TN 38201
  (731)352-3107

Hall, Patsy
(Charles R. Hall)
  185 Mockingbird
  Selmer, TN 38375
  (731)645-8231

Hicks, Ruby
(Willam D. Hicks)
  3938 Cardinal Drive
  Union City, TN 38261
  (731)885-5887

Hull, Kathryn Sue
(Robert L. Hull)
  11 The Boulevard
  New Rochelle, NY 10801
  731-352-5552
  rkhull@charter.net

Knight, Helen
(James Knight)
  8081 Jills Creek Drive
  Bartlett, TN 38133
  (901)387-0675

Laurence, Brenda
(G. Larry Laurence)
  2823 Nine Mile Road
  Enville, TN 38332
  (731)687-2022
  southernmoma@hotmail.com

Leslie, Cheryl
(Randall Leslie)
  3374 Walnut Grove Road
  Memphis, TN 38111
  (901)458-4413

Lynch, Van
(Jerry Lynch)
  73 Baseline Road
  Dyer, TN 38330

McMahen, Sandra
(Rowe Gene McMahen)
  92 Stonewall Circle
  McKenzie, TN 38201
  (731)352-3067

Stott, Beverly
(Melvin Buddy Stott)
  200 E Main Street
  Dresden, TN 38225
  (731)364-5863
  bevstott@frontiernet.net

Terrell, Mary
(Harold Terrell)
  4302 Elaine Avenue
  Memphis, TN 38122
  (901)761-7194

CUMBERLAND PRESBYTERIANS
SERVING OUTSIDE THE UNITED STATES

Please e-mail missionaries before mailing anything to them to determine the best way to send them letters or packages. If you want to communicate with missionaries in closed countries, first e-mail the Missions Ministry Team (Lthomas@cumberland.org) and we will forward your e-mail to the missionary.

Lawrence & Loretta Fung—Asia
email: revfung@gmail.com
skype: Lawrence Fung

N B—China
email: Lthomas@cumberland.org

S & L—China
email: Lthomas@cumberland.org

Boyce & Beth Wallace—Colombia
e-mail: hbwcali@yahoo.com
oovoo and facetime: Boyce Wallace

Anay Ortega—Guatemala
e-mail: anayortegamonroy@hotmail.com
skype: Anay Ortega Monroy
oovoo: Anay Ortega

Fhanor & Socorro Penjendino—Guatemala
email: pastorfhanor@gmail.com
skype: Fhanor Pejendino Arcos
oovoo: pastorestulua

Glenn Watts—Hong Kong
email: hongkongbrother@hotmail.com
skype: HongKongBROTHER

T & T—Kyrgyzstan
email: Lthomas@cumberland.org

D & S—Laos
email: Lthomas@cumberland.org

Carlos & Luz Dary Rivera—Mexico
email: caralrifra@une.lnet.co
oovoo: Carlos Rivera

M & H—Myanmar
email: Lthomas@cumberland.org

P T—Nepal
email: Lthomas@cumberland.org

Daniel & Kay Jang—Philippines
Ilollo Cumberland Mission Church
email: goingup129@hanmail.net

Kenneth & Delight Hopson—Uganda
e-mail: ken.hopson@wgm.org
skype: Delight Hopson
oovoo: Kenneth Hopson

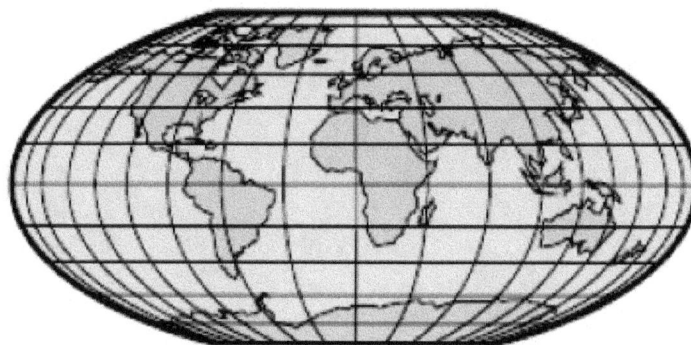

The Cumberland Presbyterian Church
has five families working in closed countries as
humanitarian workers.

NEW CHURCH DEVELOPMENTS & MISSION PROBES

ANDES

Aguadas
Cra 3 #7-14
Aguadas, Caldas
Colombia, SA
(576)851-4773
jeob40@hotmail.com
Pastor: Joaquin Orozco   (M2)
Began: 1996 (as re-development)

Amaga
Cra San Fernando #48-56
Amaga, Antioquia
Colombia, SA
(574)847-3250
rebcaldas@une.net.co
Pastor: Jhon Jairo Arias   (M3)
Began: 1997

Chinchina
Mz 2 Casa 21, Urb. Milan
Dosquebradas, Ris
Colombia, SA
(476)322-2177
oikoninonia@gmail.com
Pastor: Rodrigo Martinez   (M1)

Quimbaya
Cra 6 #25-54
Quimbaya, Quindio
Colombia, SA
(576)752-3570
joenjimu@yahoo.es
Pastor: Jorge Enrique Jimenez
  (M3)
Began: 04/02

Senda de Libertad
Cra 120 #39 F-91
Medellin, Antioquia
Colombia, SA
(574)496-1681
ipcsaladomedellin@gmail.com
Pastor: Cruzana Guerrero
    & Libardo Gutierrez   (M2)
Began: 1998

ARKANSAS

Bryant-Benton CP Mission Fellowship
16904 Old Mill Road
Little Rock, AR 72206
(501)888-4190
Pastor: Dwight Shanley   (M1)
Began: 2005

CAUCA VALLEY

Casa de Oracion

Dia de Salvacion
Pastor: Luis Cantor
(   )256-2835

Rios de Agua Viva
Pastor: Euripides Moreno   (M1)
(   )244-3557

COVENANT

Cadiz
Cadiz, KY
Pastor: Danny York   (M1)
Began: 2008

CUMBERLAND

Louisville Japanese Christian Fellowship (3223)
c/o Christ Lutheran Church
9212 Taylorsville Road
Louisville, KY 40299
(502)210-0852
iwaosatoh@gmail.com
Pastor: Iwao Satoh   (M1)
Began: 2010

DEL CRISTO

316 Christian Fellowship
2200 E Dartmouth Circle
Englewood, CO 80113
(303)504-0275
jeanhess@316denver.com
Pastor: Rick & Jean Hess   (M1)
Began: 08/10

Bethesda Korean Fellowship
139 Silverado Drive
Santa Teresa, NM 88008
(915)329-3451
pyongsanyu@hotmail.com
Pastor: Pyong San Yu   (M1)
Began: 03/10

Marantha East
12008 Fred Carter
El Paso, TX 79936
(915)857-1343
yaanaivitaly@yahoo.com
Pastor: Alfredo Rincon   (M1)
Began: 2012

GRACE

Naples Fellowship (0309)
842 Bent Creek Way
Naples, FL 34114
(931)273-0768
revga@hotmail.com
Pastor: Ramon Garcia   (M1

JAPAN

Ichikawa Grace Mission Point (8314)
3-19-5 Sugano
Ichikawa-shi, Chiba-ken
272-0824 JAPAN
(047)326-8675
(047)326-8675 FAX
fwgc6854@mb.infoweb.ne.jp
Pastor: Yasuo Masuda   (M2)

RED RIVER

Church of St. Giles
3500 S Peoria Avenue
Tulsa, OK 74105
(918)760-6145
Pastor: William G. Webb, Jr.   (M1)

TRINITY

Kardia Fellowship
Tyler, TX
Pastor: Mark Davenport   (M1)

WEST TENNESSEE

Grace Fellowship (9323)
9160 Tchulahoma Road
Southaven, MS 38671
(662)393-2552
tthompson393@aol.com
Pastor: Tommy Thompson   (M1)

Hope Fellowship
440 Blackmon Road
Medina, TN 38355
(731)738-0308
Pastor: Steven Rogers   (M1)

Iona Community of Faith
1790 Faxon Avenue
Memphis, TN 38112
website: www.iona.gutensite.com
(901)283-8062
wa4mff@aol.com
Pastor: Barry Anderson   (M1)

PROVISIONAL CHURCHES AND PROVISIONAL FELLOWSHIPS

"A provisional fellowship is a pre-existing non-English congregation that is being received into the Cumberland Presbyterian Church through an authorized assimilation process.

ARKANSAS

_____ (2135)
Arkansas Korean Loving Church
8201 Frenchmans Lane
Little Rock, AR 72209
Pastor: Sun Wan Cho   (M1)

COVENANT

_____ (3420)
Zion CP Fellowship
1347 S 6th Street
Paducah, KY 42003
(270)442-6414
zioncpcinfo@gmail.com
Pastor: Steve/Teresa Shauf (M1)
Began: 10/2012

CUMBERLAND EAST COAST

_____
Comeback Church

_____
True Love Church of New York
42-40 208th Street 1
Bayside, NY 11361
(347)308-4333
ingodswill@gmail.com
Pastor: Taeho Oh   (M1)

EAST TENNESSEE

_____ (2321)
Iloilo Cumberland Mission Church
    PO Box #5, Aduana Street
    Iloilo City 5000, Philippine
    Pastor: WonJeon (Daniel) Jang
                              (M1)
_____ (2322)
Mok-Yang Presbyterian Church
    #304-28 Sinlim-Dong
    Kwanak-Gu
    Seoul, Korea
    02-884-3474
    Pastor: Bo-Seong Park   (M1)
_____ (2323)
Sae-Sam Presbyterian Church
    #325-1 DongHyen-Dong
    Jenchen-city
    Choongbuk, Korea
    043-652-0540
    lifeyu@hanmail.net
    Pastor: Wn-Young Yu   (M1)
_____ (2324)
Ye-Il Presbyterian Church
    #1304 Kakyeng-Dong
    Sangdang-Gu
    Cheongju-City
    Choongbuk, Korea
    043-235-0219
    Pastor: Da-Wit (David) Ahn
_____ (2325)
Young-Kwang Presbyterian Church
    #1342 Seocho-2dong
    Seocho-Gu
    Seoul, Korea
    02-3474-8405
    Pastor: Sango-Do Lee

MISSOURI

_____
First CPC Korean Mission
    4216 Charleston Avenue
    Springfield, MO 65408
    (417)883-4248
    Pastor: Sang H Park   (M1)

RED RIVER

_____
Casa del Alfarero
    Calle Norte 12 Aesquino Oriente 53
    Colonia Union de Guadalupe Chaico
    MEXICO
    54-4-627-5570
    alaprep28@hotmail.com
    Pastor: Alejandro Alejo (M1)

_____
Iglesia Presbiterana Marantha
    Calle 21 Lote 22 Mzn DlI
    Colonoa Guadalupe Proleteria
    C P 07670 Mexico City
    MEXICO
    54-53-67-9103
    jessevega69@gmail.com
    Pastor: Jedidiah Vega   (M1)

_____
Restauracion de Vida
    Calle C numero 24
    Cononia San Marcos
    Delegacion Azcapotzalco C P 02020
    MEXICO
    54-5-318-7622
    castro_dan@hotmail.com
    Pastor: Jose Dan Castro (M1)

TENNESSEE GEORGIA

_____
Baek Seok Church
    3075 Landington Way
    Duluth, GA 30096
    (404)398-8469
    kpc0191@gmail.com
    Pastor: Seung Chon Han   (M1)
_____
Divinity Church
    1 Clyde Orr Drive
    Norcross, GA 3093
    Pastor: Rev. Frederick Nah
    Began: 2013
_____ (2130)
Korean Livingstone Presbyterian Church
    3340 Bentbill xing
    Cumming, GA 30041
    (770)912-8477
    barkmoksa@hanmail.net
    Pastor: Rev Young Rae Park (M1)
_____
New York Chowon Mission Church
    254-18 Northern Boulevard
    Little Neck, NY 11362
    (917)992-5200
    lovedasol@gmail.com
    Pastor: Si Hoon Park   (M1)

_____
Our Good Presbyterian Church
    32132 Huntly Circle
    Salisbury, MD 21804
    (443)783-3809 (cell)
    Pastor: Hyoung Sik Choi (M1)
    Began: 2001
_____
Phillipians Church
    2310 His Way
    Lawrenceville, GA 30044
    (678)462-7526
    agatopia@hanmail.net
    Pastor: Jin Koo Kang   (M1)
_____
Trinity Church
    1050 Grace Drive
    Lawrenceville, GA 30043
    (678)622-2717
    Pastor: Rev. Min Soo Kim (M1)
_____
Walking with God Presbyterian Church
    3299 Highway 120
    Duluth, GA 30096
    (678)600-2787
    jaeyu117@yahoo.com
    Pastor: Jae Hyung Yu   (M1)
_____
We Community Church
    302 Satellite Boulevard
    Suwanee, GA 30024
    (678)908-9191
    powerment@hotmail.com
    Pastor: Hyang Koo Lee

TRINITY

_____
Ye Rang Korean Church (8602)
    6800 Woodrow Avenue
    Austin, TX 78757
    (512)474-2646
    Pastor: Sung In Park   (M1)

WEST TENNESSEE

_____
ACTS Church
    6524 Summer Avenue
    Memphis, TN 38134
    (901)381-4790
    usyoun61@hotmail.com
    Pastor: Daniel Youn
_____
Redeemer Evangelical Church
    7011 Poplar Avenue
    Germantown, TN 38138
    (901)737-3370
    jimmylatimer@redeemerevangelical.com
    Pastor: James M. Latimer

MISSION CHURCHES AND PASTORS
UNDER CARE OF MISSIONS MINISTRY TEAM
(General Assembly Ministry Council)

GUATEMALA

Iglesia Evangelica de Fe y Jubilo
(Provisional)
  6a avenida 3-56 Zona 19
  Colonia La Florida
  Guatemala City, Guatemala
  Pastor: Edgar Buni Avalos   (M1)

Casa de Fe y Oracion
(Provisional)
  31 calle 9-75 Colonia Miralvally
  Zona 6 de Mixco
  Guatemala

Comunidad de Fe
(Provisional)
  29 calle 14-41 Zona 12
  Coonia Santa Rosa II
  Guatemala City, Guatemala

PROVISIONAL PASTORS:

Avalos, Edgar Buni
  6a avenida 3-56 Zona 19
  Colonia La Florida
  Guatemala City, Guatemala

PHILIPPINES

Iloilo Cumberland Presbyterian
(Church)
  PO Box 5
  Aduana Street
  Iloilo City 5000, Philippines
  Pastor: Wond Jeon (Daniel) Jang
                             (M1)

Pavia Cumberland Presbyterian
(Mission)
  Jabonillo Street
  Pavia, Iloilo
  Pastor: Manual Job Baldevia (M2)

Oton Cumberland Presbyterian
(Mission)
  Cabang
  Oton, Iloilo
  Pastor: Alexander Duyac, Jr. (M1)

PASTORS:

Duyac, Alexander, Jr.
  Brgy, Cabang, Oton, Iloilo

LICENTIATES:

Baldevia, Manuel Job
Saim, J Sean Espanueva
Tagurigan, Alpha Faith Singcuenco

CANDIDATES:

Agana, Romeo G, Jr.
Bonete, Harold Henry D
Dyuac, Aldrandreb D
Garnica, Darrel Von
Yutig, Lucelle E

SOUTH KOREA

_____(2221)
First Cumberland Presbyterian Church
of Korea
(Church)
  Hyundai I-park B-02
  Burim-dong 113
  Dongan-gu, Anyang-si
  Gyeonggi-do, Korea 431-787
  Phone: 82-70-8872-8033
  Pastor: Heungsoo Kang   (M2)
  Clerk: Yoon JinSub
  303-101 Raenian Ever heim Apt
  Naeson 2-dong, Uiwangsi
  Gyeonggi-do, Korea 437-761
  jinsyoon@gmail.com

Glory Church
(Mission)
  302 Si-Bum Building
  1342 Seocho 2-dong, Seocho-gu
  Seoul, Korea 137-861
  Phone: 82-2-3474-8405
  Pastor: Geumtaek Lim   (M1)

New Life Church
(Mission)
  325-1 Donghyeon-dong
  Jecheon-si
  Chungcheongbud-do, Korea 390-190
  Phone: 82-10-6655-9188
  Pastor: Woonyong Yu   (M1)

Ye-II Church
(Mission)
  15 Seogyeong-ro, 28beong-gil
  Heungdeok-gu, Cheongiu-si
  Chungcheongbuk-do, Korea 361-803
  Phone: 82-42-232-6000
  Pastor: Dawie Ahn   (M1)

PASTORS:

Ahn, Dawie
  606-304 Gapyeong Jugong Apt
  Jungnim-dong, Heungdeck-gu
  Cheongju-si
  Chungcheongbuk-do, Korea 361-850
  Phone: 82-10-2421-0219
  ankim91@hanmail.net
Lee, Sangdo
  507-1501 Samik Green Apt
  Myeongil 1-dong, Gngdong-gu
  Seoul, Korea 134-782
  Phone: 82-10-3353-2907
  humanolsd@hanmail.net
Lim, Geumtaek
  302-si-Bum Building
  1342 Seocho 2dong, Seccho-gu
  Seoul, Korea 137-861
  Phone: 82-11-9044-5250
  limkt114@hanmail.net
Yu, Woonyong
  325-1 Donghyeon-dong, Jecheon-si
  Chungcheongbuk-do, Korea 390-190
  Phone: 82-10-6655-9188
  lifeyu@hanmail.net

LICENTIATES:

Choi, Justin
  823-4 Naeson 1-dong, Uiwang-si
  Gyeonggi-do, Korea 437-838
  Phone: 82-10-2668-8795
  rev.choi@hotmail.com
Kang, Huengsoo
  Hyundai I-park B-02, Burim-dong 113
  Dongan-gu, Anyang-si
  Gyeonggi-do, Korea 431-787
  Phone: 82-10-8428-0084
  halieus@hanmail.net

CAMP GROUNDS

ARKANSAS PRESBYTERY

Camp Peniel
Jim Fisk
311 Merril Drive
Benton, AR 72015
(870)367-3086

CHOCTAW PRESBYTERY

Camp Israel Folsom
Box 158
Broken Bow, OK 74728
(580)584-2099

COLUMBIA PRESBYTERY

Crystal Springs Camp, Inc.
21 Crystal Springs Camp Road
Kelso, TN 37348
(931)937-8621
Medley@cafes.net
Camp Manager: Carol Medley

PRESBYTERY OF EAST TENNESSEE

Camp Chilhowee
c/o Darres & Juanita Craig
1920 Old Chilhowee Loop Road
Maryville, TN 37865
(865)983-7084

Camp John Speer
c/o Dennis Elwell
2154 Viking Mountain Road
Greeneville, TN 37743
(423)636-1366
dpelwell@gmail.com
www.campjohnspeer.com

GRACE PRESBYTERY

Camp Bailey
Route 1 Box 386
Union, MS 39365

Caretaker: Mr. Lynn Frederick
P. O. Box 574
Carthage, MS 39051

MISSOURI PRESBYTERY

Camp Cumberland
South Greenfield, Missouri
(417)637-2059
Renee Rogers, Business Manager

MURFREESBORO PRESBYTERY

Crystal Springs
21 Crystal Springs Camp Road
Kelso, TN 37348
(931)937-8621

NASHVILLE PRESBYTERY

Camp Crystal Springs
21 Crystal Springs Camp Road
Kelso, TN 37348
(931)937-8621
Carol Medley, Director

TENNESSEE-GEORGIA PRESBYTERY

Camp Glancy
1370 Coppinger Cove Road
Sequatchie, TN 37374

TRINITY PRESBYTERY

Camp Gilmont
Rt. 6, Box 254
Gilmer, TX 75644
(903)797-6400

WEST TENNESSEE PRESBYTERY

Camp Clark Williamson
390 Mason Road
Humboldt, TN 38343
(800)655-8204
(731)784-3221
Mike Hannaford, Administrator
www.campclarkwilliamson.com

Explanation of Symbols

MC=
  Abbreviation for name of county or state if more than one church in the presbytery has the same name.

4= The number of Sundays each month the church engages in worship
M= Manse
E= Every Home Plan for The Cumberland Presbyterian
W= Organized women's ministry

P = Provisional Church
C = Church
F = Fellowship
U = Union Church

Synod/Presbytery Abbreviations

Church Number

Church Name

Telephone Number

Little Brown Church (MC) (4MEWC) GRWT9450
2307 Country Lane
Pleasant Valley, TN 37001
(901)654-0058 <Kingdom>

County

PA: John Doe
     1 Church St.
     Pleasant Valley, TN 37001
     (901)654-3210   <M1>

AP: Mary Smith
     20 Serenity Lane
     Pleasant Valley, TN 37001
     (901)654-0123   <M1>

CL: Jane Doe
     30 Charity Rd.
     Pleasant Valley, TN 37001
     (901)654-2345

CL= Clerk of Session
CO= Chair of commission appointed to govern church

AP = Associate/AssistantPastor
IP = Interim Pastor
LS = Layperson serving church
OD= Member of another denomination
PA = Installed Pastor
SS = Stated Supply

DE = Denominational Employee
ED = Editor
FM = Former Moderator
IT = In Transit to another Presbytery
M1 = Ordained Minister
M2 = Licentiate
M3 = Candidate
M4 = Minister of another denomination enrolled as a member through reciprocal agreement (Constitution 5.3)
M5 = Member of another denomination
M6 = Layperson serving church
M7 = Associate or Assistant Pastor
M8 = Military Chaplain
M9 = Non-Military Chaplain
M0 = Mentored Minister
MY = Missionary
OM = Other approved ministry
OP = Member of another presbytery
PR = Professor, Teacher
RT = Retired or HR (honorably retired)
ST = Student

SUMMARY OF STATISTICS OF PRESBYTERIES BY SYNODS

GENERAL	MEMBERSHIP				CHANGES				FINANCES				
(Number of Ministers)	1.Church Number	2.Active	3.Total	4.Church School	5.Prof. of Faith	6.Gains	7.Losses	8.Children Baptized	9. OUR UNITED OUT-REACH	10. Total Out-Reach Giving	11. All Other Expenses	12. Total Income Received	13. Value Church Prop. 1=1000
	1	2	3	4	5	6	7	8	9	10	11	12	13
GR: SYNOD OF GREAT RIVERS													
Arkansas (40)	57	2,126	3,236	1,176	59	115	201	18	135,923	416,409	1,936,671	2,342,163	22,579
Missouri (19)	23	687	1,183	446	22	48	50	6	52,644	178,616	641,034	753,266	6,230
West Tennessee (111)	96	6,282	9,842	3,357	76	166	191	38	317,671	779,437	5,152,089	6,054,683	55,677
SYNOD TOTALS (170)	176		14,257		157		446		506,238		7,768,259		84,486
		9,091		4,980		329		62		1,383,350		9,197,999	
MI:SYNOD OF THE MIDWEST													
Covenant (43)	47	2,802	5,133	1,753	49	119	233	26	176,697	536,425	2,407,889	3,173,125	23,680
Cumberland (60)	65	2,983	4,999	1,791	64	217	157	27	110,972	285,325	2,571,452	2,703,236	24,637
North Central (35)	33	1,144	2,100	958	48	61	118	9	79,707	279,115	836,398	1,126,931	11,444
SYNOD TOTALS (138)	145		12,232		161		508		367,376		5,815,739		59,761
		6,929		4,502		397		62		1,100,865		7,003,292	
MS:MISSION SYNOD													
Andes (16)	10	1,837	1,939	869	166	177	161	0	11,700	971,922	903,347	839,121	1,526
Cauca Valley (16)	20	2,854	3,444	2,010	1,108	775	298	0	12,930	118,865	476,861	754,135	3,300
Choctaw (5)	7	71	138	78	0	0	3	0	1,187	6,073	17,106	24,982	230
del Cristo (52)	11	1,559	3,845	650	21	47	138	10	100,529	496,469	3,092,796	3,760,896	11,224
Hong Kong (7)	10	1,375	2,034	544	56	110	23	30	14,985	276,008	2,252,990	2,691,538	4,384
Japan (18)	14	1,254	2,309	782	31	26	31	4	43,755	260,553	1,616,830	1,782,477	3,138
Red River (61)	27	2,369	3,838	1,303	43	188	150	26	126,830	655,470	4,589,254	5,306,419	33,108
Trinity (44)	24	1,771	2,595	629	22	89	166	19	132,785	544,425	2,500,752	3,042,494	25,535
SYNOD TOTALS (219)	123		20,142		1,447		970		444,701		15,449,936		82,445
		13,090		6,865		1,412		89		3,329,785		18,202,062	
SE:SYNOD OF THE SOUTHEAST													
Cum East Coast (??)	5	113	147	68	14	6	53	11	0	25,288	246,997	240,558	255
East Tennessee (56)	39	2,899	4,931	1,728	35	96	364	17	272,445	559,710	3,561,860	4,042,536	33,014
Grace (104)	38	2,601	3,685	1,467	79	169	372	28	154,187	413,289	2,848,844	3,282,300	31,081
Hope (10)	17	872	1,409	542	18	23	116	9	48,044	149,711	1,130,125	1,227,135	9,679
Robert Donnell (27)	17	981	1,739	427	18	42	28	9	58,515	183,502	1,133,104	1,267,921	13,340
Tennessee-Georgia (37)	26	1,876	2,357	799	34	51	137	15	68,748	207,548	1,687,604	2,188,526	20,235
SYNOD TOTALS (234)	142		14,268		198		1,070		601,939		10,608,534		107,604
		9,342		5,031		387		89		1,538,898		12,248,976	
TN:TENNESSEE SYNOD													
Columbia (32)	38	1,459	2,612	1,006	33	95	487	9	84,382	276,617	1,991,864	2,350,034	19,893
Murfreesboro (43)	45	3,010	4,707	2,129	84	181	168	22	260,967	505,902	2,889,701	3,516,544	31,579
Nashville (52)	39	3,272	5,143	2,078	81	172	260	36	206,649	518,679	4,237,618	5,014,191	48,448
SYNOD TOTALS (127)	122		12,462		198		915		551,998		9,119,183		99,920
		7,741		5,213		448		67		1,301,198		10,880,769	
GRAND TOTALS (888)	708		73,782		2,139		3,716		2,429,736		48,195,895		435,880
		46,241		26,625		2,924		353		8,493,372		56,506,978	

Andes Presbytery
MISSION SYNOD

GENERAL		MEMBERSHIP			CHANGES				FINANCES			
1.Church Number	2.Active	3.Total	4.Church School	5.Prof. of Faith	6.Gains	7.Losses	8.Children Baptized	9. OUR UNITED OUT-REACH	10. Total Out-Reach Giving	11. All Other Expenses	12. Total Income Received	13. Value Church Prop. 1=1000
1	2	3	4	5	6	7	8	9	10	11	12	13
Armenia*	8903	545	545	245	60	71	23	0		390,762	390,724	350,044	450
Cartago	8906	160	169	69	29	29	10	0		65,405	61,654	61,658	0
Dosquebradas	8907	210	213	120	50	24	24	0		99,752	98,966	98,887	112
El Rebano	8905	272	282	20	0	7	6	0		94,610	90,609	89,445	161
Horeb-Central	8915	90	101	30	7	23	10	0		143,180	82,364	75,564	111
La Rosa DeSaron	8911	65	70	95	4	8	7	0		39,762	39,724	28,315	28
La Virginia Mis*	8913	30	30	20	5	3	0	0		18,494	20,333	16,966	21
Manizales*	8914	15	126	70	8	0	75	0		63,588	63,141	62,225	13
Pereira	8916	250	289	150	No Report Received			0		0	0	0	500
Zamora	8918	100	114	50	3	12	6	0		56,369	55,832	56,017	130
Presbytery	8900								11,700				
TOTALS	10	1,837	1,939	869	166	177	161	0	11,700	971,922	903,347	839,121	1,526

*Math error corrected. **Purged roll..

CHURCHES, PASTORS, AND CLERKS:

Armenia   (4MWC)MSAN8903
  Cra 15 #16-39
  Armenia, Quindio
  Colombia, South America
  (574)745-4860   <S America>
  FAX: (574)745-4895
  ipc-armenia@hotmail.com
PA: John Jairo Correa   <M1>
  Calle 2 Norte #16-39
  Armenia, Quindio
  Colombia, South America
  (574)745-0496
  jjcedp07@hotmail.com
AP: Esperanza Diaz   <M1>
  Calle 2 Norte #16-19
  Armenia, Quindio
  Colombia, South America
  (576)745-0496
CL: Jose Leobardo Castro
  Calle 16 #14-43
  Armenia, Quindio
  Colombia, South America
  57(310)-389-2361

Cartago   (4MW C)MSAN8906
  Cra 12 #8-47
  Cartago, Valle
  Colombia, South America
  (572)214-5060   <S America>
  FAX: (572)214-5060
  presbicartago@gmail.com
PA: Cenobia Rivera   <M1>
  Cra 12 #8-47
  Cartago, Valle
  Colombia, South America
  57(310)500-1791
  zenobiadedaza@yahoo.com.mx
PA: Edilberto Daza   <M1>
  Cra 12 #8-47

Cartago, Valle
Colombia, South America
57(314)794-1905
presbicartago@gmail.com
CL: Verney Lopez
  Calle 25C #36-15
  Cartago, Valle
  Colombia, South America
  57(314)715-3075

Dosquebradas   (4MWC)MSAN8907
  Calle 51 #15-32 (mailing)
  Cra 15 A #50-31 (physical)
  barrio Los Naranjos
  Dosquebradas, Risaralda
  Colombia, South America
  (574)322-2938   <S America>
PA: Juan Esteban Blandon   <M1>
  Calle 51 #15-32
  barrio Los Naranjos
  Dosquebradas, Risaralda
  Colombia, South America
  (574)322-2938
  juanestebanblandon@yahoo.com
CL: Alba Rodriguez
  Cra 15 A #50-31
  barrio Los Naranjoa
  Dosquebradas, Risaralda
  Colombia, South America
  (574)322-4899

El Rebano-Caldas (4WMCF)MSAN8905
  Calle 128 Sur #48-13
  barrio Central
  Caldas, Antioquia
  Colombia, South America
  (574)278-0787   <S America>
  FAX: (574)278-0787
  rebcaldas@une.net.co
SS: Juan Alexander Castano   <M3 ST>
  Calle 127 sur #42-38 Apto 301
  Caldas, Antioquia

Colombia, South America
(574)306-4435
FAX: (574)278-0787
juanalexandercastanovelez@yahoo.com
CL: Consuelo Pena
  Calle 130 Sur #57-09, Int 301
  Caldas, Antioquia
  Colombia, South America
  (574)338-6190
  FAX: (574)278-0787
  chelitopeco@hotmail.com

Horeb-Central   (4WMC)MSAN8915
  Carrera 50D #62-69, Prado Centro
  Medellin, Antioquia
  Colombia, South America
  (574)263-2154   <S America>
  ipchoreb@hotmail.com
PA: Ricardo Castaneda   <M1>
  Calle 65 #98-45 (Interior 174)
  Altos de la Macarena-Robledo La Campina
  Medellin, Antioquia
  Colombia, South America
  (574)577-0717
  rijcah@gmail.com
AP: Diana Valdez   <M1>
  Cra 50 D#62-69
  Medellin, Antioquia
  Colombia, South America
  (574)263-2154
  dianamariavaldezduque@gmail.com
CL: Lina Velasquez
  Calle 49E #83A91
  Recinto de La Arboleda, Calazans
  Medellin, Antioquia
  Colombia, South America
  (574)422-6698
  velasquezlina@yahoo.es

La Rosa de Saron   (4F)MSAN8911
  Calle 100 #50C-09
  Barrio Santa Cruz Sector La Rosa
  Medellin, Antioquia

ANDES PRESBYTERY CONTINUED

Colombia, South America
(574)236-6509   <S America>
SS: Andres Giraldo   <M2>
   Calle 76 #87-14 Apto 202
   Medellin, Antioquia
   Colombia, South America
   (574)422-6669
   andresgiraldo@une.net.co
CL: Claudia Cordoba
   Calle 100 #50C-35
   Barrio Santa Cruz Sector La Rosa
   Medellin, Antioquia
   Colombia, South America
   57(315)605-0011

La Virginia   (4WMF)MSAN8913
   Cra 4 bis #10-35
   La Virginia, Risalda
   Colombia, South America
   (576)368-3589   <S America>
CL: Nora Patricia Diaz
   Cra 4 bis #10-35
   LaVirginia, Risalda
   Colombia, South America
   (311)312-2349
   noris_1985@hotmail.com

Manizales   (4WMC)MSAN8914
   Calle 22 #25-33
   Manizales, Caldas
   Colombia, South America
   (576)883-0383   <S America>
   FAX: (576)833-0383
   manizales50ipc@hotmail.com
PA: William Diaz   <M1>
   Calle 42 #26B-68
   Manizales, Caldas
   Colombia, South America
   (574)890-2972
   manizales50ipc@hotmail.com
CL: Luz Dary Herrera
   Calle 5 #22-56
   Manizales, Caldas
   Colombia, South America
   (576)889-0994

Pereira   (4MWC)MSAN8916
   Cra 12 bis #11-69
   Pereira, Risaralda
   Colombia, South America
   (574)333-9295   <S America>
   FAX: (574)324-4110
   cumberlandpres@une.net.co
PA: David Montoya   <M1>
   Cra 12 bis #11-69
   Pereira, Risaralda
   Colombia, South America
   (574)324-4109
   FAX: (574)324-4110
   adamonva@gmail.com
AP: Luz Maria Heilbron   <M1>
   Cra 12 bis #11-51
   Pereira, Risaralda
   Colombia, South America
   (576)333-9295
   pastorapresbi@hotmail.com
AP: Rodrigo Martinez   <M1>
   Mz2 Casa 21 Urb Casas De Milan
   Dosquebradas, Risaralda
   Colombia, South America
   (576)322-2177

oikoinonia@gmail.com
CL: Shirley Murillo
   Cra 12 bis #11-69
   Pereira, Risaralda
   Colombia, South America

Zamora   (4WC)MSAN8918
   Calle 20D #42C-56 (physical)
   Cra 58 #32A-41 Apt 420 (mailing)
   Bello, Antioquia
   Colombia, South America
   (574)461-0069   <S America>
   ipczamora@gmail.com
PA: Alejandro Vasquez   <M1>
   Cra 58 #32A-41 Apt 420
   Bello, Antioquia
   Colombia, South America
   (574)451-4816
   almaesda@une.net.co
CL: Amparo Hoyos
   Calle 120D #42C-56
   Bello, Antioquia
   Colombia, South America
   57(315)424-4547
   chilalu1147@hotmail.com

OTHERS ON MINISTERIAL ROLL:

Daza, Johan   <M1>
   1844 Eagle Shore Drive
   Cordova, TN 38016
   (330)703-2855
   jdaza@cumberland.org
Gentry, Michele   <M1 M9>
   Calle 3 Norte #12-87
   Armenia, Quindio
   Colombia, South America
   (576)745-1614
   gentry.andes@yahoo.com
Guerrero, Luz Dary   <M1 MY>
   Calle 22 #25-33
   Manizales, Caldas
   Colombia, South America
   (576)888-4203
   clementinajacobo7@hotmail.com
Martinez, Dagoberto   <M1 RT>
   Cra 62D #71-113
   Bello, Antioquia
   Colombia, South America
   (574)452-3466
Ortiz, Jaime   <M1 RT>
   Cra 50D #62-69
   Medellin, Antioquia
   Colombia, South America
   (574)421-6339
Taborda, Arturo   <M1 RT>
   Cra 43 #20D-46
   Zamora, Medellin, Antioquia
   Colombia, South America
   (574)267-1351
   chilalu1147@hotmail.com
Valencia, Nulbel   <M1 RT>
   Diag 11D Casa 11 urbGemelas
   Dosquebradas, Risaralda
   Colombia, South America
   (576)330-7704
   nava1928@hotmail.com
Velez, Gabriel   <M1 RT>
   Calle 8A #16A-26, Villa Fanny
   Dosquebradas, Risaralda
   Colombia, South America
   (576)330-1168

OTHER LICENTIATES ON ROLL:

Guerrero, Cruzana   <M2>
   Calle 83 #74-179
   Medellin, Antioguia
   Colombia, South America
   (574)257-0613
Guerrero, Josue   <M2>
   Calle 76 #88-65
   Medellin, Antioquia
   Colombia, South America
   (574)412-3504
   josueggutierrez@yahoo.es
Gutierrez, Libardo   <M2>
   Calle 83 #74-179
   Medellin, Antioquia
   Colombia, South America
   (314)600-2020
   guzlibar@yahoo.es
Hoyos, Amparo   <M2>
   Cra 43 #20D-26
   Zamora, Antioquia
   Colombia, South America
   (574)278-0784
   chilalu1147@hotmail.com
Orozco, Joaquin   <M2>
   Cra 3 #7-14
   Aguadas, Caldas
   Colombia, South America
   (576)851-4773
   jeob40@hotmail.com

OTHER CANDIDATES ON ROLL:

Arias, John Jairo   <M3>
   Calle 144 sur #196-08 / Apto 202
   Caldas, Antioquia
   Colombia, South America
   (57)317-693-1162
   sajoarias@hotmail.com
Cardona, Nancy   <M3 ST>
   Calle 51 #15-32
   Dosquebradas, Risaralda
   Colombia, South America
   (576)322-2938
   nancycardona10@yahoo.com
Galvis, Alexander   <M3 ST>
   Calle 76 #87-63 Apto 211
   Medellin, Antioquia
   Colombia, South America
   (300)778-4354
   alexgt7@hotmail.com
Giraldo, Juan Pablo   <M3>
   Calle 51 #15-32
   barrio Los Naranjos
   Dosquebradas, Risaralda
   Colombia, South America
   (576)322-2938
Giraldo, Marcela   <M3>
   Calle 68 D #40-15
   Manizales, Caldas
   Colombia, South America
   (576)878-5412
Jimenez, Jorge Enrique   <M3>
   Urb Manantiales MzC Casa 6
   Armenia, Quindio
   Colombia, South America
   (321)643-0693
   joenjimu@yahoo.es
Laverde, Alina   <M3>
   Calle 100 #50C-09
   Barrio Santa Cruz Sector La Rosa

ANDES PRESBYTERY CONTINUED

Medellin, Antioquia
Colombia, South America
(574)236-6509
Lopez, Carlos Geovanny <M3>
Cra 12 bis #11-69
Pereira, Risaralda
Colombia, South America
(576)333-9295
Morales, Juan Fernando <M3>
Calle 100 #50C-09
Barrio Santa Cruz Sector La Rosa
Medellin, Antioquia
Colombia, South America
(574)236-6509
Ortega, Juan <M3>
Colombia, South America
(574)323-9305
Porras, Rene Wilgen <M3>
Cra 4 bis #10-51
La Virginia, Risalda
(576)367-9529

Vargas, Lida Patricia <M3>
Carrera 50D #62-69, Prado Centro
Medellin, Antioquia
Colombia, South America
(574)263-2154
lidapavargas@hotmail.com
Varilla, Adan Manuel <M3>
Calle 48 D E #96A-30
Medellin, Antioquia
Colombia, South America
(57)313-691-1923
Velez, Gloria Patricia <M3>
Cra 4 bis #10-51
LaVirginia, Risaralda
Colombia, South America
(576)385-4517
renewilgen@hotmail.com

Arkansas Presbytery
GREAT RIVERS SYNOD

GENERAL		MEMBERSHIP			CHANGES				FINANCES				
	1.Church Number	2.Active	3.Total	4.Church School	5.Prof. of Faith	6.Gains	7.Losses	8.Children Baptized	9. OUR UNITED OUT-REACH	10. Total Out-Reach Giving	11. All Other Expenses	12. Total Income Received	13. Value Church Prop. 1=1000
	1	2	3	4	5	6	7	8	9	10	11	12	13
Appleton	1202	14	29	25	0	0	2	0	350	2,534	10,525	14,470	40
Arkansas Loving	2135	45	63	2	No Report Received			0	0	0	0	0	700
Barren Fork	1501	90	103	57	1	2	1	0	6,957	13,411	64,480	77,891	400
Ben Lomond	1301	29	29	20	0	0	2	0	0	3,926	15,949	22,650	70
Bethesda	1302	42	62	40	2	2	12	0	0	10,529	85,556	77,825	957
Booneville	1401	50	56	7	2	6	33	0	6,274	12,953	54,937	65,545	375
Byron	1508	11	11	25	2	2	2	0	300	2,994	8,571	11,565	287
Calico Rock	1503	87	109	62	2	4	2	0	14,022	50,721	88,401	139,122	1,276
Camden	1303	37	89	40	4	4	0	0	5,929	7,788	67,976	60,088	330
Camp Ground	1101	51	123	17	0	1	5	0	6,720	14,086	49,180	68,804	600
Caulksville	1402	203	225	30	3	8	3	2	11,913	55,012	11,074	131,966	800
Dilworth	1304	7	13	13	1	0	0	1	0	1,751	22,974	20,961	125
Dover	1203	22	29	13	1	3	0	0	2,787	9,357	52,945	58,028	210
E. T. Allen	1307	17	17	12	0	0	0	0	0	3,750	38,228	33,903	225
Faith-Hopewell	1502	101	114	79	1	10	55	1	9,374	15,746	84,851	101,207	1,400
Falls Chapel	1308	32	32	28	4	6	2	0	0	10,204	39,208	57,261	n/a
Fellowship (BC)	1505	97	182	61	3	13	4	1	13,400	21,708	157,298	133,721	1,326
Fellowship (OC)	1309	31	36	57	9	10	0	9	4,338	10,649	35,632	43,384	117
Fomby	1310	5	31	6	0	0	0	0	0	4,529	10,682	17,808	138
Fort Smith*	1406	47	176	14	3	3	1	0	1,386	2,362	62,737	23,621	800
Grace	1405	56	56	14	0	0	0	0	5,090	12,101	46,244	58,345	272
Gum Springs (WC)	1205	9	9	13	0	0	0	0	0	637	7,500	8,200	n/a
Gum Springs (YC)	1206	18	23	10	0	6	0	0	0	150	26,710	20,654	250
Hector	1207	18	51	12	0	0	0	0	0	2,227	14,777	22,412	93
Lake Hamilton*	1221	66	88	10	5	0	3	1	0	5,572	59,381	69,454	350
Lockesburg	1311	3	3	0	No Report Received			0	0	0	0	0	162
Lucas Community	1407	8	11	17	No Report Received			0	0	0	0	0	65
Marietta	1408	48	48	48	0	0	1	0	0	7,122	36,174	48,354	350
Mars Hill	1211	15	35	0	0	0	1	0	500	2,949	23,417	26,355	200
Milligan C. G.	1516	6	10	5	No longer having services 10/30/13			0	0	0	0	0	61
Mt. Carmel*	1212	41	41	17	3	0	5	0	8,083	16,888	68,514	79,980	75
Mt. Olive	1517	31	39	9	2	2	0	0	1,802	17,401	20,215	35,368	230
New Hope	1510	13	18	9	0	0	0	0	2,685	4,380	13,424	27,278	350
Old Union*	1409	31	48	13	0	1	0	1	2,758	4,059	13,874	31,177	115
Oxford	1511	28	28	25	3	3	0	1	325	5,743	7,745	13,416	85
Palestine*	1103	87	121	50	1	10	4	0	4,200	13,859	79,833	111,350	1,575
Pilot Prairie	1411	8	14	6	No longer CPC 10/30/13			0	0	0	0	0	50
Pine Bluff, 1st	1104	13	103	0	Financial Figures Not Available			0	0	0	0	0	766
Pine Ridge*	1105	20	25	12	0	5	0	1	3,346	3,128	40,352	39,641	381
Pineville	1512	56	72	35	1	2	0	0	7,428	21,632	64,006	86,029	300
Pleasant Grove	1214	5	9	5	No Report Received			0	0	0	0	0	70
Prairie Grove	1412	14	14	13	No Report Received			0	0	0	0	0	530
Provo	1314	11	38	25	No Report Received			0	0	0	0	0	125
Rodney	1513	18	18	12	0	0	0	0	0	2,606	18,410	20,243	65
Rose Hill	1106	53	53	35	0	0	1	0	6,368	1,300	56,896	63,237	1,000
Russellville	1216	225	225	45	0	0	4	0	1,184	263	153,974	172,564	1,701
Salem (FC)	1514	28	29	15	0	0	0	0	1,535	4,207	16,206	18,976	250
Searcy	1218	30	56	22	2	2	2	0	1,200	5,390	21,040	25,400	500
Shaver	1413	1	1	0	No longer having services			0	0	0	0	0	10
Shell Chapel	1108	8	31	4	1	1	1	0	1,300	2,520	14,501	14,161	500
Sherwood	1220	20	184	6	0	3	3	0	0	0	57,910	51,494	777
Sidney	1515	9	18	9	No Report Received			0	0	0	0	0	200
Sulphur Springs	1315	16	47	11	0	0	1	0	0	2,083	26,446	28,529	30
Trimble Camp G**	1504	35	20	33	0	0	20	0	4,369	19,483	27,891	47,115	365
Trinity*	1219	15	35	0	0	0	31	0	0	2,949	23,417	26,355	200
Walkerville	1317	13	27	10	No Report Received			0	0	0	0	0	150
Walnut Grove	1414	32	59	18	3	6	0	0	0	3,750	36,610	36,256	200
TOTALS	57	2,126	3,236	1,176	59	115	201	18	135,923	416,409	1,936,671	2,342,163	22,579

*Math error corrected. **Purged roll.

ARKANSAS PRESBYTERY CONTINUED

CHURCHES, PASTORS, AND CLERKS:

Appleton   (W4C)GRAR1202
171 Tate Street (mailing)
320 Tate Street (physical)
Atkins, AR 72823
(   )   <Pope>
CL: Sue Bartlett
171 Tate Street
Atkins, AR 72823
(479)284-4357
msbart@thebartlettpage.com

Arkansas Loving   (P)GRAR2135
1603 Coolhurst Avenue
Sherwood, AR 72120
(501)247-5953   <Pulaski>
swcho100491@gmail.com
PA: Sung Wan Cho   <M1>
1603 Coolhurst Avenue
Sherwood, AR 72120
(501)247-5953
swcho100491@gmail.com
CL: Eun Hi Lee
110 Beaulieu Court
Maumelle, AR 72113
(501)247-4545

Barren Fork   (4MWC)GRAR1501
782 Barren Fork Road
Mount Pleasant, AR 72561
(870)346-5121   <Izard>
CL: Connie Crafton
1275 Barren Fork Road
Mount Pleasant, AR 72561
(870)346-5349

Ben Lomond   (4C)GRAR1301
180 LR 39 (mailing)
Ogden, AR 71853
495 N Main Street (physical)
Ben Lomond, AR 71823
(   )   <Sevier>
OD: Herman R Welch   <M5>
180 LR 39
Ogden, AR 71853
(903)748-2126
herawe@yahoo.com
CL: Teresa L Welch
180 LR 39
Ogden, AR 71853
(903)748-2126
tlwelch63@gmail.com

Bethesda   (4MW C)GRAR1302
395 Ouachita 47
Camden, AR 71701
(870)231-4909   <Ouachita>
CL: Ben Fields
451 Ouachita 47
Camden, AR 71701
(870)231-5080
bfields2011@hotmail.com

Booneville   (4MEW C)GRAR1401
PO Box 163 (mailing)
355 Sharp Street (physical)
Booneville, AR 72927
(   )   <Logan>
church@boonevillecpc.com

PA: Henry Jenkins   <M1>
PO Box 148 (mailing)
90 W Grove (physical)
Magazine, AR 72943
(479)969-8351
henryj@magtel.com
CL: Janet Bedene
PO Box 7 (mailing)
113 Pine Street(physical)
Ratcliff, AR 72951
(479)847-6746
phaparis@magtel.com

Byron   (4WC)GRAR1508
PO Box 524 (mailing)
Byron Road, Viola, AR (physical)
Calico Rock, AR 72519
(870)291-8542   <Fulton>
calicowild@hotmail.com
CL: Session Clerk
PO Box 524
Calico Rock, AR 72519
(870)291-8542
calicowild@hotmail.com

Calico Rock   (4MEWC)GRAR1503
PO Box 315 (mailing)
692 AR 56 Highway E (physical)
Calico Rock, AR 72519
(870)297-3931   <Izard>
FAX: (870)297-3151
crcpc@centurytel.net
PA: Thomas D Campbell   <M1>
PO Box 343
Calico Rock, AR 72519
(870)297-3931
FAX: (870)297-3151
tdcampbellar@gmail.com
CL: Carolyn Jeffery
PO Box 183
Calico Rock, AR 72519
(870)297-8530
cjeffery6@gmail.com

Camden   (4MEWC)GRAR1303
1545 California Avenue
Camden, AR 71701
(870)836-8712   <Ouachita>
CL: Deanie Tate
138 Ouachita 571
Camden, AR 71701
(870)403-4847
tdtate38@yahoo.com

Camp Ground   (4WMC)GRAR1101
1548 E AR 274 Highway
Hampton, AR 71744
(870)798-4302   <Calhoun>
PA: Garland Skidmore   <M1>
2083 US Highway 278 E
Hampton, AR 71744
(870)798-4634
CL: Shirley Strickland
1783 E AR 274 Highway
Hampton, AR 71744
(870)918-2344
strick6@sat-co.net

Caulksville   (4MWC)GRAR1402
PO Box 2 (mailing)
23 W Main, Caulksville, AR (physical)

Ratcliff, AR 72951
(479)635-4301   <Logan>
PA: Bill Van Meter   <M1>
10626 Highway 41
Charleston, AR 72933
(479)965-2998
revbill46@gmail.com
CL: Cherre Nietert
10201 Nietert Lane
Branch, AR 72928
(479)438-0673

Dilworth   (4C)GRAR1304
305 N 6th Street (mailing)
De Queen, AR 71832
2517 N Red Bridge Road (physical)
Horatio, AR 71842
(870)642-8051   <Sevier>
mtcarmel2@windstream.net
OD: Byron G Sullivan   <M5>
305 N 6th Street
De Queen, AR 71832
(870)642-8051
mtcarmel2@windstream.net
CL: Nita Sue Sullivan
305 N 6th Street
De Queen, AR 71832
(870)642-8051
mtcarmel2@windstream.net

Dover   (4MWC)GRAR1203
29 Maple Street (mailing)
Hector, AR 72843
96 Waters Street (physical)
Dover, AR 72837
(479)331-3130   <Pope>
markoe@centurytel.net
OD: Mike Galloway   <M5>
2821 Linker Mount Road
Dover, AR 72837
(479)331-0254
markoe@centurytel.net
CL: Beth McAlister
29 Maple Street
Hector, AR 72843
beth.ann56@hotmail.com

E T Allen   (4WC)GRAR1307
PO Box 822 (mailing)
153 Highway 71 N
Ashdown, AR 71822
(   )   <Little Rive>
CL: Glen Ray Bowman
1050 Oak Place
Ashdown, AR 71822
(903)824-5000
botech64@aol.com

Faith-Hopewell   (4WC)GRAR1502
3895 Harrison Street
Batesville, AR 72501
(870)612-5949   <Independence>
CL: Ionna Hess
3075 O'Neal Road
Batesville, AR 72501
(870)793-5530
ionnahess@yahoo.com

Falls Chapel   (4MC)GRAR1308
182 Hunter Falls Loop (mailing)
127 LW Davis Road (physical)

ARKANSAS PRESBYTERY CONTINUED

Lockesburg, AR 71846
( )   <Sevier>
CL: Ann Keith
  182 Hunter Falls Loop
  Lockesburg, AR 71846
  (870)289-6834
  memaplayground@windstream.net

———————————
Fellowship (BC)   (4EWC)GRAR1505
  PO Box 866 (mailing)
  1206 E 9th Street (physical)
  Mountain Home, AR 72653
  (870)425-5419   <Baxter>
  info@fellowshipcumberland.org
PA: Gary Robert Tubb   <M1>
  103 Forest Drive
  Mountain Home, AR 72653
  grtubb@yahoo.com
  (870)424-0603
CL: Andy Marts
  393 County Road 1085
  Mountain Home, AR 72653
  (870)481-6092
  amarts@centurytel.net

———————————
Fellowship (OC)   (4WC)GRAR1309
  478 Ouachita 54 (mailing)
  2855 Ouachita 3 (physical)
  Camden, AR 71701
  ( )   <Ouachita>
SS: Roberta Smith Johnson   <M1>
  397 Ouachita 54
  Camden, AR 71701
  (870)231-5827
CL: Charles T Jeffus
  478 Ouachita 54
  Camden, AR 71701
  (870)231-9994
  charlesjeffus@yahoo.com

———————————
Fomby   (4C)GRAR1310
  704 Highway 317 (mailing)
  1215 Highway 32 E (physical)
  Ashdown, AR 71822
  (870)898-2856   <Little Rive>
  carole4485@att.net
CL: Carole C Booth
  704 Highway 317
  Ashdown, AR 71822
  (870)898-2856
  carole4485@att.net

———————————
Fort Smith   (4MEWC)GRAR1406
  605 N 47th Street
  Fort Smith, AR 72903
  (479)782-0454   <Sebastian>
  FAX: (479)782-0454
  ksstamps@msn.com
OD: Randall Cross   <M5>
  608 N Crest Drive
  Fayetteville, AR 72701
  (870)917-9303
  rkcross@cox.net
CL: Janie Stamps
  4008 Logan Lane
  Fort Smith, AR 72903
  (479)478-0161
  bjstamps@msn.com

———————————
Grace   (4C)GRAR1405
  2451 Wedington Drive

Fayetteville, AR 72701
  (479)442-6772   <Washington>
CL: Robin Thomas
  1195 N White Rock Lane
  Fayetteville, AR 72704
  (479)521-0371
  rthomas@mman.com

———————————
Gum Springs(WC)   (4C)GRAR1205
  1717 W Arch Avenue (mailing)
  Gum Springs Road (physical)
  Searcy, AR 72143
  (501)268-2615   <White>
SS: Jim Bradberry   <M3>
  120 Hummingbird Lane
  Searcy, AR 72143
  (501)278-9750
CL: J C Holleman
  1717 W Arch Avenue
  Searcy, AR 72143
  (501)268-2615

———————————
Gum Springs(YC)   (4MC)GRAR1206
  10146 Crescent Drive (mailing)
  10048 Blessed Road (physical)
  Dardanelle, AR 72834
  (479)229-4140   <Yell>
  wesides@centurytel.net
CL: Marilyn Roberts
  10742 Gum Springs Road
  Dardanelle, AR 72834
  (479)229-3017

———————————
Hector   (4MWC)GRAR1207
  PO Box 53 (mailing)
  29 Maple (physical)
  Hector, AR 72843
  (479)747-7561   <Pope>
CL: Beth McAlister
  PO Box 53
  Hector, AR 72843
  (479)747-7561

———————————
Lake Hamilton   (4 C)GRAR1221
  2891 Airport Road
  Hot Springs, AR 71913
  (501)760-3800   <Garland>
  lakehamiltonchurch@att.net
PA: Duawn Mearns   <M1>
  107 Westoak Place
  Hot Springs, AR 71913
  (501)276-1266
  lakehamiltonchurch@att.net
CL: Phyllis Pipkin
  197 Cobbleridge Trail
  Hot Springs, AR 71913
  (501)318-3462
  sephpipkin@aol.com

———————————
Lockesburg   (1C)GRAR1311
  279 N Park Avenue (mailing)
  114 W Walnut (physical)
  Lockesburg, AR 71846
  ( )   <Sevier>
CL: Joe E Bush
  279 N Park Avenue
  Lockesburg, AR 71846
  (870)289-2433

———————————
Lucas Community   (4C)GRAR1407
  Rt 1 Box 260

Booneville, AR 72927
  ( )   <Logan>
CL: Nell Hattabaugh
  1227 Dizzy Dean Road
  Booneville, AR 72927
  (479)675-3219

———————————
Marietta   (4C)GRAR1408
  623 Church Street (mailing)
  2604 West Main (physical)
  Charleston, AR 72933
  (479)965-0224   <Franklin>
SS: Vondal Davenport   <M1>
  PO Box 823
  Lavaca, AR 72941
  (479)965-2036
CL: Tim Aldridge
  623 Church Street
  Charleston, AR 72933
  (479)965-7639
  dcotim58@live.com

———————————
Mars Hill   (4WC)GRAR1211
  172 Thompson Lane (mailing)
  1224 State Route 363 (physical)
  Pottsville, AR 72858
  ( )   <Pope>
PA: Jo Warren   <M1>
  811 Wall Street
  Morrilton, AR 72110
  (501)354-4139
  pastorjo47@ymail.com
CL: Gary Thompson
  172 Thompson Lane
  Pottsville, AR 72858
  (479)970-4652
  thompgary@gmail.com
——————————(no services 10/30/13)
Milligan C G   (2C)GRAR1516
  Strawberry, AR 72469
  ( )   <Sharp>
PA: Alan Meinzer   <M1>
  25 Rosewood Road
  Batesville, AR 72501
  (870)793-3915
CL:Geraldine Poskey
  1976 Arkansas Highway 230
  Strawberry, AR 72469
  (870)528-3292

———————————
Mt Carmel   (4C)GRAR1212
  1470 Mt Carmel Road W
  London, AR 72847
  (479)293-4447   <Pope>
  mtcarmel@centurylink.net
PA: Thomas (Tom) Deere   <M1>
  460 Yukon Drive
  Russellville, AR 72811
  (479)498-0318
  tdeere@suddenlinkmail.com
CL: Jennifer Metz
  276 Metz Lane
  London, AR 72847
  (479)293-4229
  jmetz54@hotmail.com

———————————
Mt Olive   (4EC)GRAR1517
  214 Bear Trail Hollow (mailing)
  5539 Mt Olive Road (physical)
  Melbourne, AR 72556
  (870)368-4923   <Izard>

ARKANSAS PRESBYTERY CONTINUED

bobeth@centurytel.net
SS: Stan Mars   <M2>
PO Box 274
Mt Pleasant, AR 72561
(217)254-5120
smars2@liberty.edu
CL: Mary Beth Jeffery
214 Bear Trail Hollow
Melbourne, AR 72556
(870)368-4923
bobeth@centurytel.net

New Hope   (2C)GRAR1510
25 Pine Hill Road (mailing)
3655 Bethesda Road (physical)
Batesville, AR 72501
( )   <Independence>
verenaherrin@yahoo.com
CL: Verena Herrin
25 Pine Hill Road
Batesville, AR 72501
(870)793-6145
verenaherrin@yahoo.com

Old Union   (4C)GRAR1409
PO Box 477 (mailing)
Old Union Road (physical)
Magazine, AR 72943
( )   <Logan>
PA: Henry Jenkins   <M1>
PO Box 148
Magazine, AR 72943
(479)969-8352
henryj@magtel.com
CL: Lee Strickland
PO Box 477
Magazine, AR 72943
(479)849-0198
eljws1@live.com

Oxford   (4U)GRAR1511
618 Camp Ground Road (mailing)
211 Main Street (physical)
Oxford, AR 72565
( )   <Izard>
SS: Bobby D Coleman   <M1>
704 E Webb Street
Mountain View, AR 72560
(870)213-5410
bobbycoleman@gmail.com
CL: Willetta Everett
618 Camp Ground Road
Oxford, AR 72565
(870)258-7798
weverett@centurytel.net

Palestine   (4MEWC)GRAR1103
PO Box 98 (mailing)
223 South Main Street (physical)
Palestine, AR 72372
(870)581-2600   <St. Francis>
FAX: (870)581-2600
CL: Lisa Alldredge
PO Box 803
Palestine, AR 72372
(870)581-2913
lsatmall@yahoo.com

Pilot Prairie   (4MC)GRAR1411
PO Box 1873
Waldron, AR 72958

(479)637-3938   <Scott>
(no longer CPC per Janie Stamps)

Pine Bluff 1st   (4W C)GRAR1104
2401 Camden Road
Pine Bluff, AR 71603
( )   <Jefferson>
CL: Catherine Currington
205 Moss Road
White Hall, AR 71602
(870)247-3839

Pine Ridge   (4C)GRAR1105
4890 Grant 14
Grapevine, AR 72057
(870)942-1827   <Grant>
PA: James (Jim) Bradshaw   <M1>
415 S Red Street
Sheridan, AR 72150
(870)942-2525
CL: Buren Walker
336 Grant 748
Sheridan, AR 72150
(870)942-4790

Pineville   (4MWC)GRAR1512
PO Box 256 (mailing)
1229 AR 223 Highway (physical)
Pineville, AR 72566
(870)297-4104   <Izard>
PA: Isaac Gray   <M1>
1211 AR 233 Highway
Pineville, AR 72566
(870)373-4731
revgray08@gmail.com
CL: Janie Jenkins
PO Box 504
Calico Rock, AR 72519
(870)297-3991
djjenkins@centurytel.net

Pleasant Grove   (2C)GRAR1214
1083 Highway 305 S
Searcy, AR 72143
(501)796-3466   <White>
CL: Robbie Stroud
1922 Highway 31 N
Beebe, AR 72012
(501)882-3262

Prairie Grove   (4C)GRAR1412
200 West Buchanan
Prairie Grove, AR 72753
(479)846-3914   <Washington>
PA: George Woodliff   <M1>
310 W Cleveland Street Apt A3
Prairie Grove, AR 72753
(479)410-1933
mwoodliff@kih.net
SS: Richard Niswonger   <M1>
20941 Highway 16 E
Siloam Springs, AR 72761
(479)524-4081
rniswonger@cox.net
CL: Jonathan Woodliff
310 W Cleveland Street Apt A3
Prairie Grove, AR 72753
(479)410-1933
mwoodliff@kih.net

Provo   (4C)GRAR1314

131 LR 47 (mailing)
Ashdown, AR 71822
125 Dooley Road (physical)
Lockesburg, AR 71846
( )   <Sevier>
CL: Mica Crow
131 LR 47
Ashdown, AR 71822
(870)898-8588

Rodney   (2EC)GRAR1513
117 Flint Rock Trail (mailing)
1333 Rodney Road (physical)
Jordan, AR 72519
( )   <Baxter>
PA: Dave Williamson   <M1>
PO Box 67
Dolph, AR 72528
(870)499-7448
CL: Yvonne Southard
117 Flint Rock Trail
Jordan, AR 72519
(870)499-7365
FAX: (870)499-5109
ysouthard@hotmail.com

Rose Hill   (4MWC)GRAR1106
1031 Binns Drive (mailing)
2133 Highway 83 N (physical)
Monticello, AR 71655
(870)367-5114   <Drew>
gsaray@att.net
CL: Stephanie Ray
122 E Shelton Avenue
Monticello, AR 71655
(870)723-3785
gsaray@att.net

Russellville   (4WC)GRAR1216
1200 N Arkansas Avenue
Russellville, AR 72801
(479)968-1061   <Pope>
FAX: (479)880-0071
fcpcrussellville@yahoo.com
PA: Steve Mosley   <M1>
320 N Sherman Circle
Russellville, AR 72801
(479)968-1061
FAX: (479)880-0071
stevemosley@hotmail.com
CL: Deanna Boston
721 Kovel Court
Russellville, AR 72801
(479)890-3880
fcpcrussellville@yahoo.com

Salem (FC)   (4MWC)GRAR1514
1003 Flint Springs Road (mailing)
Viola, AR 72583
Highway 5 S, Salem, AR (physical)
( )   <Fulton>
salemcumberlandchurch@gmail.com
SS: Bobby D Coleman   <M1>
704 E Webb Street
Mountain View, AR 72560
(870)269-6010
bobby.coleman@gmail.com
CL: Bonnie Brown
1003 Flint Springs Road
Viola, AR 72583
(870)458-2657

ARKANSAS PRESBYTERY CONTINUED

bbrown325@centurytel.net

Searcy (4MWC)GRAR1218
100 E Race Street
Searcy, AR 72143
(501)268-8278 <White>
SS: Jim Bradberry <M3>
120 Hummingbird Lane
Searcy, AR 72143
(501)278-9750
CL:Howard Johnson
2180 Holmes Road
Searcy, AR 72143
(501)268-3071
howardwjohnson@gmail.com

Shaver (1C)GRAR1413
(no longer has services 10/30/13)
401 Shaver Road (mailing)
1448 Shaver Road (physical)
Paris, AR 72855
( ) <Logan>

Shell Chapel (4WC)GRAR1108
2143 Grider Field Road (mailing)
3110 Highway 425 (physical)
Pine Bluff, AR 71601
(870)535-5408 <Jefferson>
PA: Barbara Jean Brewer <M1>
1360 White Oak Bluff Road
Rison, AR 71665
(870)325-6449
CL: Joyce Shell
2143 Grider Field Road
Pine Bluff, AR 71601
(870)535-5408
mkshell@earthlink.net

Sherwood (4WC)GRAR1220
1402 E Kiehl Avenue
Sherwood, AR 72120
(501)835-8889 <Pulaski>
CL: Olive Snow
5907 Woodview Drive S
Sherwood, AR 72120
(501)835-7819
ladysnow64@yahoo.com

Sidney (2U)GRAR1515
Batesville, AR 72501
( ) <Sharp>
PA: Alan Meinzer <M1>
25 Rosewood Road
Batesville, AR 72501
(870)793-3915
natsdad@suddenlink.net
CL: Jodi Moody
127 Arkansas Highway 58
Sidney, AR 72577
(870)283-6766

Sulphur Springs (4C)GRAR1315
3225 Ouachita 2 (mailing)
3086 Ouachita 2 (physical)
Louann, AR 71751
(870)689-3598 <Ouachita>
mdarden@oeccwildblue.com
CL:Paula G Darden
3225 Ouachita 2
Louann, AR 71751
(870)689-3598

mdarden@oeccwildblue.com

Trimble Camp G (4WC)GRAR1504
PO Box 150 (mailing)
Trimble Camp Ground Road (physical)
Dolph, AR 72528
(870)297-8088 <Izard>
PA: Joel Snyder <M1>
224 Lord Lane
Mountain View, AR 72560
(870)269-9743
synyder.joel@ymail.com
CL: Jana Cowgill
1037 Chriswood Drive
Clarkridge, AR 72623
(870)421-2106

Trinity (4MEWC)GRAR1219
809 W Wall Street
Morrilton, AR 72110
(501)354-4139 <Conway>
PA: Gordon Warren <M1>
811 Wall Street
Morrilton, AR 72110
(501)208-1120
jogordonwarren@suddenlink.net
CL: Jammie Bonds
809 Wall Street
Morrilton, AR 72110
(501)354-4139

Walkerville (4MEWC)GRAR1317
10160 Highway 19 S
Magnolia, AR 71753
( ) <Columbia>
PA: Michael Suttle <M1>
159 Ouachita 593
Camden, AR 71701
(870)836-0008
m_s_suttle@msn.com
CL: Jim Edwards
10570 S Highway 19
Emerson, AR 71740
(870)696-3973
jse10570@gmail.com

Walnut Grove (4WC)GRAR1414
4724 N State Highway 23 (mailing)
1294 Six Mile Road (physical)
Magazine, AR 72943
( ) <Logan>
danekas@centurytel.net
SS: Don Kennedy <M3>
5335 Dizzy Dean Road
Booneville, AR 72927
(479)675-4418
donkennedy@centurytel.net
CL: Debbie Danekas
4724 N State Highway 23
Booneville, AR 72927
(479)675-5004
danekas@centurytel.net

OTHERS ON MINISTERIAL ROLL:

Blackburn, Samuel N <M1 WC>
6706 S 6th Street
Fort Smith, AR 72908
(479)649-9436
Blanton, D B <M1 RT>
ADDRESS UNKNOWN

Bowling, Andrew <M1 WC>
20945 Highway 16 E
Siloam Springs, AR 72761
(479)524-6576
Chambers, Jason <M1 WC>
131 E Woods Street
Palestine, AR 72372
(870)807-1930
jmchambers@memphisseminary.edu
Chang, Leo <M1 WC>
819 W Division SE
Springfield, MO 65803
(901)287-9901
Cook, Carl <M1 WC>
475 Western Hills Loop
Mountain Home, AR 72653
(870)425-2570
carlc@suddenlink.net
Fisk, James R <M1 WC>
311 Merril Drive
Benton, AR 72015
jimfisk95@yahoo.com
(870)367-3086
Fleming, Patrick T <M1 WC>
616 N Border Street
Benton, AR 72015
(501)944-4678
ptfleming@live.com
Guthrie, William <M1 WC>
11130 Frenchmen Loop Apt B
Maumelle, AR 72113
(501)584-0019
billybarloe@yahoo.com
Halford, Angela <M1 OM>
PO Box 191466
Little Rock, AR 72219
(501)407-0065
Hamlink, Ronald L <M1 WC>
PO Box 923
Fairacres, NM 88033
(505)525-9867
hamronelink@yahoo.com
Holley, Ann <M1 WC>
PO Box 345
Lockesburg, AR 71846
(870)289-3421
FAX: (870)289-2914
ladyrev1115@yahoo.com
Jeffrey, Sarah Ann <M1 WC>
5271 Highway 202 E
Yellville, AR 72687
(870)453-7076
FAX: (870)715-9229
annjeffrey2001@yahoo.com
Jones, Michael <M1 WC>
120 Jennifer Lane
Branson, MO 65616
(417)334-2058
Jones, Victor <M1 WC>
7017 Highway 177 S
Jordan, AR 72519
(870)499-5882
pam.jones@centurytel.net
Martin, William E, Jr <M1 WC>
PO Box 98
131 E Wood Avenue
Palestine, AR 72372
(870)581-2530
juniormartin@yahoo.com
McSpadden, Nancy <M1 M9>
2011 Woodridge Drive

ARKANSAS PRESBYTERY CONTINUED

St Peters, MO 63376
(870)612-0067
revnancy77@gmail.com

Moore, Angela   \<M1 WC\>
   3756 Douglass Avenue
   Memphis, TN 38111
   (870)581-2509

O'Neal Danhof, Clair   \<M1 WC\>
   301 Whispering Hills Street
   Hot Springs, AR 71901
   acglenn@aol.com

Pedigo, Russell   \<M1 WC\>
   1002 Haney Avenue
   El Dorado, AR 71730
   (870)862-4689
   russell_pedigo@hotmail.com

Ryan, Jack   \<M1 WC\>
   8806 Kennesaw Mountain Drive
   Mabelvale, AR 72103
   (501)749-8572

Shanley, Dwight   \<M1 WC\>
   16904 Old Mill Road
   Little Rock, AR 72206
   (501)888-4190
   dwightshanley@att.net

Shauf, Steve   \<M1 WC\>
   3032 Monroe Street
   Paducah, KY 42001
   (870)346-5021
   sshauf@hotmail.com

Shauf, Teresa   \<M1 WC\>
   3032 Monroe Street
   Paducah, KY 42001
   (870)291-2938
   theshaufs@hotmail.com

Sweigart, John M   \<M1 WC\>
   PO Box 876
   Dover, AL 72837
   (479)229-4041

Treadaway, Kenneth A   \<M1 WC\>
   172 Miller County 494
   Texarkana, AR 71854
   treadaways@ark.net
   (870)574-1609

Wood, Wayne   \<M1 WC\>
   HC 61 Box 600
   Calico Rock, AR 72519
   (870)297-2205
   FAX: (870)297-3151
   bexarwood@centurytel.net

Wooten, Wallace   \<M1 WC\>
   1152 Melrose Road
   Lockesburg, AR 71846
   (870)289-2224

OTHER LICENTIATES ON ROLL:

Brown, Amy   \<M2\>
   679 Freeze Bend Road
   Newport, AR 72112

Burns, Garrett   \<M2 ST\>
   387 Forrest Avenue
   McKenzie. TN 38201
   (731)535-3126
   gburns2888@gmail.com

Terrell, Elizabeth   \<M2\>
   2073 Vinton Avenue
   Memphis, TN 38104
   (901)647-2788

OTHER CANDIDATES ON ROLL:

Anderson, Christopher   \<M3 ST\>
   131 Roberta Drive
   Memphis, TN 38112
   (870)805-0886
   csanderson@memphisseminary.edu

Anderson, Kyle   \<M3\>
   828 E Main Street
   Batesville, AR 72501
   (870)834-5799
   kanderson@memphisseminary.edu

Brodbent, Josh   \<M3\>
   PO Box 587
   Wynne, AR 72397

Harbour, Ethan   \<M3\>
   1044 Alta Vista Road
   Louisville, KY 40205
   (479)849-6329
   ethanharbour@hotmail.com

Horst, Gail F, Jr.   \<M3\>
   14624 Lonepine Road
   N Little Rock, AR 72118
   (501)240-4034
   gail_horst@yahoo.com

Walsh, Devin   \<M3\>
   801 East "M" Street
   Russellville, AR 72801
   (479)890-6716

Washburn, Gloria   \<M3\>
   PO Box 2484
   Jordan, AR 72519
   (870)321-4596
   grwashburn07@gmail.com

Cauca Valley Presbytery
MISSION SYNOD

GENERAL		MEMBERSHIP			CHANGES				FINANCES				
1.Church Number	2.Active	3.Total	4.Church School	5.Prof. of Faith	6.Gains	7.Losses	8.Children Baptized	9. OUR UNITED OUT-REACH	10. Total Out-Reach Giving	11. All Other Expenses	12. Total Income Received	13. Value Church Prop. |1=1000
1	2	3	4	5	6	7	8	9	10	11	12	13
Betania Mission**8204	38	38	20	0	0	132	0		1,793	4,995	8,708	110
Bethel 8205	186	200	230	3	14	0	0		3,500	15,873	19,300	135
Caleb Mission* 8223	90	95	50	10	0	2	0		1,827	4,599	13,771	90
Central 8208	220	220	76	0	12	42	0		14,523	93,214	79,327	350
Divino Redentor* 8206	159	159	90	46	0	30	0		7,405	4,615	51,530	200
Emaus 8219	55	64	60	8	5	1	0		1,653	8,500	10,689	95
Filadelphia 8224	65	62	30	CLOSED 2013								
Filipos* 8211	72	72	50	3	0	39	0		887	7,900	8,870	100
Getsemani* 8210	31	34	15	0	3	0	0		1,464	3,548	7,810	90
Maranatha 8220	81	124	115	23	10	16	0		3,207	15,527	18,151	150
Nueva Esperanza 8221	80	96	70	0	20	0	0		3,100	15,600	22,300	200
Nueva Jerusalen 8222	99	177	140	0	20	0	0		2,300	5,935	8,300	150
Popayan* 8227	750	810	350	350	360	0	0		18,776	13,374	164,988	300
Principe De Paz* 8201	50	75	31	4	5	0	0		1,866	11,466	13,333	130
Renacer 8225	467	570	450	566	226	24	0		32,045	193,992	226,038	350
Samaria 8217	62	66	38	0	6	12	0		2,344	11,666	13,888	150
San Lucas* 8215	38	56	45	8	30	0	0		6,847	6,931	9,492	200
San Marcos 8218	90	129	60	0	10	0	0		3,945	17,200	21,200	150
San Pablo* 8212	136	217	50	87	24	0	0		4,083	30,426	36,140	200
Tulua Mission 8226	85	180	40	0	30	0	0		7,300	11,500	20,300	150
Presbytery 8200								12,930				
TOTALS 20	2,462	2,972	1,659	1,013	421	209	0	12,930	80,383	527,162	651,765	3300

*Math error corrected. **Purged roll.

CHURCHES, PASTORS, AND CLERKS:

Betania Mission   (4WF)MSCA8204
  Av 5 No 20-12
  (Aereo 851)
  Cali
  Colombia, South America
  ( )894-0624   <S America>
SS: Samuel Guanaquillo   <M3>
  Aereo 10701
  Cali
  Colombia, South America
  FAX: (408)255-5938
  samijg@hotmail.com
CL: Ana Bechara de Montoya
  Aereo 851
  Cali
  Colombia, South America

Bethel   (4MWC)MSCA8205
  Calle 14 Oeste No 48-17
  Cali
  Colombia, South America
  ( )554-7514   <S America>
SS:Rodrigo Torres   <M3>
  Aereo 6365
  Cali
  Colombia, South America
  (011)882-8372
CL: Ana Leyda Meneses

  Aereo 10701
  Cali
  Colombia, South America

Caleb Mission   (4F)MSCA8223
  Av 47 Oeste No 9 A-24
  Montebello
  Colombia, South America
  ( )323-8070   <S America>
PA: Gildardo Agudelo   <M1>
  Cra 73C # 1A-54
  Cali
  Colombia, South America
CL: Carmen Rosa
  Ave 47 Oe 9-51
  Montebello
  Colombia, South America

Central   (4MWC)MSCA8208
  Av Las Americas 19N 18
  Cali
  Colombia, South America
  ( )668-7109   <S America>
PA: Sergio Betancur   <M1>
  Iglesia El Rebano
  Calle 128 sur #48-13
  Caldas,Antioquia
  Colombia, South America
  ( )334-2904
  sergiobetancurposada@hotmail.com
CL: Rocio Triana
  Aereo 6365

  Cali
  Colombia, South America

Divino Redentor   (4MWC)MSCA8206
  Cra 3 No 36-29
  Juan XXIII
  Buenaventur Valle
  Colombia, South America
  ( )242-8399   <S America>
PA: Wilfrido Quinonez   <M1>
  Cra 3 No 36-29
  Juan XXIII
  Buenaventur Valle
  Colombia, South America
  (310)412-1711
  ipc.divinoredentor@gmail.com
CL: Marlen Palacios
  Cra 3 No 36-29
  Juan XXIII
  Buenaventur Valle
  Colombia, South America

Emaus   (4WC)MSCA8219
  Diag 1 sur Cra 49-1
  Buenaventura
  Colombia, South America
  ( )244-2624   <S America>
PA: Manuel Medina   <M1>
  Diag 1 sur Cra 49-1
  Buenaventura
  Colombia, South America
  ( )244-2624

CAUCA VALLEY PRESBYTERY CONTINUED

CL: Omairo Valasco Cosme
Aereo 969
Buenaventura
Colombia, South America

_____

Filadelphia   (4WF)MSCA8224
CLOSED 2013

_____

Filipos   (4WF)MSCA8211
Calle 34 #24A-36
(Aereo 6365)
Cali
Colombia, South America
(   )438-2563   <S America>
PA: Joel Cuartas   <M0>
Calle 34 #24A-36
Cali
Colombia, South America
(000)438-2512
CL: Adriana Gonzalez
Calle 34 #24A-36
Cali
Colombia, South America

_____

Getsemani   (ARC)MSCA8210
Cra 15 No 8-43
El Cerrito Valle
Colombia, South America
(   )256-4261   <S America>
SS: Gilberto Arteaga   <M3>
Aereo 794
Buenaventura
Colombia, South America
(000)256-4261
pastorgilbertoa@hotmail.com
CL: Amparo Rengifo
Cra 15 No 8-43
El Cerrito
Colombia, South America

_____

Maranatha   (4WF)MSCA8220
Calle 12 No 4-69
Guapi
Colombia, South America
(092)840-0940
FAX (092)840-0120   <S America>
PA: Alejandro Madrid   <M1>
Calle 12 No 4-69
Guapi
Colombia, South America
CL: Magali Angulo
Calle 12 No 4-69
Guapi
Colombia, South America

_____

Nueva Esperanza   (F)MSCA8221
Cra 89 4C-35
Cali
Colombia, South America
(   )332-5849   <South America>
nuevaesperanza1983@hotmail.com
PA: William Diaz   <M1>
Calle 5 Con Cra 89
Cali
Colombia, South America
(   )332-5849
nuevaesperanza1983@hotmail.com
CL: Fabiola Ariza
Avenida de las Americas
#19N-18 Presbiterio del Valle
Cali

Colombia, South America
(316)419-8414
fatvioleta@hotmail.com

_____

Nueva Jerusalen   (4F)MSCA8222
Cra 73 CN No 1 A 54 Lourdes
Cali
Colombia, South America
(   )323-3009   <S America>
SS: Fabian Florez   <M3>
Cra 73 CN No 1 A 54 Lour des
Cali Valle
Colombia, South America
(   )323-4447
fabianflorezpastor@yahoo.es
CL: Adriana Montenegro
Aereo 6365
Cali Valle
Colombia, South America

_____

Popayan   (ARC)MSCA8227
Cra 9 No 6 6N 87 Bello Horizonte
Popayan
Colombia, South America
(092)823-8988   <S America>
SS: Jhony Montano   <M3>
Cra 9 No 6 6N 87 Bello Horizonte
Popayan
Colombia, South America
(092)823-8988
CL: Irma Cecilia Medina
Cra 5 #19N-56
Popayan
Colombia, South America

_____

Principe De Paz   (4WC)MSCA8201
Cra 27 #7-48
Cali
Colombia, South America
(   )556-6527   <S America>
PA: Mario Gaviria   <M1>
Cra 27 No 7-48
Cali
Colombia, South America
(   )372-3869
pastormariogaviria@hotmail.com
CL: Holber Molina
Carrera 27 #7-48
Cali
Colombia, South America

_____

Renacer   (4WF)MSCA8225
Diag 26M Trv 73A-69
Cali
Colombia, South America
(   )422-3940   <S America>
SS: Wilson Lopez   <M3>
Diag 26 M Trv 73 A 69
Cali
Colombia, South America
(   )327-2543
CL: Maria Onix Lopez
Diag 26K #73 A-66
Cali
Colombia, South America

_____

Samaria   (4MWC)MSCA8217
Tranv 30 No 17F-122
(Aereo 4290)
Cali
Colombia, South America

(   )448-5880   <S America>
PA: Juan Bautista   <M1>
Tranv 30 No 17F-122
Cali
Colombia, South America
(   )442-4562
CL: Maria Josefa Martinez
Aereo 4290
Cali
Colombia, South America

_____

San Lucas   (4WC)MSCA8215
Cll 26 No 29 53
Palmira
Colombia, South America
(   )272-7584   <S America>
SS: Fernando Osorio   <M3>
Cll 26 No 29 53
Palmira
Colombia, South America
(   )272-7584
sanlucaspalmira@hotmail.com
CL: Janneth Naranto
Aereo 329
Palmira
Colombia, South America

_____

San Marcos   (4MWC)MSCA8218
Cll 46 A No 4N-25
(Aereo 6453)
Cali
Colombia, South America
(   )446-3311   <S America>
PA: Roberto Fonseca   <M1>
Cll 46 A No 4N 25
Colombia, South America
(   )446-7370
CL: Luz Dazy Ceballos
Cll 46 A No 4N-25
Aereo 6453
Cali
Colombia, South America

_____

San Pablo   (4MWC)MSCA8212
Cra 8 No 5-27
Guacari
Colombia, South America
(   )253-2751   <S America>
PA: Aldrin Calero   <M1>
Cra 8 No 5-27
Colombia, South America
(   )253-0453
SS: Alexander Quintero   <M3>
Carrera 13 #3-81
Guacari
Colombia, South America
CL: Luis Mayorga
Carrera 13 # 3-81
Guacari
Colombia, South America

_____

Tulua Mission   (4WF)MSCA8226
Cll 41A No 26-26
Tulua
Colombia, South America
(   )224-5004   <S America>
PA: Fhanor Pejendino   <M1>
Cll 41 A No 26-26
Tulua
Colombia, South America
(317)654-5750

CAUCA VALLEY PRESBYTERY CONTINUED

CL: Arnaldo Tajama
  Cra 26 #36-40
  Tulua
  Colombia, South America

OTHERS ON MINISTERIAL ROLL:

Ariza, Fabiola   \<M1 WC>
  Ave 3 Norte 19N-18
  Cali
  Colombia, South America
  fatvioleta@hotmail.com
  (316)419-8414

De Jimenez, Luciria Aguirre   \<M1 WC>
  Ave 3 Norte 19N-18
  Cali
  Colombia, South America
  (300)686-9161
  pastorluciana50@yahoo.com.co

Giraldo, William   \<M1 WC>
  CLL 62 No 1B 11
  Buenaventura
  Colombia, South America
  ( )439-5436

Racines, Jairo   \<M1 WC>
  CLL 39 No 13-40
  Cali
  Colombia, South America
  (311)385-6546

Rodriguez, Jairo Hernan   \<M1 WC>
  Cll 42 No 80B 64
  Cali-Valle
  Colombia, South America
  jairo.hrodriguez@hotmail.com
  (572)377-8741

Solis, Arcadio   \<M1 WC>
  Crr 42 D1 No 55-69
  Cali
  Colombia, South America

( )328-5486
Valencia, Jorge   \<M1 WC>
  Cra 89 4C-35
  Cali
  Colombia, South America
( )332-5840
Wallace, Boyce   \<M1 MY>
  Cra 101 No 15-93
  Cali
  Colombia, South America
( )339-1579
  hbwcali@yahoo.com

OTHER LICENTIATES ON ROLL:

Orozeo Ariza, Juan Carlos   \<M2>
  Aereo 6365
  Cali Vale
  Colombia, South America

OTHER CANDIDATES ON ROLL:

Caicedo, Efrain   \<M3>
  Aereo 6365
  Cali
  Colombia, South America
Hoyos, Javier   \<M3>
  Calle 34 24A-36
  Cali

  Colombia, South America
Lubo, Jaime   \<M3>
  AA 6365
  Montebello
  Colombia, South America
Paredes, Fabio   \<M3>
  Carerra 7 # 1-76
  La Cruztala
  Ipiales
  Colombia, South America
Piamba, Juan Carlos   \<M3>
  Cra 7 #21N-35
  Popayan
  Colombia, South America

Choctaw Presbytery
MISSION SYNOD

	GENERAL		MEMBERSHIP			CHANGES				FINANCES				
	1.Church Number	2.Active	3.Total	4.Church School	5.Prof. of Faith	6.Gains	7.Losses	8.Children Baptized	9. OUR UNITED OUT-REACH	10. Total Out-Reach Giving	11. All Other Expenses	12. Total Income Received	13. Value Church Prop. 1=1000
	1	2	3	4	5	6	7	8	9	10	11	12	13
Coal Creek	6102	6	28	10	0	0	0	0	87	432	4,042	5,413	11
Lone Star	6105	8	22	16	0	0	0	0	147	418	4,272	4,688	50
McGee Chapel*	6106	37	37	20	0	0	2	0	652	2,943	5,292	8,235	100
Panki Bok	6108	2	4	2	No Report Received			0	33	0	0	0	6
Pigeon Roost	6109	5	22	6	0	0	0	0	114	590	3,500	4,500	35
Rock Creek	6111	4	16	4	0	0	1	0	49	1,690	0	2,146	25
Round Lake	6112	9	9	20	No Report Received			0	105	0	0	0	3
TOTALS	7	71	138	78	0	0	3	0	1,187	6,073	17,106	24,982	230

CHURCHES, PASTORS, AND CLERKS:

Coal Creek   (4WC)MSCH6102
  Route 1 Box 1215
  Coalgate, OK 74538
  ( )   <Atoka>
PA: Nathan Scott   <M1>
  960 S Katy Road
  Atoka, OK 74525
  (580)364-6155
CL: Lola John
  Route 1 Box 1215
  Coalgate, OK 74538
  (580)258-8244

Lone Star   (2WC)MSCH6105
  PO Box 44 (mailing)
  206 S Newell Street (physical)
  Coalgate, OK 74538
  ( )   <Atoka>
SS: Hannah Bryan   <M1>
  32 Trenton Lane
  Mead, OK 73449
  (580)775-4955
  hbryan@choctawnation.com
CL: Evangeline Robinson
  PO Box 44
  Boswell, OK 74727
  (580)513-0170
  erobinson@choctawarchiving.com

McGee Chapel   (2EW C)MSCH6106
  PO Box 158
  Broken Bow, OK 74728
  (580)584-2099   <McCurtain>
  FAX: (580)584-2099
  chocpres@pine-net.com
PA: Randy Jacob   <M1>
  PO Box 158
  Broken Bow, OK 74728
  (580)236-2374
  FAX: (580)584-2099
  chocpres@pine-net.com
CL: Betty Jacob
  PO Box 158

Broken Bow, OK 74728
(580)584-2099
FAX: (580)584-2099
chocpres@pine-net.com

Panki Bok   (2C)MSCH6108
  PO Box 375
  Eagletown, OK 74734
  ( )   <McCurtain>
PA: Randy Jacob   <M1>
  610 W Adams Street
  Broken Bow, OK 74728
  (580)584-2099
  FAX: (580)584-2099
  chocpres@pine-net.com
CL: Mildred Ashalintubbi
  PO Box 375
  Eagletown, OK 74734
  (580)835-7336

Pigeon Roost   (2C)MSCH6109
  960 S Katy Road
  Atoka, OK 74525
  (580)889-2292   <Choctaw>
PA: Virginia Espinoza   <M1>
  PO Box 132
  Boswell, OK 74727
  (580)775-4138
  vespinoza@choctawnation.com
CL: Linda Scott
  960 S Katy Road
  Atoka, OK 74525
  (580)889-2292

Rock Creek   (2WC)MSCH6111
  c/o Betty Walton (mailing)
  PO Box 126
  Talihina, OK 74571
  Honobia, OK (physical)
  (918)567-2370   <LeFlore>
PA: Nathan Scott   <M1>
  960 S Katy Road
  Atoka, OK 74525
  (580)364-6155
CL: Betty Walton
  PO Box 126
  Talihina, OK 74571

(918)567-2370

Round Lake   (1WC)MSCH6112
  Box 127
  Tupelo, OK 74572
  (580)317-7427   <Coal>
PA: Hannah Bryan   <M1>
  32 Trenton Lane
  Mead, OK 73449
  (580)775-4955
  hbryan@choctawnation.com
CL: Vickie McClure
  Box 127
  Tupelo, OK 74572
  (580)317-7427

OTHERS ON MINISTERIAL ROLL:

OTHER CANDIDATES ON ROLL:

Crosby, Ronald   <M3>
  407 N "A" Street
  Calera, OK 74730
Scott, Linda   <M3>
  960 S Katy Road
  Atoka, OK 74525
  (580)889-2292

Columbia Presbytery
TENNESSEE SYNOD

	GENERAL	MEMBERSHIP			CHANGES				FINANCES				
	1.Church Number	2.Active	3.Total	4.Church School	5.Prof. of Faith	6.Gains	7.Losses	8.Children Baptized	9. OUR UNITED OUT-REACH	10. Total Out-Reach Giving	11. All Other Expenses	12. Total Income Received	13. Value Church Prop. 1=1000
	1	2	3	4	5	6	7	8	9	10	11	12	13
Ash Hill	7101	38	67	30	0	0	1	0	3,080	7,639	23,174	30,812	275
Belleview*	7104	16	25	7	0	0	1	0	250	4,198	15,514	20,299	500
Boonshill	7106	25	63	25	0	2	0	0	800	2,950	22,942	28,200	321
Champ*	7108	13	20	9	0	1	0	0	0	500	18,714	18,252	40
Chapel Hill	7109	30	30	25	2	2	5	0	1,000	3,800	44,200	52,000	410
Columbia**	7110	119	119	38	5	5	169	0	6,000	20,434	185,161	160,886	1,500
Elora	7111	5	5	6	0	0	0	0	0	100	7,829	11,341	150
Fayetteville*	7112	116	267	63	2	6	6	2	14,400	22,650	161,556	190,166	2,300
Fiducia	7113	14	14	14	No Report Received			0	396	0	0	0	100
Flintville*	7115	7	7	14	0	0	2	0	0	1,836	9,087	10,364	25
Franklin	7116	34	34	6	0	3	3	0	0	4,883	57,840	62,551	800
Grace*	7145	12	12	0	2	0	18	0	966	966	40,082	19,328	10
Green Hill	7118	14	14	13	0	0	3	0	1,574	4,832	31,644	35,086	86
Harpeth Lick	7119	25	40	13	0	3	3	0	1,300	5,934	43,061	37,355	200
Hohenwald*	7120	12	64	0	0	32	0	0	0	0	26,049	18,568	250
Howell	7121	58	124	71	1	1	2	1	3,000	20,634	50,492	77,155	750
Jenkins**	7144	96	211	75	3	3	114	0	16,699	32,574	205,466	230,481	3,387
Kelso	7122	35	94	26	0	0	1	0	700	4,473	65,666	64,660	180
Kingdom	7123	10	10	7	0	2	2	0	520	520	9,130	15,888	175
Lawrenceburg**	7124	29	53	15	0	0	113	0	0	1,000	177,903	309,426	1,100
Lewisburg, 1st	7125	68	182	91	3	3	0	2	500	5,200	119,737	118,300	800
McCains	7126	48	78	20	0	1	3	0	6,000	21,112	49,007	65,382	464
Mt. Carmel	7127	74	114	30	0	0	1	0	1,000	7,825	94,797	86,610	1,000
Mt. Hebron	7128	6	6	0	0	0	0	0	0	691	9,667	8,580	53
Mt. Joy	7129	67	106	26	7	7	4	0	1,164	1,164	38,006	67,650	300
Mt. Lebanon	7130	50	50	25	4	14	2	1	0	7,916	31,038	37,130	125
Mt. Moriah	7131	53	117	35	0	1	1	0	0	16,478	30,179	55,012	250
Mt. Nebo	7132	7	7	7	0	0	3	0	529	1,124	17,577	17,843	90
Mt. Pleasant	7133	46	97	19	0	1	10	1	2,396	5,576	46,678	51,811	1,000
New Bethel	7134	8	8	8	No Report Received			0	236	0	0	0	75
Petersburg	7135	43	49	48	0	1	0	0	10,200	22,996	52,667	75,663	230
Pleasant Mount	7136	34	86	32	0	0	4	1	2,200	7,700	53,700	57,400	500
Richland	7137	58	125	54	0	1	0	0	1,500	8,210	58,850	67,982	150
Santa Fe*	7138	28	28	23	0	0	14	0	0	2,733	21,700	31,745	0
Swan	7140	9	17	0	0	0	0	0	100	300	24,240	28,230	500
Union Grove	7141	8	8	12	0	0	0	0	0	1,206	8,897	13,222	100
Waynesboro	7142	58	58	21	0	0	2	1	7,872	21,090	48,693	78,149	697
West Point*	7143	86	203	98	4	6	0	0	0	5,373	90,921	96,507	1,000
TOTALS	38	1,459	2,612	1,006	33	95	487	9	84,382	276,617	1,991,864	2,350,034	19,893

*Math error corrected. **Purged roll.

(615)599-6764   (615)395-4935

CHURCHES, PASTORS, AND CLERKS:

Ash Hill   (4WC)TNCO7101
4930 Ash Hill Road
Spring Hill, TN 37174
(931)381-3367   <Williamson>
PA: James R Miller   <M1>
1214 Whitney Drive
Columbia, TN 38401
(931)215-2108
rev.james.miller@charter.net
CL: Helen Logue
1603 Emerald Court
Franklin, 37064

Belleview   (4WC)TNCO7104
1752 Burke Hollow Road (mailing)
Nolensville, TN 37135
4724 Murfreesboro Road (physical)
Franklin, TN 37064
( )   <Williamson>
PA: James R Miller   <M1>
1214 Whitney Drive
Columbia, TN 38401
(931)381-3367
rev.james.miller@charter.net
CL: David C Hughes
1752 Burke Hollow Road
Nolensville, TN 37135

Boonshill   (4C)TNCO7106
91 Red Oak Road (mailing)
Petersburg, TN 37144
Rt 2 (physical)
Boonshill, TN
( )   <Lincoln>
OD: Thomas Smith   <M5>
467 Gunter Hollow Drive
Fayetteville, TN 37334
(931)732-5426
CL: Sammy Luna
91 Red Oak Road
Petersburg, TN 37144
(931)703-0536

COLUMBIA PRESBYTERY CONTINUED

srluna@ardmore.net

_____

Champ   (2C)TNCO7108
290 Sullenger Bend Road (mailing)
Belvidere, TN 37306
61 Tucker Creek Road (physical)
Mulberry, TN
( )   <Lincoln>
CL: Diann Adams
2800 Hillsboro Road
Huntsville, AL 35805
(256)534-6076

_____

Chapel Hill   (4MWC)TNCO7109
4801 Eagleville Pike (mailing)
302 N Horton Parkway (physical)
Chapel Hill, TN 37034
(931)364-7819   <Marshall>
PA: Joe Wiggins   <M1>
2734 US Highway 41A S
Eagleville, TN 37060
(615)274-2011
CL: Spence Walls
4521 Polaris Drive
Chapel Hill, TN 37034
(931)364-2573
walls.family95@yahoo.com

_____

Columbia   (4MWC)TNCO7110
1106 Nashville Highway
Columbia, TN 38401
(931)388-9177   <Maury>
pastor@fcpccolumbia.com
PA: Calvin Lunn   <M1>
859 Cranford Hollow Road
Columbia, TN 38401
(931)381-2397
pastor@fcpccolumbia.com
CL: Brian Keith Tilghman
1036 Theta Pike
Columbia, TN 38401
(931)698-0141
tilghmanphoto@aol.com

_____

Elora   (2C)TNCO7111
69 Bear Wallow Road (mailing)
Flintville, TN 37335
Elora, TN 37328 (physical)
( )   <Lincoln>
SS: John Blair   <M1>
108 Cliff Drive
Lawrenceburg, TN 38464
(931)762-2480
jnbblair@charter.net
CL: Jim Ramsey
69 Bear Wallow Road
Flintville, TN 37335
(931)937-8765
jim.brenda.ramsey710@gmail.com

_____

Fayetteville   (4WC)TNCO7112
1015 Lewisburg Highway
Fayetteville, TN 37334
(931)433-5441   <Lincoln>
FAX: (931)433-0056
cpc@fpunet.com
PA: Timothy Smith   <M1>
712 Morningside Drive
Fayetteville, TN 37334
(931)438-2820
FAX: (931)433-0056
tims38@hotmail.com
CL: Larry Ventress

1003 First Avenue
Fayetteville, TN 37334
(931)433-5053
FAX: (931)433-0056
dooda49@fpunet.com

_____

Fiducia   (2EW C)TNCO7113
1342 Bethel Road (mailing)
Pulaski, TN 38478
1695 Fiducia Road (physical)
Prospect, TN 38477
( )   <Giles>
PA: John Blair   <M1>
108 W Cliff Drive
Lawrenceburg, TN 38464
(931)766-2480
jnbblair@charter.net
CL: Ewing Brooks
1429 Crooked Hill Road
Pulaski, TN 38478
(931)363-5985

_____

Flintville   (2C)TNCO7115
35 Well Lee Road (mailing)
9 Flintville School Road (physical)
Flintville, TN 37335
( )   <Lincoln>
PA: John Blair   <M1>
108 W Cliff Drive
Lawrenceburg, TN 38464
(931)766-2480
CL: Jimmie D Wicks
35 Wells Lee Road
Flintville, TN 37335
(931)937-8562
bfwicks@bellsouth.net

_____

Franklin   (4MC)TNCO7116
PO Box 1134 (mailing)
615 West Main Street (physical)
Franklin, TN 37065
(615)599-0029   <Williamson>
FAX: (615)807-2959
cp1876@hotmail.com
PA: John Hyden   <M1>
6525 Peytonsville Arno Road
College Grove, TN 37046
(615)975-9584
cp1876@hotmail.com
CL: Dorris Douglass
724 Fair Street
Franklin, TN 37064
(615)790-7914
FAX: (615)595-1247
ansercher@aol.com

_____

Grace   (4C)TNCO7145
1153 Lewisburg Pike
Franklin, TN 37064
(615)794-0370   <Williamson>
gracecpchurchpastor@gmail.com
PA: Fonda Blair   <M1>
PO Box 11093
Murfreesboro, TN 37129
(615)491-2432
blairfonda2010@comcast.net
CL: Lee Bagby
311 E Chownings Court
Franklin, TN 37064
(615)794-9532
bagbyl@bellsouth.net

_____

Green Hill   (3WC)TNCO7118

1900 Unionville-Deason Road
Bell Buckle, TN 37020
(931)294-2040   <Bedford>
SS: Lawrence (Larry) Kelly   <M1>
3471 Highway 41 A North Apt 5
Unionville, TN 37180
(615)934-1517
CL: Angelia Burns
328 Dunnaway Road
Shelbyville, TN 37160
(931)294-5105

_____

Harpeth Lick   (4C)TNCO7119
6981 Arno Allisona Road
College Grove, TN 37046
( )   <Williamson>
SS: Larry Guin   <M1>
125 Glider Loop
Eagleville, TN 37060
(615)668-5236
lguin43@hotmail.com
CL: Virginia Lou Rogers
8876 Horton Highway
College Grove, TN 37046
(615)368-2202
mudpuddle42@gmail.com

_____

Hohenwald   (4MWC)TNCO7120
PO Box 456 (mailing)
201 Park Avenue S (physical)
Hohenwald, TN 38462
(931)796-3657   <Lewis>
CL: Byrne Dunn
617 Oakdale Drive
Hohenwald, TN 38462
(931)796-2806
FAX: (931)796-2153
marvinwilkins@msn.com

_____

Howell   (4MWC)TNCO7121
43 Brown Teal Road
Fayetteville, TN 37334
(931)433-0818   <Lincoln>
PA: Todd Gaskill   <M1>
430 Haysland Road
Petersburg, TN 37144
(931)580-2708
tgaskill@pens.com
CL: Tim Porter
85 Icy Bank Road
Fayetteville, TN 37334
(931)433-8306

_____

Jenkins   (4MWC)TNCO7144
PO Box 518 (mailing)
2501 York Road (physical)
Nolensville, TN 37135
(615)776-2339   <Williamson>
FAX: (615)776-3520
jenkinspastor@gmail.com
PA: Jonathan Watson   <M1>
4017 Claude Drive
Smyrna, TN 37167
jenkinspastor@gmail.com
(615)630-9153
CL: Joyce A Allemore
2442 Fly Road
Nolensville, TN 37135
(615)776-2985
jallemore@yahoo.com

_____

Kelso   (4MWC)TNCO7122
16 Teal Hollow Road

COLUMBIA PRESBYTERY CONTINUED

Kelso, TN 37348
( )   <Lincoln>
PA: Kirk Smith   <M1>
   813 1st Avenue
   Fayetteville, TN 37334
   (931)438-8649
   revkirk@fayettevilleelectric.net
CL: Bill Dickey
   1501 Swanson Boulevard
   Fayetteville, TN 37334
   (931)433-2462

Kingdom   (4C)TNCO7123
   4532 Barfield Crescent Road (mailing)
   Murfreesboro, TN 37128
   800 Kingdom Road (physical)
   Unionville, TN 37180
   ( )   <Bedford>
SS: Larry Guin   <M1>
   125 Glider Loop
   Eagleville, TN 37060
   (615)668-5236
   lguin43@hotmail.com
CL: Thelma Shockey
   4532 Barfield Crescent Road
   Murfreesboro, TN 37128
   (615)896-1890

Lawrenceburg   (4MWC)TNCO7124
   228 S Military Avenue
   Lawrenceburg, TN 38464
   (931)762-4343   <Lawrence>
   cumberlandpresby@bellsouth.net
PA: Dwight Liles   <M1>
   8467 Joy Road
   Mount Pleasant, TN 38474
   (931)379-0326
   dwightliles@att.net
CL: Kaye Luffman
   5 Powell Circle
   Five Points, TN 38457
   (931)556-2252
   kluffman@hotmail.com

Lewisburg 1st   (4MWC)TNCO7125
   210 Haynes Street (mailing)
   402 2nd Avenue N (physical)
   Lewisburg, TN 37091
   (931)359-3857   <Marshall>
   FAX: (931)270-8624
   fcpclewisburg@bellsouth.net
PA: Roger Reid   <M1>
   1505 Experiment Farm Road
   Lewisburg, TN 37091
   (931)422-5257
   drrtr@yahoo.com
CL: Tammy Caneer-Carter
   1400 Green Valley Road
   Pulaski, TN 38478
   (931)637-7374
   FAX: (931)270-8624
   cantam@bellsouth.net

McCains   (4MWC)TNCO7126
   PO Box 29 (mailing)
   3532 McCains Lane (physical)
   Columbia, TN 38401
   (931)540-0160   <Maury>
SS: David McGregor   <M1>
   (deceased 1/23/14)
CL: Gary Weatherford
   3926 Campbellsville Pike
   Columbia, TN 38401

(931)388-0599
gmweatherford@cs.com

Mt Carmel   (4C)TNCO7127
   4810 Ash Hill Road (mailing)
   Spring Hill, TN 37174
   2300 Lewisburg Pike (physical)
   Franklin, TN 37064
   (615)591-3930   <Williamson>
PA: John Eatherly   <M1>
   1377 Moss Road
   Chapel Hill, TN 37034
   (931)364-2087
   jrev@united.net
CL: Peggy S Fisher
   4810 Ash Hill Road
   Spring Hill, TN 37174
   (615)944-9300
   fishpest@ymail.com

Mt Hebron   (4C)TNCO7128
   59 Giles Hollow Road (mailing)
   927 Shelbyville Highway (physical)
   Fayetteville, TN 37334
   ( )   <Lincoln>
PA: Todd Gaskill   <M1>
   430 Haysland Road
   Petersburg, TN 37144
   (931)580-2708
   tgaskill@pens.com
CL: Jimmy Buchanan
   59 Giles Hollow Road
   Fayetteville, TN 37334
   (931)433-6446

Mt Joy   (4MWC)TNCO7129
   8364 Mt Joy Road
   Mount Pleasant, TN 38474
   ( )   <Maury>
CL: Evelyn Luckett
   8432 Mount Joy Road
   Mount Pleasant, TN 38474
   (931)379-4600

Mt Lebanon   (4EC)TNCO7130
   4497 Kedron Road
   Spring Hill, TN 37174
   ( )   <Maury>
   mortonco@bellsouth.net
PA: Patric Fife   <M1>
   73 Jordan Road
   Lawrenceburg, TN 38464
   (931)629-8146
   pnlfifernak@gmail.com
CL: Judy L Morton
   1272 John Sharp Road
   Columbia, TN 38401
   (931)381-1140
   mortonco@bellsouth.net

Mt Moriah   (4C)TNCO7131
   485 Agnew Road (mailing)
   463 Big Dry Creek Road (physical)
   Pulaski, TN 38478
   ( )   <Giles>
PA: Steve Nave   <M1>
   5172 Fall River Road
   Leoma, TN 38468
   (931)424-0020
   thenaves@wildblue.net
CL: Dickson Marks
   485 Agnew Road
   Pulaski, TN 38478

(931)363-2432

Mt Nebo   (4C)TNCO7132
   84 S Old Military Road (mailing)
   Saint Joseph, TN 38481
   473 Mt Nebo Road (physical)
   Iron City, TN 38463
   ( )   <Lawrence>
LS: Sean Richardson   <M6>
   4227 Highway 43 N
   Ethridge, TN 38456
   (931)829-2094
   sean@misterrichardson.com
CL: William B Gabel
   104 Spring Street
   Saint Joseph, TN 38481
   (931)845-4203
   stjoemerry@gmail.com

Mt Pleasant   (4EWC)TNCO7133
   PO Box 689 (mailing)
   504 Florida Avenue (physical)
   Mount Pleasant, TN 38474
   (931)379-3662   <Maury>
PA: Robert Mullenix   <M1>
   1408 Azalee Lane
   Chapel Hill, TN 37034
   (931)364-4611
   glonix@live.com
CL: Rickey Massey
   609 Circle Drive
   Mount Pleasant, TN 38474
   (931)379-3617
   rickeymassey@bellsouth.net

New Bethel   (2C)TNCO7134
   5060 Reynolds Road
   Columbia, TN 38401
   (931)364-2378   <Marshall>
SS: John Eatherly   <M1>
   1377 Moss Road
   Chapel Hill, TN 37034
   (931)364-2087
   jrev@united.net
CL: James W Hood
   1532 Lewisburg Pike
   Franklin, TN 37064
   (615)591-8689

Petersburg   (4MWC)TNCO7135
   PO Box 82 (mailing)
   303 Russell Street (physical)
   Petersburg, TN 37144
   (931)607-1859   <Lincoln>
   petersburgpreacher@att.net
PA: Troy Green   <M1>
   105 Cobb Hollow Lane
   Petersburg, TN 37144
   (931)659-6627
   thegreens101@att.net
CL: Ann Hemphill
   803 Washington Street W Apt B
   Fayetteville, TN 37334
   (931)433-8380
   ahemphill@fpunet.com

Pleasant Mount   (4WC)TNCO7136
   609 Woods Drive (mailing)
   1620 Fountain Heights Road (physical)
   Columbia, TN 38401
   ( )   <Maury>
PA: William L Rolman, Jr   <M1>
   602 Canyon Drive

COLUMBIA PRESBYTERY CONTINUED

Columbia, TN 38401
(931)388-2611
wmrolmanjr@att.net
CL: James H Rochell, Jr
609 Woods Drive
Columbia, TN 38401
(931)388-1947
tnpappy53@yahoo.com

Richland   (4C)TNCO7137
3452 Spring Place Road
Lewisburg, TN 37091
(931)270-6135   <Marshall>
PA: Charles (Buddy) Pope   <M1>
2391 Fairfield Pike
Shelbyville, TN 37160
(931)205-6897
pope6897@yahoo.com
CL: Douglas A Looney
3045 Monte Murrey Road
Lewisburg, TN 37091
(931)359-3781
ld.looney@yahoo.com

Santa Fe   (4WC)TNCO7138
PO Box 58 (mailing)
2630 Santa Fe Pike (physical)
Santa Fe, TN 38482
(931)682-3555   <Maury>
SS: Sherry Ladd   <M1>
4521 Turkey Creek Road
Williamsport, TN 38487
(931)682-2263
revsherryladd@gmail.com
CL: Whitney Seaton
111 W Hardin Drive
Columbia, TN 38401
(931)388-9319

Swan   (4C)TNCO7140
4521 Turkey Creek Road (mailing)
Williamsport, TN 38487
Swan Creek Road (physical)
Centerville, TN 37033
(931)682-2263   <Hickman>
revsherryladd@gmail.com
PA: Sherry Ladd   <M1>
4521 Turkey Creek Road
Williamsport, TN 38487
(931)682-2263
revsherryladd@gmail.com
CL: George C Ladd
4521 Turkey Creek Road
Williamsport, TN 38487
(931)682-2263
gladd@hughes.net

Union Grove   (4C)TNCO7141
2409 Green Mills Road Lot 30 (mailing)
1452 Cliff White Road (physical)

Columbia, TN 38401
(931)486-2799   <Maury>
patricia.cates@att.net
SS: Scott Yates   <M1>
8818 New Town Road
Rockvale, TN 37153
(615)274-3000
scott@scottyates.net
CL: Patricia Cates
2409 Green Mills Road Lot 30
Columbia, TN 38401
(931)486-2799
patricia.cates@att.net

Waynesboro   (4MEWC)TNCO7142
PO Box 234 (mailing)
110 North High Street (physical)
Waynesboro, TN 38485
(931)722-5621   <Wayne>
rainsr@tds.net
CL: Robert (Bob) Raines
105 E Songer Street
Waynesboro, TN 38485
(931)722-5621
rainsr@tds.net

West Point   (4MC)TNCO7143
1431 Spainwood Street (mailing)
1533 Theta Pike (physical)
Columbia, TN 38401
(931)388-7268   <Maury>
PA: Terry Peery   <M1>
1431 Spainwood Street
Columbia, TN 38401
(931)381-6871
coppreacher@gmail.com
CL: Mike McCord
4543 Snow Creek Road
Santa Fe, TN 38482
(931)682-2500
mmccord59@bellsouth.net

OTHERS ON MINISTERIAL ROLL:

Clark, Tommy   <M1 WC>
124 Roberta Drive
Memphis, TN 38112
(615)430-9158
fattire77@gmail.com
Cole, Dwayne   <M1 RT>
6460 Village Parkway
Anchorage, AK 99504
(814)602-2685
tadpolejr@aol.com
Denton, Clyde M   <M1 RT>
(NO ADDRESS AVAILABLE)
Columbia, TN 38401
(931)388-7154
Green, Odis G   <M1 RT>
18 Oakwood Street NW

Rome, GA 30165
Heflin, Robert   <M1 DE>
4144 Meadow Court Drive
Bartlett, TN 38135
(901)382-8198
rdheflin@bellsouth.net
Kinnaman, Richard Terry   <M1 WC>
2018 Spring Meadow Circle
Spring Hill, TN 37174
(615)302-3321
kinnaman91@att.net
Trotter, Wendell   <M1 RT>
1516 Fell Avenue NE
Huntsville, AL 35811
(256)519-6571
wendelltrotter@knology.net

OTHER LICENTIATES ON ROLL:

Tucker, Paul   <M2 ST>
3801 Brush Hill Pike
Nashville, TN 37216
(615)430-9158
paultucker@gmail.com

OTHER CANDIDATES ON ROLL:

Galvan, Melinda   <M3>
205 Spring Creek Street
Chapel Hill, TN 37034
(931)364-3341
mgalvan@united.net

Covenant Presbytery
MIDWEST SYNOD

GENERAL	1.Church Number	2.Active	3.Total	4.Church School	5.Prof. of Faith	6.Gains	7.Losses	8.Children Baptized	9. OUR UNITED OUT-REACH	10. Total Out-Reach Giving	11. All Other Expenses	12. Total Income Received	13. Value Church Prop. 1=1000
	1	2	3	4	5	6	7	8	9	10	11	12	13
Bayou de Chien	3401	40	77	28	0	1	1	0	0	7,690	59,000	71,049	516
Benton	3403	12	40	7	No Report Received			0	0	0	0	0	215
Bethel	3404	185	367	101	3	10	2	0	12,567	41,192	293,483	325,066	2,500
Calvary	3405	23	52	25	No Report Received			0	0	0	0	0	0332
Camp Ground	5103	23	53	26	0	1	0	0	3,203	8,565	28,286	29,486	243
Chandler	5302	109	384	96	4	9	5	1	10,370	35,363	121,195	157,041	1,502
Ebenezer	5105	20	25	15	No Report Received			0	0	0	0	0	50
Ebenezer Hall	5106	1	11	5	0	0	2	0	956	2,830	4,419	9,537	48
Flat Lick	3606	55	100	40	No Report Received			0	4,955	14,939	105,776	120,715	400
Fredonia	3608	100	237	70	0	1	1	0	16,899	37,550	134,496	172,046	675
Galatia	5109	39	150	44	CLOSED 4/30/13		0	0	0	0	0	0	350
Gilead	5110	29	150	90	0	0	2	0	1,674	12,640	44,019	53,900	350
Good Spring	3609	23	52	18	0	0	0	0	2,400	18,990	26,059	46,450	140
Highland	3414	93	202	75	4	12	4	2	7,200	35,714	138,065	207,583	1,120
Hopewell	3610	45	139	32	No Report Received			0	720	0	0	0	120
Hopkinsville	3611	46	73	40	0	0	2	0	2,656	6,254	92,614	40,776	850
Liberty*	3406	101	112	59	0	2	0	0	0	12,215	86,469	98,684	700
Lisman	3613	27	45	22	4	5	2	0	1,268	5,843	46,474	45,927	225
Macedonia	3614	35	41	30	No Report Received			0	0	0	0	0	300
Madisonville	3615	40	150	25	No Report Received			0	1,741	0	0	0	356
Margaret Hank	3415	65	99	40	No Report Received			0	5,500	0	0	0	400
Marion First	3616	65	131	25	No Report Received			0	3,559	0	0	0	658
Milburn Chapel	3416	399	399	72	No Report Received			0	0	0	0	0	1,800
Mt. Carmel	3617	90	136	20	5	6	2	0	0	3,345	61,512	41,502	600
Mt. Pleasant	3618	16	27	15	1	1	1	0	0	2,442	18,257	20,062	50
Mt. Sterling	5117	170	252	80	No Report Received			0	0	0	0	0	340
Mt. Zion	5118	10	10	0	0	0	0	0	2,150	7,368	12,731	20,099	35
New Hope	3410	165	236	159	No Report Received			0	14,375	0	0	0	1,550
No. Pleasant Gr	3411	23	53	31	No Report Received			0	0	0	0	0	200
Oak Grove	3412	60	98	40	No Report Received			0	0	0	0	0	400
Oak Grove Union	3619	30	58	30	0	0	0	0	2,883	8,593	28,412	40,085	200
Oakland	3413	45	132	32	No Report Received			0	0	0	0	0	1,250
Piney Fork	3620	45	83	32	No Report Received			0	1,703	0	0	0	250
Pleasant Valley	3418	25	25	11	No Report Received			0	0	0	0	0	150
Providence	5122	12	91	17	No Report Received			0	0	0	0	0	70
Providence 1st*	3621	8	51	0	0	12	0	0	1,200	2,850	22,500	20,350	80
Rose Creek	3622	31	66	20	No Report Received			0	2,485	0	0	0	600
Rozzell Chapel	3419	56	95	50	1	1	0	2	3,250	13,415	51,926	92,329	380
Sturgis	3625	110	215	68	2	2	5	3	19,061	52,453	210,452	232,801	2,000
Sugar Grove	3626	71	150	32	No Report Received			0	2,700	0	0	0	700
Union Chapel	5123	33	54	19	No Report Received			0	0	0	0	0	150
Unity	3422	107	180	62	No Report Received			0	2,200	0	0	0	225
Vaughn's Chapel	3423	48	63	12	No Report Received			0	2,565	0	0	0	400
Village	5125	10	10	11	0	0	1	0	1,000	4,460	29,312	33,852	10
Wheatcroft	3627	32	57	10	No Report Received			0	2,741	0	0	0	110
Woodlawn	3417	73	306	46	3	2	5	2	0	40,990	226,676	267,665	1,744
Covenant Presbytery									200				
TOTALS	47	2,850	5,554	1,787	27	70	40	10	134,181	375,701	1,842,133	2,147,005	25,344

*Math error corrected. **Purged roll.

COVENANT PRESBYTERY CONTINUED

CHURCHES, PASTORS, AND CLERKS:

Bayou de Chine   (4MWC)MICO3401
  2 Kingston Road
  Water Valley, KY 42085
  (270)355-2089   <Graves>
PA: Kenneth Richards   <M1>
  2 Kingston Road
  Water Valley, KY 42085
  (270)355-2089
  kenrich111443@hotmail.com
CL: Mark Crass
  1990 Kingston Road
  Water Valley, KY 42085
  (270)355-2381
  jimcrassauto10@bellsouth.net

Benton   (4WC)MICO3403
  2968 Aurora Highway (mailing)
  Hardin, KY 40248
  Kentucky Highway 58 (physical)
  Benton, KY 42025
  ( )   <Marshall>
PA: Donna Davenport   <M1>
  3539 State Route 339
  Wingo, KY 42088
  (270)376-5488
  chamberdonna@yahoo.com
CL: Michele Shearer
  2969 Aurora Highway
  Hardin, KY 42048
  (270)354-8656
  mshearer92858@hotmail.com

Bethel   (4WC)MICO3404
  12304 Wickliffe Road
  Kevil, KY 42053
  (270)876-7239   <Ballard>
  FAX: (270)876-7513
  bethelcpchurch@gmail.com
PA: Olen (Bud) Russell   <M1>
  9595 Wickliffe Road
  Wickliffe, KY 42087
  (270)876-7272
  olen552@aol.com
CL: Teresa Higdon
  230 Lake Point Drive
  Paducah, KY 42003
  (270)554-5003
  teresa@qservicesco.com

Calvary   (4MC)MICO3405
  98 Calvary Church Road
  Mayfield, KY 42066
  (270)376-5525   <Graves>
CL: Darla Jo Tucker
  665 McNutt Road
  Wingo, KY 42088
  (270)376-2065

Camp Ground   (4C)MICO5103
  2645 Lick Creek Road (mailing)
  70 Tunnel Lane (physical)
  Anna, IL 62906
  (618)833-9000   <Union>
OD: Dwight Kaylor   <M5>
  9393 Hamlettsburg Road
  Brookport, IL 62910
  (270)366-6881
  dkaylor70@gmail.com

CL: Sandra Boaz
  2645 Lick Creek Road
  Anna, IL 62906
  (618)833-8216
  skboaz@yahoo.com

Chandler   (4MWC)MICO5302
  338 S State Street
  Chandler, IN 47610
  (812)925-6175   <Warrick>
  FAX: (812)925-3628
  chandlercpc2@hotmail.com
PA: Jesse Thornton   <M1>
  122 E Cherry Street
  Chandler, IN 47610
  (812)925-6475
  FAX: (812)925-3628
  jessthornton@msn.com
CL: Robert Hooper
  PO Box 351
  Chandler, IN 47610
  (812)925-6965
  rwhooper@yahoo.com

Ebenezer   (C)MICO5105
  Thompsonville, IL 62890
  ( )   <Saline>
CL: Pat Fletcher
  24535 Kaskaskia Road
  Thompsonville, IL 62890
  (618)627-2288

Ebenezer Hall   (4WC)MICO5106
  9850 Lick Creek Road (mailing)
  750 Grand View (physical)
  Buncombe, IL 62912
  (618)833-8280   <Union>
CL: Carolyn Hammon
  9850 Lick Creek Road
  Buncombe, IL 62912
  (618)833-8280

Flat Lick   (4WC)MICO3606
  415 Bennetttown Street (mailing)
  Herndon, KY 42236
  9355 Lafayette Road (physical))
  Herndon, KY 42236
  (270)885-1350   <Christian>
  pastorsteve88@yahoo.com
PA: Stephen H Guarneros   <M1>
  506 Clifton Court
  Hopkinsville, KY 42240
  (270)869-7544
  pastorsteve88@yahoo.com
CL: Mike Barbee
  415 Bennetttown Street
  Herndon, KY 42236
  (270)498-3664

Fredonia   (4MEWC)MICO3608
  204 West Pierson Street (mailing)
  303 Cassidy Avenue (physical)
  Fredonia, KY 42411
  (270)545-3481   <Caldwell>
SS: Larry Buchanan   <M1>
  730 Shelby Road
  Salem, KY 42078
  (270)988-1880
  lbuchanan.tse@gmail.com
CL: Cindy Cruce
  46 Penn Drive

  Marion, KY 42064
  (270)965-4520
  ccruce@fredoniavalleybank.com

Galatia   (4MWC)MICO5109
  111 S Hickory
  Galatia, IL 62935
  (618)268-4026   <Saline>
  (closed 4-30-13)(left CP)

Gilead   (4EC)MICO5110
  3470 Gilead Church Road (mailing)
  4385 Gilead Church Road (physical)
  Simpson, IL 62985
  (618)695-2653   <Johnson>
  tim-arm@live.com
PA: William E Martin, Jr   <M1>
  741 Chapel Hill Road
  Marion, KY 42064
  (870)270-3344
  juniormartin@yahoo.com
CL: Tim Armstrong
  745 Webb Town Road
  Tunnel Hill, IL 62972
  (618)559-7021
  tim-arm@live.com

Good Spring   (2WC)MICO3609
  1800 Old Fredonia Road (mailing)
  Princeton, KY 42445
  4142 Good Spring Road (physical)
  Fredonia, KY 42411
  ( )   <Caldwell>
SS: N Ray Board   <M1>
  267 State Route 293 N
  Princeton, KY 42445
  (270)365-3850
  rayboard@att.net
CL: Mike Stephens
  1800 Old Fredonia Road
  Princeton, KY 42445
  (270)559-6032
  mstephens@pepb.net

Highland   (4MWC)MICO3414
  3950 Lovelaceville Road
  Paducah, KY 42001
  (270)554-3572   <McCracken>
  hcpsec@bellsouth.net
PA: Brent Ballow   <M1>
  140 Windmill Drive
  Paducah, KY 42001
  (270)564-8891
  hcppastor@bellsouth.net
CL: Elaine S Overton
  3915 Lovelaceville Road
  Paducah, KY 42001
  (270)554-1259
  jred3915@bellsouth.net

Hopewell   (4C)MICO3610
  768 Lola Road (mailing)
  1235 Lola Road (physical)
  Salem, KY 42078
  (270)988-3859   <Livingston>
SS: Larry Buchanan   <M1>
  730 Shelby Road
  Salem, KY 42078
  (270)988-1880
  lbuchanan.tse@gmail.com
CL: Michael Heneisen

COVENANT PRESBYTERY CONTINUED

1162 Hampton Road
Salem, KY 42078
(270)988-4856
heneisen@vci.net

_____
Hopkinsville   (4MWC)MICO3611
2701 Faircourt
Hopkinsville, KY 42240
(270)886-1464   <Christian>
FAX: (270)885-1531
cumberland1@bellsouth.net
PA: Jason Heidel   <M1>
218 Morningside Drive
Hopkinsville, KY 42240
(270)498-7380
heidelj@hotmail.com
CL: Marcia Ballard
306 Lucky Debonair
Hopkinsville, KY 42240
(270)839-5482

_____
Liberty   (4C)MICO3406
510 Richardson Street (mailing)
150 Liberty Road (physical)
Murray, KY 42071
( )   <Calloway>
OD: Gary Vacca   <M5>
2203 Creekwood Drive
Murray, KY 42071
(270)978-0818
garyvacca@spiritualliving.com
CL: Brenda Lawson
441 Old Shiloh Road
Murray, KY 42071
(270)227-5872
bsnip10@hotmail.com

_____
Lisman   (4EC)MICO3613
2085 State Route 270 W
Clay, KY 42404
( )   <Webster>
PA: John R Shoulta   <M1>
1154 Mt Carmel Road
White Plains, KY 42464
(270)676-3563
johnshoulta@bellsouth.net
CL: Nancy Burnett
451 Jim Villines Road
Dixon, KY 42409
(270)639-6204

_____
Macedonia   (4WC)MICO3614
18030 Beulah Road (mailing)
Princeton, KY 42445
Highway 291 (physical)
Dalton, KY
( )   <Hopkins>
CL: Narvin Darnall
18030 Beulah Road
Princeton, KY 42445
(279)836-7089
narvin-d@yahoo.com

_____
Madisonville   (4MWC)MICO3615
PO Box 392 (mailing)
1540 Anton Road (physical)
Madisonville, KY 42431
(270)821-5970   <Hopkins>
PA: Jeff French   <M1>
5 Rose Petal Lane
Dawson Springs, KY 42408

(270)993-0855
brojeff7@bellsouth.net
CL: Jean Duncan
330 S Daves Street
Madisonville, KY 42431
(270)821-5138
jduncan42431@att.net

_____
Margaret Hank   (4WC)MICO3415
1526 Park Avenue
Paducah, KY 42001
(270)443-3689   <McCracken>
holyday@vci.net
PA: Christopher Fleming   <M1>
133 Minerva Place
Paducah, KY 42001
(615)424-8561
holyday@vci.net
CL: Amy Fleming
133 Minerva Place
Paducah, KY 42001
(270)443-3689
holyday@vci.net

_____
Marion First   (4MEWC)MICO3616
PO Box 323 (mailing)
224 W Bellville Street (physical)
Marion, KY 42064
(270)965-4746   <Crittenden>
firstcpchurch@mchsi.com
PA: Dee Ann Thompson   <M1>
226 W Bellville Street
Marion, KY 42064
(270)445-0310
deethomp5@hotmail.com
CL: Jo Ann McClure
PO Box 92
Marion, KY 42064
(270)965-3323

_____
Milburn Chapel   (4EC)MICO3416
3760 Metropolis Lake Road
West Paducah, KY 42086
(270)488-2588   <McCracken>
milburnchapel@gmail.com
PA: Douglas Hughes   <M1>
5545 Hocker Road
Paducah, KY 42001
(270)488-2588
milburnchapel@gmail.com
CL: Joe Neal Neftzger
903 E 6th Street
Metropolis, IL 62960
(618)524-5349
milburnchapel@gmail.com

_____
Mt Carmel   (4MW C)MICO3617
11504 Mt Carmel Road (mailing)
11410 Mt Carmel Road (physical)
White Plains, KY 42464
(270)676-3563   <Hopkins>
bshoulta@bellsouth.net
PA: John R Shoulta   <M1>
11504 Mt Carmel Road
White Plains, KY 42464
(270)676-3563
johnshoulta@bellsouth.net
CL: Larry Putman
1319 Mt Carmel Pond River Road
White Plains, KY 42464
(270)676-3628

Mt Pleasant   (4 C)MICO3618
16647 State Route 109
Sullivan, KY 42460
( )   <Union>
PA: Dale Williams   <M1>
3156 State Route 2837
Clay, KY 42404
(270)664-2044
CL: Richard White
2465 State Route 270 E
Sturgis, KY 42459
(270)333-6109
whitefarms1@att.net

_____
Mt Sterling   (4MWC)MICO5117
1780 Mt Sterling Road
Brookport, IL 62910
(618)564-2616   <Massac>
FAX: (618)564-2616
PA: David LeNeave   <M1>
8725 Hamletsburg Road
Brookport, IL 62910
(618)564-2437
leneavedavid@yahoo.com
CL: Gary N Angelly
8646 Independence Road
Brookport, IL 62910
(618)564-2874
FAX: (618)564-2874
angelly@djklink.net

_____
Mt Zion   (4WC)MICO5118
PO Box 383 (mailing)
1159 Mt Zion Road (physical)
Dongola, IL 62926
(618)827-4463   <Union>
jsr487@frontier.com
SS: Donna Davenport   <M1>
3539 State Route 339
Wingo, KY 42088
chamberdonna@yahoo.com
(270)376-5488
SS: Philip Brown   <M3 ST>
540 Mt Pisgah Road
Dongola, IL 62926
(618)697-0972
brownlp75@yahoo.com
CL: Sharon R. Resch
PO Box 383
Dongola, IL 62926
(618)827-4463
jsr487@frontier.com

_____
New Hope   (4MWC)MICO3410
7620 Cross Mill Road
Paducah, KY 42001
(270)554-0473   <McCracken>
newhopecpchurch@hotmail.com
PA: Curtis Franklin   <M1>
7620 Cross Mill Road
Paducah, KY 42001
(270)625-1898
brocurtis@fredonia.biz
CL: Scott Webber
6155 McNutt Drive
Paducah, KY 42001
(270)554-7345
scott.webber@comcast.net

_____
North Pleasant Grove (4WC)MICO3411

COVENANT PRESBYTERY CONTINUED

Murray, KY 42071
( )   <Calloway>
SS: Charles K Westfall   <M1>
94 Honeysuckle Drive
Gilbertsville, KY 42044
(270)362-0816
CL: Fred Kemp
276 Airport Road
Murray, KY 42071

Oak Grove   (4MWC)MICO3412
2465 Magness Road
Benton, KY 42025
(270)437-4606   <Calloway>
PA: Randy Lowe   <M1>
222 McDougal Drive
Murray, KY 42071
(270)753-8255
loweshodle@aol.com
CL: Jeff Gordon
2465 Magness Road
Benton, KY 42025
(270)437-4613
jgordon@wk.net

Oak Grove Union   (4C)MICO3619
Highway 132
Clay, KY 42404
(270)664-0008   <Webster>
jvfulton@wk.net
SS: James V Fulton   <M1>
1520 Oak Grove Road
Benton, KY 42025
(270)437-4320
CL: Daniel M Heady
2564 State Route 132 W
Dixon, KY 42409
(270)748-6848
danielheady@kycourts.net

Oakland   (4MWC)MICO3413
9104 US Highway 68 W
Calvert City, KY 42029
(270)898-2630   <Marshall>
PA: Danny York   <M1>
5420 State Routh 902 W
Fredonia, KY 42411
(270)350-7262
nonnieyork@yahoo.com
CL: John Jenkins
1265 Elva Loop Road
Symsonia, KY 42082
(270)705-3229

Piney Fork   (4WC)MICO3620
4294 Coppers Spring Road
Marion, KY 42064
( )   <Crittenden>
SS: Daniel Hopkins   <M3 ST>
887 Penny Road
Hardin, KY 42048
(270)205-1847
CL: Ercel Edward Rushing
7550 State Route 506
Marion, KY 42064
(270)313-7841

Pleasant Valley   (4C)MICO3418
111 College Drive
Kevil, KY 42053
(270)224-2497   <Ballard>

SS: April Watson   <M2 ST>
529 W Bellville
Marion, KY 42064
(270)965-2850
aprilwatson@hotmail.com
CL: William E Kilby
PO Box 413
La Center, KY 42056
(270)665-5405

Providence   (4WC)MICO5122
335 Providence Road
Carriers Mills, IL 62917
(618)994-2146   <Saline>
CL: Oliver W Holmes
PO Box 414
Carrier Mills, IL 62917
(618)994-2146

Providence 1st   (4MEWC)MICO3621
305 Locust Street (mailing)
119 Locust Street (physical)
Providence, KY 42450
(270)667-2485   <Webster>
chalit@apex.net
SS: Paul Stone   <M1>
3490 State Route 2837
Clay, Kentucky 42404
(270)664-6244
stonepstc@aol.com
CL: Paul Northern
317 N Broadway
Providence, KY 42450
(270)667-2636

Rose Creek   (4WC)MICO3622
7650 Island Ford Road (mailing)
Hanson, KY 42413
7220 Rose Creek Road (physical)
Nebo, KY 42441
( )   <Hopkins>
PA: Paul Stone   <M1>
3490 State Route 2837
Clay, KY 42404
(270)664-6244
CL: Joseph E Peyton
7650 Island Ford Road
Hanson, KY 42413
(270)619-0636
jepeyton@madisonville.com

Rozzell Chapel   (4C)MICO3419
1258 Rozzell Church Road
Mayfield, KY 42066
(270)623-6866   <Graves>
PA: D Frederick (Fred) Fahl   <M1>
500 3rd Street
Fulton, KY 42041
(270)472-1476
dffahl@gmail.com
CL: Donna Davenport   <M1>
3539 State Route 339
Wingo, KY 42088
(270)804-3526
chamberdonna@yahoo.com

Sturgis   (4MWC)MICO3625
PO Box 86 (mailing)
504 N Main Street (physical)
Sturgis, KY 42459
(270)333-2851   <Union>

FAX: (270)333-3118
sturgiscpc@att.net
PA: Victor Hassell   <M1>
510 N Main Street
Sturgis, KY 42459
(270)333-9170
FAX: (270)333-3118
hassellvictor@hotmail.com
CL: Barbara B Sutton
849 State Route 950
Morganfield, KY 42437
(270)333-4385

Sugar Grove   (4MWC)MICO3626
585 Sugar Grove Church Road
Marion, KY 42064
(270)965-4435   <Crittenden>
PA: Terra Sisco   <M1>
6918 State Route 120
Marion, KY 42064
(270)965-0176
CL: Gladys Brown
6781 State Route 120
Marion, KY 42064
(270)965-2969
gbrown6781@live.com

Union Chapel   (4C)MICO5123
2210 Droit Road
Galatia, IL 62935
( )   <Saline>
PA: Kevin Peyton   <M1>
580 S Timothy Lane
Galatia, IL 62935
(618)841-0076
kevinp21@frontier.com
CL: Phyllis Ann Peyton
575 Allentown Road
Harrisburg, IL 62946
(618)252-7767
peytonfarms@wildblue.net

Unity   (4MWC)MICO3422
1503 Story Avenue (mailing)
Murray, KY 42071
1929 E Unity Church Road (physical)
Hardin, KY 42048
(270)354-8216   <Marshall>
cprevbhayes@gmail.com
PA: Brian Hayes   <M1>
69 Cactus Drive
Benton, KY 42025
(270)210-8165
cprevbhayes@gmail.com
CL: Jonathan Whisman
5352 Murray Highway
Hardin, KY 42048
(270)437-3949
jwhisman@wk.net

Vaughn's Chapel   (4MWC)MICO3423
4775 Calvert City Road
Calvert City, KY 42029
(270)395-7318   <Marshall>
PA: Wendell Ordway   <M1>
4775 Calvert City Road
Calvert City, KY 42029
(270)395-7318
CL: John P Case
93 W Second Avenue
Calvert City, KY 42029

COVENANT PRESBYTERY CONTINUED

(270)395-4203

_____

Village   (4C)MICO5125
324 County Road 250 N
Norris City, IL 62869
(618)962-3256   <White>
SS: Rudolph Barnett   <M1>
RR 5 Box 267
McLeansboro, IL 62859
(618)643-3253
CL: Charles F Edwards
324 County Road 250 N
Norris City, IL 62869
(618)962-3256
(618)962-3256   <White>

_____

Wheatcroft   (4WC)MICO3627
PO Box 7 (mailing)
47 Hammock Street E (physical)
Wheatcroft, KY 42463
( )   <Webster>
PA: Dale Williams   <M1>
3156 State Route 2837
Clay, KY 42404
(270)664-2802
dalewilliams@roadrunner.com
CL: Jackie Gass
147 Blackford-Sullivan Road
Clay, KY 42404
(270)664-9310

_____

Woodlawn   (4MWC)MICO3417
3402 Old Benton Road
Paducah, KY 42002
(270)442-7713   <McCracken>
woodlawnchurch@live.com
PA: David Fackler   <M1>
3409 Benton Road
Paducah, KY 42003
(270)442-7713
woodlawnpastor@live.com
CL: Todd Belt
3402 Old Benton Road
Paducah, KY 42002
(270)442-7713
woodlawnyouth@msn.com

_____

OTHERS ON MINISTERIAL ROLL:

Aden, Dare   <M1 WC>
1280 Kimber Road
Dongola, IL 62926
(618)827-3625
FAX: (618)827-4612
dare_aden@hotmail.com
Gerard, Eugene S   <M1 OM>
615 N 42nd Street
Paducah, KY 42001
(270)443-2889
Graham, Steve   <M1 WC>
2223 US Highway 641
Marion, KY 42064
(270)825-4700
Lawson, James   <M1 OM>

1003 West 3rd Street
Fulton, KY 42041
(270)472-5272
ridgepointefarm@bellsouth.net
Lively, Louella   <M1 WC>
196 Vicksburg Estate Road
Benton, KY 42025
(270)527-3776
Mays, Ronald B   <M1 PR>
1100 Cindy Lane
Mayfield, KY 42066
(270)247-0070
rbmays@wk.net
Moore, Hillman C   <M1 RT>
465 Russell Road
Jackson, TN 38301
(270)876-7163
hillmancm@att.net
Murrie, Willard   <M1 RT>
506 11th Street
Vienna, IL 62995
(618)658-2430
Potts, Danny   <M1 WC>
418 Eddings Street Apt 2
Fulton, KY 42041
(270)376-2901
Prewitt, Curtis   <M1 WC>
3712 Carmel Lane
Paducah, KY 42003
(270)554-9779
prewitt@apex.net
Rudolph, Allie D   <M1 WC>
855 Old Rosebower Church Road
Paducah, KY 42003
(270)898-4903
rallie307@aol.com
Shirey, John   <M1 RT>
10181 State Route 56 W
Sturgis, KY 42459
(270)389-3562
amshirey7@ips.com
Vasseur, Terry   <M1 WC>
121 Crossland Road
Murray, KY 42071
(270)554-2468
tvasseur@bellsouth.net
White, Charles   <M1 RT>
PO Box 44
Galatia, IL 62935
(618)268-4562
Wilkerson, Patrick   <M1 WC>
3419 Jaydens Nest Way Apt 202
Powell, TN 37849
(865)617-9126
patrickwilkerson3@gmail.com
Williams, David J   <M1 WC>
20 Acorn Drive
Harrisburg, IL 62946
(618)252-1851

_____

OTHER LICENTIATES ON ROLL:

Quinton, Noah   <M2 ST>
2912 Waller Omer Road
Sturgis, KY 42459
(270)952-3875
noah.quinton@gmail.com

_____

OTHER CANDIDATES ON ROLL:

Cain, Greg   <M3>
155 Greggstown
Calvert City, KY 42029
(270)816-5259
Hopkins, Wayne   <M3>
1413 E Unity Church Road
Hardin, KY 42048
(270)437-4481
Hunt, Shelley   <M3>
6035 State Route 506
Marion, KY 42064
sheljean@kynet.biz
(270)704-2189
Impastato, Paulino   <M3>
1547 Mt Zion Church Road
Marion, KY 42064
(270)965-9528
Kerner, Leanne   <M3 ST>
156 State Route 348
W Symsonia, KY 42082
(270)851-9709
cooldoll@bellsouth.net

Cumberland Presbytery
MIDWEST SYNOD

GENERAL		MEMBERSHIP			CHANGES			FINANCES				
	1.Church Number	2.Active	3.Total	4.Church School	5.Prof. of Faith	6.Gains	7.Losses	8.Children Baptized	9. OUR UNITED OUT-REACH	10. Total Out-Reach Giving	11. All Other Expenses	12. Total Income Received	13. Value Church Prop. 1=1000
	1	2	3	4	5	6	7	8	9	10	11	12	13
Antioch*	3101	30	30	16	2	1	0	0	0	0	23,822	22,240	300
Auburn	3301	57	100	30	No Report Received			0	0	0	0	0	405
Bald Knob*	3302	40	143	32	4	120	0	1	0	4,596	50,414	46,506	250
Bethel*	3102	62	62	28	4	14	1	2	2,000	4,684	23,379	29,744	0
Bethel #1	3103	15	71	10	0	4	2	1	1,000	2,170	29,557	29,431	200
Beulah	3501	28	39	35	0	0	0	1	2,454	2,454	40,685	25,441	100
Boiling Springs	3303	16	19	14	No Report Received			0	0	0	0	0	27
Bowling Green	3304	433	433	120	3	8	2	3	14,909	29,961	223,639	253,600	1,829
Bridgeport 1st	3131	108	108	23	0	0	2	0	0	14,820	132,736	100,022	651
Brier Creek	3503	80	163	60	0	5	2	0	7,638	16,229	72,073	88,302	300
Campbellsville	3104	100	212	75	3	3	3	1	0	1,391	128,931	134,710	1,000
Caneyville*	3201	5	5	28	2	0	9	0	0	2,529	12,175	15,143	1,990
Casey's Fork	3105	14	19	14	No Report Received			0	1,198	0	0	0	37
Cedar Flat	3106	26	63	25	0	0	0	0	0	1,513	16,587	19,094	90
Clear Point	3107	27	67	37	0	0	0	0	1,897	1,916	21,745	18,996	100
Clifton Mills	3202	16	39	53	1	0	2	0	0	1,831	20,145	23,612	264
Coyle	3203	40	143	32	4	2	1	1	0	4,596	50,414	46,506	250
Dukes	3204	12	49	7	0	0	1	0	0	2,365	14,702	17,938	300
Ephesus	3205	13	59	24	No Report Received			0	0	0	0	0	85
Fairview	3504	7	28	0	0	0	0	0	1,172	998	10,196	11,918	20
Freedom*	3207	67	91	54	0	0	3	0	1,531	8,248	87,659	92,066	450
Garfield	3208	68	109	44	14	5	0	0	0	9,443	171,857	110,635	495
Gasper River	3306	36	49	20	No Report Received			0	0	0	0	0	105
Gill's Chapel	3307	7	24	0	0	0	0	0	0	1,583	14,038	14,779	35
Glasgow	3108	220	220	121	2	11	2	1	0	17,534	289,535	265,526	1,928
Good Hope	3109	24	24	24	2	2	0	2	1,720	2,491	19,392	16,891	50
Green Ridge	3308	47	102	30	No Report Received			0	5,880	0	0	0	400
Greensburg	3110	130	180	52	2	3	3	2	11,189	11,998	105,928	116,889	1,000
Greenville	3505	17	49	0	1	0	0	0	600	3,957	44,685	50,273	525
Harrodsburg	3111	1	135	15	1	0	2	1	2,170	3,472	10,616	27,231	325
Heartsong*	3222	25	25	0	No Report Received			0	0	0	0	0	1,650
High Point	3314	25	25	6	0	0	0	0	100	1,256	26,614	25,454	482
Hopewell	3112	14	25	14	0	0	3	0	0	2,030	18,266	16,296	60
Irvington	3210	15	25	15	No Report Received			0	0	0	0	0	86
Leitchfield	3211	50	78	26	2	3	0	1	300	5,552	54,107	61,380	550
Lewisburg	3309	32	73	29	1	2	1	0	1,500	7,447	69,335	65,209	300
Liberty	3116	30	55	21	0	0	1	0	0	2,197	57,632	53,831	750
Lick Branch	3117	64	191	38	1	1	1	0	1,250	5,131	21,730	24,309	90
Little Muddy	3310	19	19	17	0	1	0	0	2,591	6,591	26,421	36,192	119
Louisville 1st**	3212	64	126	38	0	0	51	1	0	5,790	102,157	108,028	1,000
Magnolia	3214	71	176	40	1	6	5	0	0	9,755	59,531	69,286	550
Monroe Chapel	3119	24	55	24	0	1	10	0	1,730	1,730	15,879	18,746	150
Morgantown	3311	21	21	6	No Report Received			0	0	0	0	0	80
Mt. Moriah	3120	14	30	12	0	0	0	0	0	0	10,395	15,435	62
Mt. Olive	3216	15	15	8	0	0	2	1	0	977	10,273	9,100	74
Mt. Olivet	3312	30	41	20	2	2	1	0	1,250	4,089	34,089	38,177	1,121
Mt. Pleasant	3217	45	63	30	2	3	0	1	3,338	4,862	30,104	33,408	175
Mt. Vernon*	3218	25	37	15	0	0	10	2	0	1,827	20,766	39,876	70
Mt. Zion (AC)	3121	5	18	8	No Report Received			0	0	0	0	0	0
Mt. Zion (DC)	3507	33	62	30	0	0	1	0	3,103	9,200	40,124	53,300	255
Neal's Chapel*	3122	20	47	17	0	0	3	2	0	3,611	0	23,952	150
Needham*	3219	23	23	10	0	0	1	0	0	684	29,825	29,452	6
New Cypress	3508	19	41	10	0	0	0	0	1,179	2,987	3,887	16,652	122
Oak Forest	3123	104	218	78	7	0	6	0	7,706	15,372	56,095	73,070	115
Owensboro	3509	138	149	58	2	11	14	4	7,043	18,353	172,413	190,766	1,646
Pleasant Hill*	3510	4	5	4	No Report Received			0	0	0	0	0	230
Point Pleasant*	3313	5	5	0	No Report Received			0	0	0	0	0	0

Cumberland Presbytery   (Continued)
MIDWEST SYNOD

GENERAL	MEMBERSHIP			CHANGES				FINANCES				
1.Church Number	2.Active	3.Total	4.Church School	5.Prof. of Faith	6.Gains	7.Losses	8.Children Baptized	9. OUR UNITED OUT-REACH	10. Total Out-Reach Giving	11. All Other Expenses	12. Total Income Received	13. Value Church Prop. 1=1000
1	2	3	4	5	6	7	8	9	10	11	12	13
Poplar Grove	3511	9	42	6	0	0	0	0	2,134	2,762	21,502	21,344	90
Radcliff	3220	28	28	14	No Report Received			0	0	0	0	0	237
Sacramento	3512	104	209	90	No Report Received			0	11,855	0	0	0	134
Salem	3127	9	32	0	No Report Received			0	0	0	0	0	35
Seven Springs	3128	16	35	18	No Report Received			0	0	0	0	0	267
Shiloh*	3129	85	85	32	0	0	9	0	7,821	16,164	54,275	66,174	300
Short Creek	3221	22	55	22	0	3	0	0	2,714	6,024	20,967	27,139	95
Wisdom	3130	30	30	12	1	6	2	0	0	155	155	9,167	75
TOTALS	65	2,983	4,999	1,791	64	217	157	27	110,972	285,325	2,571,452	2,703,236	24,637

*Math error corrected. **Purged roll.

CHURCHES, PASTORS, AND CLERKS:

Antioch   (4C)MICU3101
103 Clarksdale Circle (mailing)
Glasgow, KY 42141
68 Antioch Church Road (physical)
Knob Lick, KY 42154
( )   <Metcalfe>
SS: Michael E Fancher   <M3>
356 Breeding Road
Edmonton, KY 42129
(270)432-3138
princo1975@live.com
CL: Kathy B Nason
103 Clarksdale Circle
Glasgow, KY 42141
(270)670-4796
cblr@coldwellbankerbg.com

Auburn   (4MWC)MICU3301
Box 6
Auburn, KY 42206
(270)542-4304   <Logan>
PA: Grant Minton   <M1>
PO Box 270
Auburn, KY 42206
(270)542-7991
FAX: (270)271-4603
gminton@logantele.com
CL: Ashley Engler
695 Howlett Road
Auburn, KY 42206
(270)542-6730

Bald Knob   (4C)MICU3302
102 Bald Knob Church Road
Russellville, KY 42276
( )   <Logan>
PA: Byron Dumas   <M1 OP>
1775 Theresa Drive
Clarksville, TN 37043
(931)358-3348

lodumas7346@aol.com
CL: Kathleen Tynes
3175 Caney Fork Road
Lewisburg, KY 42256
(270)755-4218

Bethel   (2WC)MICU3102
454 Iron Mountain Road (mailing)
Center, KY 42214
( )   <Metcalfe>
SS: Keith G Atwell   <M1>
7688 Hardyville Road
Hardyville, KY 42746
(270)528-3667
CL: Steven McMullen
454 Iron Mountain Road
Center, KY 42214
(270)565-5440
mcmfarm@yahoo.com

Bethel #1   (4MWC)MICU3103
1259 Perryville Road (mailing)
2586 Perryville Road (physical)
Harrodsburg, KY 40330
( )   <Mercer>
PA: John Contini   <M1>
4344 Poor Ridge Pike
Lancaster, KY 40444
(859)339-0747
john@hillsideheritagefarm.com
CL: James L Wheeler
1259 Perryville Road
Harrodsburg, KY 40330
(859)734-2045
jlwheeler@roadrunner.com

Beulah   (4WC)MICU3501
PO Box 233 (mailing)
320 Beulah Church Road (physical)
Hartford, KY 42347
(270)298-3352   <Ohio>
FAX: (270)298-7007
cmwsaw2@bellsouth.net

PA: Michael Justice   <M1>
112B Vance Lane
Russellville, KY 42276
(270)726-6673
CL: Chuck Westerfield
PO Box 233
Hartford, KY 42347
(270)298-3352
FAX: (270)298-7007
cmwsaw2@bellsouth.net

Boiling Springs   (4C)MICU3303
3360 Highway 259 (mailing)
2412 Highway 259 (physical)
Portland, TN 37148
(615)325-2618   <Sumner>
PA: Chris Darland   <M1>
582 Ada Drive
Harrodsburg, KY 40330
(859)734-2254
CL: Pearl Kepley
3380 Highway 259
Portland, TN 37148
(615)325-3645

Bowling Green   (4MWC)MICU3304
807 Campbell Lane
Bowling Green, KY 42104
(270)781-3295   <Warren>
FAX: (270)781-2368
bgcpc@insightbb.com
PA: Steve Delashmit   <M1>
2705 Garrett Drive
Bowling Green, KY 42104
(270)796-8822
FAX: (270)781-2368
steve.delashmit@twc.com
CL: Hoy Hodges
295 Carver Lane
Alvaton, KY 42122
(270)843-4008
hhlaw319@aol.com

CUMBERLAND PRESBYTERY CONTINUED

Bridgeport 1st   (4C)MICU3131
515 DeKalb Street
Bridgeport, PA 19405
(610)275-6942   <Philadelphi>
PA: Donald Grey Barnhouse, Jr   <M1>
51 Harristown Road
Paradise, PA 17562
(717)768-0048
donaldbarnhouse@gmail.com
CL: William McLay
9 E Brown Street
Norristown, PA 19401
(610)277-8295
wjm999@verizon.net

Brier Creek   (4MWC)MICU3503
3467 State Route 175 N
Bremen, KY 42325
(270)525-3611   <Muhlenberg>
PA: Marc Bell   <M1>
811 Campbell Lane
Bowling Green, KY 42104
(270)846-4203
marcbell@insightbb.com
CL: Sherry Skimehorn
59 Whitmer Street
Central City, KY 42330
(270)525-3472
skimehor@bellsouth.net

Campbellsville   (4MWC)MICU3104
500 Cumberland Way
Campbellsville, KY 42718
(270)465-4091   <Taylor>
FAX: (270)469-9651
firstcpchurch@windstream.net
PA: Wayne E Brooks   <M1>
1505 Parkview Drive
Campbellsville, KY 42718
(270)465-9235
webrooks@windstream.net
CL: Faye Adams
902 Rosecrest Avenue
Campbellsville, KY 42718
(270)789-1791
newlifeblessed@yahoo.com

Caneyville   (4EWC)MICU3201
PO Box 334 (mailing)
203 River Park Drive (physical)
Caneyville, KY 42721
( )   <Grayson>
CL: Mary Alice Woosley-Logsdon
PO Box 334
Leitchfield, KY 42721
(270)230-2818
FAX: (270)879-9211
alicewoosley71@yahoo.com

Casey's Fork   (1C)MICU3105
PO Box 186 (mailing)
Highway 90 (physical)
Marrowbone, KY 42759
(502)864-3129   <Cumberland>
CL: Jimmy Mosby
210 Bombshell Creek Road
Burkesville, KY 42717

Cedar Flat   (C)MICU3106
1444 Milam Clark Road (mailing)
Summer Shade, KY 42166

Cedar Flat - Curtis Road (physical)
Edmonton, KY 42129
( )   <Metcalfe>
CL: Janet A Proffitt
1444 Milam Clark Road
Summer Shade, KY 42166
(270)428-4379

Clear Point   (4MWEC)MICU3107
7895 S Jackson Highway
Horse Cave, KY 42749
( )   <Hart>
PA: Darrell Pickett   <M1>
113 Woods Drive
Glasgow, KY 42141
(270)834-6102
dpickett@glasgow-ky.com
CL: Barbara Ogden
7895 S Jackson Highway
Horse Cave, KY 42749
(270)786-2695

Clifton Mills   (4WC)MICU3202
521 Butler Hobbs Road (mailing)
Hardinsburg, KY 40143
6406 W Highway 86 (physical)
Irvington, KY 40146
(270)547-5717   <Breckinridge>
PA: Don Bruington   <M1>
PO Box 105
Falls of Rough, KY 40119
(270)257-2228
CL: Edna M Hobbs
521 Butler Hobbs Road
Hardinsburg, KY 40143
(270)756-2592
tejthbs@att.net

Coyle   (4C)MICU3203
1285 Centerview Rough River Lane
Hudson, KY 40145
(270)257-0851   <Breckinridge>
tucker_rd@bellsouth.net
PA: Billy Ray Carter   <M1>
33 Mockingbird Drive
Leitchfield, KY 42754
(270)259-3897
cartercbc@windstream.net
CL: Ralph D Tucker
1285 Centerview Rough River Lane
Hudson, KY 40145
(270)257-0851
tucker_rd@bellsouth.net

Dukes   (4C)MICU3204
4743 Happy Hollow Road (mailing)
7814 State Route 144 E (physical)
Hawesville, KY 42348
(270)927-9577   <Hancock>
kimwilborn@yahoo.com
SS: Kimberley Wilborn   <M3>
4743 Happy Hollow Road
Hawesville, KY 42348
(270)927-9577
kimwilborn@yahoo.com
CL: Joe Wilborn
4743 Happy Hollow Road
Hawesville, KY 42348
(270)927-9577
joeandkimwilborn@bellsouth.net

Ephesus   (4EC)MICU3205
2300 Ephesus Church Road (mailing)
30 Ephesus Church Loop (physical)
Harned, KY 40144
( )   <Breckinridge>
bridget.keesee@ky.gov
PA: Jerrell M Underwood   <M1>
PO Box 9
Garfield, KY 40140
(270)536-3706
CL: Bridget Keesee
2300 Ephesus Church Road
Harned, KY 40144
(270)756-9278
bridget.keesee@ky.gov

Fairview   (4C)MICU3504
PO Box 195 (mailing)
Sacramento, KY 42372
Fairview Road (physical)
Bremen, KY
(270)736-5189   <Muhlenberg>
SS: James E Talley   <M1>
203 Browning Place
Hopkinsville, KY 42240
(270)886-4184
CL: Ottis E Markwell
PO Box 195
Sacramento, KY 42372
(270)736-5189

Freedom   (4MWC)MICU3207
224 John Drane Lane (mailing)
394 John Drane Lane (physical)
Harned, KY 40144
(270)617-4016   <Breckinridge>
PA: Jeff McMichael   <M1>
224 John Drane Lane
Harned, KY 40144
(270)617-4016
revmcmichael@outlook.com
CL: Larry Collard
4634 Highway 261 N
Hardinsburg, KY 40143
(270)617-0609

Garfield   (4MWC)MICU3208
PO Box 39 (mailing)
90 W Highway 86 (physical)
Garfield, KY 40140
(270)580-4796   <Breckinridge>
mccallum@bbtel.com
PA: Frank McCallum   <M1>
PO Box 56
Garfield, KY 40140
(270)580-4796
mccallum@bbtel.com
CL: Stephen J Tabor
PO Box 39
Garfield, KY 40140
(270)536-3297
btabor@bbtel.com

Gasper River   (4C)MICU3306
3201 Bucksville Road (mailing)
3005 Bucksville Road (physical)
Auburn, KY 42206
(270)542-8998   <Logan>
SS: Byron Dumas   <M1 OP>
1775 Theresa Drive
Clarksville, TN 37043

CUMBERLAND PRESBYTERY CONTINUED

(931)358-3348
CL: Sandy Tinsley
3201 Bucksville Road
Auburn, KY 42206
(270)542-7900
tinsley@logantele.com

_____

Gill's Chapel   (4EC)MICU3307
1733 Stokes Chapel Road (mailing)
Elkton, KY 42220
955 Hermon Road (physical)
Guthrie, KY 42234
(270)755-4282   <Todd>
sam60romines@hotmail.com
PA: Sam Romines   <M1>
PO Box 127
Lewisburg, KY 42256
(270)755-4282
sam60romines@hotmail.com
CL: Sam Romines
PO Box 127
Lewisburg, KY 42256
(270)755-4282
sam60romines@hotmail.com

_____

Glasgow   (4MWC)MICU3108
101 Cumberland Street
Glasgow, KY 42141
(270)651-3308   <Barren>
gcpc@glasgow-ky.com
SS: Nicholas Smith   <M3>
101 Cumberland Street
Glasgow, KY 42141
(270)651-3308
pastornic@gcpchurch.tv
CL: Buelon R (Pete) Moss
101 Cumberland Street
Glasgow, KY 42141
(270)651-3308

_____

Good Hope   (2C)MICU3109
700 Dutton Creek Road (mailing)
Lemon Bend Road (physical)
Campbellsville, KY 42718
(270)789-1482   <Taylor>
glwgaw@windstream.net
CL: Gayle Whitley
700 Dutton Creek Road
Campbellsville, KY 42718
(270)789-1482
glwgaw@windstream.net

_____

Green Ridge   (4MWC)MICU3308
7424 Highland Lick Road
Lewisburg, KY 42256
(270)726-8497   <Logan>
brojoe2@logantele.com
PA: Joseph R Vaught   <M1>
7424 Highland Lick Road
Lewisburg, KY 42256
(270)726-8497
brojoe2@logantele.com
CL: Shannon Wells
1720 Crawford Road
Lewisburg, KY 42256
(270)277-9977
chps@bellsouth.net

_____

Greensburg   (4MEWC)MICU3110
699 Old Hodgenville Road
Greensburg, KY 42743

(270)932-4864   <Green>
greensburgcpc@windstream.net
PA: Kevin T Brantley   <M1>
729 Old Hodgenville Road
Greensburg, KY 42743
(270)932-3780
kbrantley1971@windstream.net
CL: Amy Beard
699 Old Hodgenville Road
Greensburg, KY 42743
(270)932-4864
greensburgcpc@windstream.net

_____

Greenville   (4WC)MICU3505
234 Sunset Park (mailing)
108 S Cherry Street (physical)
Greenville, KY 42345
(270)338-0882   <Muhlenberg>
PA: Arthur L Burrows, Jr   <M1>
PO Box 511
Hopkinsville, KY 42241
(270)886-1301
CL: Joseph Harris
234 Sunset Park
Greenville, KY 42345
(270)338-6555
josephharris234@yahoo.com

_____

Harrodsburg   (4MWC)MICU3111
1113 Louisville Road
Harrodsburg, KY 40330
(   )   <Mercer>
PA: Geoff Barrett   <M1>
155 Maude Lane
Harrodsburg, KY 40330
(859)748-0450
glbarrett@live.com
CL: Nancy R Tatum
4955 Louisville Road
Salvisa, KY 40372
(859)865-4482

_____

Heartsong   (4C)MICU3222
6322 Labor Lane (mailing)
6800 S Hurstbourne Parkway (physical)
Louisville, KY 40291
(502)635-8587   <Jefferson>
PA: Jim Butler   <M1>
6322 Labor Lane
Louisville, KY 40291
(502)635-8587
jbutler54@insightbb.com
CL: Susan Lawson
6322 Labor Lane
Louisville, KY 40291
(502)968-0006

_____

High Point Community   (C)MICU3314
PO Box 753 (mailing)
Burnside, KY 42519
190 Longview Drive (physical)
West Somerset, KY 42503
(606)271-0842   <Pulaski>
highpointcpc@gmail.com
PA: Fred Michael (Mike) Adams   <M1>
42 Julies Way
Somerset, KY 42503
(606)451-9155
fma46@twc.com
CL: Betty Huffman
PO Box 753

Burnside, KY 42519
(606)561-3645
betty.huffman@hotmail.com

_____

Hopewell   (4C)MICU3112
1012 N Jackson Highway (mailing)
Hardyville, KY 42746
Hopewell Church Road (physical)
Canmer, KY 42722
(   )   <Hart>
CL: Kaye Atwell
1012 N Jackson Highway
Hardyville, KY 42746
(270)528-5341
mkatwell@yahoo.com

_____

Irvington   (4MWC)MICU3210
4108 Highway 477 (mailing)
Webster, KY 40176
111 W Walnut Street (physical)
Irvington, KY 40146
(   )   <Breckinridge>
PA: Charles Meredith   <M1>
144 Barbara Circle
Elizabethtown, KY 42701
(270)307-0607
CL: Ruby Bell
4108 Highway 477
Webster, KY 40176
(270)547-7455
rrbells@bbtel.com

_____

Leitchfield   (4MC)MICU3211
501 W Chestnut Street
Leitchfield, KY 42754
(270)259-3835   <Grayson>
PA: Brenda Wilson   <M1>
35 Collins Drive
Elizabethtown, KY 42701
(270)249-3835
susieq2007@windstream.net
CL: Arita French
245 Embry Road
Leitchfield, KY 42754
(270)259-4457
kenarita@windstream.net

_____

Lewisburg   (4MWC)MICU3309
PO Box 127 (mailing)
101 Church Street (physical)
Lewisburg, KY 42256
(270)755-4282   <Logan>
PA: Sam Romines   <M1>
PO Box 127
Lewisburg, KY 42256
(270)755-4282
sam60romines@hotmail.com
CL: Ralph Cropper
178 Cardinal Street
Lewisburg, KY 42256
(270)755-2357
ralph.cropper@novelis.com

_____

Liberty   (4WC)MICU3116
PO Box 4105 (mailing)
4139 Old Columbia Road (physical)
Campbellsville, KY 42718
(270)849-7377   <Taylor>
PA: Earl West   <M1>
246 Maple Avenue
Greensburg, KY 42743

CUMBERLAND PRESBYTERY CONTINUED

(207)932-5010
west5010@windstream.net
CL: Barbara Davenport
216 Happy Hill Drive
Campbellsville, KY 42718
(270)465-3633
teebdee@windstream.net

_____
Lick Branch　　　　(4C)MICU3117
50 B Jones Road (mailing)
7318 Lecta Kino Road (physical)
Glasgow, KY 42141
(270)670-6698　　　　<Barren>
doncynem@gmail.com
OD: Jerry D Martin　　　　<M5>
292 Bristletown Road
Glasgow, KY 42141
(270)678-2476
doncynem@glasgow-ky.com
CL: Nancy Jolly
2979 Kino Road
Glasgow, KY 42141
(270)428-5722
jollyfarms@scrtc.com

_____
Little Muddy　　　　(4MC)MICU3310
1061 Sugar Grove Road (mailing)
170 Little Muddy Church Road (physical)
Morgantown, KY 42261
(　)　　　　<Butler>
SS: Carlton Hatcher　　　　<M1>
2111 Robin Road
Bowling Green, KY 42101
(270)842-8488
CL: William Gabe Keen
822 Sugar Grove Road
Morgantown, KY 42261
(270)526-5895

_____
Louisville 1st　　　　(4MWC)MICU3212
4610 Manslick Road
Louisville, KY 40216
(502)368-4709　　　　<Jefferson>
FAX: (502)368-4709
firstcumberland@att.net
PA: Rodney E Harris　　　　<M1>
7420 Conjar Court
Louisville, KY 40214
(502)368-5501
rodneypat@insightbb.com
CL: Carrie Roth
4610 Manslick Road
Louisville, KY 40216
(502)368-4709
firstcumberland@att.net

_____
Magnolia　　　　(4MWC)MICU3214
PO Box 1 (mailing)
235 Old L and N Turkpike (physical)
Magnolia, KY 42757
(270)324-3472　　　　<LaRue>
magnoliacpchurch@gmail.com
SS: Anthony Harris　　　　<M2>
1604 Parkview Drive
Campbellsville, KY 42718
(270)403-1126
aharris044@gmail.com
CL: Charlotte Tucker
1080 Greensburg Road
Hodgenville, KY 42748
(270)358-3090

charlotte.tucker@larue.kyschools.ust

_____
Monroe Chapel　　　　(4C)MICU3119
7688 Hardyville Road (mailing)
Rt 2 Highway 88 (physical)
Hardyville, KY 42746
(270)528-3667　　　　<Hart>
jbuggforbis@hotmail.com
PA: Keith G Atwell　　　　<M1>
7688 Hardyville Road
Hardyville, KY 42746
(270)528-3667
CL: Janie B Forbis
2465 Possum Trot Road
Hardyville, KY 42746
(270)528-3873
jbuggforbis@hotmail.com

_____
Morgantown　　　　(4MWC)MICU3311
308 Helm Lane (mailing)
118 W Ohio Street (physical)
Morgantown, KY 42261
(　)　　　　<Butler>
SS: David Hocker　　　　<M3>
309 N Taylor Street
Morgantown, KY 42261
(270)526-6027
dhocker@hocker.com
CL: Carolyn Henderson
308 Helm Lane
Morgantown, KY 42261
(270)526-3439

_____
Mt Moriah　　　　(2C)MICU3120
107 James Street (mailing)
Edmonton, KY 42129
2038 Mt Moriah Road (physical)
Summer Shade, KY 42166
(　)　　　　<Metcalfe>
CL: Sandy England
107 James Street
Edmonton, KY 42129
(270)432-3778
englandsim@scrtc.com

_____
Mt Olive　　　　(4WC)MICU3216
1295 Solway Meeting Road (mailing)
Mt Olive Church Road (physical)
Big Clifty, KY 42712
(　)　　　　<Hardin>
CL: Gayle Johnson
1295 Solway Meeting Road
Big Clifty, KY 42712
(270)862-4313
vonnie.g0000@yahoo.com

_____
Mt Olivet　　　　(4MEWC)MICU3312
2640 Mt Olivet Road
Bowling Green, KY 42101
(270)843-0223　　　　<Warren>
SS: Robert (Bob) Bunnell　　　　<M1>
329 Lexington Drive
Glasgow, KY 42141
(270)629-6209
bob_bunnell@yahoo.com
CL: Betty Grammer
180 Sir Wilburn Way
Alvaton, KY 42122
(270)781-4435
thememaw02@walmartconnect.com

_____

Mt Pleasant　　　　(4C)MICU3217
364 E Big Reedy Road (mailing)
E Big Reedy Road (physical)
Caneyville, KY 42721
(　)　　　　<Edmonson>
CL: Gloria Slaughter
364 E Big Reedy Road
Caneyville, KY 42721
(270)286-9372
gslaughter@mtownbank.com

_____
Mt Vernon　　　　(4WC)MICU3218
1870 Brandenburg Road (mailing)
2373 Brandenburg Road (physical)
Leitchfield, KY 42754
(　)　　　　<Grayson>
PA: William M Macy　　　　<M1>
1358 Ephesus Church Road
Harned, KY 40144
(270)756-2775
CL: Marcella Lucas
1870 Brandenburg Road
Leitchfield, KY 42754
(270)259-9215

_____
Mt. Zion (AC)　　　　(1C)MICU3121
c/o Lena Bryson
1925 Loren Collins Road
Glens Fork, KY 42741
(　)　　　　<Adair>
CL: Lena Bryson
214 Buell Collins Road
Glens Fork, KY 42741
(502)378-6172

_____
Mt Zion (DC)　　　　(4MWC)MICU3507
7447 Knottsville Mt Zion Rd (mailing)
8001 Knottsville Mt Zion Rd (physical)
Philpot, KY 42366
(　)　　　　<Daviess>
PA: Dennis J Preston　　　　<M1>
7447 Knottsville Mount Zion Road
Philpot, KY 42366
(270)925-8144
dennis.preston@daviess.kyschools.us
CL: Shirley L Bratcher
3815 Locust Hill Drive
Owensboro, KY 42303
(270)993-4056
slbratcher24@yahoo.com

_____
Neal's Chapel　　　　(4C)MICU3122
62 Oscar Gilpin Road (mailing)
860 Lecta Kino Road (physical)
Glasgow, KY 42141
(　)　　　　<Barren>
LS: Bob White　　　　<M6>
313 Cleveland Avenue
Glasgow, KY 42141
(270)651-8529
drbwhite@glasgow-ky.com
CL: Pam H Browning
62 Oscar Gilpin Road
Glasgow, KY 42141
(270)670-1047
pshbrowning@hotmail.com

_____
Needham　　　　(4WC)MICU3219
3179 Meeting Creek Road (mailing)
State Route 84 (physical)
Eastview, KY 42732

CUMBERLAND PRESBYTERY CONTINUED

( )
PA: Shelby O Haire   \<M1>
   3179 Meeting Creek Road
   Eastview, KY 42732
   (270)862-3887
CL: Odelia Dewall
   2548 Meeting Creek Road
   Eastview, KY 42732
   (270)862-4362

New Cypress   (4C)MICU3508
   127 W 23rd Street (mailing)
   Owensboro, KY 42303
   4814 Highway 81 S (physical)
   Rumsey, KY 42371
( )   \<McLean>
PA: Terry Fortner   \<M1>
   1079 Luzerne Depoy Road
   Greenville, KY 42345
   (270)836-3635
   terryfortner@att.net
CL: Phyllis Davis
   127 W 23rd Street
   Owensboro, KY 42303
   (270)926-6033
   phyllisdavis966@hotmail.com

Oak Forest   (4MWC)MICU3123
   170 Milby Rattliff Road
   Summersville, KY 42782
   (270)932-4685   \<Green>
OD: Robert Knight   \<M5>
   1360 Free Union Road
   Columbia, KY 42728
   (270)384-0677
CL: Mike Durrett
   170 Milby Rattliff Road
   Summersville, KY 42782
   (270)932-4685
   thedurretts@windstream.net

Owensboro   (4C)MICU3509
   910 Booth Avenue
   Owensboro, KY 42301
   (270)683-4479   \<Daviess>
   brotim.cpc@gmail.net
PA: Timothy McGuire   \<M1>
   PO Box 42
   Mt Sherman, KY 42764
   (270)766-9027
   brotim.cpc@gmail.com
CL: Mike Tooley
   729 Greenbriar Street
   Owensboro, KY 42301
   (270)570-1372
   tooleyma@gmail.com

Pleasant Hill   (4MEC)MICU3510
   10851 Highway 593
   Owensboro, KY 42301
   (386)689-9340   \<Daviess>
CL: Carole Robertson
   4709 Forrest Drive
   Owensboro, KY 42303
   (270)315-5288

Point Pleasant   (1C)MICU3313
   7030 State Route 269
   Beaver Dam, KY 42320
( )   \<Butler>
SS: David Hocker   \<M3>

   309 N Taylor Street
   Morgantown, KY 42261
   (270)526-6027
CL: Kathy Pharris
   7030 State Route 269
   Beaver Dam, KY 42320
   (270)274-7418
   kathyspharris@yahoo.com

Poplar Grove   (4WC)MICU3511
   2929 Kentucky 254 W (mailing)
   5112 State Highway 1155 (physical)
   Sacramento, KY 42372
( )   \<McLean>
PA: James E Talley   \<M1>
   203 Browning Place
   Hopkinsville, KY 42240
   (270)886-4184
CL: Gibson H Riggs
   PO Box 224
   Calhoun, KY 42327
   (270)273-3280
   FAX: (270)273-3280
   riggsg@bellsouth.net

Radcliff   (4U)MICU3220
   1751 S Logsdon Parkway
   Radcliff, KY 40159
   (270)351-6199   \<Hardin>
   radpres@bbtel.com
OD: John Lentz   \<M5>
   1876 Highway 44 E
   Shepherdsville, KY 40165
   (502)543-2659
   lentzhome@aol.com
CL: Patricia T. Crosby
   851 S Archer Street
   Radcliff, KY 40160
   (270)351-8548
   ptcrosby@bbtel.com

Sacramento   (4MWC)MICU3512
   PO Box 257 (mailing)
   40 Lyons Lane (physical)
   Sacramento, KY 42372
   (270)736-5176   \<McLean>
   butler8134@bellsouth.net
PA: John Butler   \<M1>
   PO Box 257
   Sacramento, KY 42372
   (270)736-2268
   butler8134@bellsouth.net
CL: Brenda Lee
   386 Dillahay Dame Loop
   Island, KY 42350
   (270)736-5160

Salem   (2C)MICU3127
   1570 Old Salem Church Road (mailing)
   291 Clay Wright Road (physical)
   Greensburg, KY 42743
( )   \<Green>
CL: Joan Cook
   1570 Old Salem Church Road
   Greensburg, KY 42743
   (502)932-5717

Seven Springs   (2C)MICU3128
   1607 Seven Springs Church Road
   Center, KY 42214
   (270)565-4865   \<Metcalfe>

PA: Randall Gray   \<M1>
   1230 New Liberty Big Meadow Road
   Knob Lick, KY 42154
   (270)432-5322
CL: Louise London
   2466 Highway 1048
   Center, KY 42214
   (270)565-3015

Shiloh   (4MEWC)MICU3129
   252 Tabernacle Road (mailing)
   1186 Shiloh Road (physical)
   Campbellsville, KY 42718
   (270)789-2346   \<Taylor>
   ferree047@windstream.net
PA: Ronald L Ferree   \<M1>
   2475 Fallen Timber Road
   Campbellsville, KY 42718
   (270)465-1150
   ferree047@windstream.net
CL: Sue Campbell
   333 Campbell Road
   Campbellsville, KY 42718
   (270)465-5492

Short Creek   (4WC)MICU3221
   9312 Owensboro Road (mailing)
   Hollow Church Road (physical)
   Falls of Rough, KY 40119
( )   \<Grayson>
CL: George Fentress
   11680 Owensboro Road
   Falls of Rough, KY 40119
   (270)879-8883

Wisdom   (2C)MICU3130
   254 Echo Road (mailing)
   State Route 640 (physical)
   Knob Lick, KY 42129
( )   \<Metcalfe>
CL: Frances Royse
   491 Cave Ridge Road
   Knob Lick, KY 42154
   (270)432-0112
   froyse@scrtc.com

OTHERS ON MINISTERIAL ROLL:

Akai, Anum   \<M1 WC>
   458 Dean Taylor Court
   Simpsonville, KY 40067
   (502)405-3120
Barton, Robert   \<M1 WC>
   22460 Klines Resort Road #290
   Three Rivers, MI 49093
   (859)613-2686
   csm2ndinfbde2002@yahoo.com
Blevins, Tom   \<M1 WC>
   50 Blevins Road
   Center, KY 42214
   (270)565-1792
Boggs, Robert   \<M1 WC>
   89 Maple Leaf Lane
   Leitchfield, KY 42754
   (270)259-5546
Byrd, James F   \<M1 WC>
   1158 Cornishville Road
   Harrodsburg, KY 40330
   (859)734-0534
   jfbyrd@bluezoomwifi.com
Chesnut, Walter   \<M1 RT>

CUMBERLAND PRESBYTERY CONTINUED

114 Cherrydale Drive
Greeneville, TN 37745
(270)259-4429
lc1916@yahoo.com

Clark, Tom   <M1 WC>
62 Oak Trace
Campbellsville, KY 42718
(270)469-4377

Cottingim, Tom   <M1 WC>
353 Atwood Drive
Lexington, KY 40515
(859)273-3800
FAX: (859)272-4315
t.cottingim@insightbb.com

Ferree, Carole   <M1 WC>
2475 Fallen Timber Road
Campbellsville, KY 42718
(270)465-1150
ferree047@wildblue.net

Gary, Brian   <M1 WC>
105 Wilma Avenue
Radcliff, KY 40160
(502)351-6938

Jones, Joseph M   <M1 RT>
405 Lakeview Drive
Campbellsville, KY 42718
joepegjones@windstream.net

Love, James R   <M1 WC>
14382 Sonora Hardin Springs Road
Eastview, KY 42732
(502)862-4119

Milby, Elizabeth L   <M1 WC>
207 Summersville Road
Greensburg, KY 42743
(270)932-5659

Neafus, Kenneth R   <M1 WC>
237 Richland Church Road
Morgantown, KY 42261
(270)526-6835

Norris, Freddie   <M1 WC>
330 Lexington Drive
Glasgow, KY 42141
(270)651-7932

Perkins, William H   <M1 WC>
PO Box 632
Central City, KY 42330
(270)754-5333

Powell, Omer T   <M1 RT>
11856 Sonora Hardin Springs Road
Eastview, KY 42732
(270)862-4720

Ranson, Doris   <M1 WC>
9440 Fenwick Road
Owensboro, KY 42301
(270)229-2875
dorisranson@bellsouth.net

Renner, Wallace   <M1 WC>
1648 Griffith Avenue
Owensboro, KY 42303
(270)685-4359
pwrenner@adelphia.net

Ricketts, Roger   <M1 WC>
205 Contantz Drive
Canton, MO 63435

Thompson, Eugene   <M1 WC>
2825 Albatross Road
Del Ray Beach, FL 33444

Thompson, W Fay   <M1 WC>
210 Macbeth Lane
Glasgow, KY 42141
(270)646-2218

Tucker, James D   <M1 WC>
PO Box 34
Mc Daniels, KY 40152
(270)257-8971

OTHER LICENTIATES ON ROLL:

Watts, Glenn David   <M2 ST>
7400 Willowbend Drive
Crestwood, KY 40014
(502)241-0436
hongkongbrother@hotmail.com

OTHER CANDIDATES ON ROLL:

Craddock, Barry   <M3>
147 Moss Way
Glasgow, KY 42141

Johnson, Alan F   <M3>
10809 State Route 593
Owensboro, KY 42301
(386)689-9340
ajatlantic@yahoo.com

Pursley, Andrew   <M3>
1608 Pearl Street
Owensboro, KY 42303

Cumberland East Coast Presbytery
SOUTHEAST SYNOD

GENERAL		MEMBERSHIP			CHANGES				FINANCES				
1.Church Number	2.Active	3.Total	4.Church School	5.Prof. of Faith	6.Gains	7.Losses	8.Children Baptized	9. OUR UNITED OUT-REACH	10. Total Out-Reach Giving	11. All Other Expenses	12. Total Income Received	13. Value Church Prop. 1=1000
1	2	3	4	5	6	7	8	9	10	11	12	13
Hope Korean Outreach	2131	15	19	1	1	3	11	1	0	15,488	63,127	65,382	63
One Way	2137	78	104	57	12	0	23	2	0	4,800	135,870	120,176	190
Sharing	2141	20	24	10	1	3	19	8	0	5,000	48,000	55,000	2
Sunnyside													
TOTALS	5	113	147	68	14	6	53	11	0	25,288	246,997	240,558	255

*Math error corrected. **Purged roll.

New Presbytery for 2012
-- data incomplete

CHURCHES, PASTORS, AND CLERKS:

Hope Korean   (C)SECE2131
 1189 Hope Road
 Tinton Falls, NJ 07724
 ( )   <Monmouth>
PA: Buhwan Yang   <M1>
 19 Taylors Run
 Tinton Falls, NJ 07712
 (732)918-0011
 yangmoksa@gmail.com
CL: Session Clerk
 1189 Hope Road
 Tinton Falls, NJ 07724

One Way   (C)SECE2137
 9 Carlton Avenue
 Port Washington, NY 11050
 (516)815-1164   <Queens>
 FAX: (516)921-2821
PA: Jin Soo Park   <M1>
 37 Arizona Avenue
 Syosset, NY 11791
 (516)558-7298
 owcasa@hanmail.net
AP: Si Hoon Park   <M1>
 511 4th Street #B
 Palisades Park, NJ 07650
 (201)944-7913
CL: Session Clerk
 PO Box 56
 Syosset, NY 11791
 (516)815-1164
 FAX: (516)558-7298
 owcusa@hanmail.net

Outreach   (C)SECE2143
 800 Silver Lane Room 205
 East Hartford, CT 06118
 (860)830-6808
 lovejcamen@yahoo.com
PA: Sansook Cho   <M1>
 7 Falmouth Court
 Middletown, CT
 lovejcamen@yahoo.com
 (860)830-6808
CL: Session Clerk
 800 Silver Lane Room 205
 East Hartford, CT 06118
 (860)830-6808
 lovejcamen@yahoo.com

Sharing   (C)SECE2141
 35-24 Union Street 1C
 Flushing, NY 11354
 (718)460-1118   <Queens>
 spcko1188@gmail.com
PA: John Jae Ko   <M1>
 13955 35th Avenue #5A
 Flushing, NY 11354
 (718)460-1118
 spcko@hanmail.net
CL: Session Clerk
 35-24 Union Street 1C
 Flushing, NY 11354
 spcko1188@gmail.com

Sunnyside   (C)SECE0000
 27-27 Bayside Lane
 Flushing, NY 11354
 (718)809-5191
PA: Kio Seob Kim   <M1>
 14430 35th Avenue Apt A62
 Flushing, NY 11354
 (718)539-3476

OTHER LICENTIATES ON ROLL:

Sung, John   (M2)
 26 Old Orchard Road
 Cherry Hill, NJ 08003
 (856)751-0227

Presbytery del Cristo
MISSION SYNOD

	GENERAL		MEMBERSHIP			CHANGES				FINANCES				
	1.Church Number	2.Active	3.Total	4.Church School	5.Prof. of Faith	6.Gains	7.Losses	8.Children Baptized	9. OUR UNITED OUT-REACH	10. Total Out-Reach Giving	11. All Other Expenses	12. Total Income Received	13. Value Church Prop. 1=1000	
	1	2	3	4	5	6	7	8	9	10	11	12	13	
Chinese	8501	575	575	205	0	19	56	0	30,936	30,936	943,518	960,187	3,500	
Desert Gardens*	8705	18	24	0	0	0	2	0	2,167	8,585	37,997	54,134	180	
El Paso First	8704	22	29	11	0	2	1	0	2,073	10,259	54,890	66,885	1,000	
Grace Fellowship	8510	143	143	90	0	0	3	2	43,333	212,642	382,013	655,259	700	
Heights	8701	382	2,495	95	10	6	37	0	5,833	162,915	734,235	971,456	1,852	
Lubbock First	8702	121	137	35	3	10	7	2	2,500	8,596	399,863	407,780	2,467	
Maranatha	8706	100	100	60	0	0	17	0	0	5,000	30,000	37,000	0	
Redeemer	8512	40	40	60	0	0	0	2	5,000	21,487	182,159	209,605	0	
St. Andrew	8703	110	204	47	6	6	4	4	7,963	28,981	224,039	295,456	1,200	
Trona	8503	5	35	9	0	0	5	0	174	623	11,006	13,115	125	
Westside	8709	43	63	38	2	4	6	0	550	6,445	93,076	90,019	200	
TOTALS	11	1,559	3,845	650	21	47	138	10	100,529	496,469	3,092,796	3,760,896	11,224	

*Math error corrected. **Purged roll.

CHURCHES, PASTORS, AND CLERKS:

Chinese   (4C)MSDC8501
865 Jackson Street
San Francisco, CA 94133
(415)421-1624   <San Francisco>
FAX: (415)421-1874
church@cumberlandsf.org
PA: Walter Lau   <M1>
865 Jackson Street
San Francisco, CA 94133
(415)421-1624
FAX: (415)421-1874
walter@cumberlandsf.org
AP: Steven Chen   <M1>
865 Jackson Street
San Francisco, CA 94133
(415)421-1624
psalm1305@yahoo.com
AP: Pek Hua Tan   <M1>
7 Belhaven Avenue
Daly City, CA 94015
(415)515-0076
ptan27@yahoo.com
AP: Sonny Wan   <M1>
13 Wexford Place
Aladema, CA 94502
(415)421-1624
sonny@cumberlandsf.org
AP: Alexis Yu   <M1>
1761 Willow Way
San Bruno, CA 94066
(415)421-1624
alexis.yu.k@gmail.com
CL: John Fang
2362 - 39th Avenue
San Francisco, CA 94116
(415)665-3721
johnfang@pacbell.net

Desert Gardens   (4C)MSDC8705

10851 E Old Spanish Trail
Tucson, AZ 85748
(520)296-0703   <Pima>
PA: Gerald (Jerry) Hagelin   <M1>
10851 E Old Spanish Trail
Tucson, AZ 85712
(520)275-8110
azcef@cs.com
CL: Bonnie Kopke
10851 E Old Spanish Trail
Tucson, AZ 85748
(520)647-4700
bkopke@cox.net

El Paso First   (4WC)MSDC8704
11299 Pebble Hills Boulevard
El Paso, TX 79936
(915)592-6138   <El Paso>
FAX: (915)592-3538
fcpcelp@sbcglobal.net
PA: Alfredo Rincon   <M1>
12008 Fred Carter
El Paso, TX 79936
(915)857-1343
yaanaivitaly@yahoo.com
CL: Norma Frye
3317 Funston Place
El Paso, TX 79936
(915)633-6877
cherokee80@sbcglobal.net

Grace Fellowship   (4C)MSDC8510
3265 16th Street
San Francisco, CA 94103
(415)703-6090   <San Francisco>
FAX: (415)864-1543
PA: Sharon Huey   <M1>
3265 16th Street
San Francisco, CA 94103
(415)703-6090
sharon_huey@yahoo.com
AP: Douglas Lee   <M1>

3265 16th Street
San Francisco, CA 94103
(415)703-6090
dlee@gum.org
CL: Matthew Denson
3265 16th Street
San Francisco, CA 94103
(415)247-9421 ext 17
FAX: (415)864-5830
matthew@densons.org

Heights   (4WC)MSDC8701
8600 Academy Road NE
Albuquerque, NM 87111
(505)821-1993   <Bernalillo>
FAX: (505)797-8599
info@heightscpc.org
PA: Lloyd Aaron McMillan   <M1>
8600 Academy Road NE
Albuquerque, NM 87111
(505)821-1993
FAX: (505)797-8599
amcmillan@heightscpc.org
AP: Jerry Smyrl   <M1>
3421 Montreal Street NE
Albuquerque, NM 87111
(505)293-0108
jwsmyrl@hotmail.com
AP: Marty Goehring   <M1>
8600 Academy NE
Albuquerque, NM 87111
(505)821-3628
FAX: (505)797-8599
mgoehring@heightscpc.org
AP: Justin Richter   <M1>
8600 Academy Road NE
Albuquerque, NM 87111
(505)363-8738
richteryp@gmail.com
CL: Barbara J Cok
8600 Academy Road NE
Albuquerque, NM 87112

PRESBYTERY DEL CRISTO CONTINUED

(505)275-0108
FAX: (866)280-0731
barbara@lobo.net

_____
Lubbock First   (4WC)MSDC8702
7702 Indiana Avenue
Lubbock, TX 79423
(806)792-3553   <Lubbock>
joy@cpclubbock.com
PA: Steve Doles   <M1>
7702 Indiana Avenue
Lubbock, TX 79423
(806)787-7551
steve@cpclubbock.com
CL: Diana K Akins
4712 63rd Street
Lubbock, TX 79414
(806)797-5246
FAX: (806)744-0640
dkakins48@yahoo.com

_____
Maranatha   (4C)MSDC8706
PO Box 1040 (mailing)
San Elizario, TX 79849
11497 Socorro Road (physical)
Socorro, TX 79927
(915)851-8349   <El Paso>
hectoryliz@att.net
PA: Hector Mata   <M1>
PO Box 1040
San Elizario, TX 79849
(915)851-5354
hectoryliz@att.net
AP: Isaac Mata   <M1>
PO Box 1040
San Elizaro, TX 79849
(915)851-5354
isaacmata96@yahoo.com
AP: Lyvia Rincon   <M1>
12008 Fred Carter
El Paso, TX 79936
(915)857-1343
yaanaivitaly@yahoo.com
CL: Miguel Flores
PO Box 1040
San Elizario, TX 79849
(915)346-2071

_____
Redeemer   (4C)MSDC8512
1224 Fairfax Avenue
San Francisco, CA 94124
(415)671-2194   <San Francisco>
info@redeemersf.org
PA: Danny Fong   <M1>
1224 Fairfax Avenue
San Francisco, CA 94124
(415)671-2194
dfong@redeemersf.org
CL: Daniel Kim
1224 Fairfax Avenue
San Francisco, CA 94124
(415)596-6400
dannydhkim@gmail.com

_____
St Andrew   (4MEWC)MSDC8703
1415 N Grandview
Odessa, TX 79761
(432)367-8603   <Ector>
FAX: (432)367-8605
standrewcp@sbcglobal.net
PA: Jimmy Braswell   <M1>

1514 E 10th Street
Odessa, TX 79761
(432)335-9346
jjcgbraz@cableone.net
AP: Sharon Notley   <M1>
16500 S Grey Wolf Apt 5
Odessa, TX 79766
(432)210-9059
sharon_standrewcp@sbcglobal.net
CL: Linda Anglley
309 E 89th Street
Odessa, TX 79765
(432)550-8569
anglley@yahoo.com

_____
Trona   (4C)MSDC8503
PO Box 1105 (mailing)
83456 Argus Avenue (physical)
Trona, CA 93592
(760)382-8636   <San Bernardino>
PA: Dennis Benadom   <M1>
13314 Sage Street
Trona, CA 93562
(760)372-4536
galerose91@msn.com
CL: Cindy Barton
83426 Argus Avenue
Trona, CA 93562
(760)372-4033
cbarton53@hotmail.com

_____
Westside   (4C)MSDC8709
PO Box 15209 (mailing)
4110 Sabana Grande Avenue (physical)
Rio Rancho, NM 87174
(505)620-2427   <Sandoval>
nancye320@aol.com
PA: Harry W Chapman   <M1>
4908 El Picador Court
Rio Rancho, NM 87124
(505)620-2427
wrightrev@gmail.com
CL: Sherry Meier
7113 Hartford Hills Drive NE
Rio Rancho, NM 87144
(505)771-0418
sjmeier53@aol.com

_____
OTHERS ON MINISTERIAL ROLL:

Bondurant, Lee   <M1 WC>
1453 Paseo Del Sur Court
El Paso, TX 79928
(915)309-7269
leebondurant@yahoo.com
Bower, Clay   <M1 WC>
221 Waterlemon Way
Monroe, NC 28110
(704)575-9497
cblower@lzbsoutheast.com
Chang, John   <M1 RT>
1753 Castro Drive
San Jose, CA 95130
(408)370-0643
FAX: (405)370-0643
Collins, Paul   <M1 WC>
915 Warm Sands Drive SE
Albuquerque, NM 87123
(505)294-3842
FAX: (505)254-7707
chapp3@comcast.net

Estes, George R   <M1 RT>
7910 Cloverbrook Lane
Germantown, TN 38138
(901)755-6673
geoestes@gmail.com
Estes, Sam R, Jr   <M1 RT>
3026 54th Street Apt 311
Lubbock, TX 79413
(806)748-6116
Freund, Henry O   <M1 RT>
913 Sam Houston Drive
Dyersburg, TN 38024
(731)285-1744
freundly@att.net
Fung, David   <M1 WC>
1846 Gunston Way
San Jose, CA 95124
(408)266-3398
Giron, Francisco   <M1 OM>
3451 Los Mochis Way
Oceanside, CA 92056
(760)203-0381
FAX: (760)414-1236
thegirons@cox.net
Gonzales, Homer   <M1 WC>
8924 Armistice NE
Albuquerque, NM 87109
(505)821-4376
FAX: (505)841-4267
hgabq1985@gmail.com
Green, Paul   <M1 RT>
5228 Anchorage Avenue
El Paso, TX 79924
(915)751-7960
Hess, Jean   <M1 WC>
2200 E Dartmouth Circle
Englewood, CO 80113
(303)504-0275
jeanhess@316denver.com
Hess, Rick   <M1 WC>
2200 E Dartmouth Circle
Englewood, CO 80113
(303)504-0275
rick@densem.edu
Hom, Paul   <M1 RT>
722 24th Avenue
San Franciso, CA 94121
(415)751-9766
Kim, Byong Sam   <M1 RT>
6290 Dawnridge Court
Paradise, CA 95969
(530)877-4651
Knight, Melissa   <M1 M9>
5730 Haley Road
Meridian, MS 39305
(530)632-6472
revlissa@gmail.com
Lui, Stephen   <M1 RT>
512 16th Avenue
San Francisco, CA 94118
(415)386-2302
FAX: (415)386-2302
Luo, Tian-en   <M1 WC>
87 Berta Circle
Daly City, CA 94015
(650)754-9885
FAX: (650)754-9885
tianenyang555@gmail.comt
Maddux, Cynthia   <M1 WC>
15042 Tinker Street
Houston, TX 77084
(832)343-8867

PRESBYTERY DEL CRISTO CONTINUED

cmaddux1962@gmail.com

Martinez, Soledad <M1 WC>
5809 Calloway
El Paso, TX 79927
(915)319-8407
ismael3233@sbcglobal.net

Mata, Pablo <M1 WC>
PO Box 1040
San Elizaro, TX 79849
(915)851-8348
pablomata@yahoo.com

Matlock, Joe <M1 RT>
5905 Hickory Grove Lane
Memphis, TN 38134
(901)937-8457

O'Mara, Shelia <M1 M8>
533 Loughton Lane
Arnold, MD 21012
(410)757-5713
chaplainshelia@aol.com

Patterson, Jerry <M1 WC>
7007 Whitaker Avenue
Van Nuys, CA 91406
(818)994-5828

Shin, Kyung I <M1 WC>
1805 Gallinas Road NE
Rio Rancho, NM 87144
(505)453-5461
pastorkshin@gmail.com

Sze, Joseph <M1 WC>
Rau Sao Joaquim, 382
Liberdale, Sao Paulo, SP
CEP 015068-000 Brazil
pastorsze@yahoo.com

Tsujimoto, Mark <M1 WC>
88 S Broadway Unit 3210
Millbrae, CA 94030
(650)697-6901
mltsujimoto@gmail.com

Wilson, Don <M1 RT>
7300 Calle Montana NE
Albuquerque, NM 87113
(505)823-2594

don-wilson07@comcast.net

Wong, Bruce <M1 WC>
822 Sunnyarbor Court
Campbell, CA 95008
(408)628-4643
(415)290-1101 (cell)
revbwong@gmail.com

Yu, Pyong San (Sonny) <M1 WC>
139 Silverado Drive
Santa Teresa, NM 88008
(915)329-3451
pyongsanyu@hotmail.com

OTHER LICENTIATES ON ROLL:

Chamberlin, Edwin (Joey) <M2 ST>
7385 W Grant Ranch Boulevard Apt 1636
Littleton, CO 80123
ejcham@gmail.com
(817)929-9876

George, Thomas <M2>
908 N Brown Avenue
Casa Grande, AZ 85222
(640)447-2676
tgeorge@aerogram.net

Mata, Elizabeth <M2>
PO Box 1040
San Elizaro, TX 79849
(915)851-5354
hectoryliz@att.net

Mata, Jose <M2>
230 Flor Blanca
Socorro, TX 79927
(915)694-8099

Saldana, Manuel <M2>
536 Telop
El Paso, TX 79927
(915)317-9349
campe13@yahoo.com

OTHER CANDIDATES ON ROLL:

Barton, Cindy <M3>
83426 Argus Avenue
Trona, CA 93562
(760)372-4033
cbarton53@hotmail.com

Bell, Michelle <M3>
8643 Dry Creek Road Unit 1226
Centennial, CO 80112
(720)344-4040
mabbell@comcast.net

Coati, DeAngelo <M3 ST>
11280 Pebble Hills Boulevard #165
El Paso, TX 79936
(915)504-9032
spccoatie@yahoo.com

Sotak, Max <M3>
7805 W 62nd Place
Arvada, CO 80004
(303)423-5525
msotak@regis.edu

Presbytery of East Tennessee
SOUTHEAST SYNOD

	GENERAL	MEMBERSHIP			CHANGES				FINANCES				
	1.Church Number	2.Active	3.Total	4.Church School	5.Prof. of Faith	6.Gains	7.Losses	8.Children Baptized	9. OUR UNITED OUT-REACH	10. Total Out-Reach Giving	11. All Other Expenses	12. Total Income Received	13. Value Church Prop. 1=1000
	1	2	3	4	5	6	7	8	9	10	11	12	13
Beaver Creek	2301	500	786	275	2	10	12	0	49,326	82,058	422,983	497,997	2,900
Bethesda	2201	35	50	42	0	0	28	0	2,408	8,682	36,111	47,480	170
Casa De Fe	2220	45	100	25	2	6	6	3	1,000	8,862	68,339	61,671	0
Cedar Hill	2202	53	178	38	0	1	3	0	7,553	15,336	71,809	78,442	850
Clark's Grove	2302	36	120	38	1	2	1	2	5,440	5,970	43,707	55,045	500
Corntassel	2304	22	49	10	0	0	1	0	2,513	4,605	21,377	25,158	250
Dover	2203	64	71	37	0	2	5	0	7,749	15,566	78,627	75,034	1,250
Fairview	2204	54	105	65	7	26	2	1	4,868	9,270	82,041	98,555	602
FaithFellowship	2319	86	144	52	0	1	6	0	14,887	24,174	299,254	249,454	2,769
Gass Memorial	2205	3	7	5	0	0	1	0	385	1,726	7,161	8,887	160
Greeneville	2206	407	571	99	2	7	6	1	40,321	86,365	400,804	470,207	3,803
Heartland	2306	60	114	25	4	4	0	0	3,866	9,169	78,049	98,450	550
Knoxville**	2305	97	282	67	1	0	113	1	2,100	13,243	232,885	242,108	2,500
Korea 1st	2221	89	132	55	Under Care of Missions Ministry Team				0	0	0	0	0
Lebanon	2207	19	19	10	0	0	1	0	2,596	6,970	50,757	32,930	300
Loudon**	2307	151	211	88	4	6	97	4	0	4,668	192,804	210,491	2,201
Marietta	2308	100	199	60	0	0	1	0	20,838	38,781	198,552	220,786	600
Maryville 1st	2309	90	232	63	1	3	6	2	2,400	3,050	119,382	101,632	1,561
Mercy	2320	16	26	27	No Report Received			0	0	0	0	0	5
Mohawk	2208	24	62	25	0	1	0	0	1,364	2,455	18,615	19,777	300
Mt. Carmel	2310	55	89	25	0	3	3	0	4,723	17,384	37,251	50,721	375
Mt. Pleasant	2209	28	68	22	0	4	2	0	2,754	5,841	21,346	28,473	100
New Bethel*	2210	16	32	25	0	0	2	0	1,241	1,838	22,478	24,316	333
New Hope*	2311	36	36	14	0	2	2	0	2,052	5,383	15,461	20,523	575
Oak Ridge	2313	141	141	42	2	3	6	0	27,381	42,516	152,092	283,620	1,650
Oakland**	2211	10	25	20	0	0	20	0	0	2,400	12,230	27,906	100
Oliver Springs	2314	7	9	6	No Report Received			0	0	0	0	0	180
Philadelphia	2212	27	27	27	0	0	3	0	600	2,657	18,694	19,339	300
Pilot Knob	2213	9	9	27	No Report Received			0	718	0	0	0	100
Pleasant Hill	2214	25	31	25	0	0	1	0	3,064	7,331	22,616	29,947	400
Pleasant Vale	2215	11	11	26	No Report Received			0	313	0	0	0	250
Salem	2216	7	37	55	No Report Received			0	0	0	0	0	104
Shiloh	2217	119	221	90	4	5	2	0	10,417	22,429	128,338	146,871	1,021
Sumkim Presby	2222				Under Care of Missions Ministry Team				0	0	0	0	5
Talbott	2218	69	93	35	0	0	5	0	10,102	13,374	33,601	99,748	1,100
Union	2315	193	356	68	3	5	6	1	8,624	32,941	379,943	365,099	2,296
Virtue	2316	67	83	34	0	0	17	2	15,193	17,477	131,305	159,170	1,604
Willoughby	2219	13	15	13	No Report Received			0	1,548	0	0	0	250
Young's Chapel	2317	115	190	68	2	5	6	0	14,101	47,189	163,248	192,699	1,000
TOTALS	39	2,899	4,931	1,728	35	96	364	17	272,445	559,710	3,561,860	4,042,536	33,014

*Math error corrected. **Purged roll.

PRESBYTERY OF EAST TENNESSEE CONTINUED

CHURCHES, PASTORS, AND CLERKS:

Beaver Creek   (4WC)SEET2301
 7225 Old Clinton Pike
 Knoxville, TN 37921
 (865)938-7245   <Knox>
 FAX: (865)938-1465
 tsweet1@comcast.net
PA: Thomas Sweet   <M1>
 7225 Old Clinton Pike
 Powell, TN 37849
 (865)938-7245
 tsweet1@comcast.net
AP: Fran Vickers   <M1>
 7225 Old Clinton Pike
 Knoxville, TN 37921
 (865)859-0805
 franv3@comcast.net
CL: John Todd
 4912 Montmorency Drive
 Powell, TN 37849
 (865)938-7211
 jtodd4912@comcast.net

Bethesda   (4C)SEET2201
 155 Old Shiloh Road (mailing)
 Greeneville, TN 37745
 16340 Kingsport Highway (physical)
 Fall Branch, TN 37656
 (423)620-7753   <Greene>
 FAX: (423)798-2042
 kcor_98@yahoo.com
PA: Rocky L Johnson   <M1>
 321 Hope Road
 Greeneville, TN 37745
 (423)638-2771
 kcor_98@yahoo.com
CL: Jeff H Hayes
 155 Old Shiloh Road
 Greeneville, TN 37745
 (423)639-8404
 mdlpilot@yahoo.com

Casa De Fe   (PRESC)SEET2220
 493 Main Street, 2nd Floor
 Malden, MA 02148
 (781)322-2685   <Middlesex>
 casadefepastores@verizon.net
PA: Ricardo Franco   <M1>
 7 Hancock Street
 Melrose, MA 02176
 (781)662-0267
 casadefericardo@verizon.net
AP: Josefina Sanchez   <M1>
 7 Hancock Street
 Melrose, MA 02176
 (479)970-8654
 fsfamily64@gmail.com
CL: Myriam Santizo
 125 Pennsylvania Avenue
 Somerville, MA 02145
 (617)666-6763

Cedar Hill   (4EWC)SEET2202
 4170 Newport Highway
 Greeneville, TN 37743
 (423)639-0268   <Greene>
 cedarhill@centurylink.net
PA: Casey Nicholson   <M1>
 1020 Tusculum Boulevard

Greeneville, TN 37745
 (423)639-0268
 caseynicholson@mac.com
CL: Carolyn Harmon
 4435 Newport Highway
 Greeneville, TN 37743
 (423)639-3037
 richardharmon09@comcast.net

Clark's Grove   (4WC)SEET2302
 1662 Peppertree Drive (mailing)
 Alcoa, TN 37701
 3137 Old Knoxville Highway (physical)
 Maryville, TN 37802
 (865)982-5280   <Blount>
 FAX: (865)273-8726
 lwaters111@aol.com
OD: Danny Davis   <M5>
 3137 Old Knoxville Highway
 Maryville, TN 37804
 (865)661-6723
 dannydavis617@yahoo.com
CL: Lynn Waters
 1662 Peppertree Drive
 Alcoa, TN 37701
 (865)982-9083
 FAX: (865)379-0654
 lwaters111@aol.com

Corntassel   (4C)SEET2304
 933 Kahite Trail (mailing)
 Vonore, TN 37885
 2100 Povo Road (physical)
 Madisonville, TN 37354
 (423)884-3909   <Monroe>
 miriamf23@tds.net
PA: Gary Hartman   <M1>
 3001 Hines Valley Road
 Lenoir City, TN 37771
 (865)986-4949
 g37771@att.net
CL: Miriam Fisher
 933 Kahite Trail
 Vonore, TN 37885
 (423)884-3909
 miriamf23@tds.net

Dover   (4MEWC)SEET2203
 1550 Dover Road
 Morristown, TN 37813
 (423)581-4719   <Hamblen>
 dovercp@comcast.net
CL: John Ayers
 4371 Danbury Drive
 Morristown, TN 37813
 (423)586-6883
 bigorange@charter.net

Fairview   (4MWC)SEET2204
 4720 Snapps Ferry Road
 Afton, TN 37616
 (423)639-9011   <Greene>
PA: Ronnie Duncan   <M1>
 146 Deseree Broyles Road
 Chuckey, TN 37641
 (423)552-0321
 ronkduncan@icloud.com
CL: Rick Taylor
 175 Stone Dam Road
 Chuckey, TN 37641
 (423)470-0216

Faith Fellowship   (4EWC)SEET2319
 PO Box 24162 (mailing)
 Knoxville, TN 37934
 14025 Highway 70 E (physical)
 Lenoir City, TN 37772
 (865)988-8522   <Knox>
 info@faithfellowshipcp.org
PA: Jeff Sledge   <M1>
 241 Long Bow Road
 Knoxville, TN 37934
 (865)288-3375
 pastorjeff@faithfellowshipcp.org
CL: Larry Byars
 1412 Dempsey Road
 Knoxville, TN 37932
 (865)850-2925
 larry@byars-consulting.com

Gass Memorial   (4C)SEET2205
 PO Box 1767 (mailing)
 815 Gass Memorial Road (physical)
 Greeneville, TN 37744
 (423)278-7610   <Greene>
 FAX: (423)638-3452
 gassch@comcast.net
PA: Rex Brown   <M1>
 134 Everhart Drive
 Greeneville, TN 37745
 (423)639-4298
CL: George C Mays
 PO Box 1767
 Greeneville, TN 37744
 (423)638-8624
 FAX: (423)638-3452
 g.mays@comcast.net

Greeneville   (4MEWC)SEET2206
 201 N Main Street
 Greeneville, TN 37745
 (423)638-4119   <Greene>
 FAX: (423)636-1017
 office@gcpchurch.org
PA: James W Lively   <M1>
 906 Lyle Circle
 Greeneville, TN 37745
 (423)798-1959
 FAX: (423)636-1017
 jlively@gcpchurch.org
AP: Roy E Blakeburn   <M1>
 111 Park Place
 Greeneville, TN 37743
 (423)787-9609
 FAX: (423)636-1017
AP: Abby Cole Keller   <M1>
 4415 Fieldstone Drive
 Kingsport, TN 37664
 (423)863-6565
 colekeller@yahoo.com
AP: Melissa Malinoski   <M1>
 9087 Fenmore Cove
 Cordova, TN 38016
 (420)620-0089
 FAX: (423)636-1017
 mmalinoski@memphisseminary.edu
CL: Dick Parrack
 201 N Main Street
 Greeneville, TN 37745
 (423)638-4119
 FAX: (423)636-1017
 parrackd@embarqmail.com

PRESBYTERY OF EAST TENNESSEE CONTINUED

Heartland   (4MWC)SEET2306
160 Harrison Road
Lenoir City, TN 37772
(865)986-3018   <Loudon>
lccpc@icx.net
PA: Kenneth P Phillips   <M1>
6419 Town Creek Road East
Lenoir City, TN 37772
(865)986-7344
CL: Jennifer L Smith
1085 Crestview Circle
Lenoir City, TN 37772
(865)986-5099
jlleslie@chartertn.net

Knoxville   (4WC)SEET2305
6900 Nubbin Ridge Drive
Knoxville, TN 37919
(865)588-8581   <Knox>
FAX: (865)588-8581
firstcpc@earthlink.net
PA: Michael Wilkinson   <M1>
2861 Pine Acres Street
Millbrook, AL 36054
(334)517-6568
mwilkinson1@elmore.rr.com
PA: J David Hester   <M1 RT>
1212 Woodbury Court
Knoxville, TN 37922
(865)769-0540
FAX: (865)769-0540
jdavebar@icx.net
CL: Dianne Pipkin
1725 Covey Rise Trail
Knoxville, TN 37922
(865)675-2872
pndpip@aol.com

Korea First   (PRESC)SEET2221
Seoul
South Korea
( )   <Korea >
CL: Jin Ho Kim
c/o Ernest Gillis
605-3 Anyang 8 Dong
South Korea
sergiobetancur@starmedia.com

Lebanon   (4MEC)SEET2207
2117 Murray Street (mailing)
Morristown, TN 37814
714 Lebanon Road (physical)
Jefferson City, TN 37760
( )   <Jefferson>
PA: Howard E Shipley   <M1>
3800 Dan Drive
Morristown, TN 37814
(423)581-1092
hshipley@charter.net
CL: Frances McCarter
2117 Murray Street
Morristown, TN 37814
(423)586-6292
lofmcar@aol.com

Loudon   (4MWC)SEET2307
PO Box 373 (mailing)
503 College Avenue (physical)
Loudon, TN 37774
(865)458-2270   <Loudon>

FAX: (865)458-5360
loudoncpc@bellsouth.net
PA: Robert N Coker   <M1>
721 Lakeview Drive
Loudon, TN 37774
(865)458-8791
FAX: (865)458-5360
nickcoker@bellsouth.net
CL: Joseph J Malloy, Jr
7866 E Lee Highway
Loudon, TN 37774
(865)458-5951
FAX: (865)458-5360
malloyusmc@att.net

Marietta   (4MC)SEET2308
11402 Hardin Valley Road (mailing)
1922 Marietta Church Road (physical)
Knoxville, TN 37932
(865)693-0080   <Knox>
mariettacpc@comcast.net
PA: Randall Mayfield   <M1>
12470 Daisywood Drive
Knoxville, TN 37932
(865)769-4756
FAX: (865)769-4756
mayfield07@comcast.net
CL: Virgil R Hubbard
2122 Campbell Station Road
Knoxville, TN 37932
(865)740-4863
vrhubbard@comcast.net

Maryville First   (4MWC)SEET2309
1301 E Broadway
Maryville, TN 37804
(865)982-7860   <Blount>
firstcumberland@gmail.com
PA: Ronald L Longmire   <M1>
2041 Eckles Drive
Maryville, TN 37804
(865)984-1647
ronaldlongmire@charter.net
CL: Tom Longmire
630 Garfield Street
Alcoa, TN 37701
(865)983-3604

Mercy   (4C)SEET2320
634 Martel Road
Lenoir City, TN 37772
(865)660-7579   <Knox>
iglesiapcmisericordia@gmail.com
PA: Alfonso Oscar Marquez   <M1>
389 Bethel Drive
Lenoir City, TN 37772
(865)660-7579
amarquez61@bellsouth.net
CL: Miguel Angel Gonzalez
200 Bethel Drive
Lenor City, TN 37772
(865)227-2710
mgonzalez865@bellsouth.net

Mohawk   (4MWC)SEET2208
PO Box 7 (mailing)
50 Soville Loop (physical)
Mohawk, TN 37810
( )   <Greene>
SS: Chris Franklin   <M2>
104 Delta Circle

Greeneville, TN 37743
(423)972-3609
chrisfranklin104@comcast.net
CL: Velta Rhea Riley
2149 Phillipe Road
Mohawk, TN 37810
(423)235-6179

Mt Carmel   (4EC)SEET2310
PO Box 4 (mailing)
Coalfield, TN 37719
5515 Knoxville Highway (physical)
Oliver Springs, TN 37840
(865)435-9247   <Morgan>
PA: Donald W Acton   <M1>
1186 Jenkins Lane
Knoxville, TN 37922
(865)966-5132
CL: Lisa Layne
714 Back Valley Road
Oliver Springs, TN 37840
(865)382-8817
lalayne64@yahoo.com

Mt Pleasant   (4MWC)SEET2209
3945 Babbs Mill Road
Afton, TN 37616
( )   <Greene>
PA: James L Carter   <M1>
6155 Hummingbird Lane
Whitesburg, TN 37891
(423)587-8423
jandjmt@comcast.net
CL: Louise Gass
701 Franklin Street
Greeneville, TN 37745
(423)639-3731

New Bethel   (3WC)SEET2210
2820 Blue Springs Parkway (mailing)
90 Cox Road (physical)
Greeneville, TN 37743
( )   <Greene>
PA: Rex Brown   <M1>
134 Everhart Drive
Greeneville, TN 37745
(423)639-4298
firstcumberland@gmail.com
CL: Coriece Baxter
2820 Blue Springs Parkway
Greeneville, TN 37743
(423)638-4089

New Hope   (4C)SEET2311
904 Acorn Gap Road
Madisonville, TN 37354
( )   <Monroe>
PA: David L Koopman   <M1>
5606 Brandon Park Drive
Maryville, TN 37804
(865)660-2440
racewthrev@aol.com
CL: Yvonne Wolfe
139 Old Loudon Road
Sweetwater, TN 37874
(423)442-3045

Oak Ridge   (4EWC)SEET2313
PO Box 4836 (mailing)
127 Lafayette (physical)
Oak Ridge, TN 37831

PRESBYTERY OF EAST TENNESSEE CONTINUED

(865)483-8433   \<Anderson\>
FAX: (865)483-8445
1stcpc@comcast.net
PA: Jim Buttram   \<M1\>
103 Golfcrest Lane
Oak Ridge, TN 37830
(865)938-7418
FAX: (865)483-8445
littlejimb@gmail.com
CL: Sarah Makin
378 New Henderson Road
Clinton, TN 37716
(865)945-3104
makin1too@aol.com

Oakland   (4C)SEET2211
694 Oakland Road
Telford, TN 37690
(423)257-2258   \<Washington\>
OD: Parker Street   \<M5\>
353 Old Stagecoach Road
Jonesborough, TN 37659
CL: Freda Graham
959 Bowmantown Road
Limestone, TN 37681
(423)257-5050

Oliver Springs   (4C)SEET2314
PO Box 175 (mailing)
400 Spring Street (physical)
Oliver Springs, TN 37840
firstcumberland@gmail.com
( )   \<Roane\>
PA: Ken Johnson   \<M1\>
122 Ridge Lane
Clinton, TN 37716
(865)463-7090
kenjoxav122@bellsouth.net
CL: Sid Thurmer
PO Box 175
Oliver Springs, TN 37840
(865)435-5438

Philadelphia   (4MWC)SEET2212
509 Snapp Bridge Road (mailing)
757 Snapp Bridge Road (physical)
Limestone, TN 37681
( )   \<Washington\>
CL: Greg Stafford
509 Snapp Bridge Road
Limestone, TN 37681
(423)257-3796
gregandlesa509@comcast.net

Pilot Knob   (2C)SEET2213
515 Marvin Mountain Road (mailing)
445 Gap Creek Road (physical)
Bulls Gap, TN 37711
( )   \<Greene\>
LS: Richard Snowden   \<M6\>
PO Box 6004
Morristown, TN 37815
(423)235-5914
FAX: (423)254-3206
richard.snowden@wallacehardware.com
CL: Joyce Lamb
4185 Gap Creek Road
Bulls Gap, TN 37711
(423)235-6858

Pleasant Hill   (4WC)SEET2214

13385 Kingsport Highway
Chuckey, TN 37641
( )   \<Greene\>
PA: Rex Brown   \<M1\>
134 Everhart Drive
Greeneville, TN 37745
(423)639-4298
firstcumberland@gmail.com
CL: Genevieve M Bolton
15440 Kingsport Highway
Chuckey, TN 37641
(423)234-7942

Pleasant Vale   (4C)SEET2215
525 Pleasant Vale Road
Chuckey, TN 37641
( )   \<Greene\>
OD: Gene Swatzell   \<M5\>
2342 Buckingham Road
Greeneville, TN 37745
(423)639-8289
CL: Howard Collins
3750 Rheatown Road
Chuckey, TN 37641
(423)278-6072

Salem   (4C)SEET2216
695 West Pines Road (mailing)
Afton, TN 37616
1927 Lost Mountain Pike (physical)
Greeneville, TN 37745
( )   \<Greene\>
OD: Billy Moore   \<M5\>
880 Black Bear Road
Greeneville, TN 37745
(423)552-1594
CL: Helen Starnes
695 West Pines Road
Afton, TN 37616
(423)234-0281
cehwstarnes@comcast.net

Shiloh   (4WC)SEET2217
1121 Shiloh Road
Greeneville, TN 37745
(423)639-3763   \<Greene\>
shilohcpc@embarqmail.com
PA: Tammy L Greene   \<M1\>
109 Armitage Drive
Greeneville, TN 37745
(423)972-5525
tg6386@aol.com
CL: Jimmy Ricker
1304 Kenney Street
Greeneville, TN 37745
(423)525-7962
jimmyricker@hotmail.com

Sumkim Presbyterian   (GESC)SEET2222
#876-15 Dokok-1dong
Kangam-Gu
Seoul, Korea
(023)463-3939   \<Korea\>
PA: Byung-Jae Choe   \<M1\>
876-15 Dokok-1dong
Kangnam-Gu
Seoul, Korea
(023)463-3939
CL: Session Clerk Sumkim Presbyterian
#876-15 Dokok-1dong
Kangam-Gu

Seoul, Korea
(023)461-8615

Talbott   (4C)SEET2218
PO Box 116 (mailing)
7410 W Andrew Johnson Hwy (physical)
Talbott, TN 37877
(865)475-1221   \<Hamblen\>
FAX: (865)475-1221
talbottchurch@bellsouth.net
LS: Richard Snowden   \<M6\>
PO Box 6004
Morristown, TN 37815
(423)235-5914
FAX: (423)254-3206
richard.snowden@wallacehardware.com
CL: Lon Barry Knight
950 Rocktown Road
Jefferson City, TN 37760
(865)548-8449
lonknight1@hughes.net

Union   (4WC)SEET2315
400 Everett Road
Knoxville, TN 37934
(865)966-9040   \<Knox\>
FAX: (865)675-3787
union@unioncpchurch.com
PA: Leonard E Turner, Jr   \<M1\>
12651 Wagon Wheel Circle
Knoxville, TN 37934
(865)966-9040
FAX: (865)675-3787
pastor@unioncpchurch.com
CL: Hugh Turpin
101 E Passmore Lane
Oak Ridge, TN 37830
(865)272-5116
FAX: (865)675-3787
turpinhk@cs.com

Virtue   (4MWC)SEET2316
725 Virtue Road
Knoxville, TN 37934
(865)966-1491   \<Knox\>
FAX: (865)966-0558
virtuecpchurch@tds.net
AP: Robert T Spurling Jr   \<M1\>
127 Wellington Circle
Oak Ridge, TN 37830
(865)803-8582
CL: Jack A Watson
12309 Turkey Creek Road
Knoxville, TN 37934
(865)966-5998
jwatson423@aol.com

Willoughby   (4C)SEET2219
240 Wheeler Road (mailing)
220 Willoughby Road (physical)
Bulls Gap, TN 37711
( )   \<Greene\>
SS: Chris Franklin   \<M2\>
104 Delta Circle
Greeneville, TN 37743
(423)638-5600
chrisfranklin104@comcast.net
CL: Charles Clowers
240 Wheeler Road
Bulls Gap, TN 37711
(423)235-5249

PRESBYTERY OF EAST TENNESSEE CONTINUED

Young's Chapel   (4WC)SEET2317
1705 Lawnville Road
Kingston, TN 37763
(865)376-2192   <Roane>
FAX: (865)376-2196
info@youngschapel.net
PA: Dale Watson   <M1>
1705 Lawnville Road
Kingston, TN 37763
(865)376-2192
revdwatson@comcast.net
CL: Paul McCallie
3340 Kingston Highway
Kingston, TN 37763
(865)376-9199
pt57466@bellsouth.net

OTHERS ON MINISTERIAL ROLL:

Ahn, Da-Wit (David)   <M1 OM>
1304 Kakyeng-Dong
Sangdang-Gu Cheongju-City
Choongbook, Korea
(043)235-0219
Dobson, H Wallis   <M1 WC>
150 Liberty Way
Greeneville, TN 37745
(423)798-8947
Fly, William   <M1 OM>
1146 Paradise Drive
Powell, TN 37849
(865)938-6273
Freeman, A Daniel   <M1 WC>
210 Dogwood Drive
Greeneville, TN 37743
(423)638-5925
Gillis, Ernest H   <M1 WC>
3273 Bruckner Boulevard
Snellville, GA 30078
(770)982-6587
professorgil64@hotmail.com
Greenwell, James C   <M1 WC>
7165 Wind Whisper Boulevard
Knoxville, TN 37924
(865)742-1653
FAX: (865)742-1653
greenwelljc@comcast.net
Hester, Mark S   <M1 WC>
763 Finn Long Road
Friendsville, TN 37737
(865)995-1541
markshester@att.net
Hubbard, Donald   <M1 RT>
2128 N Campbell Station Road
Knoxville, TN 37932
(865)693-0264
djhubbard@mindspring.com
Ivey, Billy F   <M1 RT>
409 Rodeo Drive
Knoxville, TN 37922
(865)966-5946
iveybe@tds.net
Jang, WonJeon   <M1 OM>
Lot2-C Teresa Subdivision
Tabucan Mandurriao
Iloilo City 5000, Phillippine
Johnson, Beverly B   <M1 RT>
801 Riverhill Drive Apt 308
Athens, GA 30606
(865)977-0405

bevloujohnson@aol.com
Kelly, Patrick L   <M1 M9>
1449 Rainbow Road
Mountain City, TN 37681
(423)727-4067
Keown, Gale J   <M1 RT>
2130 Cason Lane
Murfreesboro, TN 37128
(865)805-5451
Kim, YoungHo (Steve)   <M1 WC>
B02 Hyundai I-Space 1608-2
Burim Dong, Dong An Gu
AnYang City, Kyunggi Do S Korea
(231)348-8033
paidion4377@naver.com
Lee, Sang-Do   <M1 OM>
1342 Seocho-2dong
Seocho-Gu
Seoul, Korea
(023)474-8405
Lim, Keum-Taek   <M1 WC>
1342 Seocho-2dong
Seocho-Gu
Seoul, Korea
(023)474-8405
limkt114@hanmail.net
Malinoski, T J   <M1 DE>
9087 Fenmore Cove
Cordova, TN 38016
(423)972-1239
mlmalinoski@comcast.net
Marquez, Martha   <M1 WC>
389 Bethel Drive
Lenoir City, TN 37772
(865)660-7579
McBeth, David L   <M1 M8>
PSC Box 20085
Camp LeJeune, NC 28542
(910)451-2375
david.mcbeth@usmc.mil
McConnell, Donald R   <M1 RT>
147 Confederacy Circle
Knoxville, TN 37934
(865)288-0230
donjoyce515@hotmail.com
McGuire, James D   <M1 WC>
220 Southwind Circle #2
Greenville, TN 37745
(423)638-6380
jmcguire915@comcast.net
Middleton, Bill S   <M1 RT>
12826 Union Road
Knoxville, TN 37922
(865)966-1706
revbill@charter.net
Ortiz, Milton   <M1 DE>
817 Radiance Drive
Cordova, TN 38018
(901)276-4572
mortiz@cumberland.org
Park, Bo-Seong   <M1 OM>
304-28 Sinlim-Dong, Kwanak-Gu
Seoul, Korea
(002)884-3474
Pickard, Ronald   <M1 WC>
6292 Golden Drive
Morristown, TN 37814
(423)587-9735
Reid, Richard   <M1 WC>
1211 Provost Drive
Jefferson City, TN 37760

(865)475-3452
rjreid1964@msn.com
Richardson, W Jean   <M1 RT>
7533 Lancashire Boulevard
Powell, TN 37849
(865)947-3111
jeanandregena@frontier.com
Scott, Jerry   <M1 M9>
2310 Sentell Drive
Maryville, TN 37803
(865)803-3669
dmjlscott@yahoo.com
Sweet, Don   <M1 RT>
3008 Shropshire Boulevard
Powell, TN 37849
(865)938-7435
mariondon77@netscape.com
West, Fred E, Jr   <M1 WC>
510 Cedaredge Drive
New Smyrna, FL 32168
(206)409-8321
jwest616@earthlink.net
Wood, Kevin L   <M1 WC>
1116 Park Hill Circle
Knoxville, TN 37909
(865)588-8581
FAX: (865)588-8581
revkev7285@earthlink.net
Yu, Wn-yong   <M1 OM>
325-1 DongHyen-Dong
Jecheon-city
Choongbuk, Korea
(043)652-0540
lifeyu@hanmail.net

OTHER LICENTIATES ON ROLL:

Choi, Justin   <M2 ST>
605 Arbor Hollow Circle Apt 203
Cordova, TN 38018
(901)605-4542
flymetothemoon@hotmail.com
Choi, Sean   <M2 ST>
7565 Macon Road
Cordova, TN 38016
(901)826-2993
esloveh2@hotmail.com
Overton, Twanda   <M2 ST>
616 S Cox Street
Memphis, TN 38104
(865)591-8881
tdeeov@yahoo.com

OTHER CANDIDATES ON ROLL:

Brown, Whitney   <M3 ST>
137 Roberta Drive
Memphis, TN 38112
(865)387-0002
Choi, Ezra   <M3>
605 Arbor Hollow Circle #203
Cordova, TN 38018
(901)236-82635
Craig, Aaron   <M3>
325 Cherry Avenue
McKenzie, TN 38201
(731)352-6718
Frazier, Shawn   <M3 ST>
459 Forrest Avenue
McKenzie, TN 38201
(865)414-8394

PRESBYTERY OF EAST TENNESSEE CONTINUED

Gonzales, Miguel   <M3 ST>
200 Bethel Drive
Lenoir City, TN 37772
(865)988-4238

Hamby, Gary   <M3>
700 W 6th Avenue
Lenoir City, TN 37771
(731)986-2635

Mejia, Salvador   <M3 ST>
7618 S Highway 72
Loudon, TN 37774
(865)661-8267

Sweet-Brockman, Anna   <M3>
210 E Main Street Apt B
Greenfield, TN 38230
(865)803-8582

Wright, Tim   <M3>
165 Quaker Knob Road
Chuckey, TN 37641
(423)639-0634
tdwright1123@yahoo.com

Grace Presbytery
SOUTHEAST SYNOD

GENERAL		MEMBERSHIP			CHANGES				FINANCES				
	1.Church Number	2.Active	3.Total	4.Church School	5.Prof. of Faith	6.Gains	7.Losses	8.Children Baptized	9. OUR UNITED OUT-REACH	10. Total Out-Reach Giving	11. All Other Expenses	12. Total Income Received	13. Value Church Prop. 1=1000
	1	2	3	4	5	6	7	8	9	10	11	12	13
Antioch	0701	33	40	25	0	0	0	1	1,642	4,517	9,632	16,476	150
Beersheba	0702	147	185	79	1	9	2	0	16,752	52,414	178,788	210,938	1,150
Branchville	0106	152	166	46	12	21	11	3	0	3,600	87,400	89,000	1,650
Brooksville (x)	0703	8	8	5	CLOSED 2013		0	0	0	0	0	0	169
Cairo*	0704	6	23	7	0	0	0	0	0	3,066	15,659	25,754	135
Christ*	0303	70	93	25	4	0	8	1	4,280	3,514	91,678	99,255	1,346
Coker	0705	51	102	25	0	4	5	0	1,186	8,026	75,982	85,810	1,935
Columbus	0706	143	143	65	0	4	3	0	2,000	2,800	132,561	124,486	1,800
Crestline	0102	30	32	19	0	1	0	0	6,000	12,411	59,070	92,108	1,500
El Camino*	0310	55	67	22	0	1	10	0	500	4,050	70,668	70,503	530
Enon	0707	167	250	131	1	7	6	1	1,200	16,850	248,502	272,986	1,050
Erin	0601	57	101	42	1	1	1	2	0	7,717	56,639	56,847	221
First Hispanic+*	0307	78	76	21	4	6	0	2	0	700	94,277	95,935	175
Forrest Avenue	0403	116	116	8	0	0	1	0	2,888	4,700	27,876	28,437	240
Gadsden	0402	91	156	64	0	2	4	2	8,250	32,363	135,915	168,081	800
Glencoe	0404	85	247	70	5	17	4	0	500	0	0	0	2,000
Grace Commun**	0407	82	125	65	15	4	43	0	10,070	16,447	129,434	133,339	1,200
Greens Chapel	0208	40	71	25	0	5	13	3	8,277	15,865	57,354	83,686	820
Groverton	0602	14	14	14	1	4	0	0	0	3,553	4,200	8,112	0
Helena*	0108	44	45	26	2	0	43	1	2,000	10,500	83,000	106,000	550
Homewood*	0111	77	117	46	0	0	125	0	12,600	24,094	207,563	235,240	2,025
Hope	0308	101	115	20	2	9	1	2	5,337	12,648	143,901	155,718	1,985
Hopewell	0101	20	25	13	0	2	17	0	3,600	7,640	42,822	38,076	1,240
House of Prayer	0214	180	180	180	No Report Received			0	0	0	0	0	450
Hueytown 1st*	0109	20	102	6	No Report Received			0	0	0	0	0	385
Immanuel	0311	24	20	10	2	4	8	1	2,559	1,816	50,610	25,374	
McLeod Chapel	0708	15	20	10	2	0	6	0	0	1,072	16,864	18,249	350
Mt. Zion	0709	22	22	20	0	0	1	0	3,990	8,795	18,261	38,568	650
New Hope	0104	181	218	80	13	13	2	1	28,050	75,834	204,663	280,497	2,000
Oldham Chapel	0405	14	14	10	No Report Received			0	805	0	0	0	325
Piedmont	0406	59	75	71	5	8	8	0	2,700	5,100	81,978	81,305	1,009
Pleasant Hill	0710	15	33	7	0	2	2	0	100	100	28,224	24,232	160
Roca DeSalvacion	0115	31	56	0	3	36	10	0	0	850	3,258	44,408	41
Rocky Ridge	0105	83	227	35	2	5	2	2	22,788	29,184	152,083	198,013	1,200
Salem	0607	30	60	15	0	0	1	0	600	5,199	43,994	32,215	150
Spring Creek	0113	160	163	87	2	4	3	3	3,900	24,400	205,900	233,300	1,100
Steam Mill**	0608	50	97	73	2	0	32	3	0	13,314	90,088	109,352	340
Union	0114	50	81		No Report Received			0	1,613	0	0	0	250
TOTALS	38	2,601	3,685	1,467	79	169	372	28	154,187	413,139	2,848,844	3,282,300	31,081

*Math error corrected. **Purged roll (x)Closed 2013 +Union church

GRACE PRESBYTERY CONTINUED

CHURCHES, PASTORS, AND CLERKS:

Antioch (2C)SEGR0701
2994 Antioch Church Road
Reform, AL 35481
( ) <Pickens>
PA: William L Benson <M1>
137 W Lowndes Drive
Columbus, MS 39701
(662)386-3433
willardb715@gmail.com
CL: Reba Carpenter
3951 County Road 45
Reform, AL 35481
(205)375-6042
rebarform@aol.com

Beersheba (4MEWC)SEGR0702
1736 Beersheba Road
Columbus, MS 39702
(662)327-9615 <Lowndes>
FAX: (662)324-8320
officebeersheba@att.net
PA: Timothy Daniel Lee <M1>
186 Blasingame Drive
Columbus, MS 39702
(601)433-3714
eelmit@bellsouth.net
CL: Charles Studdard
95 Studdard Drive
Columbus, MS 39702
(662)328-8844
FAX: (662)327-8773
clstuddard@emssonline.com

Branchville (4MWC)SEGR0106
80 Hurst Road
Odenville, AL 35120
(205)629-3258 <St Clair>
FAX: (205)629-3258
session@branchvillechurch.org
PA: Keith L. Mariott <M1>
155 Ridgewood Lane
Odenville, AL 35120
(205)903-5251
kjmariott@windstream.net
CL: Steve Smith
80 Hurst Road
Odenville, AL 35120
session@branchvillechurch.org

Brooksville (2EC)SEGR0703
CHURCH CLOSED 03/2013

Cairo (4MC)SEGR0704
3836 Highway 50 W (mailing)
West Point, MS 39773
Cairo Road (physical)
Cedar Bluff, MS 39741
( ) <Clay>
CL: Judy Chrismond
3836 Highway 50 W
West Point, MS 39773
(662)494-7290
tjchrismond@gmail.com

Christ (4EWC)SEGR0303
19501 Holly Lane
Lutz, FL 33548
(813)909-9789 <Hillsborough>

ccpclutz@verizon.net
PA: Michael Laperche <M1>
3867 Evergreen Oaks Drive
Lutz, FL 33558
(813)948-8016
pastor-mike@earthlink.net
CL: Jeannie Vaughn
16107 Carden Drive
Odessa, FL 33556
(813)926-6631
jvaughn1@tampabay.rr.com

Coker (4MEWC)SEGR0705
PO Box 262 (mailing)
14705 Romulus Road (physical)
Coker, AL 35452
(205)339-1178 <Tuscaloosa>
cokercpgreg@att.net
SS: Greg Tucker <M2>
PO Box 262
Coker, AL 35452
(205)541-7484
cokercpgreg@att.net
CL: Retha Channell
15535 Lisenba Drive
Coker, AL 35452
(205)339-8125
rechannell@aol.com

Columbus (4EWC)SEGR0706
2698 Ridge Road
Columbus, MS 39705
(662)328-2692 <Lowndes>
fcpcsecretary@att.net
PA: Luke Lawson <M1>
270 N Ridgeland Circle
Columbus, MS 39705
(662)295-9322
luke_lawson03@hotmail.com
CL: Carol Carley
71 Little Tom Road
Columbus, MS 39705
(662)328-4589
carleyr@bellsouth.net

Crestline (4MWC)SEGR0102
605 Hagood Street
Birmingham, AL 35213
(205)879-6001 <Jefferson>
FAX: (205)968-8105
jan@crestlinechurch.org
PA: Janice M Overton <M1>
3320 Pipeline Road
Birmingham, AL 35243
(205)281-6819
FAX: (205)968-8105
jan@crestlinechurch.org
CL: Birki Cvacho
1214 Regal Avenue
Birmingham, AL 35213
(205)592-3023
blcvacho@bellsouth.net

El Camino (C)SEGR0310
6248 SW 14th Street (mailing)
6790 SW 12th Street (physical)
West Miami, FL 33144
(305)261-6200 <Dade>
lucatha@aol.com
PA: Luciano Jaramillo <M1>
6249 SW 14th Street

West Miami, FL 33144
(305)264-1074
ljara@aol.com
CL: Hedemarrie Dussan
6248 SW 14th Street
Miami, FL 33144
(054)812-0613

Enon (4MWC)SEGR0707
PO Box 294 (mailing)
9000 Highway 12 (physical)
Ackerman, MS 39735
(662)285-3303 <Choctaw>
enoncpchurch@dtcweb.net
PA: Jerry L Lawson <M1>
6039 MS Highway 415
Ackerman, MS 39735
(662)285-8295
lawson@dtcweb.net
CL: Raymond D Gillon Jr
PO Box 294
Ackerman, MS 39735
(601)916-3589
rgillon@dtcweb.net

Erin (4WC)SEGR0601
PO Box 574, Carthage, MS (mailing)
590 Pete Freeman Road (physical)
Union, MS 39051
( ) <Newton>
OD: Scott Engle <M5>
PO Box 1023
Decatur, MS 39327
(601)683-9586
CL: Lynn Federick
PO Box 574
Carthage, MS 39051
(601)267-4954

First Hispanic (4MWU)SEGR0307
2828 W Kirby Street
Tampa, FL 33614
(813)932-9684 <Hillsborough>
FAX: (813)932-9700
fhpctampafla@aol.com
PA: Alexandri Sosa <M1>
8601 Huron Court
Tampa, FL 33614
(813)562-4289
FAX: (813)932-9700
sosapcus@gmail.com
CL: Nivaria F Neff
3845 S Lake Drive U-186
Tampa, FL 33614
(813)765-2745
nivys7@yahoo.com

Forrest Avenue (4MWC)SEGR0403
2316 Forrest Avenue
Gadsden, AL 35904
(256)547-2833 <Etowah>
SS: Lem Lockmiller Jr <M1>
5068 Louise Street
Hokes Bluff, AL 35903
(256)490-3021
CL: Joe Neal
1110 Cabot Avenue
Gadsden, AL 35904
(256)547-2833
jnwr@aol.com

GRACE PRESBYTERY CONTINUED

Gadsden   (4MWC)SEGR0402
PO Box 2055 (mailing)
1200 Piedmont Cutoff (physical)
Gadsden, AL 35903
(256)492-2556   <Etowah>
FAX: (256)492-2525
office@gadsdencp.com
PA: Daniel Barkley   <M1>
2732 Rexford Street
Hokes Bluff, AL 35903
daniel@gadsdencp.com
(256)478-0397
CL: Grace Whitfield
245 Monterey Circle
Gadsden, AL 35901
(256)442-1860
FAX: (256)492-2525
gracenaomi@aol.com

Glencoe   (4WC)SEGR0404
200 N College Street
Glencoe, AL 35905
(256)492-1584   <Etowah>
FAX: (256)492-1584
glencoecpchurch@yahoo.com
PA: Rodney McInnis   <M1>
280-B Coley Road
Glencoe, AL 35905
(256)454-2399
mcinnisrodneyand@bellsouth.net
CL: Scott Stewart
200 N College Street
Gadsden, AL 35905
(256)492-1584
stewie242@hotmail.com

Grace Community   (4C)SEGR0407
3515 Highway 14
Millbrook, AL 36054
(334)285-4655   < >
millbrookgcc@gmail.com
CL: Debbie Silva
3515 Highway 14
Millbrook, AL 36054
(334)290-3884
quilter.deb@charter.net

Greens Chapel   (4WC)SEGR0208
PO Box 729 (mailing)
81 Greens Chapel Road (physical)
Cleveland, AL 35049
(205)559-7671   <Blount>
SS: W Ray Lathem   <M1>
452 County Road 1462
Cullman, AL 35055
(256)708-1247
lathemray@bellsouth.net
CL: Ben Royal
148 Truman Drive
Cleveland, AL 5049
(205)274-7503
broyal@otelco.net

Groverton   (2C)SEGR0602
222 Leon Harrell Road
Morton, MS 39117
( )   <Scott>
OD: Ronnie Spears   <M5>
101 Shirley Drive
Pelahatchie, MS 39145
CL: Judy Thompson

1824 Irby Road
Morton, MS 39117
(601)732-3572

Helena   (4MC)SEGR0108
PO Box 566 (mailing)
3396 Helena Road (physical)
Helena, AL 35080
(205)663-2174   <Shelby>
helenacpchurch@bellsouth.net
SS: Mike Emsinger   <M3>
4910 Cox Cove
Helena, AL 35080-3424
(205)620-4699
me0573@att.com
CL: Michelle Burt
PO Box 566
Helena, AL 35080
(205)663-2174
michelle.burt@regions.com

Homewood   (4WC)SEGR0111
513 Columbiana Road
Homewood, AL 35209
(205)942-3051   <Jefferson>
FAX: (205)945-0677
hcpc@homewoodcpc.com
PA: Mathew Derek Jacks   <M1>
341 Shadeswood Drive
Hoover, AL 35226
(205)903-8469
pastorderek@homewoodcpc.com
CL: Kim Moore
5514 Pearl Drive SE
Bessemer, AL 35023
(205)428-9151
kmoore@cwcd.com

Hope   (4WC)SEGR0308
826 S Miller Road
Valrico, FL 33594
(813)684-4689   <Hillsborough>
FAX: (813)655-7919
hopecpc@verizon.net
PA: William E (Eddie) Jenkins   <M1>
1836 S Ridge Drive
Valrico, FL 33594
(813)651-3802
hopechurch4@aol.com
CL: Donna Cachia
4122 Helene Place
Valrico, FL 33594
(813)684-8391
djc1948@msn.com

Hopewell   (4MWC)SEGR0101
2139 Cumberland Drive SE
Bessemer, AL 35023
(205)425-2126   <Jefferson>
SS: James Scott Edwards   <M3>
226 Jasmine Drive
Alabaster, AL 35007
(205)837-4069
jedwards53163@bellsouth.net
CL: Beverly Edwards
226 Jasmine Drive
Alabaster, AL 35007
(205)529-4507
jedwards53163@bellsouth.net

House of Prayer   (4C)SEGR0214

405 E Moulton Street (mailing)
Decatur, AL 35601
170 County Road 730 (physical)
Cullman, AL 35055
(256)355-0947   <Cullman>
FAX: (256)355-0947
nlajap@yahoo.com
PA: Neil Aguiar   <M1>
405 E Moulton Street
Decatur, AL 35601
(256)616-1318
nlajap@yahoo.com
CL: Andres Esteban
405 E Moulton Street
Decatur, AL 35601
(256)355-0947
FAX: (256)355-0947

Hueytown First   (4MWC)SEGR0109
2711 Clyburne Street (mailing)
4846 15th Street Road (physical)
Hueytown, AL 35023
( )   <Jefferson>
CL: Thomas S Neel
2711 Clyburne Street
Hueytown, AL 35023
(205)491-6772
tardistom@hotmail.com

Immanuel   (4MC)SEGR0311
10235 US Highway 301
Dade City, FL 33525
(352)567-7427   <Pasco>
PA: Charles Reed   <M1>
10235 US Highway 301
Dade City, FL 33525
instchuck@embarqmail.com
(352)567-7427
CL: Chad Reed
36821 Indian Lake Cemetary Road
Dade City, FL 33523
(352)567-8755
chadrreed@embarqmail.com

McLeod Chapel   (4MC)SEGR0708
305 E Minor Street (mailing)
Macon-Lynn Creek Road (physical)
Macon, MS 39341
(662)726-4609   <Noxubee>
PA: Samuel L Foreman   <M1>
13700 Highway 488
Philadelphia, MS 39350
(601)562-1415
slfcpc@yahoo.com
CL: James B Moore III
305 E Minor Street
Macon, MS 39341
(662)726-4609

Mt Zion   (4C)SEGR0709
3044 Wolfe Road
Columbus, MS 39705
(662)328-3778   <Lowndes>
mmims@muw.edu
CL: Martha Jo Mims
3011 Wolfe Road
Columbus, MS 39705
(662)328-3778
mmims@muw.edu

New Hope   (4EWC)SEGR0104

GRACE PRESBYTERY CONTINUED

5521 Double Oak Lane
Birmingham, AL 35242
(205)991-5252   <Shelby>
FAX: (205)991-5159
jessie@newhopecpc.org
PA: Donny Acton   <M1>
5521 Double Oak Lane
Birmingham, AL 35242
(205)991-5252
FAX: (205)991-5259
donny@newhopecpc.org
AP: Mindy Acton   <M1>
1413 Oak Ridge Drive
Birmingham, AL 35242
(205)991-3204
FAX: (205)991-5259
mindy@newhopecpc.org
AP: Sherrlyn Frost   <M1>
5557 Surrey Lane
Birmingham, AL 35242
(205)408-0729
FAX: (205)991-5259
sherrlyn@newhopecpc.org
CL: Jessie R Dunnaway
120 Virginia Way
Birmingham, AL 35242
(205)991-7434
FAX: (205)991-5259
jessie@newhopecpc.org

_____

Oldham Chapel   (4EC)SEGR0405
PO Box 537 (mailing)
8767 Greensport Road (physical)
Ashville, AL 35953
(205)594-5727   <St Clair>
SS: Rodney McInnis   <M1>
280-B Coley Road
Glencoe, AL 35905
(256)454-2399
CL: Faye Bowling
PO Box 537
Ashville, AL 35953
(205)594-7171

_____

Piedmont   (4MWC)SEGR0406
23746 AL Highway 9 N
Piedmont, AL 36272
(256)447-7275   <Calhoun>
PA: Jacob Sims   <M1>
23716 Alabamaa Highway 9 N
Piedmont, AL 36272
(205)907-8273
jacobdsims@gmail.com
CL: Charles Needham
201 Needham Drive
Piedmont, AL 36272
(256)447-6897
cneedham_99@yahoo.com

_____

Pleasant Hill   (4MC)SEGR0710
115 Westwood Drive SW (mailing)
7782 CR 181, Eutaw, AL (physical)
Bessemer, AL 35022
(205)425-9659   <Greene>
williambetts7177@gmail.com
LS: William H Betts   <M6>
115 Westwood Drive SW
Bessemer, AL 35022
(205)425-9659
CL: Greg Espey
12034 County Road 60

Eutaw, AL 35462
(205)372-2260
gregandmichel@bellsouth.net

_____

Roca De Salvacion   (C)SEGR0115
2404 Altadena Road
Birmingham, AL 35243
(205)705-3145   <Jefferson>
cpcrocadesalvacion@gmail.com
PA: William Alas   <M1>
612 King Valley Circle
Pelham, AL 35124
(205)966-9411
alas3542085@yahoo.es
CL: Carlos Solito
106 Highway 63
Calera, AL 35040
(205)329-8514

_____

Rocky Ridge   (4WC)SEGR0105
2404 Altadena Road
Birmingham, AL 35243
(205)823-2719   <Jefferson>
rockyridgechurch@bellsouth.net
SS: David Ferguson   <M2>
1841 Pebble Lake Drive
Birmingham, AL 35232
(205)200-9205
fergusondavid15@yahoo.com
AP: Don H Thomas   <M1 RT>
4829 Caldwell Mill Road
Birmingham, AL 35242
(256)742-0785
dhtatn4ybc@cs.com
CL: Cheryl Riley
2416 Altadena Road
Birmingham, AL 35243
(205)790-4342
crsallyfay@aol.com

_____

Salem   (4WC)SEGR0607
PO Box 121 (mailing)
Sebastopol, MS 39359
1220 Highway 487 E (physical)
Walnut Grove, MS 39189
(601)253-2678   <Leake>
sondragould@att.net
PA: Linda Howell   <M1>
PO Box 278
Sebastopol, MS 39359
(601)942-2015
lshowell1000@yahoo.com
CL: Virginia Gould
1220 Highway 487 E
Walnut Grove, MS 39189
(601)253-2678
sondragould@att.net

_____

Spring Creek   (4MWC)SEGR0113
3411 Spring Creek Road (mailing)
3455 Spring Creek Road (physical)
Montevallo, AL 35115
(205)665-4184   <Shelby>
sccpchurch@yahoo.com
PA: Scott Fowler   <M1>
1900 Alex Mill Road
Montevallo, AL 35115
(205)901-8478
springcreekcp@aol.com
CL: Ben Ingram
15 Quincy Lane

Montevallo, AL 35115
(205)665-4145
ben_ingram@msn.com

_____

Steam Mill   (4WC)SEGR0608
593 Pine Grove Road (mailing)
Walnut Grove, MS 39189
11551 Road 101 (physical)
Union, MS 39365
( )   <Neshoba>
nchambers@hughes.net
PA: Nicholas Chambers   <M1>
11300 Road 101
Union, MS 39365
(601)900-3684
nachambrs@hotmail.com
CL: Myra Bankston
593 Pine Grove Road
Walnut Grove, MS 39189
(601)616-0436
mbankston@ecmhci.com

_____

Union   (4MWC)SEGR0114
PO Box 64 (mailing)
11633 Bama Rock Garden Road (physical)
Vance, AL 35490
( )   <Tuscaloosa>
LS: Herbie Gray   <M6>
2554 A Rocky Ridge
Birmingham, AL 35243
CL: Clifford Odell
11491 Bama Rock Garden Road
Vance, AL 35490
wjsrabbit@aol.com

_____

OTHERS ON MINISTERIAL ROLL:

Acton, Wade   <M1 RT>
1615 Estes Drive
Glencoe, AL 35905
(256)492-8542
ginnyacton@juno.com
Black, Gary G   <M1 WC>
503 S Main Street
Piedmont, AL 36272
(205)447-7142
Carter, Patricia   <M1 M9>
2509 Decatur Stratton Road
Decatur, MS 39327
(601)604-3813
revtree@yahoo.com
Clark, J Don   <M1 RT>
1601 Lake Ridge Circle
Birmingham, AL 35216
(205)942-4054
jdsjcl@charter.net
Crawford, Roger B   <M1 RT>
541 Highway 25 N
Carthage, MS 39051
(601)298-1899
Davis, C Timothy   <M1 WC>
8880 Childress Road
West Paducah, KY 42086
(850)995-8383
FAX: (904)994-6003
charles0828@earthlink.net
Edmonds, Wayne   <M1 RT>
112 Dogwood Trail
Eclectic, AL 36024
(334)857-2202
sweetpea@comlinkinc.net

GRACE PRESBYTERY CONTINUED

English, Don W <M1 WC>
4311 Guys Court
Bessemer, AL 35022
(205)428-4790

Gaither, Randy <M1 WC>
No 3 Pacific Street
Belmopan City
Belize, Central America
rgaither@valuelinx.net

Garcia, Ramon <M1 OM>
2714 Callista Court Apt 104
Naples, FL 34114
(239)200-5714
revga@hotmail.com

Hartung, J Thomas <M1 M9 ST>
2291 Americus Boulevard W Apt 1
Clearwater, FL 33763
(727)797-2882
revtom6@aol.com

Headrick, Anthony <M1 M8>
3327 N Eagle Road Ste 110-132
Meridian, ID 83646
(619)524-8821
chaps2a@yahoo.com

Headrick, Christopher <M1 WC>
1913 Vestavia Court Apt B
Vestavia Hills, AL 35216
(205)240-0979
bravespop@gmail.com

Headrick, Jerry <M1 RT>
9950 Old Stage Road
Stockton, AL 36579
(251)377-9744
willjheadrick@gmail.com

Hunley, Jearl <M1 RT>
2618 Canterbury Road
Columbus, MS 39705
(662)329-1516
jdhunley@cableone.net

Johnson, Thomas (Tommy) C <M1 RT>
PO Box 566
Helena, AL 35080
(205)936-1350
revtomjohnson@aol.com

Lefavor, David <M1 M8>
414 S Monroe Siding Road
Xenia, OH 45385
(813)613-4133
david.lefavor@med.va.gov

Maynard, Terrell D <M1 RT>
639 Timber Creek Drive
Columbus, MS 39702
(662)244-0416
terrellmaynard@bellsouth.net

Moore, James R, Sr <M1 RT>
2778 Marguerite Street S
Hokes Bluff, AL 35903
(256)494-9030
jmoore@microxl.com

Morrow, Charles <M1 RT>
5032 Pine Grove Road
Union, MS 39365
(601)479-0288
morrowp7@yahoo.com

Payne, Robert (Bob) <M1 WC>
1660 3rd Street NW
Birmingham, AL 35215
(205)856-2427
payne.bob.emmet@gmail.com

Ros, Ramiro <M1 WC>
107 Bracken Lane

Brandon, FL 33511
(813)633-1548
bethel@gte.net

Rowlett, Ron <M1 WC>
22 Diana Drive
Savannah, GA 31406
(912)351-0736

Schultz, Don <M1 RT>
708 Gateway Lane
Tampa, FL 33613
(813)960-1473

Talley, Ed <M1 WC>
404 Serenity Circle
Walland, TN 37886
(205)854-1886
vellate@att.net

Thomas, Lynn <M1 DE>
4833 Caldwell Mill Lane
Birmingham, AL 35242
(205)601-5770
lynndont@gmail.com

Tobler, Garth <M1 WC>
136 Boat Landing Road
Oneonta, AL 35121
(205)683-0298
gatobler@gmail.com

Travieso, Julio <M1 WC>
15910 Countrybrook Street
Tampa, FL 33624
(813)963-3727
jutra98@aol.com

Weldon, Mark <M1 WC>
1515 Chambliss Drive
Birmingham, AL 35226
(205)330-8580
weldonm@bellsouth.net

Wilson, James <M1 WC>
2449 Sardis Airport Road
Addison, AL 35540
(256)338-0095

Yarce, Omar <M1 WC>
10925 Neptune Drive
Cooper City, FL 33026
alphavida@gmail.com
(205)919-9685

OTHER LICENTIATES ON ROLL:

Moro, Wilfredo <M2>
15292 SW 104th Street Apt 11-22
Miami, FL 33196
(786)554-1478
moraw@bellsouth.net

Rojas, Antonio Mena <M2>
1421 1st Street NW
Cullman, AL 35055
(256)531-8193
antonio.mena.7@facebook.com

Sumerlin, Larkin <M2>
174 Brookgreen Lane
Indian Springs, AL 35124
(334)357-00007
larkin_sumerlin72@hotmail.com

Thomas, Micaiah <M2>
PO Box 5204 SBN 499
Princeton, NJ 08543
(205)478-5985
micaiah.thomas@gmail.com

OTHER CANDIDATES ON ROLL:

Byford, Ken <M3>
58 Quincy Lane
Montevallo, AL 35115
(205)665-5753
kenabyford@gmail.com

Linski, David <M3>
1060 Alpine Way
Indian Springs, AL 35124
(205)677-8163
david.linski@gmail.com

Prevost, Abigail <M3>
4731 Lafayette Road
Hopkinsville, KY 42240
(731)343-5386
abbyprevost@gmail.com

Solito, Carlos <M3>
106 Highway 63
Calera, AL 35040
(205)329-8514
fcg9700@gmail.com

Yarce, Virginia <M3>
10925 Neptune Drive
Cooper City, Fl 33026
(205)919-9685
ginnyyarce@gmail.com

Hong Kong Presbytery
MISSION SYNOD

	1.Church Number	2.Active	3.Total	4.Church School	5.Prof. of Faith	6.Gains	7.Losses	8.Children Baptized	9. OUR UNITED OUT-REACH	10. Total Out-Reach Giving	11. All Other Expenses	12. Total Income Received	13. Value Church Prop. 1=1000
	1	2	3	4	5	6	7	8	9	10	11	12	13
Cheung Chau	8801	25	38	24	0	5	1	0	206	7,032	45,974	40,132	128
Kowloon Chapel	8803	116	290	58	0	7	1	2	1,710	35,323	186,322	200,890	154
Macau	8804	68	142	36	4	3	1	0	1,049	14,208	73,621	117,369	761
Mu Min*	8810	241	271	60	18	29	2	14	257	1,589	332,202	454,032	0
N. Point Chapel	8805	51	117	40	1	1	2	1	1,746	29,780	113,348	147,780	100
Po Lam	8808	79	129	20	5	6	1	0	258	6,080	121,920	128,000	0
Shatin	8807	171	196	25	14	18	1	4	1,518	15,000	350,000	485,000	385
Tao Hsien	8806	400	529	200	0	11	7	5	2,575	129,600	592,172	721,779	2,856
Xi Lin	8809	85	156	45	0	11	3	2	3,863	16,936	247,431	191,026	0
Yao Dao	8811	139	166	36	14	19	4	2	1,803	20,460	190,000	205,530	0
TOTALS	10	1,375	2,034	544	56	110	23	30	14,985	276,008	2,252,990	2,691,538	4,384

CHURCHES, PASTORS, AND CLERKS:

Cheung Chau   (4C)MSHK8801
11 On Wing Centre 2/F
Pak She Back Street
Cheung Chau, HONG KONG
(852)2981-4933   <Hong Kong>
cccpcmail@yahoo.com.hk
SS: Kelvin Ho   <M2>
11 On Wing Centre 2/F
Pak She Back Street
Cheung Chau, HONG KONG
(852)2981-4933
kelvinskho@gmail.com
CL: Wing Hin Cheung
11 On Wing Centre 2/F
Pak She Back Street
Cheung Chau, HONG KONG
(852)2981-4933
cccpcmail@yahoo.com.hk

Kowloon Chapel   (4WC)MSHK8803
338-340 Castle Peak Road
Flat A-D 2/F
Kowloon, HONG KONG
(852)2386-6563   <Hong Kong>
FAX: (852)3020-0365
kcumber@biznetvigator.com
SS: Ting Bong Ha   <M2>
338-340 Castle Peak Road
Flat D 2/FL
Kowloon, HONG KONG
(852)2386-6563
FAX: (852)3020-0365
kcumber@biznetvigator.com
CL: Lai Seung AU
338-340 Castle Peak Road
Flat D 2/Fl
Kowloon, HONG KONG
(852)2386-6563
FAX: (852)3020-0365
kcumber@biznetvigator.com

Macau   (4WC)MSHK8804
258 Carlos D'Assumpcao
Ed Kin Heng Long 4 Andar LMN
MACAU
(853)2892-1702   <Macau>
cpc_macau@yahoo.com.hk
SS: Eva Watt   <M3>
258 Carlos D'Assumpcao
Ed Kin Heng Long 4 Andar LMN
MACAU
(853)2892-1702
eva6e@hotmail.com
CL: Sok Yi Leong
258 Carlos D'Assumpcao
Ed Kin Heng Long 4 Andar LMN
MACAU
(853)2892-1702
cpc_macau@yahoo.com.hk

Mu Min   (C)MSHK8810
2/F Fu Tung Shopping Center
Tung Chung
Lantau Island, HONG KONG
(852)2109-1738   <Hong Kong>
FAX: (852)2109-1737
mmcpc@cumberland.org.hk
PA: Patrick Tat Wing So   <M1>
2/F Fu Tung Shopping Center
Tung Chung
Lantau Island, HONG KONG
(852)2109-1738
FAX: (852)2109-1737
pattwso1@gmail.com
CL: Lai Yuet Liu   <M2>
2/F Fu Tung Shopping Center
Tung Chung
Lantau Island, HONG KONG
(852)2109-1738
FAX: (852)2109-1737
lyliu0914@gmail.com

N Point Chapel   (4WC)MSHK8805
14-16 Tsat Tsz Mui Road
1/Fl Block B

North Point, HONG KONG
(852)2562-2148   <Hong Kong>
FAX: (852)2564-2898
northpointcpc@yahoo.com.hk
SS: Eliza Yuk Lan Yau   <M2>
14-16 TsatTsz Mui Road
1/Fl Block B
North Point, HONG KONG
(852)2562-2148
FAX: (852)2564-2898
elizaylyau@yahoo.com.hk
CL: Bankie Ching
14-16 Tsat Tsz Mui Road
1/Fl Block B
North Point, HONG KONG
(852)2562-2148
FAX: (852)2564-2898
northpointcpc@yahoo.com.hk

Po Lam   (ARC)MSHK8808
Wing B&C, G/F, Ming Wik House
Kin Ming Estate
Tseung Kwan O NT, HONG KONG
(852)2706-0111   <Hong Kong>
FAX: (852)2706-0114
polamcpc@yahoo.com.hk
SS: Yim Ngar Wong   <M2>
Wing B&C G/F Ming Wik House
Kin Ming Estate
Tseung Kwan O NT, HONG KONG
(852)2706-0111
FAX: (852)2706-0114
yimngar@yahoo.com.hk
CL: Yim Ngar Wong
Wing B&C G/F Ming Wik House
Kin Ming Estate
Tseung Kwan O NT, HONG KONG
(852)2706-0111
FAX: (852)2706-0114
yimngar@yahoo.com.hk

Shatin   (ARC)MSHK8807
G/1F 251 Tin Sam Village
Shatin NT, HONG KONG

HONG KONG PRESBYTERY CONTINUED

(852)2693-3444   <Hong Kong>
FAX: (852)2607-2245
cpcshatin@yahoo.com.hk
PA: Jonathan Chor K Siu   <M1>
  G/1F 251 Tin Sam Village
  Shatin NT, HONG KONG
  (852)2693-3444
  FAX: (852)2607-2245
  cpccksiu@yahoo.com.hk
CL: Gigi Fung
  G/1F 251 Tin Sam Village
  Shatin NT, HONG KONG
  (852)2693-3444
  FAX: (852)2607-2245
  cpcshatin@yahoo.com.hk

Tao Hsien   (4F)MSHK8806
  2/F Welland Plaza
  188 Nam Cheong Street
  Sham Shui Po, Kowloon, HONG KONG
  (852)2783-8923   <Hong Kong>
  FAX: (852)2771-2726
  thchurch@taohsien.org.hk
PA: Amos Pui Chung Yuen   <M1>
  2/F Welland Plaza
  188 Nam Cheong Street
  Sham Shui Po, Kowloon, HONG KONG
  (852)2783-8923
  FAX: (852)277-1272
  revyuen@taohsien.org.hk
CL: Adays Lee
  2/F Welland Plaza
  188 Nam Cheong Street
  Sham Shui Po, Kowloon, HONG KONG
  (852)2783-8923
  FAX: (852)2771-2726
  thchurch@taohsien.org.hk

Xi Lin   (4C)MSHK8809
  28 Hong Yip Street
  Yuen Long, HONG KONG
  (852)2639-9176   <Hong Kong>
  FAX: (853)2639-5620
  maywmchan8@yuenlongcpc.org
PA: William Kin Keung Yeung <M1>
  28 Hong Yip Street
  Yuen Long, HONG KONG
  (852)2639-9176
  FAX: (852)2639-5620
  william@xilincpc.org.hk
CL: Ioletta Wong
  28 Hong Yip Street
  Yuen Long, HONG KONG
  (852)2639-9176
  FAX: (852)2639-5620
  maywmchan8@yuenlongcpc.org

Yao Dao   (4C)MSHK8811
  CPC Yao Dao Primary School
  Tin Yuet Estate
  Tin Shui Wai, NT, HONG KONG
  (852)2617-7872   <Hong Kong>
  FAX: (852)2617-0287
  ydgrowth@yaodaocpc.org
PA: Grace Siu Tim Yu Leung <M1>
  2/F Welland Plaza
  188 Nam Cheong Street
  Sham Shui Po, Kowloon, HONG KONG
  (852)2783-8923
  FAX: (852)2771-2726
  yuleungsiutim@netvigator.com

CL: Kwong Lung Leung
  CPC Yao Dao Primary School
  Tin Yuet Estate
  Tin Shui Wai, NT, HONG KONG
  (852)2617-7872
  FAX: (852)2617-0287
  ydgrowth@yaodaocpc.org

OTHERS ON MINISTERIAL ROLL:

Cheung, Luke   <M1 WC>
  2/F Weeland Plaza
  188 Nam Cheong Street
  Sham Shui Po Kowloon, HONG KONG
  (852)2783-8923
  FAX: (852)2771-2726
  luke.cheung@cgst.edu
Fung, Lawrence   <M1 WC>
  2/F Weeland Plaza
  188 Nam Cheong Street
  Sham Shui Po Kowloon, HONG KONG
  (852)2783-8923
  FAX: (852)2771-2726
  revfung@yahoo.com
Yu, Carver Tat Sum   <M1 WC>
  2/F Welland Plaza
  188 Nam Cheong Street
  Sham Shui Po, Kowloon, HONG KONG
  (852)2783-8923
  FAX: (852)2771-2726
  carver.yu@cgst.edu

OTHER LICENTIATES ON ROLL:

Cheung, Percy   <M2>
  G/F & 1/F 251 TinSam Village
  Tai Wai, Shatin, NT, HONG KONG
  (852)2693-3444
  FAX: (852)2607-2245
  percycheung@hotmail.com
Hung, Ella Siu Kei   <M2>
  2/F Welland Plaza
  188 Nam Cheong Street
  Sham Shui Po, Kowloon, HONG KONG
  (852)2783-8923
  FAX: (852)2771-2726
  siukee@taohsien.org.hk
Lam, Janice   <M2>
  G/F & 1/F 251 Tin Sum Village
  Tai Wai, Shatin NT, HONG KONG
  (852)2693-3444
  FAX: (852)2607-2245
  janiceyeung929@gmail.com
Lee, Ted Shu Tak   <M2>
  2/F Welland Plaza
  188 Nam Cheong Street
  Sham Shui Po, Kowloon, HONG KONG
  (852)2783-8923
  FAX: (852)2771-2726
  tedlee@taohsien.org.hk
Li, Chun Wai   <M2>
  1/Fl Block B
  14 TsatTsz Mui Road
  North Point, HONG KONG
  (852)2562-2148
  FAX: (852)2564-2898
  cwli2000hk@yahoo.com.hk
Lim, Abraham   <M2>
  2/F Welland Plaza
  188 Nam Cheong Street
  Sham Shui Po, Kowloon, HONG KONG

(852)2783-8923
FAX: (852)2771-2726
abraham@taohsien.org.hk
Liu, Lai Yuet   <M2>
  2/F Fu Tung Shopping Centre
  Tung Chung
  Lantau Island NT, HONG KONG
  (852)2109-1738
  FAX: (852)2109-1737
  laiyuet0914@gmail.com
Mak, Daphne Suet Chung <M2>
  2/F Welland Plaza
  188 Nam Cheong Street
  Sham Shui Po, Kowloon, HONG KONG
  (852)2783-8923
  FAX: (852)2771-2726
  daphne@taohsien.org.hk
Tang, Po Kau   <M2>
  2/F Welland Plaza
  188 Nam Cheong Street
  Sham Shui Po, Kowloon, HONG KONG
  (852)2794-2382
  FAX: (852)2771-2726
  cpc_pokau@yahoo.com.hk
Tsui, Jackson   <M2>
  258 Carlos D'Assumpcao
  Ed Kin Heng Long 4 Andar LMN
  MACAU
  (853)2892-1702
  tsuih@yahoo.com
Wong, So Li   <M2>
  2/F Fu Tung Shopping Center
  Tung Chung
  Lantau Island, HONG KONG
  (852)2109-1738
  FAX: (852)2109-1737
  soliwong@gmail.com
Yau, Chat Ming   <M2>
  G/F 251 Tin Sum Village
  Shatin NT, HONG KONG
  (852)2693-3444
  FAX: (852)2607-2245
  summerycm@yahoo.com.hk
Yung, Karen Wing Man   <M2>
  Flat D 2/F
  338-340 Castle Peak Road
  Kowloon, HONG KONG
  (852)2386-6563
  FAX: (852)3020-0365
  yungyungmiss@yahoo.com.hk

OTHER CANDIDATES ON ROLL:

Cheung Kam Ho   <M3>
  G/1F 251 Tin Sam Village
  Shatin NT, HONG KONG
  (852)2607-3414
  FAX: (852)2607-2245
  percycheung@hotmail.com
Lee, Priscilla   <M3>
  Tin Yuet Estate
  Tin Shui Wai NT, HONG KONG
  (852)2617-7872
  FAX: (852)2617-0287
  wai_yung_lee@yahoo.com.hk
Wong, Apple   <M3>
  G/F & 1/F 251 Tin Sum Village Tai Wai
  Shatin NT, HONG KONG
  (852)2693-3444
  FAX: (852)2607-2245

yunnan_apple@yahoo.com
Yuen, Susanna <M3>
28 Hong Yip Street
Yuen Long, NT, HONG KONG
(522)639-9176
FAX: (522)639-5620
susanna@yuenlongchurch.org

Hope Presbytery
SOUTHEAST SYNOD

	1.Church Number	2.Active	3.Total	4.Church School	5.Prof. of Faith	6.Gains	7.Losses	8.Children Baptized	9. OUR UNITED OUT-REACH	10. Total Out-Reach Giving	11. All Other Expenses	12. Total Income Received	13. Value Church Prop. 1=1000
Allsboro**	0501	48	78	27	0	1	19	0	0	11,881	71,513	85,483	300
Baldwin Chapel	0202	36	54	21	0	0	0	0	1,510	2,505	27,797	30,306	200
Cherokee	0505	7	10	0	No Report Received			0	0	0	0	0	130
Faith	0213	49	107	31	0	0	0	0	0	1,500	58,860	69,175	600
Florence 1st	0506	89	130	61	0	2	4	4	12,667	28,398	127,648	167,429	1,200
Hickory Grove	0507	26	37	16	No Report Received			0	1,200	0	0	0	150
Hurricane*	0508	60	92	30	4	6	0	0	0	4,909	82,777	111,408	300
Maud	0509	10	4	0	No Report Received			0	0	0	0	0	90
Mt. Hester	0510	10	10	7	0	0	0	0	0	0	12,847	10,994	200
Mt. Pleasant	0511	13	13	10	0	0	0	0	0	1,995	15,734	16,465	70
Nebo	0512	34	42	24	1	1	39	0	0	2,000	66,961	68,294	1,250
Old Mt Bethel*	0513	30	38	25	0	0	7	1	0	2,937	22,396	26,216	65
Park Terrace*	0514	30	33	20	4	4	27	0	0	1,335	57,544	62,953	671
Rogersville 1st	0517	119	268	84	2	2	6	2	16,837	20,095	254,042	195,396	1,028
Springfield	0515	89	168	52	1	1	0	0	0	10,753	96,410	116,604	1,000
Union Hill	0516	74	105	50	3	3	11	1	0	14,721	87,926	94,341	1,500
Welti	0212	148	220	84	3	3	3	1	15,830	46,682	147,670	172,071	925
TOTALS	17	872	1,409	542	18	23	116	9	48,044	149,711	1,130,125	1,227,135	9,679

*Math error corrected. **Purged roll.

CHURCHES, PASTORS, AND CLERKS:

Allsboro (4MEWC)SEHO0501
515 Iuka Road (mailing)
1925 Allsboro Road (physical)
Cherokee, AL 35616
(256)360-2919 <Colbert>
SS: Don F Thomas <M1 OP>
400 Park Hill Road
Collierville, TN 38017
(901)861-6398
thomas63981@comcast.net
CL: Dale Johnson
515 Iuka Road
Cherokee, AL 35616
(256)360-2973
djohnson@bibank.com

Baldwin Chapel (4MEWC)SEHO0202

381 County Road 404 (mailing)
126 County Road 1153 (physical)
Cullman, AL 35057
(256)737-1850 <Cullman>
PA: Howard Rodgers <M1>
336 County Road 1216
Vinemont, AL 35179
(256)739-6296
djbr421@yahoo.com
AP: Gary Carter <M1>
310 River Bluff Drive
Sheffield, AL 35660
(256)443-8389
garycarter51@gmail.com
CL: Bonnie Marty
381 County Road 404
Cullman, AL 35057
(256)734-6399
brmarty45@yahoo.com

Cherokee (4MEC)SEHO0505
(CLOSED 4/2013)

Faith (4WC)SEHO0213
5821 County Road 1114 (mailing)
Vinemont, AL 35179
6880 AL Highway 157 (physical)
Cullman, AL 35057
(256)734-0893 <Cullman>
SS: Philip Nickles <M1>
5821 County Road 1114
Vinemont, AL 35179
(256)620-1977
nickles.phil@yahoo.com
CL: Philip Nickles
5821 County Road 1114
Vinemont, AL 35179
(256)620-1977
nickles.phil@yahoo.com

HOPE PRESBYTERY CONTINUED

Florence First　　　　(4WC)SEHO0506
　2422 Darby Drive
　Florence, AL 35630
　(256)766-0471　　　　　<Lauderdale>
　FAX: (256)766-0736
　fcpoffice@comcast.net
PA: Dwayne McDuff　　　　<M1>
　9770 County Road 5
　Florence, AL 35633
　(256)764-6354
　FAX: (256)766-0736
　fcpdmcduff@comcast.net
CL: Philip Gambrell
　1045 Piedmont Street
　Florence, AL 35630
　(256)443-8924
　pgambrell@ffcuonline.com

Hickory Grove　　　　(4MC)SECU0507
　75 County Road 59
　Moulton, AL 35650
　(256)306-0025　　　　　<Lawrence>
　dhtatn4ybc@cs.com
PA: Tony Gaskin　　　　<M1>
　479 County Road 1157
　Cullman, AL 35057
　(256)338-7893
　tgaskin46@hotmail.com
CL: Noah Williamson
　655 County Road 38
　Mount Hope, AL 35651
　(256)974-9413
　mwilliamson@lawrenceal.org

Hurricane　　　　(4EWC)SEHO0508
　1331 County Road 86 (mailing)
　1000 County Road 156 (physical)
　Rogersville, AL 35652
　(256)247-7483　　　　　<Lauderdale>
PA: Jimmy R Cox　　　　<M1>
　2250 County Road 156
　Anderson, AL 35610
　(256)710-1702
　dcox01@msn.com
CL: Bryan Belue
　1331 County Road 86
　Rogersville, AL 35652
　(256)247-7175
　rbeluebigboy@aol.com

Maud　　　　(4MWC)SEHO0509
　2280 Maud Road (mailing)
　Gypsy Loop (physical)
　Cherokee, AL 35616
　(256)360-2811　　　　　<Colbert>
CL: Paula Pardue
　2280 Maud Road
　Cherokee, AL 35616
　(256)360-2811

Mt Hester　　　　(4MEWC)SEHO0510
　PO Box 174 (mailing)
　14720 Mount Hester Road (physical)
　Cherokee, AL 35616
　(　)　　　　　<Colbert>
CL: Leigh Ann Malone
　2625 Sutton Hill Road
　Cherokee, AL 35616
　(256)359-6134
　leighmalone05@yahoo.com

Mt Pleasant　　　　(4MC)SEHO0511
　30 Carolyn Road (mailing)
　13575 County Line Road (physical)
　Muscle Shoals, AL 35661
　(256)446-5397　　　　　<Colbert>
SS: Tony Gaskin　　　　<M1>
　479 County Road 1157
　Cullman, AL 35057
　(256)338-7893
　tgaskin46@hotmail.com
CL: James Letsinger
　8285 2nd Street
　Leighton, AL 35646
　(256)446-9367

Nebo　　　　(4MEWC)SEHO0512
　9491 Highway 101
　Lexington, AL 35648
　(256)577-5952　　　　　<Lauderdale>
　nebo9491@gmail.com
PA: Terry Herston　　　　<M1>
　390 County Road 95
　Rogersville, AL 35652
　(256)247-3004
　tpaw51@gmail.com
CL: Gerald A McGee
　9491 Highway 101
　Lexington, AL 35648
　(256)577-5952
　nebo9491@gmail.com

Old Mt Bethel　　　　(4C)SEHO0513
　County Road 51
　Rogersville, AL 35652
　(　)　　　　　<Lauderdale>
PA: Terry Herston　　　　<M1>
　390 County Road 95
　Rogersville, AL 35652
　(256)247-3004
　tpaw51@gmail.com
CL: Tommy Word
　620 County Road 521
　Lexington, AL 35648
　(256)247-3182
　tword1956@gmail.com

Park Terrace　　　　(4MEWC)SEHO0514
　100 E Wheeler Avenue
　Sheffield, AL 35660
　(256)383-8052　　　　　<Colbert>
　pastor@parkterracechurch.org
PA: George Lee　　　　<M1>
　104 Parc Circle
　Florence, AL 35630
　(256)740-0809
　butchleeautos@yahoo.com
CL: Peggy Vickers
　112 Pasadena Avenue
　Muscle Shoals, AL 35661
　(256)383-1992

Rogersville First　　　　(4WC)SEHO0517
　16751 Highway 72
　Rogersville, AL 35652
　(256)247-3339　　　　　<Lauderdale>
　fcprogersville@yahoo.com
PA: James P Driskell　　　　<M1>
　154 Mountain Way
　Anderson, AL 35610
　(256)648-6758
　FAX: (256)247-3339

　patprespax@yahoo.com
CL: Kathy W Ezell
　275 McGraw Circle
　Anderson, AL 35610
　(256)247-3625
　kwhiteheadezell@aol.com

Springfield　　　　(4MWC)SEHO0515
　5400 Highway 101
　Rogersville, AL 35652
　(256)247-1424　　　　　<Lauderdale>
　FAX: (256)247-1424
　kennymorgan330@hotmail.com
PA: Kenneth P Morgan　　　　<M1>
　5400 Highway 101
　Rogersville, AL 35652
　(256)247-3890
　FAX: (256)247-1424
　kennymorgan330@hotmail.com
CL: Charles G Lash
　170 Meadow Ridge Lane
　Rogersville, AL 35652
　(256)247-0040

Union Hill　　　　(4MEWC)SEHO0516
　6535 Bailey Road
　Anderson, AL 35610
　(256)233-1841　　　　　<Limestone>
PA: Charles Hood　　　　<M1>
　1200 County Road 519
　Anderson, AL 35610
　(256)229-6251
　hooddad11@gmail.com
CL: Curtis Usery
　28341 Easter Ferry Road
　Lester, AL 35647
　(256)232-9237

Welti　　　　(4MWC)SEHO0212
　8817 County Road 747
　Cullman, AL 35055
　(256)737-9138　　　　　<Cullman>
　weltipastor@welticpchurch.com
PA: James L Peyton　　　　<M1>
　1455 County Road 643
　Cullman, AL 35055
　(256)735-3620
　jakjpeyton@att.net
CL: Lee Holder
　6589 County Road 747
　Cullman, AL 35055
　(256)739-5136
　lholder@tvpinc.com

OTHERS ON MINISTERIAL ROLL:

Brock, Dudley　　　　<M1 WC>
　490 County Road 1184
　Cullman, AL 35057
　(256)734-0893
　preacherbrock@att.net
Craig, Peggy Jean　　　　<M1 WC>
　1659 Briar Cliff Road #2308
　Atlanta, GA 30306
　(256)277-1147
　pjfpeggy@gmail.com
Deaton, John　　　　<M1 WC>
　277 School Lane
　Springfield, PA 19064
　(215)906-7067
　deatonjr11@gmail.com

HOPE PRESBYTERY CONTINUED

Malone, John W   <M1 RT>
    3693 Highway 67 South
    Sommerville, AL 35670
    (256)778-8237

Parker, Susan   <M1 WC>
    655 York Drive
    Rogersville, AL 35652
    (256)247-3877
    park9301@bellsouth.net

Yaple, George H   <M1 RT>
    2051 Lost Creek Road
    Carbon Hill, AL 35549
    (205)924-9921

OTHER LICENTIATES ON ROLL:

OTHER CANDIDATES ON ROLL:

Japan Presbytery
MISSION SYNOD

GENERAL	1.Church Number	MEMBERSHIP 2.Active	3.Total	4.Church School	CHANGES 5.Prof. of Faith	6.Gains	7.Losses	8.Children Baptized	FINANCES 9. OUR UNITED OUT-REACH	10. Total Out-Reach Giving	11. All Other Expenses	12. Total Income Received	13. Value Church Prop. 1=1000
	1	2	3	4	5	6	7	8	9	10	11	12	13
Asahi Mission	8315	26	26	7	1	3	0	0	464	977	38,105	39,082	5
Den-en Mission	8310	19	41	25	0	3	3	0	710	1,763	61,510	37,089	70
EbinaShionNoOka	8311	113	165	47	1	2	7	0	3,749	26,892	82,960	109,852	73
Higashi Koganei	8301	28	35	5	0	1	3	0	1,161	5,084	61,833	61,685	130
Ichikawa Grace	8314	14	19	0	0	0	0	0	441	903	68,042	34,157	45
Izumi	8312	31	42	7	0	4	1	2	698	2,993	43,696	46,689	17
Kibougaoka	8302	178	334	120	2	5	4	0	6,018	39,325	199,951	242,412	467
Koza	8303	587	1,158	452	22	0	0	2	20,233	136,765	675,656	812,420	1,528
KunitachiNozomi	8306	63	105	40	0	1	1	0	2,575	13,151	82,250	95,401	170
Mata De	8313	35	60	24	2	2	2	0	351	589	60,168	30,836	17
Megumi	8309	38	49	10	0	0	1	0	1,631	6,957	57,867	65,811	73
Naruse	8305	58	118	14	1	2	1	0	2,267	10,990	76,609	88,202	96
Sagamino	8304	27	56	11	1	1	1	0	1,624	7,050	45,980	50,973	174
Shibusawa*	8307	37	101	20	1	2	7	0	1,833	7,114	62,203	67,868	273
TOTALS	14	1,254	2,309	782	31	26	31	4	43,755	260,553	1,616,830	1,782,477	3,138

*Math error corrected. **Purged roll.

JAPAN PRESBYTERY CONTINUED

CHURCHES, PASTORS, AND CLERKS:

Asahi Mission   (4F)MSJA8315
  1F Miyabi-Bldg
  1-19-21 Honcho Tsurugamine
  Asahi-ku Yokohama, Kanagawa-Ken
  241-0021 JAPAN
  (045)489-3720   <Japan>
  FAX: (045)953-2588
  asahi_ch@yahoo.co.jp
PA: Atsushi Suzuki   <M1>
  53-17 Higashi Kibogaoka Asahi-ku
  Yokohama, Kanagawa-ken
  241-0826 JAPAN
  (045)362-2603
  FAX: (045)362-2603
  asyuwa98@m10.alpha-net.ne.jp
CL: Session Clerk Asahi Mission Point
  1F Miyabi-Bldg
  1-19-21 Honcho Tsurugamine
  Asahi-ku Yokohama, Kanagawa-Ken
  241-0021 JAPAN
  (045)489-3720
  FAX: (045)953-2588
  asahi_ch@yahoo.co.jp

Den-en Mission   (4MC)MSJA8310
  9-41-2 Kamitsuruma-honcho
  Sagamihara-Shi, Kanagawa-Ken
  228-0818 JAPAN
  (042)744-6804   <Japan>
  FAX: (042)744-6804
  den-en@church.ne.jp
PA: Kazuhiko Furuhata   <M1>
  #310, 9-41-15 Kamitsurumahoncho
  Sagamihara-shi, Kanagawa-ken
  252-0318 JAPAN
  (042)814-7802
  FAX: (042)814-7802
  cpc.furuhata@gmail.com
CL: Takashi Kanazashi
  3-6-406 Shimoyuzuki
  Hachiouji-shi, Tokyo
  197-0732 JAPAN
  (042)675-6895
  fredericfchopin@gmail.com

Ebina Shion No Oka (4MWC)MSJA8311
  3-17-57 Nakashinden
  Ebina-shi, Kanagawa-ken
  243-0422 JAPAN
  (046)234-3426   <Japan>
  ebinazion@gmail.com
PA: Yukio Tamai   <M1>
  3-17-57 Nakashinden
  Ebina-shi, Kanagawa-ken
  243-0422 JAPAN
  (046)234-3426
  yukiotamai@me.com
CL: Hiroko Fushimi
  2-4-7 Rinkan Yamato-shi
  Kanagawa-ken
  242-0003 JAPAN
  (046)275-3801
  FAX: (046)725-3801
  hrkfsm@hotmail.com

Higashi Koganei   (4MWC)MSJA8301
  2-14-16 Higashi-cho
  Koganei-shi, Tokyo

  184-0011 JAPAN
  (042)231-1279   <Japan>
  FAX: (042)231-1279
PA: Shigeru Katsuki   <M1>
  2-14-16 Higashi-cho
  Koganei-shi, Tokyo
  184-0011 JAPAN
  (042)232-3640
  shigeru.katsuki@nifty.com
CL: Eiko Imai
  3-4-19 Higashi-cho
  Koganei-shi, Tokyo
  184-0011 JAPAN
  (042)232-1417

Ichikawa Grace Mission (4MF)MSJA8314
  1-11-20 Kokubu
  Ichikawa-shi, Chiba-ken
  272-0834 JAPAN
  (047)369-7540   <Japan>
  FAX: (047)369-7540
  ichikawa-grace@mbi.nifty.com
PA: Yasuo Masuda   <M1>
  1-11-20 Kokubu
  Ichikawa-shi, Chiba-ken
  272-0834 JAPAN
  (047)369-7540
  FAX: (047)369-7540
  fwgc6854@mb.infoweb.ne.jp
CL: Session Clerk Ichikawa Grace Mission
  1-11-20 Kokubu
  Ichikawa-shi, Chiba-ken
  272-0834 JAPAN
  (047)369-7540
  FAX: (047)369-7540

Izumi   (4WC)MSJA8312
  4194-13 Izumi-cho Izumi-ku
  Yokohama, Kanagawa-ken
  245-0016 JAPAN
  (045)803-1749   <Japan>
  FAX: (045)361-4351
  izumi@kyokai.org
PA: Kenji Ushioda   <M1>
  2-47-3 Akuwa-higashi Seya-ku
  Yokohama, Kanagawa-ken
  243-0023 JAPAN
  (046)361-4351
  ushioda@jc.ejnet.ne.jp
CL: Kenji Ushioda
  2-47-3 Akuwa-higashi Seya-ku
  Yokohama, Kanagawa-ken
  246-0023 JAPAN
  (046)361-4351
  FAX: (045)361-4351
  ushioda@jc.ejet.ne.jp

Kibougaoka   (4WMC)MSJA8302
  72-2 Naka Kibogaoka
  Asahi-ku Yokohama, Kanagawa-ken
  241-0825 JAPAN
  (045)391-6038   <Japan>
  FAX: (045)391-6653
PA: Ryuzo Matsuya   <M1>
  72-2 Naka Kibogaoka Asahi-ku
  Yokohama, Kanagawa-ken
  241-0825 JAPAN
  (045)364-8297
  matsuya.r@woody.ocn.ne.jp
CL: Kazuhiro Ohashi
  2-50-16 Akuwa-Higashi

Seya-ku Yokohama, Kanagawa-ken
  246-0023 JAPAN
  (045)363-4923
  k_0084@nifty.com

Koza   (4MWC)MSJA8303
  2-14-1 Minami Rinkan
  Yamato-shi, Kanagawa-ken
  242-0006 JAPAN
  (046)724-1370   <Japan>
  FAX: (046)276-9685
  cpckoza@koza-church.jp
PA: Masahiro Matsumoto   <M1>
  2-14-1 Minami Rinkan
  Yamato-shi, Kanagawa-ken
  242-0006 JAPAN
  (046)275-2767
  matsumoto@koza-church.jp
CL: Yutaka Shibata
  1-18-3 Rinkan Yamato-shi
  Kanagawa-ken
  241-0003 JAPAN
  (046)272-0579
  shibata@koza-church.jp

Kunitachi Nozomi   (4MWC)MSJA8306
  3-15-9 Higashi
  Kunitachi-shi, Tokyo
  186-0002 JAPAN
  (042)572-7616   <Japan>
  FAX: (042)572-7616
  nozomi-ch@ceres.ocn.ne.jp
PA: Kenta Karasawa   <M1>
  3-15-10 Higashi
  Kunitachi-shi, Tokyo
  186-0002 JAPAN
  (042)575-5549
  FAX: (042)575-5549
  k-kenta@roy.hi-ho.ne.jp
CL: Keita Komine
  3-26-16 Higashi
  Kunitachi-shi, Tokyo
  186-0002 JAPAN
  (042)507-9971
  bgmgb65@gmail.com

Mata De Sao Joao   (4MC)MSJA8313
  Nucleo Colonial JK
  Lote 56 Mata De Sao Joao
  48280-000, Bahia, BRAZIL
  (5571)9641-1307   <JAPAN>
PA: Keishi Ishitsuka   <M1>
  Nucleo Colonial JK
  Lote 56 Mata De Sao Joao
  48280-000, Bahia, BRAZIL
  (5571)9641-1307
  kishitsuka@hotmail.com
SS: Atsushi Miyajima   <M2>
  Rua Araja
  58 Paraiso Sao Joa
  48280-000, Bahia, BRAZIL
  (5571)3664-1037
  ariel.atsushi@gmail.com
CL: Shinnichi Hizumi
  Nucleo Colonial JK
  Lote 56 Mata De Sao Joao
  48280-000, Bahia, BRAZIL
  (5571)3664-1037
  hizumi@uol.com.br

Megumi   (4MWC)MSJA8309

JAPAN PRESBYTERY CONTINUED

3-355-4 Kami Kitadai Higashi
Yamato-shi, Tokyo
207-0023 JAPAN
(042)564-0593   <Japan>
FAX: (042)567-2977
megumikyokai@gmail.com
PA: Makihiko Arase   <M1>
  3-355-4 Kamikitadai Higashi
  Yamato-shi, Tokyo
  207-0023 JAPAN
  (042)567-2977
  FAX: (042)567-2977
  viator@cb3.so-net.ne.jp
CL: Shigeru Yanagawa
  2-68-25 Sunagawa-cho
  Tachikawa-shi, Tokyo
  190-0031 JAPAN
  (042)536-5332
  FAX: (042)536-5473
  punisumo33noa@tbz.t-com.ne.jp

Naruse   (4WC)MSJA8305
  7-20-12 Tamagawa Gakuen
  Machida-shi, Tokyo
  194-0041 JAPAN
  (042)725-9909   <Japan>
  FAX: (042)725-9909
  cpc-naruse@nifty.com
PA: Yoshimasa Niwa   <M1>
  15-402 Narakita Danchi
  2913 Naramachi Aoba-ku
  Kanagawa-ken, Yokohama
  227-0036 JAPAN
  (045)961-1540
  rsb09335@nifty.com
CL:Toru Abe
  5-18-14 Nara Aboba-ku
  Yokohama-shi, Kanagawa-ken
  227-0038 JAPAN
  (045)961-8620
  FAX: (045)961-8620
  abe.tooru@rouge.plala.or.jp

Sagamino   (4MWC)MSJA8304
  4-13-24 Higashihara
  Zama-shi, Kanagawa-ken
  228-0004 JAPAN
  (046)255-6441   <Japan>

FAX: (046)255-6441
sagamino@church.jp
PA: Takehiko Miyai   <M1>
  A-201 2-2-48 Higashihara Zama-shi
  Kanagawa-ken
  228-0004 JAPAN
  (046)207-6558
  FAX: (046)256-3212
CL: Akimasa Nakano
  1-105 Sagaminosakura 5-1
  Higashihara Zama-shi
  Kanagawa-ken
  228-0004 JAPAN
  (046)254-8564
  nakano.a.ipt@gmail.com

Shibusawa   (4MWC)MSJA8307
  1-8-50 Magarimatsu
  Hadano-shi, Kanagawa-ken
  259-1321 JAPAN
  (046)387-1203   <Japan>
  FAX: (046)387-1203
PA: Keitaro Ohi   <M1>
  1-8-50 Magarimatsu
  Hadano-shi, Kanagawa-ken
  259-1321 JAPAN
  (046)387-1203
  FAX: (046)387-1203
  keitaro_o@hotmail.com
CL: Kiyoshi Kumon
  3-26-5 Shibusawa
  Hadano-shi, Kanagawa-ken
  259-1322 JAPAN
  (046)388-3609
  kiyokumon@yahoo.co.jp

OTHERS ON MINISTERIAL ROLL:

Asayama, Masaharu   <M1 RT>
  6-3-2-308 Toyogaoka
  Tama-shi, Tokyo
  206-0031 JAPAN
  (042)373-2710
  asa@ipcc-21.com
Hamazaki, Takashi   <M1 RT>
  1551-1-202 Inokuchi
  Nakai-cho Ashigarakami-gun

Kanagawa-ken
259-0151 JAPAN
(046)387-1203
FAX: (046)387-1203
gen22-14@qf7.so-net.ne.jp
Ikushima, Michinobu   <M1 RT>
  2074 Nakashinden
  Ebina-Shi, Kanagawa-Ken
  243-0422 JAPAN
  (046)232-9888
  m.ikushima@tbz.t-com.ne.jp
Satoh, Iwao   <M1 OM>
  9111 Cedarwood Drive
  Pewee Valley, KY 40056
  iwaosatoh@gmail.com
  (502)210-0852
Seki, Nobuko   <M1 WC>
  Yamato City
  JAPAN   MSJA#8300
Yano, Fumitsuta   <M1 WC>
  424-4 Kamide, Fjinomiya-shi
  Shuizuika-ken   JAPAN
  (054)454-0313

OTHER CANDIDATES ON ROLL:

Suzuki, Temote   <M2>
  9-41-15-310 Honcho Kamitsuruma
  Sagamihara-shi, Kanagawa-ken
  228-0818 JAPAN
  timocsuzuki@gmail.com

OTHER CANDIDATES ON ROLL:

Inoh, Yuki   <M3>
  Tokyo Christian University
  3-301-5 Uchino Inzai-shi, Chiba
  270-1347 JAPAN
  (047)646-1141
  yuki_inoh0615@yahoo.co.jp
Wada, Ichiro   <M3>
  Tokyo Christian University
  3-301-5 Uchino Inzai-shi, Chiba
  270-1347 JAPAN
  (047)646-1141
  ichirowada@gmail.com

Missouri Presbytery
GREAT RIVERS SYNOD

	GENERAL	MEMBERSHIP			CHANGES				FINANCES				
	1.Church Number	2.Active	3.Total	4.Church School	5.Prof. of Faith	6.Gains	7.Losses	8.Children Baptized	9. OUR UNITED OUT-REACH	10. Total Out-Reach Giving	11. All Other Expenses	12. Total Income Received	13. Value Church Prop. 1=1000
	1	2	3	4	5	6	7	8	9	10	11	12	13
Bethel	4102	8	8	8	0	0	0	0	0	2,309	3,572	9,416	10
Elk Creek	4304	19	20	16	0	0	1	0	0	700	18,771	20,358	75
Greenfield	4104	5	7	8	3	3	0	0	1,661	2,675	36,671	3,489	100
Happy Home	4306	20	32	8	0	0	0	0	2,573	5,877	18,563	25,990	200
Harmony	4203	19	36	9	4	3	1	1	2,246	5,460	29,298	36,645	80
Hopewell*	4105	34	34	29	0	0	0	1	4,496	11,491	31,681	41,732	310
Lobb	4209	13	13	14	No Report Received			0	0	0	0	0	170
Mansfield	4308	54	73	30	0	9	6	0	0	0	0	0	75
Marshall	4210	95	195	40	3	13	6	0	11,118	53,030	114,060	111,177	900
Montrose	4107	2	17	0	No Report Received			0	0	0	0	0	32
New Hope (DeC)*	4309	15	15	11	0	0	9	0	0	3,597	16,924	27,148	60
Orange*	4108	39	39	47	2	1	0	0	0	4,836	74,829	69,713	546
Phillipsburg	4311	14	14	8	7	0	0	0	2,500	3,094	17,856	22,834	150
Pierson*	4312	10	13	9	0	0	6	0	938	18,623	5,539	18,368	150
Pleasant Grove	4109	8	59	0	0	0	1	0	293	418	2,797	2,930	30
Salem	4216	9	9	0	0	0	2	0	0	286	3,823	3,201	125
Seymour	4313	15	29	6	0	1	1	0	0	0	20,161	18,192	50
Shawnee Mound	4111	6	44	6	0	0	0	0	577	941	4,910	4,831	60
Spring Creek	4113	28	37	15	0	1	3	0	3,730	10,872	20,936	39,297	182
Springfield 1st	4314	76	159	38	0	6	9	2	5,060	23,087	75,135	92,302	1,500
Warrensburg	4115	61	72	26	1	6	2	1	1,875	4,548	38,974	49,908	275
White Oak Pond	4315	125	228	115	2	5	3	1	15,577	26,772	106,534	155,735	1,150
TOTALS	22	687	1,183	446	22	48	50	6	52,644	178,616	641,034	753,266	6,230

*Math error corrected. **Purged roll.

CHURCHES, PASTORS, AND CLERKS:

Bethel　　　　　　(2C)GRMI4102
  14621 Lawrence 1032 (mailing)
  Sarcoxie, MO 64862
  Crossroads Lawrence 1030 & Lawrence 2170 (physical)
  Wentworth, MO
  (417)285-6571　　　　　<Lawrence>
SS: Tim Steeley　　　　　<M3>
  PO Box 281
  Mt Vernon, MO 65712
  (417)466-4345
  tsteeley@swr5.k12.mo.us
CL: Lana Moore
  14621 Lawrence 1032
  Sarcoxie, MO 64862
  (417)285-6571
  lanajeanmoore@hotmail.com

Elk Creek　　　　　(4MEC)GRMI4304
  7423 County Road 3730 (mailing)
  Peace Valley, MO 65788
  US Highway 160 E (physical)
  West Plains, MO 65775
  (417)257-0983　　　　　<Howell>
  pastorbrown44@yahoo.com
PA: Dale M Brown　　　　<M1>
  HC 61 Box 4740
  West Plains, MO 65775
  (417)257-0983

pastorbrown44@yahoo.com
CL: Cindy Rasor
  7423 County Road 3730
  Peace Valley, MO 65788
  (417)256-7353
  rrasor@centurytel.net

Greenfield　　　　(4MC)GRMI4104
  423 Water Street (mailing)
  417 W Water Street (physical)
  Greenfield, MO 65661
  (　)　　　　　　　<Dade>
PA: John Ang　　　　　<M1>
  5843 S Farm Road 157
  Springfield, MO 65810
  (417)886-3487
  pastorcares@yahoo.com
CL: Debra Kay Bartlett
  423 Water Street
  Greenfield, MO 65661
  (417)637-5678
  debrakaybartlett@gmail.com

Happy Home　　　　(4C)GRMI4306
  510 S Newport Avenue (mailing)
  5604 State Highway ZZ (physical)
  Conway, MO 65632
  (　)　　　　　　<Webster>
SS: Linda Rodden　　　　<M1>
  363 Cornelison Street
  Lebanon, MO 65536

(417)588-2207
  linda.rodden@mercy.net
CL: Rex Luallin
  510 S Newport Avenue
  Conway, MO 65632
  (417)589-3804

Harmony　　　　(4WC)GRMI4203
  3508 Scott Street (mailing)
  Saint Joseph, MO 64507
  SE State Road Z (physical)
  San Antonio, MO 64443
  (816)279-0733　　　　<Buchanan>
  orvalschafer@aol.com
OD: Marion Cannon　　　　<M5>
  4248 SW State Route N
  Stewartsville, MO 64490
  (816)449-2437
  orvalschafer@aol.com
CL: Viola Schafer
  3508 Scott Street
  Saint Joseph, MO 64507
  (816)279-0733
  orvalschafer@aol.com

Hopewell　　　　(4EWC)GRMI4105
  248 NE 50th Road (mailing)
  273 NE 50th Road (physical)
  Lamar, MO 64759
  (417)682-2396　　　　<Barton>
  FAX: (417)682-3514

MISSOURI PRESBYTERY CONTINUED

parrishron@att.net
OD: George Haag   <M5>
  301 Gulf Street
  Lamar, MO 64759
  (417)682-3876
CL: Reba Simmons
  63 E Highway C
  Lamar, MO 64759
  (417)884-2810

___

Lobb   (4MC)GRMI4209
  1410 W Walnut Street(mailing)
  Flynn Road & 7-Highway (physical)
  Independence, MO 64050
  ( )   <Jackson>
OD: Paul J Petralie   <M5>
  1409 Granite Creek Drive
  Blue Springs, MO 64015
  (816)229-2804
CL: Pamela Markey
  1419 W Walnut Street
  Independence, MO 64050
  (816)254-1130
  pammarkey@sbcglobal.net

___

Mansfield   (4MEC)GRMI4308
  PO Box 673 (mailing)
  307 S Phelps Avenue (physical)
  Mansfield, MO 65704
  ( )   <Wright>
OD: S Larry Scott   <M5>
  2211 Airport Road
  Mansfield, MO 65704
  (417)924-4390
  revslscott@gmail.com
CL: Leon Veenstra
  4680 Highway F
  Hartville, MO 65667
  (417)741-7408
  veenstra@getgoin.net

___

Marshall   (4MWC)GRMI4210
  1000 S Miami
  Marshall, MO 65340
  (660)886-2402   <Saline>
  pastor_randy_shannon@yahoo.com
PA: Randy Shannon   <M1>
  30282 Highway H
  Marshall, MO 65340
  (660)886-9454
  pastor_randy.shannon@yahoo.com
CL: Karen L Guthrie
  1700 S Grant Avenue
  Marshall, MO 65340
  (660)886-5797
  kguthrie7878@gmail.com

___

Montrose   (4MWC)GRMI4107
  204 Kansas
  Montrose, MO 64770
  (816)693-4612   <Henry>
OD: Ron Beardon   <M5>
  214 E 3rd Street
  Appleton City, MO 64724
  (660)476-5322
CL: Kathy Collins
  1542 SW H Highway
  Montrose, MO 64770
  (660)693-4689

___

New Hope (DeC)   (4WC)GRMI4309

230 County Road 2630 (mailing)
Dent County Road 6200 (physical)
Salem, MO 65560
( )   <Dent>
CL: Fay J Haxton
  230 County Road 2630
  Salem, MO 65560
  (573)729-5524
  rafay@embarkmail.com

___

Orange   (4WC)GRMI4108
  109 Agnes (mailing)
  Crane, MO 65633
  15743 Highway K (physical)
  Aurora, MO 65605
  (417)678-5220   <Lawrence>
OD: Joe Wolven   <M5>
  1134 Carico Road
  Galena, MO 65656
  (417)357-4004
  lestesx5@centurytel.net
CL: Leah Estes
  109 Agnes
  Crane, MO 65633
  (417)723-8033
  lestesx5@centurytel.net

___

Phillipsburg   (4WC)GRMI4311
  11187 Cuba Road (mailing)
  Grovespring, MO 65662
  Grover Street (physical)
  Phillipsburg, MO 65722
  ( )   <Laclede>
CL: Cheryl Brown
  11187 Cuba Drive
  Grovespring, MO 65662
  (417)462-0813
  brownc@hartville.k12.mo.us

___

Pierson   (4C)GRMI4312
  12754 State Highway M (mailing)
  Billings, MO 65610
  45129 State Highway 413 (physical)
  Billings, MO 65610
  (417)369-2104   <Stone>
OD: George Van Hooser   <M5>
  1839 E Lark Street
  Springfield, MO 65804
CL: Kary Crumpley
  1513 Crumpley Drive
  Marionville, MO 65705
  (417)839-3552
  karycrumpley@gmail.com

___

Pleasant Grove   (4C)GRMI4109
  PO Box 97 (mailing)
  891 SE Y Highway (physical)
  Knob Noster, MO 65336
  ( )   <Johnson>
  gary.moore@reagan.com
CL:Gary M. Moore
  PO Box 97
  Knob Noster, MO 65336
  (816)830-9308
  gary.moore@reagan.com

___

Salem   (4WC)GRMI4216
  211 NW County Road OO (mailing)
  382 NW County Road H (physical)
  Warrensburg, MO 64093
  ( )   <Johnson>

CL: Anne Patrick
  211 NW County Road OO
  Warrensburg, MO 64093
  (660)747-8902
  apatrick52@hotmail.com

___

Seymour   (4C)GRMI4313
  PO Box 40 (mailing)
  222 Main Street (physical)
  Seymour, MO 65746
  (417)935-2235   <Webster>
OD: Sam Burt   <M5>
  102 E Summit Avenue
  Seymour, MO 65746
  ( )
CL: Ellen M Griechen
  PO Box 40
  Seymour, MO 65746
  (417)935-2235
  egriechen@webound.com

___

Shawnee Mound   (4WC)GRMI4111
  72 NW 1150 Road
  Chilhowee, MO 64733
  ( )   <Henry>
SS: Edward Harris   <M1 RT>
  517 Terrace Drive
  Warrensburg, MO 64093
  (660)747-7447
  ed517@earthlink.net
CL: Doris Hunter
  62 NW 1150 Road
  Chilhowee, MO 64733
  (660)885-3709
  dfhunter@embarqmail.com

___

Spring Creek   (4EWC)GRMI4113
  307 E 365th Road (mailing)
  Hwy 123 & Hwy A Junction (physical)
  Dunnegan, MO 65640
  (417)754-8498   <Polk>
OD: Scott Garner   <M5>
  1403 E Primrose Lane
  Republic, MO 65738
  (417)732-4218
CL: Gary M Roetto
  307 E 365th Road
  Dunnegan, MO 65640
  (417)754-8498

___

Springfield First   (4MWC)GRMI4314
  4216 S Charleston Avenue
  Springfield, MO 65804
  (417)883-4248   <Greene>
PA: Andrew (Andy) Eppard   <M1>
  1427 W McGee Street
  Springfield, MO 65807
  (417)862-6434
  reformedminister@yahoo.com
AP: Sang Hoon Park   <M1>
  3504 W Shawnee Drive
  Springfield, MO 65810
  (417)888-0442
CL: Carol Fare
  302 N Market Street
  Nixa, MO 65714
  (417)725-2775
  cjfare52@sbcglobal.net

___

Warrensburg   (4WC)GRMI4115
  201 Grover Street

MISSOURI PRESBYTERY CONTINUED

Warrensburg, MO 64093
(660)747-3021   <Johnson>
PA: Randy Crawshaw   <M1>
136 NE 1271 Road
Knob Noster, MO 65336
(660)563-5149
randy_crawshaw@yahoo.com
CL: Dana Moore
113 Larkin Street
Warrensburg, MO 64093
(660)747-8777
djmoore@iland.net

White Oak Pond   (4MWC)GRMI4315
16549 Highway 5 (mailing)
16551 Highway 5 (physical)
Lebanon, MO 65536
(417)532-5049   <Laclede>
wopcpc@whiteoakpond.org
PA: Terry Hansen   <M1>
16549 Highway 5
Lebanon, MO 65536
(417)533-8106
thansen@whiteoakpond.org
CL: Janie Lewis
1931 King James Drive
Lebanon, MO 65536
(417)664-6357

OTHERS ON MINISTERIAL ROLL:

Appling, John   <M1 WC>
1722 S Fairway Avenue
Springfield, MO 65804
(417)877-4643
pegblessings@sbcglobal.net
Appling, Peggy   <M1 WC>
1722 S Fairway
Springfield, Missouri 65804
(417)877-4643
pegblessings@sbcglobal.net

Bone, Leslie   <M1 M9>
16504 E George Franklin Drive
Independence, MO 64055
(816)373-6625
lesliebone@comcast.net
Campbell, Gordon C   <M1 WC>
1469 E Wayland Street
Springfield, MO 65804
(417)823-9567
gofor12@gmail.com
Cravens, Marvin L   <M1 RT>
604 N Hovis Street
Mountain Grove, MO 65711
(417)926-5778
Melson, Glenda   <M1 M9>
634 W Fremont Road
Lebanon, MO 65536
(417)588-2758
gmelson@fidnet.com
Plachte, Richard   <M1 RT>
615 Grover Street
Warrensburg, MO 64093
(660)441-4427
rap@aerobiz.org
Scott, Lisa   <M1 WC>
ADDRESS ON FILE
(816)332-0604
lascott1979@att.net
Wieland, Jack G, Jr   <M1 WC>
PO Box 116
Napoleon, MO 64074
(217)823-4331
jgwieland@hotmail.com

OTHER CANDIDATES ON ROLL:

Carr, Jill   <M3>
PO Box 1547
Lebanon, MO 65536
(417)532-6760
dig.micah.6.8@gmail.com
Gibbons, Jeannette   <M3>
6204 S Haynes Avenue
Ozark, MO 65721
(417)889-9862
Griffin, Adam   <M3>
23502 Clinton Road
Lebanon, MO 65536
(417)588-2522
plowboy3500@hotmail.com
Grounds, Clint   <M3>
918 Stonewall Apt C
McKenzie, TN 38201
(731)415-1422

Murfreesboro Presbytery
TENNESSEE SYNOD

GENERAL		MEMBERSHIP			CHANGES				FINANCES				
	1.Church Number	2.Active	3.Total	4.Church School	5.Prof. of Faith	6.Gains	7.Losses	8.Children Baptized	9. OUR UNITED OUT-REACH	10. Total Out-Reach Giving	11. All Other Expenses	12. Total Income Received	13. Value Church Prop. 1=1000
	1	2	3	4	5	6	7	8	9	10	11	12	13
Algood	7201	21	29	6	No Report Received			0	0	0	0	0	180
Banks	7202	15	15	16	1	1	9	0	0	2,435	29,965	43,517	344
Bates Hill*	7203	66	103	37	No Report Received			0	7,684	0	0	0	325
Beech Grove	7204	20	20	10	0	0	3	0	200	200	29,882	40,551	423
Belvidere	7205	7	47	7	0	0	0	0	0	427	5,672	6,743	60
Blues Hill	7207	32	32	19	0	0	1	0	2,755	6,923	24,148	30,541	80
Cloyd's	7208	107	107	83	No Report Received			0	4,500	0	0	0	1,500
Commerce	7209	62	62	40	5	8	1	1	1,000	5,721	77,035	63,488	425
Cookeville 1st	7210	558	632	260	17	30	13	3	51,046	100,832	349,168	550,000	4,570
Cowan	7211	59	58	52	1	2	11	1	11,055	14,992	88,425	107,393	1,100
Dibrell	7212	7	9	7	0	1	0	0	0	8,963	0	8,963	35
Dry Valley	7213	9	10	10	1	1	0	0	200	3,225	7,292	11,128	10
Goshen	7214	95	95	45	No Report Received			0	2,500	0	0	0	874
Gum Creek	7215	19	19	10	0	4	0	2	500	1,255	18,156	21,550	100
Harmony	7216	65	99	58	1	4	1	1	11,227	21,268	82,172	119,091	1,041
Hickory Valley*	7251	9	9	21	No Report Received			0	0	0	0	0	0
Hillsboro	7217	16	18	6	No Report Received			0	0	0	0	0	250
Jerusalem*	7218	40	132	24	0	3	0	1	7,832	18,614	60,914	78,299	275
Joywood	7250	25	36	12	No Report Received			0	0	0	0	0	375
LaGuardo	7219	25	25	3	No Report Received			0	0	0	0	0	150
Lebanon	7220	298	481	230	17	34	9	5	22,000	45,410	327,127	442,384	2,431
Liberty	7222	85	146	56	0	1	1	1	12,074	32,310	100,121	120,736	989
Livingston 1st	7223	10	42	3	0	0	2	0	0	0	10,315	11,464	250
LuzD.L.Naciones**	7252	9	20	23	12	12	40	0	0	0	37,957	12,457	0
Manchester	7224	104	233	75	1	1	3	1	18,356	25,785	146,537	183,557	1,300
McMinnville*	7225	12	14	9	1	2	0	0	911	907	19,749	22,191	225
Monteagle	7227	5	5	0	0	0	0	0	0	0	6,756	3,998	220
Mt. Carmel	7228	11	30	0	0	0	12	0	0	1,500	12,000	15,000	350
Mt. Hermon	7229	9	18	10	No Report Received			0	0	0	0	0	200
Mt. Tabor	7230	16	34	9	0	0	3	0	3,794	5,911	65,770	67,865	325
Mt. Vernon	7231	32	37	26	No Report Received			0	0	0	0	0	410
Murfreesboro	7232	149	419	108	4	6	4	0	12,064	30,191	235,670	283,000	3,234
New Hope	7233	50	66	29	1	2	2	2	0	5,177	114,220	109,000	1,022
Old Zion	7234	11	11	9	0	0	2	0	400	2,813	22,980	26,239	300
Owens Chapel	7235	55	65	19	2	7	20	0	1,000	5,236	91,595	107,706	210
Providence	7238	14	14	38	No Report Received			0	0	0	0	0	150
Rockvale	7239	86	150	58	5	18	0	0	1,700	4,946	81,457	86,403	1,308
Rocky Glade*	7240	68	76	54	3	11	0	0	3,500	11,000	47,500	54,000	300
Ruth Chapel	7241	2	5	0	No Report Received			0	0	0	0	0	3
Sewanee*	7242	22	28	12	No Report Received			0	2,155	0	0	0	225
Smithville	7243	158	248	120	6	9	16	0	24,616	41,700	202,300	248,000	1,700
Suggs Creek*	7244	9	9	6	No Report Received			0	250	0	0	0	120
Union Hill	7246	48	70	49	2	2	1	0	1,106	10,077	38,469	55,297	250
Watertown	7247	10	14	10	0	1	0	0	500	723	18,939	16,471	440
Winchester 1st	7249	480	915	450	4	21	14	4	56,042	97,361	537,410	569,512	3,500
TOTALS	45	3,010	4,707	2,129	84	181	168	22	260,967	505,902	2,889,701	3,516,544	31,579

*Math error corrected. **Purged roll.

MURFREESBORO PRESBYTERY CONTINUED

CHURCHES, PASTORS, AND CLERKS:

Algood   (4WC)TNMU7201
3617 Burton Cove Road (mailing)
Cookeville, TN 38506
Corner Harp & Main Street (physical)
Algood, TN 38506
( )   <Putnam>
PA: Richard Bond   <M1>
2425 Fisk Road, Lot 0
Cookeville, TN 38506
(931)526-7610
erbond@frontier.net
CL: Elaine Burton
3617 Burton Cove Road
Cookeville, TN 38506
(931)537-6661
e_burton@frontier.com

Banks   (4MWC)TNMU7202
846 Luttrell Avenue (mailing)
2933 Banks Pisgah Road (physical)
Smithville, TN 37166
( )   <DeKalb>
SS: Glenn Warren   <M3 OP>
903 W Old Hickory Boulevard
Madison, TN 37115
(615)426-8029
gwarren224@gmail.com
CL: Robert Joins
846 Lutrell Avenue
Smithville, TN 37166
(615)597-6366
b_joins@hotmail.com

Bates Hill   (4MEWC)TNMU7203
9957 Nashville Highway
Mc Minnville, TN 37110
(931)939-3235   <Warren>
cavecrew1979@gmail.com
SS: Blake Stephens   <M1>
9980 Nashville Highway
Mc Minnville, TN 37110
(931)939-2628
blsteph@edge.net
CL: William R Black
205 Ben Lomond Drive
Mc Minnville, TN 37110
(931)743-9809
cavecrew1979@gmail.com

Beech Grove   (4MC)TNMU7204
PO Box 26 (mailing)
471 Oscar Crowell Road (physical)
Beechgrove, TN 37018
(931)394-2387   <Coffee>
CL: Crystal B Brandon
269 French Brantley Road
Wartrace, TN 37183
(931)394-2387
no_tenn@hotmail.com

Belvidere   (4WC)TNMU7205
Walnut Hill Road
Belvidere, TN 37306
( )   <Franklin>
PA: Joseph H Butler   <M1>
56 Cline Ridge Road
Winchester, TN 37398
(931)224-8423

jhbu737@bellsouth.net
CL: Alton Smith
123 Post Oak Road
Belvidere, TN 37306
starsmith53@hotmail.com

Blues Hill   (4MWC)TNMU7207
7292 Short Mountain Road
Mc Minnville, TN 37110
( )   <Warren>
SS: Lyon Walkup   <M1>
225 Bertha Owen Road
Morrison, TN 37357
(931)607-3233
dirtroad@blomand.net
CL: Maria Mott
38 Winfree Road
Mc Minnville, TN 37110
(931)934-2425

Cloyd's   (4WC)TNMU7208
PO Box 277 (mailing)
595 West Division (physical)
Mt Juliet, TN 37121
(615)758-7434   <Wilson>
PA: Michael Reese   <M1>
404 Five Oaks Boulevard
Lebanon, TN 37087
(615)443-0457
michaelhreese@bellsouth.net
CL: Vickie Hibdon
7141 Lebanon Road
Mount Juliet, TN 37122
(615)444-6498

Commerce   (4WC)TNMU7209
351 Borum Road (mailing)
4260 S Commerce Road (physical)
Watertown, TN 37184
(615)237-9409   <Wilson>
crutchmckinwater@aol.com
SS: Denny C Shepard   <M1>
8514 Newsom Station Road
Nashville, TN 37221
(615)662-1114
CL: Jacki Crutcher
351 Borum Road
Watertown, TN 37184
(615)237-3310
crutchmckinwater@aol.com

Cookeville First   (4WC)TNMU7210
565 E 10th Street
Cookeville, TN 38501
(931)526-6585   <Putnam>
FAX: (931)528-2270
charles@cookevillecpchurch.org
PA: Charles McCaskey   <M1>
679 Canter Lane
Cookeville, TN 38501
(931)526-4885
charles@cookevillecpchurch.org
AP: Perryn Rice   <M1>
565 E 10th Street
Cookeville, TN 38501
(931)526-6585
perryn@cookevillecpchurch.org
AP: Richard Morgan   <M1>
191 Abby Lane
Baxter, TN 38544
(931)349-4474

icthuse@charter.net
CL: Lanny Knight
521 Chad Lane
Cookeville, TN 38501
(931)528-7800
alknight2@msn.com

Cowan   (4MC)TNMU7211
PO Box 277 (mailing)
206 Cowan Street W (physical)
Cowan, TN 37318
(931)967-7431   <Franklin>
cowancpchurch@bellsouth.net
PA: Richard "Rocky" Whray   <M1>
201 8th Avenue SE
Winchester, TN 37398
(931)636-4844
rocklex1017@att.net
CL: Nancy Wood
215 N Cedar Street
Winchester, TN 37398
(931)968-0893
woodnd@bellsouth.net

Dibrell   (4C)TNMU7212
128 Mitchell Road (mailing)
Mike Muncey Road (physical)
McMinnville, TN 37110
( )   <Warren>
CL: Jacqulyn S Boyd
128 Mitchell Road
McMinnville, TN 37110
(931)934-2088

Dry Valley   (4C)TNMU7213
5196 Shady Lane (mailing)
4415 Highway 70 N (physical)
Cookeville, TN 38506
( )   <Putnam>
PA: Richard Bond   <M1>
2425 Fisk Road Lot 0
Cookeville, TN 38506
(931)854-0979
CL: Janice F Bohannon
5196 Shady Lane
Cookeville, TN 38506
(931)528-7894
jandan80@gmail.com

Goshen   (4MWC)TNMU7214
PO Box 881 (mailing)
1262 Williams Cove Road (physical)
Winchester, TN 37398
(931)967-0245   <Franklin>
goshenchurch@cafes.net
PA: Steven Diamond   <M1>
1468 William Cove Road
Winchester, TN 37398
(931)636-7336
smdiam@hotmail.com
CL: Frances Hanger
251 Whipperwill Lane
Winchester, TN 37398
(931)967-7730
FAX: (931)967-7730
bhanger@bellsouth.net

Gum Creek   (4C)TNMU7215
1063 Franklin Heights Drive
Winchester, TN 37398
(931)967-6539   <Franklin>

MURFREESBORO PRESBYTERY CONTINUED

PA: Coyle Campbell   <M1>
186 Old Limestone Road
New Market, AL 35761
(256)379-4392
CL: Molly Perry
1063 Franklin Heights Drive
Winchester, TN 37398
(931)967-6539

_____
Harmony   (4MWC)TNMU7216
8891 Lynchburg Road
Winchester, TN 37398
(931)962-0842   <Franklin>
PA: Joseph H Butler, Jr   <M1>
261 Ridgefield Drive
Winchester, TN 37398
(931)224-8423
jhbu737@live.com
CL: Clare Wiseman
8555 Lynchburg Road
Winchester, TN 37398
(931)967-3932
wisrc9802@gmail.com

_____
Hickory Valley   (4U)TNMU7251
Sparta, TN 38583
(931)738-5812   <White>
PA: Richard Bond   <M1>
1528 Eastlake Drive
Cookeville, TN 38506
(931)526-7610
CL: Kathryn Adcock
1450 Oak Grove Road
Sparta, TN 38583
(931)761-5858
kadcock@blomand.net

_____
Hillsboro   (4EC)TNMU7217
PO Box 4
Hillsboro, TN 37342
(931)394-2415   <Coffee>
CL: Robert L Jenkins
68 Hillsboro Viola Road
Hillsboro, TN 37342
(931)596-2745

_____
Jerusalem   (4MWC)TNMU7218
7192 Mona Road
Murfreesboro, TN 37129
(615)895-8118   <Rutherford>
PA: Brent Wills   <M1>
4607 E Richmond Shop Road
Lebanon, TN 37090
(615)449-3258
bwills9185@yahoo.com
CL: Jimmy C Francis
4657 W Jefferson Pike
Murfreesboro, TN 37129
(615)893-8311
jcfjimmy@aol.com

_____
Joywood   (4MWC)TNMU7250
7120 Old Nashville Highway
Murfreesboro, TN 37129
(615)459-6518   <Rutherford>
joywoodchurch@yahoo.com
PA: Jeff Clark   <M1>
327 Haynes Haven Lane
Murfreesboro, TN 37129
(615)896-7733
jclark7733@aol.com

CL: Mark Tharp
5018 Willowbend Drive
Murfreesboro, TN 37128
(615)895-4772
markat52@comcast.net

_____
LaGuardo   (4WC)TNMU7219
7320 Highway 109 N
Lebanon, TN 37087
(615)444-0419   <Wilson>
OD: Gary Mraz   <M5>
8630 Highway 109 N
Lebanon, TN 37087
CL: Nancy Voight
500 Woods Ferry Pike
Lebanon, TN 37087

_____
Lebanon   (4MWC)TNMU7220
522 Castle Heights Avenue
Lebanon, TN 37087
(615)444-7453   <Wilson>
FAX: (615)444-6671
lcpsecretary@hotmail.com
PA: Kevin Medlin   <M1>
316 Dandelion Drive
Lebanon, TN 37087
(615)444-7453
FAX: (615)444-6671
kmedlin12@hotmail.com
AP: Drew Gray   <M1>
5610 Country Drive Apt 210
Nashville, TN 37211
(615)332-8360
CL: Kelly Hendricks
464 Locust Grove Road
Watertown, TN 37184
(615)443-0226
FAX: (615)444-6671

_____
Liberty   (4MWC)TNMU7222
317 Liberty Lane
McMinnville, TN 37110
(931)473-3813   <Warren>
libertycpc@gmail.com
PA: Marcus Hayes   <M1>
102 River Drive
McMinnville, TN 37110
(270)841-7576
marcus.hayes@att.net
CL: Patty Boyd
35 Lonsvale Drive
McMinnville, TN 37110
(931)473-8059
pattyboyd@blomand.net

_____
Livingston First   (4WC)TNMU7223
PO Box 393 (mailing)
110 Byrdstown Highway (physical)
Livingston, TN 38570
(931)823-5115   <Overton>
SS: Donald Ray Fossey, II   <M3>
328 Waterloo Road
Cookeville, TN 38506
(931)498-2149
dfossey@twlakes.net
CL: Helen Fossey
611 W 4th Street
Livingston, TN 38570
(931)823-9884

_____
Luz D L Naciones   (4F)TNMU7252

114 Northwood Lane
Mc Minnville, TN 37110
( )   <Warren>
PA: Jose Perez   <M1>
89 Northwood Lane Apt A102
Mc Minnville, TN 37110
(931)743-5585
jrp_rll@yahoo.com
CL: Session Clerk
114 Northwood Lane
Mc Minnville, TN 37110
(931)815-9502

_____
Manchester   (4MWEC)TNMU7224
838 McArthur Street
Manchester, TN 37355
(931)728-2975   <Coffee>
FAX: (931)728-2975
mancp@cafes.net
PA: Mark Barron   <M1>
836 McArthur Street
Manchester, TN 37355
(931)728-2975
FAX: (931)728-2975
mbarron@cafes.net
AP: Cardelia Howell Diamond   <M1>
834 McArthur Street
Manchester, TN 37355
(931)952-1122
revhd@tds.net
CL: Debbie Shelton
1255 M G England Road
Manchester, TN 37355
(931)728-9422
debbiebl@cafes.net

_____
McMinnville   (4MWC)TNMU7225
115 Peers Street
McMinnville, TN 37110
(931)474-4255   <Warren>
dwalhart@aol.com
PA: Daryl Alhart   <M1>
2187 Rutledge Ford Road
Decherd, TN 37324
(931)349-7104
dwalhart@aol.com
CL: Leota Watson
804 W Main Street
Mc Minnville, TN 37110
(931)473-7561
leotaw@blomand.net

_____
Monteagle   (4C)TNMU7227
PO Bos 243 (mailing)
343 College Street (physical)
Monteagle, TN 37356
( )   <Grundy>
PA: William F James   <M1>
2937 Arthur Drive
Murfreesboro, TN 37127
(615)653-1396
wimjim19@gmail.com
CL: Billie Faye Terrill
PO Box 243
Monteagle, TN 37356
(931)924-2787

_____
Mt Carmel   (4MEWC)TNMU7228
1484 Elora Road
Huntland, TN 37345
(931)469-7394   <Franklin>

MURFREESBORO PRESBYTERY CONTINUED

SS: B J Hancock   <M1 RT>
  103 W Cowan Street
  Cowan, TN 37318
  (931)967-8491
CL: Tina M Morrow
  714 Baxter Hollow Road
  Belvidere, TN 37306
  (931)967-3853
  ramtmm@netzero.net

Mt Hermon   (4MEWC)TNMU7229
  5544 Mt Hermon Road
  Cookeville, TN 38506
  ( )   <Putnam>
SS: Maury A Norman   <M1 OP>
  1750 Shipley Road
  Cookeville, TN 38501
  (931)526-1644
  maurynorman@yahoo.com
CL: Ruth Shubert
  6799 Cherry Creek Road
  Cookeville, TN 38506
  (931)526-5109

Mt Tabor   (4EC)TNMU7230
  3122 Donard Court (mailing)
  6000 Manchester Highway (physical)
  Murfreesboro, TN 37127
  (615)545-4695   <Rutherford>
  sheila.mcclain4695@gmail.com
PA: Brent Wills   <M1>
  4607 E Richmond Shop Road
  Lebanon, TN 37090
  (615)449-3258
  bwills9185@yahoo.com
CL: Sheila McClain
  3122 Donard Court
  Murfreesboro, TN 37128
  (615)545-4695
  sheila.mcclain4695@gmail.com

Mt Vernon   (4C)TNMU7231
  131 Hickory Hills Drive (mailing)
  Murfreesboro, TN 37128)
  11915 Mt Vernon Road (physical)
  Rockvale, TN 37153
  (615)890-9125   <Rutherford>
PA: Judy Taylor Sides   <M1>
  534 Bethany Circle
  Murfreesboro, TN 37128
  (615)895-1627
CL: Gregory L Sides
  534 Bethany Circle
  Murfreesboro, TN 37128
  (615)895-1627

Murfreesboro   (4MEWC)TNMU7232
  907 E Main Street
  Murfreesboro, TN 37130
  (615)893-6755   <Rutherford>
  FAX: (615)893-4553
  firstcp@comcast.net
PA: Christopher Warren   <M1>
  906 Prince Lane
  Murfreesboro, TN 37129
  (615)828-8719
  chris@murfreesborocpc.org
CL: Mary Healey
  2015 Red Mile Road
  Murfreesboro, TN 37127
  (615)896-6337

jomarhealey@comcast.net

New Hope   (4EWC)TNMU7233
  PO Box 1215 (mailing)
  7845 Coles Ferry Pike (physical)
  Lebanon, TN 37087
  (615)449-7020   <Wilson>
SS: Vernon Burrow   <M1 RT>
  707 Saratoga Drive
  Murfreesboro, TN 37130
  (615)406-6385
  vernonburrow@comcast.net
CL: Mary Ann Smith
  1600 Smith Road
  Lebanon, TN 37087
  (615)444-0102
  nwhpchrch0@gmail.com

Old Zion   (4C)TNMU7234
  395 Coventry Drive (mailing)
  Nashville, TN 37211
  7489 Old Kentucky Road (physical)
  Sparta, TN 38583
  ( )   <White>
PA: James A McGill   <M1>
  433 S Walnut Avenue
  Cookeville, TN 38501
  (931)526-6936
  jam7235@frontiernet.net
CL: Kay Armstrong
  268 Tulip Drive
  Sparta, TN 38583
  (615)406-3976

Owens Chapel   (4C)TNMU7235
  PO Box 532 (mailing)
  3058 Liberty Road (physical)
  Winchester, TN 37398
  (931)636-8076   <Franklin>
  ferguea9@gmail.com
PA: Elizabeth Ferguson   <M1>
  2251 Mansford Road
  Winchester, TN 37398
  (931)636-8076
  ferguea9@gmail.com
CL: Jimmy McKinney
  1310 Liberty Road
  Winchester, TN 37398
  (931)967-3679
  bigmacj37@comcast.net

Providence   (3C)TNMU7238
  c/o Pierce Dodson(mailing)
  106 Bartonwood Drive
  Lebanon, TN 37087
  Providence Road (physical)
  Hartsville, TN 37074
  ( )   <Trousdale>
CL: Session Clerk
  c/o Pierce Dodson(mailing)
  106 Bartonwood Drive
  Lebanon, TN 37087

Rockvale   (4MEWC)TNMU7239
  PO Box 67 (mailing)
  8769 Rockvale Road (physical)
  Rockvale, TN 37153
  (615)274-3143   <Rutherford>
PA: Joyce Merritt   <M1>
  3929 Snail Shell Cave Road
  Rockvale, TN 37153

(615)574-3047
CL: Martha A Lannom
  903 Sunset Avenue
  Murfreesboro, TN 37129
  (615)896-1348
  malannom@bellsouth.net

Rocky Glade   (4C)TNMU7240
  PO Box 8 (mailing)
  2017 Rocky Glade Road (physical)
  Eagleville, TN 37060
  ( )   <Rutherford>
PA: J. Tommy Jobe   <M1>
  PO Box 8
  Eagleville, TN 37060
  (615)776-7755
  cppreacher@united.net
CL: Bill Lamb
  425 River Eagleville Road
  Eagleville, TN 37060
  (615)274-2275
  billlamb1@bellsouth.net

Ruth Chapel   (2C)TNMU7241
  347 Windle Community Road (mailing)
  146 Windle Community Road (physical)
  Livingston, TN 38570
  ( )   <Overton>
SS: Donald Fossey II   <M3>
  328 Waterloo Road
  Cookeville, TN 38506
  (931)498-2149
  dfossey@twlakes.net
CL: Jo K Smith
  347 Windle Community Road
  Livingston, TN 38570
  (931)823-5916

Sewanee   (4WC)TNMU7242
  Box 11
  Sewanee, TN 37375
  (931)598-0766   <Franklin>
  smdiam@hotmail.com
PA: Steven Diamond   <M1>
  834 McArthur Street
  Manchester, TN 37355
  smdiam@hotmail.com
  (931)636-7336
CL: Paul E Mooney
  Box 11
  Sewanee, TN 37375
  (931)598-0766

Smithville   (4MWC)TNMU7243
  201 S College Street
  Smithville, TN 37166
  (615)597-4197   <DeKalb>
  FAX: (615)597-4397
  larrylgreen24@aol.com
PA: Larry Green   <M1>
  525 Dearman Street
  Smithville, TN 37166
  (615)597-5832
  larrylgreen24@aol.com
CL: Wesley A Rogers
  305 S College Street
  Smithville, TN 37166
  (615)597-5549
  wesrogers305@gmail.com

Suggs Creek   (4MWC)TNMU7244

MURFREESBORO PRESBYTERY CONTINUED

PO Box 234 (mailing)
Gladeville, TN 37071
405 Corinth Road (physical)
Mount Juliet, TN 37122
( )   <Wilson>
PA: James Diamond   <M1 M9>
PO Box 1220
Smyrna, TN 37167
(615)220-2341
FAX: (615)220-1077
james.diamond007@comcast.net
CL: Session Clerk
PO Box 234
Gladeville, TN 37071

_____

Union Hill   (4MWC)TNMU7246
235 Sykes Road
Brush Creek, TN 38547
(615)683-8327   <Smith>
brotherperry@msn.com
SS: Dennis Croslin   <M3>
165 Maple Street
Gordonsville, TN 38563
(615)934-2383
cro26110@hotmail.com
CL: Robin L Nixon
237 Temperance Hall Highway
Hickman, TN 38567
(615)418-5074
robinlpn@hotmail.com

_____

Watertown   (4WC)TNMU7247
510 W Main Street
Watertown, TN 37184
( )   <Wilson>
OD: Rodger McCann   <M5>
352 Winding River Lane
Sparta, TN 38563
(931)738-0352
CL: Emily Nix
305 Cornwell Avenue
Watertown, TN 37184
(615)237-3488
emilymckin_1@juno.com

_____

Winchester First   (4WC)TNMU7249
PO Box 176 (mailing)
200 2nd Avenue NW (physical)
Winchester, TN 37398
(931)967-2121   <Franklin>
FAX: (931)967-8444
wintncp@bellsouth.net
PA: Michael Clark   <M1>
338 Royal Oak Drive
Winchester, TN 37398
(931)967-2121
book_worm35@comcast.net
AP: Amber Clark   <M1>
338 Royal Oak Drive
Winchester, TN 37398
(931)967-2121
revamber@comcast.net
AP: Aaron Ferry   <M1>
PO Box 176
Winchester, TN 37398
(615)946-3078
amferry815@gmail.com
CL: Tom Mahler
PO Box 176

Winchester, TN 37398
twmahler@gmail.com

_____

OTHERS ON MINISTERIAL ROLL:

Benedict, Mary McCaskey   <M1 WC>
69 Lennox Court
Richmond Hill, GA 3132
(931)260-1422
marykat_61@hotmail.com
Clark, Jonathan   <M1 RT>
88 Woodcrest Drive
Winchester, TN 37398
(931)967-9613
FAX: (931)967-8444
clark3568@bellsouth.net
Estep, William   <M1 RT>
239 Skyline Drive
Harriman, TN 37748
(865)882-5114
Green, Harry   <M1 WC>
45 Wood Way
McMinnville, TN 37110
(931)815-9190
Hayes, Jennifer   <M1 WC>
102 River Drive
McMinnville, TN 37110
(205)533-1018
Jeffrey, Peter   <M1 WC>
61 Northwood Drive
McKenzie, TN 38201
(731)352-0792
jeffreyp@bethelu.edu
Johnson, Lanny   <M1 RT>
120 S Mill Street
Morrison, TN 37357
(931)212-1658
ljohnson37357@gmail.com
Labrada, Hector   <M1 WC>
74 Cumberland Drive
McMinnville, TN 37110
Logan, Jason   <M1 M8>
4895 Diggins Drive
Fort Meade, ND 20755
(410)305-8494
jason.b.logan@dix.army.mil
Malone, Michael   <M1 WC>
330 Holly Street
Johnson City, TN 37604
(865)692-2415
Martin, James W   <M1 WC>
1922 Battleground Drive
Murfreesboro, TN 37129
(615)896-4442
(615)859-1493
Matlock, Robert   <M1 RT>
156 Dovenshire Drive
Fairfield Glade, TN 38558
(921)210-0614
revbobm@msn.com
Nye, John   <M1 WC>
210 Crestview Drive
Mount Juliet, TN 37122
Oliver, Lisa   <M1 M9 OM>
110 Allen Drive
Hendersonville, TN 37075

(615)319-6466
Parks, Sam   <M1 WC>
138 Orchard Road Apt 16
Kingston, TN 37763
(423)949-3951
wsamparks@aol.com
Pittenger, Ronnie M   <M1 WC>
547 Southcrest Drive
Nashville, TN 37211
(615)832-8832
Salisbury, Rebecca   <M1 WC>
1033 Twin Oaks Drive
Murfreesboro, TN 37130
(615)410-7801
rebsalisbury@yahoo.com
Warren, Joy   <M1 WC>
907 W Main Street
Murfreesboro, TN 37129
(615)828-8719
revjoywarren@gmail.com
Wood, Bennie R   <M1 RT>
3697 S Mount Juliet Road
Hermitage, TN 37076
(615)449-8651

_____

OTHER LICENTIATES ON ROLL:

Mathis, B J   <M2>
675 Newt McKnight Road
McMinnville, TN 37110

_____

OTHER CANDIDATES ON ROLL:

Boggs, Barry   <M3>
1039 Johnnie Bud Lane
Cookeville, TN 38501
Cleek, Phillip   <M3>
188 Cleek Lane
Estill Springs, TN 37330
(931)967-2354
Gibson, Rachel   <M3>
2520 Cairo Bend Road
Lebanon, TN 37087
(615)453-2724
Heard, Robert   <M3>
527 Jack Thomas Drive
Manchester, TN 37355
(931)273-9687
Norton, Austin   <M3>
1498 Bradshaw Boulevard
Cookeville, TN 38506
(931)261-3260
Quevedo, Mariano   <M3>
289 Golf Club Lane
McMinnville, TN 37110
Whaley, Greg   <M3>
4970 Comstock Road
Chapel Hill, TN 37034
Wright, John   <M3>

Nashville Presbytery
TENNESSEE SYNOD

GENERAL		MEMBERSHIP			CHANGES				FINANCES				
	1.Church Number	2.Active	3.Total / 4.Church School		5.Prof. of Faith / 6.Gains		7.Losses	8.Children Baptized	9. OUR UNITED OUT-REACH	10. Total Out-Reach Giving	11. All Other Expenses	12. Total Income Received	13. Value Church Prop. 1=1000
	1	2	3	4	5	6	7	8	9	10	11	12	13
Arlington*	7311	24	42	22	0	0	2	0	0	7,185	36,860	79,909	403
Beech	7301	283	283	125	5	7	7	3	16,556	34,797	312,557	394,271	2,990
Bethel	7302	47	87	52	1	5	42	0	1,200	3,749	90,991	91,697	400
Brenthaven	7331	299	479	168	4	11	6	1	35,000	83,288	438,627	525,064	6,500
Brush Hill+*	7325	155	222	92	1	8	20	3	9,910	10,863	199,966	218,476	5,600
Calvary*	7342	25	25	0	0	6	0	0	250	550	54,591	56,878	416
Camp Ground*	7312	19	21	12	0	0	3	0	0	2,795	36,909	36,704	450
Cane Ridge*	7326	20	20	7	0	0	16	0	0	674	26,903	22,137	275
Charlotte+	7303	27	57	19	2	4	1	1	4,043	6,989	39,749	48,178	499
Clarksville	7304	261	261	159	1	12	11	0	38,057	53,408	359,792	415,063	2,500
Concord	7306	26	26	26	0	0	0	0	1,000	2,267	42,546	40,346	105
Cristo Vive	7314		No Report Received					0	0	0	0	0	0
Cumberland Valle	7307	29	45	20	1	1	0	0	2,841	5,498	22,867	28,423	250
Dickson	7308	338	397	148	4	6	3	4	12,000	32,300	169,064	223,889	1,500
Donelson	7327	53	117	65	6	12	5	3	2,000	7,553	65,953	76,951	1,650
Dry Fork	7309	25	19	0	0	4	8	0	1,500	4,774	12,884	12,624	75
Erin	7310	11	17	6	0	0	3	0	1,757	1,757	21,564	23,223	350
Goodlettsville	7328	346	346	310	7	21	6	2	1,025	7,665	527,582	542,546	3,500
Halls Creek	7313	54	54	42	0	0	0	0	0	6,029	25,175	44,019	350
Hendersonville*	7340	18	17	20	1	0	15	1	0	1,200	39,554	40,931	500
Liberty**	7315	54	54	55	3	0	54	0	3,469	8,723	114,577	98,435	600
Locust Grove*	7316	12	44	12	0	3	0	0	0	1,320	30,997	36,321	313
Madison 1st	7329	27	50	21	0	0	4	0	8,961	15,240	59,000	76,265	340
Mariah	7317	32	32	20	0	1	3	0	0	1,470	26,312	30,685	150
McAdoo	7318	48	48	25	4	4	2	1	2,000	8,621	115,680	100,314	646
Mt. Denson	7319	85	165	45	0	5	2	0	7,960	7,960	93,918	97,742	730
Mt. Liberty	7320	92	153	49	8	8	5	0	3,325	8,125	12,105	135,427	1,035
Mt. Sharon	7321	107	210	97	4	9	2	1	8,750	22,704	177,538	201,807	1,750
Mt. Sinai*	7330	11	11	0	3	2	8	0	0	510	13,338	14,962	300
Mt. View*	7322	73	73	16	2	2	0	0	0	2,759	0	49,690	350
New Hope	7337	7	7	12	No Report Received			0	0	0	0	0	52
New Providence	7305	33	33	15	2	0	0	0	0	1,475	42,371	46,774	700
Shiloh*	7338	41	71	18	7	0	1	4	500	53,877	53,745	120,687	850
St. Luke	7332	128	313	58	1	9	7	2	18,209	29,498	180,324	219,822	3,525
Sudanese	7341	36	48	9	No Report Received			0	0	0	0	0	24
The Connection	7335	26	26	10	1	2	1	2	1,200	3,476	9,332	53,864	1,250
Tusculum	7333	226	691	205	8	14	9	2	6,566	40,179	425,200	481,345	3,600
Waverly	7339	50	181	8	4	14	8	2	0	4,743	54,000	59,390	670
West Nashville	7334	124	398	110	1	2	6	4	18,570	34,658	305,047	269,332	3,250
TOTALS	39	3,272	5,143	2,078	81	172	260	36	206,649	518,679	4,237,618	5,014,191	48,448

*Math error corrected. **Purged roll.

NASHVILLE PRESBYTERY CONTINUED

CHURCHES, PASTORS, AND CLERKS:
_____

Arlington   (4WC)TNNA7311
PO Box 624 (mailing)
7 Knight Street (physical)
Erin, TN 37061
(931)289-3597   <Houston>
OD: Paul S Moody
600 Hurricane Loop
Tennessee Ridge, TN 37178
(931)721-3953
CL: Andrea Dillard
85 Victor Lane
Erin, TN 37061
(931)289-4004
adillard@workforceessentials.com
_____

Beech   (4MWC)TNNA7301
3216 Long Hollow Pike
Hendersonville, TN 37075
(615)824-3990   <Sumner>
FAX: (615)824-6507
office@beechcp.com
PA: Malcolm Patton   <M1>
921 Harris Drive
Gallatin, TN 37066
(615)452-5557
FAX: (615)824-6507
bpatton11@comcast.net
CL: Sarah Ezell
787 New Shackle Island Road
Hendersonville, TN 37075
(615)824-6815
sarahezell2@att.net
_____

Bethel   (4MC)TNNA7302
3375 Sango Road
Clarksville, TN 37043
(931)358-3295   <Montgomery>
PA: Stewart Salyer   <M1>
2211 Foxfire Road
Clarksville, TN 37043
(931)980-2829
stewart.salyer@gmail.com
CL: Gwen Conner
1853 Madison Street #15
Clarksville, TN 37043
(931)802-2442
gccon@charter.net
_____

Brenthaven   (4C)TNNA7331
516 Franklin Road
Brentwood, TN 37027
(615)373-4826   <Williamson>
FAX: (615)373-4869
secretary@brenthaven.org
PA: Kip J Rush   <M1>
513 Meadowlark Lane
Brentwood, TN 37027
(615)376-4563
pastor@brenthaven.org
CL: Christi Peppers
5008 Woodland Hills Drive
Brentwood, TN 37027
(615)376-9977
christi.peppers@gmail.com
_____

Brush Hill   (4MEWC)TNNA7325
3705 Brush Hill Road
Nashville, TN 37216

(615)227-2504   <Davidson>
FAX: (615)227-0039
bhcpc@birch.net
PA: Kenny Butcher   <M1>
4608 Cather Court
Nashville, TN 37214
(615)719-1887
bhpastor@birch.net
CL: Terri Peltier
403 Cunniff Parkway
Goodlettsville, TN 37072
(615)227-2504
tp1260@aol.com
_____

Calvary   (4C)TNNA7342
340 Ringgold Road
Clarksville, TN 37042
(931)645-9200   <Montgomery>
2ourchurch@gmail.com
SS: Choil Ma   <M1>
300 Ringgold Road Apt 503
Clarksville, TN 37042
(931)824-2443
choilma@yahoo.com
CL: Soonhe Jones
4630 Lylewood Road
Indian Mound, TN 37079
(931)920-1945
_____

Camp Ground   (4MWC)TNNA7312
88 Campground Road
Erin, TN 37061
(931)289-4605   <Houston>
LS: Terry Mathis   <M6>
88 Campground Road
Erin, TN 37061
(931)289-3602
ttmathis@peoplestel.net
CL: Patsy Mullins
6210 Highway 13
Erin, TN 37061
(931)289-3195
_____

Cane Ridge   (4EC)TNNA7326
6867 Burkitt Road (mailing)
13412 Old Hickory Boulevard (physical)
Cane Ridge, TN 37013
(615)941-8317   <Davidson>
FAX: (615)941-2985
gdunn6867@comcast.net
LS: Gregory (Greg) Dunn   <M6>
6867 Burkitt Road
Cane Ridge, TN 37013
(615)941-8317
FAX: (615)941-2985
gdunn6867@comast.net
CL: Eleanor Willett
145 Greenwood Drive
La Vergne, TN 37086
(615)793-5016
tuffyw9@comcast.net
_____

Charlotte   (4WC)TNNA7303
515 Mt Hebron Road (mailing)
3 Court Square (physical)
Charlotte, TN 37036
( )   <Dickson>
SS: Dean Guye   <M1>
2759 Highway 70 E
Dickson, TN 37055
(615)446-7687

deanjoy@att.net
CL: Eloise Jones
515 Mount Hebron Road
Charlotte, TN 37036
(615)789-5353
joneseloise515@bellsouth.net
_____

Clarksville   (4WC)TNNA7304
1410 Golf Club Lane
Clarksville, TN 37040
(931)648-0817   <Montgomery>
office@clarksvillecpc.com
PA: Stephen L Louder   <M1>
98 Gallant Court
Clarksville, TN 37043
(931)217-0369
pastorsteve@clarksvillecpc.com
AP: Paula Louder   <M1>
98 Gallant Court
Clarksville, TN 37043
(615)804-4809
paula.louder@cmcss.net
CL: Ashley Kettle
205 Bullock Drive
Clarksville, TN 37040
(931)624-8769
ashleykettle@gmail.com
_____

Concord   (4MC)TNNA7306
63 Gander Branch Road
Waverly, TN 37185
( )   <Humphreys>
OD: Tom Powell   <M5>
2826 Fenton Court
Clarksville, TN 37040
(931)648-2051
CL: Phyllis Webb
3571 Fire Tower Road
Erin, TN 37061
(931)289-4601
_____

Cristo Vive   (4C)TNNA7314
735 Argyle Avenue
Madison, TN 37115
(615)262-3134   <Davidson>
PA: Carlos Cinco   <M1>
611 Cheron Road
Madison, TN 37115
(615)262-3134
pastorcinco2020@gmail.com
CL: Session Clerk
735 Argyle Avenue
Madison, TN 37115
(615)262-3134
_____

Cumberland Valley   (4WC)TNNA7307
285 Cumberland Valley Road
Mc Ewen, TN 37101
(931)582-8050   <Houston>
CL: June R Hicks
1339 Highway 13 S
Waverly, TN 37185
(931)296-4284
_____

Dickson   (4WC)TNNA7308
500 Highway 70 E
Dickson, TN 37055
(615)446-8511   <Dickson>
FAX: (615)446-7827
office@cumberlandpresbyterian.org
PA: Robert D Truitt   <M1>

NASHVILLE PRESBYTERY CONTINUED

1238 Old East Side Road
Burns, TN 37029
(615)740-9180
FAX: (615)446-7827
rdtjct@aol.com
AP: Dean Guye   <M1>
2759 Highway 70 E
Dickson, TN 37055
(615)446-7687
deanjoy@att.net
CL: Mark Rolman
7106 Crestview Drive
Fairview, TN 37062
(615)740-9180
mdrolman@att.net

Donelson   (4WC)TNNA7327
2914 Lebanon Road
Nashville, TN 37214
(615)516-9427   <Davidson>
email@donelsoncpchurch.com
CL: Keith C Vanstone
3803 Plantation Drive
Hermitage, TN 37076
(615)210-5010
clerk@donelsoncpchurch.com

Dry Fork   (4C)TNNA7309
174 Dry Fork Creek Road (mailing)
1050 Dry Fork Creek Road (physical)
Bethpage, TN 37022
(615)841-3169   <Sumner>
PA: Patricia (Pat) Pickett   <M1 M9>
1460 Cheatham Dam Road
Ashland City, TN 37015
(615)792-4973
tovahtoo@aol.com
CL: Sue Carr
174 Dry Fork Creek Road
Bethpage, TN 37022
(615)841-3169
suekencarr@nctc.com

Erin   (4MWC)TNNA7310
PO Box 307 (mailing)
4793 E Main Street (physical)
Erin, TN 37061
( )   <Houston>
erincpchurch@gmail.com
SS: Timothy W Ferrell   <M1>
1850 Dunbar Road
Woodlawn, TN 37191
(931)920-2662
ferrelltw@aol.com
CL: Carolyn Zurawski
978 Scotts Chapel Road
Cumberland City, TN 37050
(931)827-3111

Goodlettsville   (4MWC)TNNA7328
226 South Main Street
Goodlettsville, TN 37072
(615)859-5888   <Davidson>
FAX: (615)859-8820
gcpc@comcast.net
PA: Tim Stutler   <M1>
1044 Mansker Farm Boulevard
Hendersonville, TN 37075
(615)859-5888
gcpctim@comcast.net
CL: Doug Newman

675 Windsor Green Boulevard
Goodlettsville, TN 37072
(615)400-4589
dougnewman@comcast.net

Halls Creek   (4EC)TNNA7313
3650 Perrywinkle Branch Road (mailing)
2803 Halls Creek Road (physical)
Waverly, TN 37185
(931)296-7758   <Humphreys>
SS: Gary Carlton   <M1>
108 Greenbrier Street
Dickson, TN 37055
(615)441-8963
gwcarlton@yahoo.com
CL: Jerry Binkley
3650 Perrywinkle Branch Road
Waverly, TN 37185
(931)296-3154
binkleys@hughes.net

Hendersonville   (4WC)TNNA7340
453 Walton Ferry Road
Hendersonville, TN 37075
(615)822-6091   <Sumner>
SS: David West   <M1 M9>
2027 Lucille Street
Lebanon, TN 37087
(217)732-7568
CL: Susan Wyatt
115 Elissa Drive
Hendersonville, TN 37075
(615)948-8242
FAX: (615)824-0195
susandwyatt@comcast.net

Liberty   (4MWC)TNNA7315
725 S Liberty Church Road
Clarksville, TN 37042
( )   <Montgomery>
PA: Ronald D Burgess   <M1>
1208 Redwood Lane
Clarksville, TN 37042
(931)906-2868
revron4@bellsouth.net
CL: Bob Del Giorno
1510 S Freestone Court
Clarksville, TN 37042
(931)647-1086
bodeno@charter.net

Locust Grove   (4WC)TNNA7316
3449 Locust Church Road
Cunningham, TN 37052
( )   <Montgomery>
SS: Timothy W Ferrell   <M1>
1850 Dunbar Road
Woodlawn, TN 37191
(931)920-2662
ferrelltw@aol.com
CL: Lawanda Black
3192 Budds Creek Road
Palmyra, TN 37142
(931)326-5298
jobee39@hughes.net

Madison First   (4MWC)TNNA7329
735 Argyle Avenue
Madison, TN 37115
(615)868-2888   <Davidson>
FAX: (615)868-2888

madisonfirst@yahoo.com
PA: Johnny Parish   <M1>
102 Trousdale Court
Hendersonville, TN 37075
(615)824-5842
johnnyparish@bellsouth.net
CL: Edith Marlin
112 Becker Avenue
Old Hickory, TN 37138
(615)847-4148
edithmarlin@live.com

Mariah   (4MWC)TNNA7317
43 Mariah Church Lane
Waverly, TN 37185
(931)296-5546   <Humphreys>
SS: Nathaniel Mathews   <M3>
1006 Woodland Drive
New Johnsonville, TN 37134
(931)209-6645
bro.nate-mathews@hotmail.com
CL: Debra Rogers
107 Truman Avenue
Waverly, TN 37185
(931)296-5101

McAdoo   (4WC)TNNA7318
3724 Ashland City Road
Clarksville, TN 37043
(931)362-3091   <Montgomery>
PA: Joe Vick   <M1>
6064 Old Hickory Boulevard
Whites Creek, TN 37189
(615)519-5249
joervick@gmail.com
CL: Sherry Jenkins
4253 Ashland City Road
Clarksville, TN 37043
(931)801-4020
tnweaver44@att.net

Mt Denson   (4MWC)TNNA7319
4558 Highway 161
Springfield, TN 37172
(615)384-3613   <Robertson>
PA: Andrew Ward   <M1>
407 Rose Hill Court
Goodlettsville, TN 37072
(615)456-9136
andrewbward@aol.com
CL: Karen C Sweatt
4946 Minnis Road
Springfield, TN 37172
(615)944-5218
kcsweatt@hotmail.com

Mt Liberty   (4MWC)TNNA7320
3655 Highway 49 E
Charlotte, TN 37036
(615)789-5916   <Dickson>
PA: Don Winn   <M1>
3655 Highway 49 E
Charlotte, TN 37036
(615)789-5916
dwinn@davidsonacademy.com
CL: Cindy Simpson
3378 Highway 49 E
Charlotte, TN 37036
(615)945-0010
cindyrsimpson@hotmail.com

NASHVILLE PRESBYTERY CONTINUED

Mt Sharon   (4MWC)TNNA7321
4634 Mount Sharon Road
Greenbrier, TN 37073
(615)384-8569   <Robertson>
pastor@mtsharoncpchurch.org
PA: Jason Mikel   <M1>
4630 Mt Sharon Road
Greenbrier, TN 37073
(615)243-8938
jasonemikel@gmail.com
AP: Fred Schott, Jr   <M1 RT>
606 Taylor Trail
Springfield, TN 37172
(615)384-8572
fws195@aol.com
CL: James D Jordan
2100 W End Avenue Ste 1150
Nashville, TN 37203
(615)329-2100
FAX: (615)329-2187
jdjordan@gjplaw.com

_____

Mt Sinai   (4WC)TNNA7330
3738 Hydes Ferry Road
Nashville, TN 37218
(615)586-7886   <Davidson>
OD: David Lomax   <M5>
1501 Robert Cartwright Drive
Goodlettsville, TN 37072
(615)753-2493
lomaxdavid53@yahoo.com
CL: Katherine B Pleas
507 Glen Echo Place
Nashville, TN 37215
(615)298-2625
pleas5@hotmail.com

_____

Mt View   (4C)TNNA7322
2359 Leatherwood Road (mailing)
Stewart, TN 37175
282 Hickman Creek Road (physical)
Dover, TN 37058
(931)217-0893   <Stewart>
mvcpchurch@gmail.com
PA: Ronald D Burgess   <M1>
1208 Redwood Lane
Clarksville, TN 37042
(931)906-2868
revron4@bellsouth.net
CL: Gail Ross
2359 Leatherwood Road
Stewart, TN 37175
(931)220-4989

_____

New Hope   (4C)TNNA7337
c/o Sharon Cook (mailing)
8009 White Oak Road
Stewart, TN 37175
60 New Hope Road (physical)
Stewart, TN 37175
( )   <Houston>
LS: G Ray Mayo   <M6>
3019 Lights Chapel Road
Greenbrier, TN 37073
(615)643-4948
CL: Sharon E Cook
8009 White Oak Road
Stewart, TN 37175
(931)721-2513
ricsha55@yahoo.com

_____

New Providence   (4MWC)TNNA7305
1307 Fort Campbell Boulevard
Clarksville, TN 37042
(931)647-4455   <Montgomery>
CL: Jeane D Morgan
60 Bel Air Boulevard
Clarksville, TN 37042
(931)647-5503

_____

Shiloh   (4C)TNNA7338
4812 Shiloh-Canaan Road
Palmyra, TN 37142
(931)387-4198   <Montgomery>
greg1013@aol.com
PA: Gregory Jones   <M1>
4808 Shiloh Canaan Road
Palmyra, TN 37142
(931)249-9512
greg1013@aol.com
CL: Judi Moore
2010 Old Harmony Church Road
Adams, TN 37010
(615)505-5206

_____

St Luke   (4MWC)TNNA7332
901 W Old Hickory Boulevard
Madison, TN 37115
(615)868-1982   <Davidson>
stlukecpchurch@gmail.com
PA: Dwayne Tyus   <M1>
901 W Old Hickory Boulevard
Madison, TN 37115
(615)720-2564
dwayne.tyus@gmail.com
CL: Angie Pinson
901 W Old Hickory Boulevard
Madison, TN 37115
(615)337-7311
stlukecpchurch@gmail.com

_____

Sudanese   (ARF)TNNA7341
c/o First UMC (mailing)
149 W Main Street
407 Owen Drive (physical)
Gallatin, TN 37066
(615)585-2842   <Sumner>
PA: Jock Tut Paleak   <M1>
614 N Water Street Apt #623
Gallatin, TN 37066
(615)585-2842
CL: John Tiang Ping
49 Millwood Drive
Nashville, TN 37217
(615)365-3274

_____

The Connection   (4WC)TNNA7335
(previously named West Side)
215 Bellevue Road
Nashville, TN 37221
(615)646-4030   <Davidson>
PA: Roger Patton Jr   <M1>
7217 Belle Chasse Drive
Nashville, TN 37221
(615)673-8108
rogerlpatton@att.net
CL: Session Clerk
215 Bellevue Road
Nashville, TN 37221

_____

Tusculum   (4MWC)TNNA7333
477 McMurray Drive

Nashville, TN 37211
(615)833-0742   <Davidson>
tusculumchurch@gmail.com
PA: Raymond De Vries   <M1>
2080 Stanford Village Drive
Antioch, TN 37013
(615)332-3587
ray.devries@comcast.net
CL: Anita Ausenbaugh
131 Antioch Pike
Nashville, TN 37211
(615)833-0579
nitaflower@aol.com

_____

Waverly   (4MWC)TNNA7339
109 N Church Street
Waverly, TN 37185
(931)296-3232   <Humphreys>
FAX: (931)296-3232
waverlycpc@att.net
SS: Glenn Warren   <M3 ST>
116 Cedar Hill Drive
Waverly, TN 37185
(931)209-5431
gwarren224@gmail.com
CL: Larry Cochran
581 Wisteria Lane
Waverly, TN 37185
(931)296-4450
cochran@hughes.net

_____

West Nashville   (4MWC)TNNA7334
6849 Charlotte Pike
Nashville, TN 37209
(615)352-2800   <Davidson>
FAX: (615)352-2801
info@wncp.org
PA: Rickey Page   <M1>
736 Rodney Drive
Nashville, TN 37205
(615)353-7850
FAX: (615)352-2801
rickey.page@wncp.org
CL: Barbara Smith
7428 George Gains Road
Nashville, TN 37221
(615)646-1307
grannyb7428@att.net

_____

OTHERS ON MINISTERIAL ROLL:

Acuff, David   <M1 M8>
4969 Quail Lane
Columbia, SC 29206
(803)727-3910
david.acuff@us.army.mil
Bane, Ted   <M1 WC>
903 W Old Hickory Boulevard
Madison, TN 37115
(615)975-9343
tedjan95@aol.com
Baranoski, Timothy   <M1 M8>
8040 Starz Loop
Killeen, TX 76544
(615)731-0138
Bennett, Alfred J   <M1 RT>
7286 Nolensville Road
Nolensville, TN 37135
(615)776-5181
Cadenbach, Mark   <M1 OM>
PO Box 66

NASHVILLE PRESBYTERY CONTINUED

Westfield, IA 51062
Cook, Lisa   <M1 M9>
  4101 Dalemere Court
  Nashville, TN 37207
  (615)830-6217
  tgoose@comcast.net
Corbin, William   <M1 PR>
  7300 N Lamar Road
  Mount Juliet, TN 37122
  (615)459-8998
  raven.rest@comcast.net
Duke, Michael E   <M1 WC>
  106 Friar Tuck Drive
  Dickson, TN 37055
  (615)446-6515
Dumas, Byron   <M1 OM>
  1775 Theresa Drive
  Clarksville, TN 37043
  (931)552-8772
  bdumas7346@aol.com
Earheart-Brown, Daniel   <M1 PR>
  866 N McLean
  Memphis, TN 38107
  jebrown@memphisseminary.edu
  (901)278-0367
Freeman, Jesse L, Jr   <M1 WC>
  270 Eastside Road
  Burns, TN 37029
  (615)441-6527
  mptc@bellsouth.net
Goodwill, James L   <M1 RT>
  205 S English Hill Lane
  Hillsborough, NC 27278
  (704)526-8729
  jim@jimgoodwill.com
Gough, Ernest E   <M1 WC>
  8366 Highway 70
  Nashville, TN 37221
  (615)646-4372
  eegough@bellsouth.net
Hurley, E C   <M1 WC>
  704 Rainswood Court
  Clarksville, TN 37043
  (931)321-8691
  FAX: (931)645-7772
  hurleyec@gmail.com
Miller, Carol   <M1 WC>
  1022 Cedar Creek Road
  Vanleer, TN 37181
  (615)763-0742
  cmiller109@juno.com
Norton, Kitty   <M1 WC>
  251 Westchase Drive
  Nashville, TN 37205
  (615)584-1464
  kitty.a.norton@vanderbilt.edu
Parrish, Steven   <M1 PR>
  4610 Dunn Avenue
  Memphis, TN 38117
  (901)743-9545
  sparrish@memphisseminary.edu
Polacek, Fred E   <M1 WC>
  907 Graham Drive
  Old Hickory, TN 37138
  (615)754-5328
  nashvillepresb.sc.treasurer@gmail.com
Rippy, James G   <M1 WC>
  442 Trina Street
  Gallatin, TN 37066
  (615)681-7086
  lrippy@live.com

Roddy, Lowell G   <M1 RT>
  2583 Hedgerow Lane
  Clarksville, TN 37043
  (931)368-1081
  FAX: (931)221-1032
  lgroddy@yahoo.com
Shepherd, Sandra   <M1 WC>
  525 Summit Oaks Court
  Nashville, TN 37221
  (256)608-8701
  woolywagon@gmail.com
Sims, Edward G   <M1 RT>
  2161 N Meadow Drive
  Clarksville, TN 37043
  (931)206-5759
  simseg@aol.com
Smith, Billy T   <M1 HR>
  49 Abby Lynn Circle
  Clarksville, TN 37043
  (931)368-0424
Smith, John Adam   <M1 WC>
  916 Allen Road
  Nashville, TN 37214
  (573)453-8455
  john.a.smith.81@gmail.com
Stefan, Gregory   <M1 WC>
  1153 Letort Road
  Conestoga, PA 17516
  (931)296-5291
  pastorstefan@att.net
Stovall, Jeff   <M1 WC>
  2829 Trelawny Drive
  Clarksville, TN 37043
  (931)993-6104
  jeffstovall@juno.com
Tabor, Don M   <M1 RT>
  9611 Mitchell Place
  Brentwood, TN 37027
  (615)776-7292
  FAX: (615)373-3356
  dontabor@comcast.net
Todd, Virgil H   <M1 HR>
  3095 E Glengarry Road
  Memphis, TN 38128
  (901)358-4336
Varner, Susan   <M1 M9>
  2766 N Rockcreek Parkway
  Cordova, TN 38016
  (901)371-1249
  smvarner76@yahoo.com
Whitworth, Gary W   <M1 RT>
  1706 Old Hickory Boulevard
  Brentwood, TN 37027
  (270)525-6311
  garywwhitworth@att.net

OTHER LICENTIATES ON ROLL:

Jones, Steve   <M2 ST>
  PO Box 368
  Burns, TN 37029
  (615)441-6159
Stowell, Andrew   <M2>
  2998 Trough Springs Road
  Clarksville, TN 37043
  andrewstowellcft@gmail.com
Wheelbarger, J J   <M2>
  PO Box 504
  Joelton, TN 37080
  (615)876-6948
  jjwheelbarger@aol.com

OTHER CANDIDATES ON ROLL:

Adams, Hunter   <M3>
  603 Red Fox Court
  Burns, TN 37029
  (615)943-7862
Cassell, C J   <M3 ST>
  825 Aimes Court
  Nashville, TN 37221
  (615)594-2693
  n4cjc@comcast.net
Chall-Hutchinson, Deborah   <M3>
  190 Ussery Road
  Clarksville, TN 37043
  (931)905-1671
  challhut@gmail.com
Stevens, Brittany   <M3>
  606 Huntington Parkway
  Nashville, TN 37211
  (615)719-3362
  bstevens5@my.apsu.edu
Wilson, Melissa   <M3 ST>
  107 Hillwood Drive
  Dickson, TN 37055
  (615)446-7523
  milzwilz@comcast.net
Young, Taylor   <M3>
  255 Willard Drive
  Nashville, TN 37211
  (615)319-8294
  brandontayloryoung@yahoo.com

North Central Presbytery
MIDWEST SYNOD

	GENERAL		MEMBERSHIP			CHANGES				FINANCES			
	1.Church Number	2.Active	3.Total	4.Church School	5.Prof. of Faith	6.Gains	7.Losses	8.Children Baptized	9. OUR UNITED OUT-REACH	10. Total Out-Reach Giving	11. All Other Expenses	12. Total Income Received	13. Value Church Prop. 1=1000
	1	2	3	4	5	6	7	8	9	10	11	12	13
Bethany	5401	115	345	105	19	19	4	0	15,465	47,645	129,796	155,539	560
Burnt Prairie	5102	16	34	6	No Report Received			0	0	0	0	0	63
Campground	5402	13	15	15	No Report Received			0	1,350	0	0	0	50
Casey	5201	20	37	13	9	9	2	0	0	6,961	32,296	33,455	60
Christ	5305	8	11	7	No Report Received			0	693	0	0	0	150
Comunidad	5212	25	25	19	No Report Received			0	1,840	0	0	0	0
Cumb. Chapel	5104	7	7	5	0	0	0	0	0	14,585	9,735	23,491	4
Ebenezer	5203	38	38	30	No Report Received			0	3,780	0	0	0	1,000
Elm River	5107	49	49	71	2	4	7	1	6,522	13,100	39,650	67,350	235
Fairfield	5108	139	317	61	3	3	1	1	1,000	39,190	172,828	218,039	1,000
Faith	5501	6	14	4	0	0	1	0	4,703	7,153	32,830	51,800	500
Fullerton	5404	28	28	21	0	0	0	0	1,951	4,473	22,287	27,172	50
Georgetown*	5204	27	78	24	3	0	2	0	3,571	3,571	32,345	35,706	111
Good Prospect**	5205	91	91	97	3	0	67	0	8,007	45,158	64,486	114,341	1,100
Grace	5502	12	29	16	No Report Received			0	159	0	0	0	245
Knights Chapel	5306	29	36	38	No Report Received			0	0	0	0	0	100
Lebanon North	5113	71	161	64	No Report Received			0	0	0	0	0	200
Lebanon South	5114				No Report Received			0	0	0	0	0	0
Lincoln 1st*	5405	39	91	25	No Report Received			0	5,400	0	0	0	575
Monroe City**	5307	8	8	0	0	0	11	0	0	1,414	29,399	29,192	200
Morningside	5304	58	80	21	0	0	3	0	1,000	0	0	0	1,600
Mt. Gilead	5406	29	49	42	0	0	0	0	1,000	3,886	18,821	23,302	145
Mt. Olivet	5308	14	28	8	0	0	0	0	438	2,001	15,759	19,769	75
Mt. Oval	5116	6	6	10	No Report Received			0	0	0	0	0	10
New Hope	5208	54	109	49	1	2	0	0	7,412	19,852	63,416	81,069	400
Oak Grove*	5120	5	5	0	CLOSED 2013			0	0	0	0	0	45
Pleasant Grove	5210	15	33	25	0	2	11	0	0	22,859	12,657	33,653	190
Shiloh	5409	28	101	26	1	3	0	0	1,000	7,470	18,965	40,099	310
Shinar*	5410	31	38	0	3	5	0	5	0	961	25,705	26,939	237
Spring Hill	5411	5	5	3	No Report Received			0	0	0	0	0	379
Union North	5124	30	26	23	1	3	4	0	3,946	14,542	34,118	42,775	60
United	5119	52	106	30	No Report Received			0	500	0	0	0	790
Willow Creek	5211	76	100	100	3	11	5	2	9,970	24,294	81,305	103,240	1,000
TOTALS	33	1,144	2,100	958	48	61	118	9	79,707	279,115	836,398	1,126,931	11,444

*Math error corrected. **Purged roll.

NORTH CENTRAL PRESBYTERY CONTINUED

CHURCHES, PASTORS, AND CLERKS:

Bethany   (4MWC)MINC5401
  PO Box 384 (mailing)
  219 S Lincoln Street (physical)
  Bethany, IL 61914
  (217)665-3034   <Moultrie>
  bethanycpc@yahoo.com
  PA: D Kevin Vanderlaan   <M1>
  12 Willow Street
  Bethany, IL 61914
  (217)620-2723
  pastorkevin2@gmail.com
  CL: Dean McReynolds
  399 County Road 1600 N
  Bethany, IL 61914
  (217)665-3420
  wdeanmcreynolds@yahoo.com

Burnt Prairie   (4MWC)MINC5102
  RR 3 Box 947 (mailing)
  Fairfield, IL 62837
  Church Street (physical)
  Burnt Prairie, IL 62820
  (618)925-1185   <White>
  LS: Scott D Smothers   <M6>
  RR 5 Box 573
  Fairfield, IL 62837
  (618)842-6009
  lsmothers@myfrontiermail.com
  CL: Andy Pottorff
  RR 3 Box 947
  Fairfield, IL 62837
  (618)925-1185
  andypottorff@yahoo.com

Campground   (4WEC)MINC5402
  1497 Hookdale Avenue (mailing)
  Route 4 (physical)
  Greenville, IL 62246
  (618)664-1547   <Bond>
  CL: Rodney Reavis
  1497 Hookdale Avenue
  Greenville, IL 62246
  (618)664-1547
  rcreavis@yahoo.com

Casey   (4C)MINC5201
  PO Box 21 (mailing)
  16 N Central (physical)
  Casey, IL 62420
  (217)932-5404   <Clark>
  OD: Ron Juenger   <M5>
  1258 Willow Street
  Neoga, IL 62447
  (217)663-0704
  CL: Mary Gard
  7810 N 400th Street
  Casey, IL 62420
  (217)932-2971
  thetoymaker@wildblue.net

Christ   (4MC)MINC5305
  6140 S Meridian
  Indianapolis, IN 46217
  (317)787-9585   <Marion>
  CL: Paula Price
  892 Geagan Street
  Greenwood, IN 46143
  (317)709-8138

Comunidad Cristina   (4F)MINC5212
  1714 S 4th Avenue (mailing)
  Maywood, IL 60153
  15N562 Vista Lane (physical)
  Dundee, IL 60118
  (708)223-2185   <Cook>
  pastorccc@clear.net
  SS: Julio Roman   <M3>
  1714 S 4th Avenue
  Maywood, IL 60153
  (312)714-6960
  pastorccc@clear.net
  CL: Noel Taveras
  809 Lexington Circle
  Hanover Park, IL 60133
  (630)965-7113
  cololo809@yahoo.com

Cumberland Chapel   (4C)MINC5104
  1075 County Road 2400E (mailing)
  Route 2 CR 1300 N, CR 1200 E (physical)
  Fairfield, IL 62837
  ( )   <Wayne>
  PA: J B Gates   <M1>
  PO Box 289
  Enfield, IL 62835
  (618)963-2306
  rjjbgate@hamiltoncom.net
  CL: Ronald E Huffman
  1075 County Road 2400E
  Fairfield, IL 62837
  (618)842-9518
  huffmanrj@hotmail.com

Ebenezer   (4WF)MINC5203
  1941 W Belmont Avenue
  Chicago, IL 60657
  (773)528-8218   <Cook>
  PA: Eduardo Montoya   <M1>
  270 Windsor Drive
  Roselle, IL 60172
  (630)980-1577
  edmontoya@hotmail.com
  CL: Samuel Alvarez
  3740 W Leland Avenue
  Chicago, IL 60625
  (773)509-9165

Elm River   (4EC)MINC5107
  2212 County Highway 2 (mailing)
  2250 County Highway 2 (physical)
  Cisne, IL 62823
  ( )   <Wayne>
  SS: Ralph Blevins   <M1>
  1623 County Road 2375 E
  Geff, IL 62842
  (618)854-2494
  pastorreblevins@gmail.com
  CL: Jack Enlow
  2212 County Highway 2
  Cisne, IL 62823
  (618)854-2492
  enlow@wabash.net

Fairfield   (4MEWC)MINC5108
  1700 W Delaware
  Fairfield, IL 62837
  (618)847-5281   <Wayne>
  FAX: (618)842-2608
  PA: Jeff Biggs   <M1>

  1504 Cumberland Drive
  Fairfield, IL 62837
  (618)842-2219
  jeffbiggsonline@gmail.com
  CL: Kevan Stum
  15 Brock Lane
  Fairfield, IL 62837
  (618)842-2705

Faith   (4C)MINC5501
  20301 E Ten Mile Road
  St Clair Shores, MI 48080
  (586)775-1524   <Macomb>
  CL: Christopher D McMacken
  20396 Erben Street
  St Clair Shores, MI 48081
  (586)771-7855
  cmcmacken@itctransco.com

Fullerton   (4WC)MINC5404
  1105 E Allen Street (mailing)
  Route 48 (physical)
  Farmer City, IL 61848
  ( )   <DeWitt>
  SS: Diane Dill   <Advisory Mem>
  1105 N State Street Apt E7
  Lincoln, IL 62656
  (217)617-4400
  diedremarie@live.com
  CL: Duane Runyon
  1105 E Allen Street
  Farmer City, IL 61848
  (309)825-3324
  dprunyon@yahoo.com

Georgetown   (4EWC)MINC5204
  201 Frazier Street
  Georgetown, IL 61846
  (217)662-6988   <Vermilion>
  CL: Stephen K Hughes
  1011 E 14th Street
  Georgetown, IL 61846
  (217)662-6988
  hughesst@sbcglobal.net

Good Prospect   (4MWC)MINC5205
  PO Box 5 (mailing)
  301 E Trilla Road (physical)
  Trilla, IL 62469
  (217)234-8529   <Coles>
  trillacp@yahoo.com
  CL: Jedd Tolen
  PO Box 8
  Trilla, IL 62469
  trillatolens@gmail.com

Grace   (4C)MINC5502
  1122 Harrison Boulevard
  Lincoln Park, MI 48146
  (313)381-3456   <Wayne>
  PA: Roger Dallwig   <M1>
  1661 Hickory Lane
  Corydon, IN 47112
  (812)705-5071
  rcd129@hotmail.com
  CL: Dorinda Boyer
  21625 Knights Lane
  Brownstown, MI 48183
  (734)675-7322

Knights Chapel   (4WC)MINC5306

NORTH CENTRAL PRESBYTERY CONTINUED

1285 S County Road 375 W
Petersburg, IN 47567
( )   <Pike>
CL: Janet Church
5541 W County Road 100 S
Petersburg, IN 47567
(812)749-3242

Lebanon North   (4C)MINC5113
Route 5
Fairfield, IL 62837
(618)842-5205
FAX: (618)842-5205   <Wayne>
PA: J C McDuffie   <M1>
RR 3 Box 574
Fairfield, IL 62837
(618)842-5624
mactrapper4@frontier.com
CL: De Young
107 W King Street
Fairfield, IL 62837
(618)516-1736

Lebanon South   (4C)MINC5114
Route 3
Galatia, IL 62935
( )   <Saline>
OD: Robert D Craig   <M5>
46030 Sunset Drive
Bay Minette, AL 36507
CL: James Patterson
RR 2
Galatia, IL 62935
(618)268-4471

Lincoln First   (4MEWC)MINC5405
PO Box 596 (mailing)
110 Broadway (physical)
Lincoln, IL 62656
(217)732-7568   <Logan>
PA: Steven Blaum   <M1>
184 900 Street
Middletown, IL 62666
(217)871-3339
strab2010@yahoo.com
CL: Ronald (Ron) Hubbard
330 3rd Street
Lincoln, IL 62656
(217)871-5453
rehubb1@gmail.com

Monroe City   (4MWC)MINC5307
PO Box 167 (mailing)
8th & Cleveland Streets (physical)
Monroe City, IN 47557
(812)743-5171   <Knox>
FAX: (812)743-5171
PA: David Parman   <M1>
5034 S Monroe School Road
Monroe City, IN 47557
(812)743-2646
FAX: (812)743-5171
CL: Marjorie Vories
PO Box 167
Monroe City, IN 47557
(812)743-5286
FAX: (812)743-5171

Morningside   (4WC)MINC5304
8419 Newburgh Road

Evansville, IN 47715
(812)473-4700   <Vanderburgh>
FAX: (812)473-4765
morningsidechurch@sbcglobal.net
PA: James Messer   <M1 M8>
3653 Old Madisonville Road
Henderson, KY 42420
(270)827-0711
jcmess@hotmail.com
CL: Karen Gossman
5077 Kenosha Drive
Newburgh, IN 47630
(812)490-6522
km56gossman@yahoo.com

Mt Gilead   (4C)MINC5406
PO Box 494 (mailing)
1077 Mt Gilead Road (physical)
Greenville, IL 62246
( )   <Bond>
CL: Elizabeth File
547 IL Route 140
Pocahontas, IL 62275
(618)664-3216

Mt Olivet   (4C)MINC5308
3153 S State Road 257 (mailing)
4299 S State Road 57 (physical)
Washington, IN 47501
(812)254-4077   <Daviess>
g9barnard@yahoo.com
CL: Karen Barnard
3153 S State Road 257
Washington, IN 47501
(812)254-4077
g9barnard@yahoo.com

Mt Oval   (2C)MINC5116
Route 2
Norris City, IL 62869
( )   <White>
CL: Edward Douglas
950 Washington Road
Omaha, IL 62871
(618)962-3362

New Hope   (4EC)MINC5208
3997 N 100th Street (mailing)
Casey, IL 62420
20955 E 2100th Avenue (physical)
Yale, IL 62481
( )   <Jasper>
royndebbie@hotmail.com
LS: Chris Parr   <M6>
9956 E 2100th Avenue
Hidalgo, IL 62438
(618)793-2704
parpar62432@yahoo.com
CL: Roy Shanks
3997 N 100th Street
Casey, IL 62420
(217)932-2995
royndebbie@hotmail.com

Oak Grove   (2C)MINC5120
(CLOSED 8/2013)

Pleasant Grove   (4EC)MINC5210
6360 E 2100th Avenue (mailing)
Martinsville, IL 62442
4125 E 200th Avenue (physical)

Annapolis, IL 62413
(618)569-4588   <Crawford>
donnie.bailey62@yahoo.com
LS: Bill Ulery   <M6>
10725 E 1500th Road
Marshall, IL 62441
(217)382-4593
CL: Donnie B Bailey
7970 E 1625th Avenue
Robinson, IL 62454
(618)569-4588
donnie.bailey62@yahoo.com

Shiloh   (4MWC)MINC5409
7722 Shiloh Road
Virginia, IL 62691
(217)452-3802   <Cass>
CL: Anna Ruth Long
6614 IL Route 78
Virginia, IL 62691
(217)883-2654
hjlong@casscomm.com

Shinar   (4WC)MINC5410
11383 147th Avenue (mailing)
West Burlington, IA 52655
19705 185th Avenue (physical)
New London, IA 52645
(319)457-2652   <Des Moines>
OD: Shane McCampbell   <M5>
109 Indian Terrace
Burlington, IA 52601
(319)457-2652
revshane777@yahoo.com
CL: Carolyn Schenk
11383 147th Avenue
West Burlington, IA 52655
(319)754-8274
carolynschenk@yahoo.com

Spring Hill   (4C)MINC5411
690 E 1800th Avenue (mailing)
9 miles SW of Beecher City (physical)
Beecher City, IL 62414
( )   <Fayette>
OD: Donald Ray Miller   <M5>
Route 2 Box 136C
Beecher City, IL 62414
(618)487-5648
CL: Nelda Kline
690 E 1800th Avenue
Beecher City, IL 62414
(618)487-5363

Union North   (4C)MINC5124
506 Lakeview Drive (mailing)
635 County Road 2400 E (physical)
Fairfield, IL 62837
(618)847-4061   <Wayne>
SS: Ron Fell   <M2>
PO Box 285
Fairfield, IL 62837
(618)638-3744
r.fell@yahoo.com
CL: Sandra Beckel
506 W Lakeview Drive
Fairfield, IL 62837
(618)842-6400
gonqwik@fairfieldwireless.net

United   (4MC)MINC5119

NORTH CENTRAL PRESBYTERY CONTINUED

204 S Powell Street
Norris City, IL 62869
(618)378-3341 <White>
FAX: (618)378-3064
tc_5854@yahoo.com
CL: Nellie Shepard
206 E Eubanks Street
Norris City, IL 62869
(618)378-3997

Willow Creek (4MWC)MINC5211
6492 E 400th Road
Martinsville, IL 62442
(618)569-4955 <Clark>
PA: Kevin Small <M1>
6492 E 400th Road
Martinsville, IL 62442
(618)569-4955
revkev61@gmail.com
CL: Mark Kannmacher
12477 E 1000th Road
Martinsville, IL 62442
(217)382-4318
kfarms5@yahoo.com

OTHERS ON MINISTERIAL ROLL:

Allen, Gail <M1 WC>
488 County Road 1650 N
Bethany, IL 61914
(217)665-3387
kallen1_61914@yahoo.com
Aros, Jeremias <M1 RT>
5649 W Roscoe Street
Chicago, IL 60634
(773)685-4395
jeremiasaros@sbcglobal.net
Axton, Durant <M1 WC>
2441 SE Browning Road
Evansville, IN 47725
(812)459-0089
FAX: (618)842-2608
Barnett, Rudolph <M1 WC>
RR 5 Box 267
McLeansboro, IL 62859
(618)643-3253
Bender, Richard J <M1 WC>
5297 Normandy Place
Evansville, IN 47715
(812)983-9597
richardjbenderjr@yahoo.com
Bunting, Geoff <M1 WC>
9229 Hedgewood Court
Evansville, IN 47725
(812)925-6630
geoff.bunting@yahoo.com
Compton, Marcia <M1 ST>
218 N Kirk W
Indianapolis, IN 46234
(317)209-9798
mcomptonma@yahoo.com
Craig, Robert A <M1 RT>
417 S Grove Avenue
Oak Park, IL 60302
(773)477-8249
v-craig@sbcglobal.net
Furr, Wayne <M1 WC>
706 E 6th Street
Coal Valley, IL 61240
(309)791-1691
prespreacher@gmail.com

Gross, Ronald <M1 RT>
2436 N 420th Street
Oblong, IL 62449
(217)932-2788
juneg@eiis.net
Hackman-Truhan, Deborah <M1 WC>
7314 N Miramar Drive
Peoria, IL 61614
(931)537-9040
cprevdeb@hotmail.com
Korb, Leon C <M1 RT>
15360 E 350 North Road
Ridge Farm, IL 61870
(217)662-8398
Lovelace, John G <M1 RT>
814 Crestwood Drive
Evansville, IN 47715
(812)476-5879
jlove1234@aol.com
Nichols, Oscar Lee <M1 RT>
1035 N County Road 650E
Trilla, IL 62469
(217)234-6551
Oliveira, Jose <M1 WC>
7310 Jasmine Drive
Hanover Park, IL 60133
(630)855-0870
valdirsoares@yahoo.com
Richards, Carroll R <M1 RT M9>
210 Allison Drive
Lincoln, IL 62656
(217)732-7894
FAX: (217)732-7894
dr_cr@comcast.net
Shirley, Betty L <M1 RT>
811 Rotherham Drive
Ballwin, MO 63011
(636)386-3174
therevbls@prodigy.net
Smith, Albert J <M1 RT>
407 W Main Street Apt 131
Wilkesboro, NC 28697
(217)452-3408
ct_alsmith@casscomm.com
Topar, Shirley <M1 WC>
2233 Cambridge Drive SE
Grand Rapids, MI 49506
(616)245-0625
s_j_topar@yahoo.com
Wallace, Andrew <M1 WC>
816 Howard Avenue
Burlingame, CA 94010
Watkins, Robert B <M1 DE>
235 Misty Drive
Somerset, KY 42503
(319)431-0990
watkr@mac.com
Yarce, Janeth <M1 WC>
3019 W Calavar Road
Phoenix, AZ 85053
(630)518-0295
janethyarce@yahoo.com

OTHER LICENTIATES ON ROLL:

OTHER CANDIDATES ON ROLL:

Alvarez, Samuel <M3>
3740 W Leland Avenue
Chicago, IL 60625
(773)509-9165
Sandiford, Holton <M3>
4227 E 300th Road
Casey, IL 62420
(217)259-3773
Stephenson, Joseph <M3>
PO Box 129
Bethany, IL 61914
(217)853-7819

Red River Presbytery
MISSION SYNOD

	GENERAL	MEMBERSHIP			CHANGES				FINANCES				
	1.Church Number	2.Active	3.Total	4.Church School	5.Prof. of Faith	6.Gains	7.Losses	8.Children Baptized	9. OUR UNITED OUT-REACH	10. Total Out-Reach Giving	11. All Other Expenses	12. Total Income Received	13. Value Church Prop. 1=1000
	1	2	3	4	5	6	7	8	9	10	11	12	13
Burns Flat*	6301	80	100	65	3	10	0	5	2,600	20,500	113,366	121,179	1,500
Clinton	6302	71	119	60	0	2	2	0	8,166	15,679	123,940	139,619	1,500
Covenant	6304	86	107	88	2	3	5	0	6,000	26,623	196,966	199,248	1,130
Denton*	8404	52	206	24	0	21	0	1	950	3,164	78,050	74,419	2,500
Eastlake	6205	44	133	33	0	1	0	0	9,384	82,879	96,720	171,220	904
Ethel	8405	0	3	0	CLOSED 10/2013		0	0	0	100	0	0	0 80
Faith	6201	39	42	4	2	2	4	0	4,161	4,635	9,622	104,429	450
Hubbard	8410	13	13	5	0	0	0	0	150	573	17,739	18,069	200
Lake Highlands+	8411	179	179	40	0	1	20	1	0	8,107	256,769	219,311	3,518
Locust Grove	6203	7	11	5	0	0	3	0	600	2,500	29,911	13,680	150
Mangum	6306	33	33	15	0	7	0	0	550	7,612	41,950	39,059	752
Marlow	6305	42	80	25	0	0	6	0	8,240	22,039	149,425	178,677	694
Mesquite	8412	44	56	14	0	4	5	0	1,000	1,175	105,135	81,482	1,208
Mt. Zion	8414	4	4	20	0	0	0	0	1,551	1,872	17,962	18,727	60
Newberry*	8415	13	13	6	0	0	18	0	500	2,772	30,268	13,898	375
Olney	8416	62	92	33	1	1	1	0	8,140	16,257	80,917	81,403	600
Sandy Springs	8420	14	35	4	0	0	0	0		2,000	12,042	13,535	200
Shiloh	8421	83	203	69	0	0	2	1	15,574	35,236	134,148	202,680	500
St. John	8413	41	77	7	5	19	5	2	5,940	10,224	64,969	73,529	916
St. Luke*	8407	83	86	60	3	0	46	1	2,100	12,520	191,412	222,132	4,743
St. Mark (TX)	8408	53	53	6	1	1	7	0	1,100	6,804	62,483	69,287	1,048
St. Matthew	8418	1,050	1,781	550	22	109	10	9	2,400	261,702	2,272,000	2,669,345	5,480
St. Timothy	8419	136	251	114	0	0	5	4	29,928	71,139	251,470	308,087	2,570
Stonegate	6307	36	37	20	1	3	2	0	7,313	7,313	93,435	83,562	520
Trinity	8409	78	97	29	2	3	3	2	9,682	22,200	1 19,648	141,668	1,300
Whitney*	8424	12	13	4	0	0	4	0	201	1,454	17,641	14,914	100
Zion Valley	8425	14	14	3	1	1	2	0	500	8,491	21,266	33,260	110
TOTALS	27	2,369	3,838	1,303	43	188	150	26	126,830	655,470	4,589,254	5,306,419	33,108

*Math error corrected. **Purged roll. +Union church

CHURCHES, PASTORS, AND CLERKS:

_____

Burns Flat (4WMC)MSRR6301
  PO Box 8 (mailing)
  205 Highway 44 (physical)
  Burns Flat, OK 73624
  (580)562-4706 <Washita>
  burnsflatcpc@windstream.net
PA: Thomas R Spence <M1>
  PO Box 802
  Burns Flat, OK 73624
  (580)562-4531
  tomspence0302@gmail.com
CL: Gene Reeves
  Route 2 Box 177
  Dill City, OK 73641
  (580)674-3763

_____

Clinton (4WMC)MSRR6302
  500 S 30th Street
  Clinton, OK 73601
  (580)323-3440 <Custer>
PA: Dale Nease <M1>
  500 S 30th Street
  Clinton, OK 73601

(580)323-7557
CL: Dave Felch
  500 S 30th Street
  Clinton, OK 73601
  (580)323-3111

_____

Covenant (4MEWC)MSRR6304
  15791 State Highway 1W
  Ada, OK 74820
  (580)332-0799 <Pontotoc>
  lindasnelling@covenantcpc.org
PA: Linda Snelling <M1>
  15791 State Highway 1W
  Ada, OK 74820
  (580)332-0799
  FAX: (580)332-9424
  lindasnelling@covenantcpc.org
CL: Randy C Davidson
  PO Box 880
  Ada, OK 74821
  (580)421-6969
  randy@d-son.com

_____

Denton (4MWC)MSRR8404
  PO Box 236 (mailing)
  1424 Stuart Road (physical)

Denton, TX 76202
  (940)387-6811 <Denton>
  gacakee12@verizon.net
PA: John V Lindsay <M1>
  2004 Burning Tree Lane
  Denton, TX 76209
  (940)387-6811
CL: Jami McQueen
  5802 Green Ivy Road
  Denton, TX 76210
  (940)390-0397
  gacakee12@verizon.net

_____

Eastlake (4C)MSRR6205
  700 SW 134th Street
  Oklahoma City, OK 73170
  (405)799-8987 <Oklahoma>
  eastlakecumberland@att.net
PA: Leslie A Johnson <M1>
  11716 Price Drive
  Oklahoma City, OK 73170
  (405)248-4232
  ljohnson275@cox.net
CL: Ray Sears
  821 SW 42nd Street
  Moore, OK 73160

RED RIVER PRESBYTERY CONTINUED

(405)703-0779
lrsears@cox.net

_____

Ethel   (4C)MSRR8405
  (CLOSED 10/19/2013)

_____

Faith   (4WC)MSRR6201
  PO Box 690715 (mailing)
  2801 S 129th East Avenue (physical)
  Tulsa, OK 74169
  (918)437-2190   <Tulsa>
  FAX: (918)437-2199
  tulsafaith@att.net
PA: Thomas R Sanders   <M1 DE>
  4201 W Kent Street
  Broken Arrow, OK 74012
  (918)269-0043
  FAX: (918)437-2199
  trsncf@msn.com
CL: Georgia Stevens
  29605 S River Ridge Drive
  Catoosa, OK 74015
  FAX: (918)437-2199
  stevenscabinets@yahoo.com

_____

Hubbard   (4MWC)MSRR8410
  404 N Magnolia
  Hubbard, TX 76648
  ( )   <Hill>
PA: Charles E Nelson   <M1>
  209 Classic Court
  Springtown, TX 76082
  (903)641-5466
  dundeal10@aol.com
CL: Brenard Nunnelley
  475 H County Road 3350 N
  Hubbard, TX 76648
  (254)576-2468
  bfn76648@aol.com

_____

Lake Highlands   (4WU)MSRR8411
  8525 Audelia Road
  Dallas, TX 75238
  (214)348-2133   <Dallas>
  lhpc@lhpres.org
CL: Maureen Ramsay
  8935 Larchwood Drive
  Dallas, TX 75238
  (214)542-6173
  FAX: (214)348-2408
  msramsay@hotmail.com

_____

Locust Grove   (4MWC)MSRR6203
  PO Box 577 (mailing)
  203 E Harriett Avenue (physical)
  Locust Grove, OK 74352
  (918)479-5613   <Mayes>
PA: R Brent Turpen   <M1>
  PO Box 577
  Locust Grove, OK 74352
  (918)479-5613
  mlturpen@hotmail.com
CL: Mayme Miley
  7847 S 438 Road
  Locust Grove, OK 74352
  (918)479-2575

_____

Mangum   (4MEWC)MSRR6306
  314 N Oklahoma
  Mangum, OK 73554
  (580)782-2560   <Greer>

FAX: (580)782-3485
OD: David Rosales   <M5>
  312 Oklahoma Avenue
  Mangum, OK 73665
CL: Jack Cossey
  606 W Sproat Street
  Mangum, OK 73554
  (580)782-2560
  jscossey@att.net

_____

Marlow   (4MWC)MSRR6305
  202 N Sixth
  Marlow, OK 73055
  (580)658-2892   <Stephens>
  rgoodman4gvn@hotmail.com
PA: Robert Goodman   <M1>
  604 N 4th Street
  Marlow, OK 73055
  (580)756-4726
  rgoodman4gvn@hotmail.com
CL: Faye Kimbrough
  1202 W Randall Court
  Duncan, OK 73533
  (580)786-4434

_____

Mesquite   (4C)MSRR8412
  819 N Town East Boulevard
  Mesquite, TX 75150
  (972)270-6923   <Dallas>
  FAX: (972)270-6923
  mcpchurch@gmail.com
IP: Wesley H Johnson   <M1>
  6222 Crestmoor Lane
  Sachse, TX 75048
  (972)429-6129
  wjohnson@transitionconsulting.com
CL: Patricia Chatt
  1705 Windmire Drive
  Mesquite, TX 75181
  (214)394-6513
  FAX: (972)270-6923
  pbchatt@sbcglobal.net

_____

Mt Zion   (2C)MSRR8414
  691 County Road 4108 (mailing)
  Greeneville, TX 75401
  15175 Texas Highway 11 W (physical)
  Cumby, TX 75433
  (903)454-3444   <Hopkins>
  bvwood10@yahoo.com
CL: Virginia Woodworth
  691 County Road 4108
  Greeneville, TX 75401
  (903)454-3444
  bvwood10@yahoo.com

_____

Newberry   (2C)MSRR8415
  PO Box 253 (mailing)
  1301 Newberry Road (physical)
  Millsap, TX 76066
  ( )   <Parker>
SS: Tim Dewhirst   <M3>
  3609 Oakbriar Lane
  Colleyville, TX 76034
  (817)605-8147
  timdew@sbcglobal.net
CL: Royce E Jordan
  1751 Newberry Road
  Millsap, TX 76066
  (940)682-4844

_____

Olney   (4MEWC)MSRR8416
  PO Box 756 (mailing)
  210 S Avenue M (physical)
  Olney, TX 76374
  (940)564-2882   <Young>
  olneycpc@brazosnet.comt
PA: David Carpenter   <M1>
  909 W Elm Street
  Olney, TX 76374
  (940)564-2339
  olneycpc@brazosnet.com
CL: Clifton W Key
  PO Box 615
  Olney, TX 76374
  (940)564-2979
  barkey8@brazosnet.com

_____

Sandy Springs   (4C)MSRR8420
  1865 Bones Chapel Road (mailing)
  Rease Road (physical)
  Whitesboro, TX 76273
  ( )   <Grayson>
CL: Billy L Morrow
  1865 Bones Chapel Road
  Whitesboro, TX 76273
  (903)564-5148

_____

Shiloh   (4MEWC)MSRR8421
  7810 Shiloh Road
  Midlothian, TX 76065
  (972)723-3758   <Ellis>
  vernon@sansom.us
PA: Vernon Sansom   <M1>
  104 Cockrell Hill Road
  Ovilla, TX 75154
  (972)825-6887
  vernon@sansom.us
CL: Lynette McCarty
  2160 Springer Road
  Midlothian, TX 76065
  (214)629-6963
  lmccarty@link.com

_____

St John   (4WC)MSRR8413
  6007 W Pleasant Ridge Road
  Arlington, TX 76016
  (817)478-6219   <Tarrant>
  FAX: (817)478-8684
  stjohncpc@att.net
SS: Richard Shugert   <M1>
  5208 Bellis Drive
  Fort Worth, TX 76244
  (817)913-7211
  shugertr@yahoo.com
CL: Patricia Long
  525 E Oak Street
  Aledo, TX 76008
  (817)441-1428
  pjlong47@aledobb.com

_____

St Luke   (4C)MSRR8407
  1404 Sycamore School Road
  Fort Worth, TX 76134
  (817)293-3778   <Tarrant>
  FAX: (817)293-2750
  office@stlukecpc.org
PA: David Kurtz   <M1>
  4709 Layla Road
  Arlington, TX 76016
  (817)683-4783
  davidk36@yahoo.com

RED RIVER PRESBYTERY CONTINUED

CL: Nancy Plattsmier
4121 Inwood Road
Fort Worth, TX 76109
(817)923-2669
moomer@charter.net

St Mark (TX)   (4MWC)MSRR8408
4101 Hardeman Street
Fort Worth, TX 76119
(817)536-1315   <Tarrant>
PA: Roosevelt Baugh   <M1>
4101 Hardeman Street
Fort Worth, TX 76119
(817)536-1315
gmf1220@charter.net
CL: Hazel F Wilson
2801 Sarah Jane Lane
Fort Worth, TX 76119
(817)536-4892
jesseewilson@charter.net

St Matthew   (4EC)MSRR8418
PO Box 182 (mailing)
380 NW Tarrant (physical)
Burleson, TX 76097
(817)295-5832   <Johnson>
FAX: (817)295-2576
info@stmattcpc.org
PA: Rick Owen   <M1>
3305 Wild Oaks Court
Burleson, TX 76028
(817)295-5832
FAX: (817)295-2576
rowen@stmattcpc.org
AP: Jeffrey A Gehle   <M1>
PO Box 182
Burleson, TX 76097
(817)295-5832
jeff.gehle@stmattcpc.org
AP: R Allan Mink   <M2>
1113 Hidden Glen Court
Burleson, TX 76028
(817)295-5832
FAX: (817)295-2576
alan.mink@stmattcpc.org
CL: Kim Perkey
2600 Embry Lane
Burleson, TX 76028
(817)235-9061
kimberley.k.perkey@wellsfargo.com

St Timothy   (4WC)MSRR8419
PO Box 210338 (mailing)
3001 Forest Ridge Drive (physical)
Bedford, TX 76095
(817)571-7474   <Tarrant>
FAX: (817)571-7714
cbrown@sttimothy-cpc.org
PA: Chuck Brown   <M1>
2908 Steve Drive
Hurst, TX 76054
(817)915-2907
cbrown@sttimothy-cpc.org
CL: Danny Washmon
PO Box 210338
Bedford, TX 76095
(817)571-7474
washmon@rocketmail.com

Stonegate   (ARC)MSRR6307
PO Box 3973 (mailing)

17101 N Western Avenue (physical)
Edmond, OK 73083
(405)340-7281   <Oklahoma>
church@stonegatechurch.org
PA: Marian Sontowski   <M1>
PO Box 3973
Edmond, OK 73083
(405)340-7281
marian.desk@gmail.com
CL: Phyllis Johnston
2708 Pinto Trail
Edmond, OK 73012
(405)330-2119
andyriah@yahoo.com

Trinity   (4MEWC)MSRR8409
7120 W Cleburne Road
Fort Worth, TX 76133
(817)292-6149   <Tarrant>
trinitycpc@sbcglobal.net
PA: Randy L Hardisty   <M1>
4908 Redondo Street
Fort Worth, TX 76180
(817)428-3513
rhardisty@sbcglobal.net
CL: Betty Jean Cooper
1108 Trinity Trail
Saginaw, TX 76131
(817)306-4877
bjjacoop@sbcglobal.net

Whitney   (4EC)MSRR8424
PO Box 582 (mailing)
108 S Colorado (physical)
Whitney, TX 76692
(254)694-3852   <Hill>
PA: Charles A Hendershot   <M1>
122 Tree Shadow
Whitney, TX 76692
(254)694-3852
CL: Lou Webb
101 Bridge Lane
Whitney, TX 76692
(254)694-2879
joelou2@windstream.net

Zion Valley   (4C)MSRR8425
2684 South FM 1655
Chico, TX 76431
( )   <Wise>
PA: Barney Hudson   <M1>
10541 Fossil Hill Drive
Fort Worth, TX 76131
(817)851-2960
barneyrev@gmail.com
CL: Priscilla Moreland
1177 N State Highway 101
Chico, TX 76431
(940)644-2462
hdpjmoreland@hotmail.com

OTHERS ON MINISTERIAL ROLL:

Aden, Marty   <M1 M9>
202 Bennington Place
Wilmington, NC 28412
(910)795-1092
maden@ec.rr.com
Baltimore, Claud G   <M1 WC>
PO Box 1358
1430 Lakehurst Drive

Ada, OK 74821
(580)332-2679
baltimorejb@earthlink.net
Brown, Stephanie S   <M1 M9>
1713 Arbor Mill Circle Apt 1424
Bedford, TX 76021
(901)729-3612
scrudderbrown7@yahoo.com
Condon, Jr, Thomas W   <M1 RT>
6508 Victoria Avenue
N Richland Hills, TX 76180
(817)656-9334
Fajardo, Jose   <M1 WC>
101 Vanderbilt
Waxahachie, TX 75165
(972)923-2955
Ferrol, Ruben   <M1 M9 RT>
1823 Straford Court
Allentown, PA 18103
(610)966-7289
rubeferrol@msn.com
Gardner, Charles   <M1 WC>
124 Dawson Street
Penrose, CO 81240
(719)784-7744
Harris, Wendell   <M1 WC>
329 N Louis Tittle Avenue
Mangum, OK 73554
(580)782-2142
wendellharris@itlnet.net
Henson, Kevin R   <M1 DE>
1121 Raleigh Path
Denton, TX 76208
(817)354-1182
khenson@cpch.org
Hong, Soon Gab   <M1 WC>
13600 Doty Avenue Apt 4
Hawthorne, CA 90250
(972)446-0350
lemuelhong@hotmail.com
Kays, Michael   <M1 WC>
2505 Canterbury Avenue
Muskogee, OK 74403
(918)577-6255
msppk@suddenlink.net
Lain, Judy   <M1 M9>
1928 Pine Ridge Drive
Bedford, TX 76021
(817)660-8020
judylane5@gmail.com
Lounsbury-Lombard, Kristi   <M1 M9>
902 Clearview
Krum, TX 76249
(940)435-5077
kristilounsbury@gmail.com
Madden, Judith Ellen   <M1 WC>
100 SW Brushy Mound
Burleson, TX 76028
(817)295-5832
jmadden@stmattcpc.org
McGee, Charles Randall   <M1 WC>
9037 Groveland Drive
Dallas, TX 75218
(214)328-2488
randallmcgee@sbcglobal.net
Morgan, Jerome H   <M1 RT>
8420 Baumgarten Drive
Dallas, TX 75228
(214)323-7557
Palmer, Walter (Pete)   <M1 WC>
1438 S 133rd East Avenue

RED RIVER PRESBYTERY CONTINUED

Tulsa, OK 74108
(918)438-0406
peteangelblue@att.net

Parkhurst, L G, Jr   <M1 WC>
409 Woodhollow Trail
Edmond, OK 73012
(405)341-7477

Petty, Linda Lee   <M1 WC>
4401 W Elgin Street
Broken Arrow, OK 74012
(918)252-4741

Rice, Keith   <M1 M9>
PO Box 582
Itasca, TX 76055
(254)087-2418
rsvkeith@yahoo.com

Rivera, Carlos A   <M1 WC>
Calle Tokio 610, Departmento 6
Colonia Portales Norte
Delegacion Benito
Juarez, C.P. 03300
(52)1-55-31058377
caralrifra@une.net.co

Ruggia, Mario (Bud)   <M1 M9 RT>
603 Rumsey Street
Kiowa, KS 67070
(620)825-4509
ruggia@aol.com

Schmoyer, Donna Marie   <M1 WC>
613 Mound Street
Monongahela, PA 15063
(817)266-6572
schmoyerdm@yahoo.com

Scrudder, Norlan   <M1 RT>
29688 S 534 Road
Park Hill, OK 74451
(918)949-1326
ndscrudder@gmail.com

Sharpe, Michael G   <M1 DE>
3423 Summerdale Drive
Bartlett, TN 38133
(901)276-4572

Shelton, Robert E   <M1 RT>
10508 Royalwood Drive
Dallas, TX 75238
(214)349-7162
bshelton67@yahoo.com

Shelton, Robert M   <M1 RT>
7128 Lakehurst Avenue
Dallas, TX 75230
(214)696-3237

Smith, Robert H   <M1 WC>
5055 S 76th East Avenue Apt D
Tulsa, OK 74145
(918)671-5520
rhsmith@sstelco.com

Thomas, Cassandra   <M1 RT>
1920 Dancy Street
Fayetteville, NC 28301
(910)488-4897
chcothomas@yahoo.com

Wagner, Hugh   <M1 WC>
12556 Timberline Drive
Garfield, AR 72732
(479)359-0021
hughawagner@gmail.com

Webb, William G   <M1 OM>
7926 S 78th East Avenue
Tulsa, OK 74133
(918)294-9117

Youngman, Betty   <M1 RT>
1471 Creekview Court
Fort Worth, TX 76112
(817)492-4100
bettyy@swbell.net

Zumbrunnen, Craig H   <M1 WC>
1210 Country Club Road Apt 3
Santa Teresa, NM 88008
(580)471-0308
craigzum1@yahoo.com

OTHER LICENIATES ON ROLL:

King, Keith   <M2 ST>
3341 S 137th East Avenue
Tulsa, OK 74134
(918)437-5464

OTHER CANDIDATES ON ROLL:

Lumpee, Daniel   <M3>
1200 Charles Court
College Station, TX 77840
dlumpee@gmail.com
(817)691-1945   MSRR#8400

Robert Donnell Presbytery
SOUTHEAST SYNOD

GENERAL		MEMBERSHIP			CHANGES				FINANCES				
1.Church Number	2.Active	3.Total	4.Church School	5.Prof. of Faith	6.Gains	7.Losses	8.Children Baptized	9. OUR UNITED OUT-REACH	10. Total Out-Reach Giving	11. All Other Expenses	12. Total Income Received	13. Value Church Prop. 1=1000	
	1	2	3	4	5	6	7	8	9	10	11	12	13
Alabaster	0107	200	368	50	4	7	5	1	0	28,778	178,143	217,319	2,300
Big Cove	0801	15	31	10	0	0	2	0	200	3,160	25,261	16,560	330
Christ Church	0814	76	107	25	0	6	2	1	9,051	12,574	82,031	84,965	650
Concord	0802	23	79	18	0	0	1	0	2,180	2,422	21,507	27,354	286
East Point	0206	23	68	20	0	0	5	0	1,100	2,331	37,143	41,643	656
Edgefield	0813	2	3	0	0	1	0	0	0	402	6,609	8,120	209
Eidson Chapel	0207	20	51	17	No Report Received			0	0	0	0	0	140
Goosepond	0803	28	48	5	0	0	1	0	1,800	7,736	25,620	33,457	250
Gurley	0804	76	76	25	0	5	3	3	5,383	26,564	124,013	150,576	751
Holly Grove	0805	3	3	1	Closed 3/2014				0	0	0	0	50
Hope+	0812	66	66	29	0	0	2	1	0	3,435	102,523	105,958	568
Huntsville, 1st	0806	55	112	28	0	5	4	0	1,250	3,074	99,058	98,402	1,500
Meridianville*	0808	33	44	24	0	3	0	0	0	600	56,972	64,164	1,350
Scottsboro	0809	267	465	120	14	14	3	3	27,910	66,828	293,694	313,275	2,880
Stevenson	0810	54	148	30	0	1	0	0	9,641	23,928	72,478	96,406	1,200
Union Grove	0211	20	27	15	No Report Received			0	0	0	0	0	200
Walnut Grove	0811	20	43	10	0	0	0	0	0	1,670	8,052	9,722	20
TOTALS	17	981	1,739	427	18	42	28	9	58,515	183,502	1,133,104	1,267,921	13,340

*Math error corrected. **Purged roll. +Union church

CHURCHES, PASTORS, AND CLERKS:

Alabaster   (4WC)SERD0107
   8828 Highway 119
   Alabaster, AL 35007
   (205)663-3152   <Shelby>
   FAX: (205)663-8323
   fpcalabaster@bellsouth.net
IP: Darren Kennemer   <M1>
   8828 Highway 119
   Alabaster, AL 35007
   (205)663-3152
   FAX: (205)663-8323
   darren.kennemer@va.gov
CL: Margaret Russo
   8828 Highway 119
   Alabaster, AL 35007
   (205)663-3152
   russorm@att.net

Big Cove   (4MWC)SERD0801
   5984 Highway 431 S
   Brownsboro, AL 35741
   (256)518-9657   <Madison>
SS: Philip Nickles   <M1 OP>
   5821 County Road 1114
   Vinemont, AL 35179
   (256)734-9847
   nickles.phil@yahoo.com
CL: Beryl Tidwell
   680 Old Big Cove Road
   Owens Cross Roads, AL 35763
   (256)518-9977
   beryl.tidwell@comcast.net

Christ Church   (4WC)SERD0814
   1580 Jeff Road
   Huntsville, AL 35806
   (256)837-6014   <Madison>
   christchurch@knology.net
PA: Cardelia Howell Diamond   <M1>
   1580 Jeff Road
   Huntsville, AL 35806
   (256)837-6014
   clhdzmhd@hotmail.com
CL: Cheryl Caldwell
   1043 Douglass Road
   Huntsville, AL 35806
   (256)837-6014
   sccz4647@att.net

Concord   (4MWC)SERD0802
   1827 Joe Quick Road
   New Market, AL 35761
   (256)828-4503   <Madison>
CL: Gayle Poole
   215 Sealey Hill Road
   New Market, AL 35761
   (256)829-1147

East Point   (4WC)SERD0206
   1441 US Highway 278 E
   Cullman, AL 35055
   (256)734-0900   <Cullman>
OD: Lee Walton   <M5>
   1441 US Highway 278 E
   Cullman, AL 35055
CL: Karen Munger
   PO Box 1773
   Cullman, AL 35056
   (256)739-0746
   karenamunger@bellsouth.net

Edgefield   (4UC)SERD0813
   411 McMahan Cove Road (mailing)
   Stevenson, AL 35772
   311 County Road 158 (physical)
   Stevenson, AL 35772
   ( )   <Jackson>
CL: Merris Powell
   7434 Alabama Highway 40
   Henagar, AL 35978
   (256)558-0715

Eidson Chapel   (4C)SERD0207
   2680 County Road 1725
   Holly Pond, AL 35083
   ( )   <Cullman>
OD: Floyd Bradford   <M5>
   351 Piney Grove Road W
   Falkville, AL 35622
   (256)784-6510
   FAX: (415)864-1543
CL: Linda Harris
   5910 County Road 747
   Cullman, AL 35058
   (256)734-6697

Goosepond   (4MWC)SERD0803
   1155 East Hancock Drive
   Scottsboro, AL 35769
   (256)259-4386   <Jackson>
   betrich76@gmail.com
PA: C E (Ed) Herring Jr   <M1>
   969 Campground Circle
   Scottsboro, AL 35769
   (256)259-2721
   edherring@scottsboro.org
CL: Bettie M Jordan
   198 County Road 46

ROBERT DONNELL PRESBYTERY CONTINUED

Hollywood, AL 35752
(256)437-1546
betrich76@gmail.com

Gurley　　　　　　　(4MEWC)SERD0804
223 Section Line Road
Gurley, AL 35748
(256)776-2331　　　　　　　<Madison>
PA: Toy E Brindley　　　　　　<M1>
PO Box 335
Gurley, AL 35748
(256)776-2331
gurleycpc@gmail.com
CL: Becky Arnold
423 Sharps Cove Road
Gurley, AL 35748
(256)776-6950
bailey@darnold.net

Holly Grove　　　　　　(2C)SERD0805
CLOSED 3/2014

Hope　　　　　　　(4WU)SERD0812
10001 Bailey Cove Road SE
Huntsville, AL 35803
(256)881-4673　　　　　　　<Madison>
hopepresby@comcast.net
PA: Christie Ashton　　　　　　<M1>
10001 Bailey Cove Road SE
Huntsville, AL 35803
(256)881-4673
pastorhope@comcast.net
CL: Cheryl D Hoard
10001 Bailey Cove Road SE
Huntsville, AL 35803
(256)881-4673
cdhoard@bellsouth.net

Huntsville First　　　　(4EWC)SERD0806
PO Box 777 (mailing)
1802 Bankhead Parkway (physical)
Huntsville, AL 35804
(256)536-9371　　　　　　　<Madison>
hsvfcpc@att.net
PA: Richard W Hughes　　　　　<M1>
2954 Bob Wade Lane
Harvest, AL 35749
(256)859-3178
hughesrichard23@gmail.com
CL: Carla Rowley
PO Box 777
2012 Brandy Court
Huntsville, AL 35811
(256)651-5916
carla.rowley4@gmail.com

Meridianville　　　　(4MWC)SERD0808
PO Box 188 (mailing)
11696 Highway 231/431 N (physical)
Meridianville, AL 35759
(256)828-0160　　　　　　　<Madison>
dptalley@hotmail.com
PA: Keith Lorick　　　　　　<M1>
127 Chesapeake Boulevard
Madison, AL 35757
(256)325-3865
keithlorick@knology.net
CL: Donna Talley
360 Monroe Road
Meridianville, AL 35759
(256)683-6111

dptalley@hotmail.com

Scottsboro　　　　　　(4WC)SERD0809
PO Box 639 (mailing)
315 S Kyle Street (physical)
Scottsboro, AL 35768
FAX: (256)259-2809
cumberland@scottsboro.org
(256)574-2575　　　　　　　<Jackson>
PA: Roy W Hall　　　　　　<M1>
87 Lee Hall Street
Scottsboro, AL 35769
(256)259-9340
royhall@scottsboro.org
CL: Norman Johnson
154 Willow Cove Drive
Scottsboro, AL 35769
(256)259-4708
njohnson@webeca.com

Stevenson　　　　　　(4MEWC)SERD0810
112 College Street
Stevenson, AL 35772
(256)437-8632　　　　　　　<Jackson>
PA: Perry Whitaker
202 College Street
Stevenson, AL 35772
(256)437-8632
brotherperry@msn.com
CL: Jen Stewart
112 College Street
Stevenson, AL 35772
(256)437-3116
jstewart306@hotmail.com

Union Grove　　　　　(4WC)SERD0211
91 County Road 1734 (mailing)
2760 County Road 1742 (physical)
Holly Pond, AL 35803
(256)796-1023　　　　　　　<Cullman>
johnson9983@att.net
SS: David Hooper　　　　　　<M3>
115 County Road 682
Cullman, AL 35055
(256)775-2419
davidhoop165@yahoo.com
CL: Glen Johnson
91 County Road 1734
Holly Pond, AL 35083
(256)796-1023
johnson9983@att.net

Walnut Grove　　　　　(4WC)SERD0811
PO Box 403 (mailing)
711 New Hope/Cedar Point Road (physical)
New Hope, AL 35760
( )　　　　　　　　　<Madison>
PA: James Smith　　　　　　<M1>
1949 Little Cove Road
Owens Cross Roads, AL 35763
dr.james.smith42@gmail.com
CL: Kathy Pegues
211 Butler Lane
New Hope, AL 35760
(256)723-8740
mcwoodpeg@nehp.net

OTHERS ON MINISTERIAL ROLL:

Alspaugh, Kevin　　　　　<M1 WC>

5102 Main Drive
New Hope AL 35760
(256)723-3808
rev.alspaugh@gmail.com
Alverson, Elmer L　　　　　<M1 WC>
354 Roy Davis Road
New Market, AL 35761
(256)828-4503
bud@alscomputers.com
Babcock, Edward S, Jr　　　　<M1 RT>
1007 San Ramone Avenue
Huntsville, AL 35802
(256)882-9339
ejsb1@aol.com
Brodeur, Evelyn　　　　　<M1 WC>
1005 Cleermont Drive SE
Huntsville, AL 35801
(256)536-1070
lifeandwater@aol.com
Bynum, Ronald H　　　　　<M1 WC>
121 Sycamore Road
Gurley, AL 35748
(256)776-9313
ronaldbynum@bellsouth.net
Davenport, Mark A　　　　　<M1 WC>
8828 Highway 119
Alabaster, AL 35007
(205)663-3152
FAX: (205)663-8323
fpcapastor@bellsouth.net
Gillis, Aubrey Thomas　　　　<M1 WC>
PO Box 869
Silverhill, AL 36576
(251)947-1638
FAX: (205)664-8323
tomgillis63@hotmail.com
Goodwin, Earl　　　　　<M1 WC>
1012 Windsor Parkway
Moody, AL 35004
(205)222-1741
FAX: (205)664-8323
earlgoodwin@yahoo.com
Hall, Brad　　　　　　<M1 WC>
1602 Toll Gate Road SE
Huntsville, AL 35801
(256)533-4845
Hall, John D　　　　　　<M1 WC>
109 Oddo Lane SE
Huntsville, AL 35802
(256)880-5129
johnhall33@comcast.net
Howton, Orvie Ray　　　　　<M1 RT>
4928 Montauk Trail SE
Owens Cross Road, AL 35763
(256)533-9224
arhowton@bellsouth.net
Hughes, Charles　　　　　<M1 RT>
114 Gaul Street
Estill Springs, TN 37330
(931)649-5189
cphugs@cafes.net
Lambert, James　　　　　<M1 RT>
224 Peabody Road
Meridianville, AL 35759
(256)828-6850
Livingston, Ronald L　　　　<M1 WC>
5851 Quantrell Avenue #201
Alexandria, VA 22312
Matthews, James N　　　　<M1 WC>
241 Morning Star Drive

ROBERT DONNELL PRESBYTERY CONTINUED

Huntsville, AL 35811
(256)851-1694
FAX: (256)828-0160
jamesnmatthews@bellsouth.net
Murphree, Hughlen   <M1 WC>
    4298 County Road 1719
    Holly Pond, AL 35083
    (256)796-5352
    hmurph@hiwaay.net

Phillips-Burk, Pam   <M1 DE>
    1065 Legacy Lake Circle 104
    Collierville, TN 38017
    (256)684-5247

pam@cumberland.org
Reeves, Donald
PO Box 528
Rainsville, AL 35986
(256)228-4057
reevesd@nacc.edu

<M1 WC>   OTHER CANDIDATES ON ROLL:

Tennessee-Georgia Presbytery
SOUTHEAST SYNOD

	GENERAL		MEMBERSHIP			CHANGES				FINANCES				
	1.Church Number	2.Active	3.Total	4.Church School	5.Prof. of Faith	6.Gains	7.Losses	8.Children Baptized	9. OUR UNITED OUT-REACH	10. Total Out-Reach Giving	11. All Other Expenses	12. Total Income Received	13. Value Church Prop. 1=1000
	1	2	3	4	5	6	7	8	9	10	11	12	13
Bartow	2101	87	149	35	3	7	3	1	9,000	32,456	120,273	126,740	913
Cedar Springs	2119	8	17	6	0	0	1	0	500	1,808	17,076	19,186	323
Charleston	2102	37	49	23	0	1	2	1	3,900	7,645	46,099	57,321	900
Chattanooga 1st	2104	578	578	206	4	9	15	3	5,000	21,738	479,912	624,818	650
Cleveland*	2108	150	178	87	3	0	3	2	14,083	28,486	272,345	223,679	2,400
Cornerstone Com	2107	12	42	9	No Report Received			0	0	0	0	0	675
Ebenezer	2110	7	7	0	No Report Received			0	0	0	0	0	75
El Redill	2149	50	55	38	7	12	13	0	0	3,723	79,000	69,798	780
Falling Water	2111	69	82	35	0	0	5	0	3,000	32,900	106,935	127,134	870
Flint Springs	2112	26	26	7	0	0	2	0	0	450	0	16,550	150
Glory Church*	2144	55	55	7	5	0	35	0	0	5,000	7,000	75,000	2,300
Jasper	2113	30	45	14	0	1	1	0	3,868	3,686	55,930	50,931	750
Kelly's Chapel	2120	13	19	17	No Report Received			0	200	0	0	0	110
Korean Living Sto	2130	30	30	8	Provisional Church			0	0	0	0	0	0
Liberty*	2114	2	3	2	Church dissolved 3/16/13			0	0	0	0	0	100
New Hope	2115	55	82	34	3	3	2	2	1,000	9,180	76,490	85,670	600
Oak Grove	2121	14	28	0	0	0	0	0	0	886	10,391	8,499	110
Our Good*	2138	22	22	8	No Report Received			0	0	0	0	0	0
Pine Hill	2117	13	13	14	No Report Received			0	0	0	0	0	70
Prospect United**	2116	41	98	22	0	0	31	0	1,500	3,190	88,622	81,149	1,400
Red Bank	2105	265	265	80	3	5	12	4	12,250	24,375	0	264,544	2,000
Richard City	2118	28	62	13	0	0	3	0	2,700	3,449	32,547	35,450	900
Silverdale	2106	103	151	52	6	11	4	2	6,647	15,146	126,514	141,763	2,643
South Pittsburg	2123	19	64	0	0	0	3	0	100	716	23,576	20,947	825
Sumach	2124	157	222	73	0	2	2	0	5,000	12,123	135,678	147,801	666
Whitwell	2122	5	15	9	0	0	0	0	0	591	9,216	11,546	25
TOTALS	26	1,876	2,357	799	34	51	137	15	68,748	207,548	1,687,604	2,188,526	20,235

*Math error corrected. **Purged roll.

TENNESSEE-GEORGIA PRESBYTERY CONTINUED

CHURCHES, PASTORS, AND CLERKS:

Bartow   (4MWEC)SETG2101
  1078 Cassville White Road (mailing)
  Cartersville, GA 30121
  2851 Highway 140 NE (physical)
  Rydal, GA 30171
  (770)382-3896   <Bartow>
  pastormarkbcpcga@gmail.com
PA: Mark Rackley   <M1>
  3060 Highway 140 NE
  Rydal, GA 30171
  (770)382-3790
  pastormarkbcpcga@gmail.com
AP: Min Young Lim   <M3 ST>
  3480 Summit Ridge Parkway
  Duluth, GA 30096
  (770)751-1148
  minyounglim63@gmail.com
CL: James Harris Bagwell
  1078 Cassville White Road
  Cartersville, GA 30121
  (770)382-0747
  shadygrovebeef@aol.com

Cedar Springs   (4C)SETG2119
  495 Cedar Springs Loop (mailing)
  6665 Old Dunlap Road (physical)
  Whitwell, TN 37397
  ( )   <Marion>
PA: Kriss McGowan   <M1>
  900 Alvin York Highway
  Whitwell, TN 37397
  (423)463-8609
  krissmcg658@gmail.com
CL: Sarah Way
  4595 Old Dunlap Road
  Whitwell, TN 37397
  (423)580-7685
  sarahway1958@aol.com

Charleston   (4MEWC)SETG2102
  PO Box 476 (mailing)
  Charleston, TN 37310
  8267 N Lee Highway (physical)
  Cleveland, TN 37312
  (423)336-5004   <Bradley>
PA: Bill Bond   <M1>
  205 Windmere Drive
  Chattanooga, TN 37411
  (423)316-0867
  bill@wcbj.net
CL: Vivian McCormack
  5502 Mouse Creek Road NW
  Cleveland, TN 37312
  (423)479-8230
  mcco6868@bellsouth.net

Chattanooga First   (4WC)SETG2104
  1505 N Moore Road
  Chattanooga, TN 37411
  (423)698-2556   <Hamilton>
  FAX: (423)629-6683
  office@firstcumberland.com
PA: Gary Carver   <M1>
  2810 Cabin Road
  Chattanooga, TN 37404
  (423)698-2556
  FAX: (423)629-6683
  sandgatthecabin@epbfi.com

CL: Christy Miller
  7853 Legacy Park Court
  Chattanooga, TN 37421
  (423)894-8220
  christymiller62@epbfi.com

Cleveland   (4WC)SETG2108
  161 2nd Street NE Ste 3 (mailing)
  200 Church Street NE (physical)
  Cleveland, TN 37311
  (423)476-6751   <Bradley>
  FAX: (423)476-6423
  gchudson3@gmail.com
PA: George Cliff Hudson   <M1>
  4782 Waverly Court
  Ooltewah, TN 37363
  (423)238-6333
  FAX: (423)476-6423
  gchudson3@gmail.com
AP: Jennifer Newell   <M1>
  2322 Maraco Circle
  Chattanooga, TN 37421
  (423)892-5834
  FAX: (423)476-6423
  newelljennifer3@gmail.com
CL: Denise Callais
  161 2nd Street NE Suite 3
  Cleveland, TN 37311
  (423)476-6751

Cornerstone Com   (4MWC)SETG2107
  9632 E Brainerd Road
  Chattanooga, TN 37421
  (423)892-3027   <Hamilton>
  cornerstone3cp@gmail.com
SS: Jerry (Butch) Hullander   <M1>
  767 Rifle Range Road
  Ringgold, GA 30736
  (706)935-4878
  jerryihs@catt.com
CL: Session Clerk
  9632 E Brainerd Road
  Chattanooga, TN 37421
  (423)892-3027
  cornerstone3cp@gmail.com

Ebenezer   (4C)SETG2110
  PO Box 424 (mailing)
  Sequatchie, TN 37374
  East Valley Road (physical)
  Jasper, TN 37347
  (423)942-3191   <Marion>
  cprevinsv@bellsouth.net
PA: Phillip Layne   <M1>
  10699 Griffith Highway
  Whitwell, TN 37397
  (423)658-5849
  cprevinsv@bellsouth.net
CL: Carol Renfro
  PO Box 434
  Sequatchie, TN 37374
  (423)942-3191

El Redill   (C)SETG2149
  875 Scenic Highway
  Lawrenceville, GA 30045
  (678)698-7971   <Monmouth>
  FAX: (678)225-0127
  mabega@juno.com
PA: Maria (Mabe) Garcia   <M1>
  875 Scenic Highway

  Lawrenceville, GA 30045
  (678)698-7971
  mabega@juno.com
CL: Francia Bryon
  3315 Crooked Stick Drive
  Cumming, GA 30041
  (678)977-8606
  elenabry1@yahoo.com

Falling Water   (4WC)SETG2111
  6534 Old Dayton Pike
  Hixson, TN 37343
  (423)843-3050   <Hamilton>
  james_barry@bellsouth.net
PA: James C Barry   <M1>
  1405 Anna Street
  Hixson, TN 37343
  (903)315-7998
  james_barry@bellsouth.net
CL: Diane J Bunch
  8212 Pierpoint Drive
  Harrison, TN 37341
  (423)802-2763
  topdog23@bellsouth.net

Flint Springs   (4WC)SETG2112
  517 Mitchell Road SE (mailing)
  Flint Springs Road (physical)
  Cleveland, TN 37311
  ( )   <Bradley>
PA: Kevin Wilson   <M1>
  2225 North East Road SE
  Cleveland, TN 37311
  (423)284-6397
  revkev1000@hotmail.com
CL: James F Mitchell, Jr
  517 Mitchell Road SE
  Cleveland, TN 37323
  (423)479-7649

Glory Church of Jesus Christ(C)SETG2144
  3480 Summit Ridge Parkway
  Duluth, GA 30096
  ( )   < >
PA: David Lee   <M1>
  (404)641-4359
  gcjcatl@gmail.com
CL: Session Clerk Glory Church
  3480 Summit Ridge Parkway
  Duluth, GA 30096

Jasper   (4MWC)SETG2113
  PO Box 877 (mailing)
  148 College Street (physical)
  Jasper, TN 37347
  (423)942-2188   <Marion>
  FAX: (423)942-2188
SS: James H. Patterson   <M1>
  1305 Falmouth Road
  Chattanooga, TN 37405
  (423)267-8568
  FAX: (423)942-2188
CL: Dorris G Ross
  214 Hancock Road
  Jasper, TN 37347
  (423)942-5224
  FAX: (423)942-2188
  ross37347@charter.net

Kelly's Chapel   (4MC)SETG2120
  3748 Alvin York Highway (mailing)

TENNESSEE-GEORGIA PRESBYTERY CONTINUED

470 Highway 27 (physical)
Whitwell, TN 37397
( )   <Marion>
carolb8667@bellsouth.net
OD: Anthony Tucker   <M5>
209 Rock City Trail
Lookout Mountain, GA 30750
CL: Stanley Doyle Davis
280 Condra Street
Whitwell, TN 37397
(423)658-5606

_____

Korean Living Stone   (P)SETG2130
4175 Buford Highway
Duluth, GA 30096
(770)912-7710
PA: Yang Rae Park   <M1>
3340 Bentbill Crossing
Cumming, GA 30041
(770)912-7710
barkmoksa@hanmail.net
CL: Session Clerk Korean Living Stone
4175 Buford Highway
Duluth, GA 30096
(770)912-7710

_____

New Hope   (4MWC)SETG2115
176 E Valley Road (mailing)
196 E Valley Road (physical)
Whitwell, TN 37397
(423)949-3951   <Sequatchie>
PA: Jimmy Byrd   <M1>
176 E Valley Road
Whitwell, TN 37397
(615)289-3347
revjimmybyrd@hotmail.com
CL: James Condra
PO Box 1001
Dunlap, TN 37327
(423)447-8126
jwcondra@bledsoe.net

_____

Oak Grove   (4C)SETG2121
872 Alvin York Highway (mailing)
8150 Griffith Highway (physical)
Whitwell, TN 37397
( )   <Marion>
PA: Phillip H Layne   <M1>
10699 Griffith Highway
Whitwell, TN 37397
(423)658-6421
cprevinsv@bellsouth.net
CL: Martha S Layne
872 Alvin York Highway
Whitwell, TN 37397
(423)658-6421

_____

Our Good   (P)SETG2138
32132 Huntly Circle
Salisbury, MD 21804
(443)783-7502   <Wilomico>
PA: Hyoung S. Choi   <M1>
32132 Huntly Circle
Salisbury, MD 21804
(443)880-6776
pastor0101@naver.com
CL: Session Clerk Our Good Church
32132 Huntly Circle
Salisbury, MD 21804

_____

Pine Hill   (4MC)SETG2117

Rt 2 Box 220 (mailing)
146 Pine Hill Road SW (physical)
McDonald, TN 37353
(423)339-2816   <Bradley>
OD: Russell Maroon   <M5>
Rt 2 Box 220
McDonald, TN 37353
(423)894-9395
CL: Russell Kelley
970 Black Fox Road SW
Cleveland, TN 37311
(423)476-7272

_____

Prospect United   (4MC)SETG2116
310 New Murraytown Road NW
Cleveland, TN 37312
(423)476-6181   <Bradley>
cloverwreathfarm@hotmail.com
CL: Betty Brakebill
3512 Windsor Circle NE
Cleveland, TN 37312
(423)479-2731

_____

Red Bank   (4WC)SETG2105
115 Morrison Springs Road
Chattanooga, TN 37415
(423)877-1383   <Hamilton>
rbcpchurch@gmail.com
CL: Mark Craven
21 Kingston Street
Chattanooga, TN 37415
(423)870-2274
cravenhaus@gmail.com

_____

Richard City   (4MWC)SETG2118
1706 Marion Avenue
South Pittsburg , TN 37380
(423)837-6533   <Marion>
SS: Carlton Harper   <M1>
8764 Cody Dan Court
Ooltewah, TN 37363
(423)238-9257
carltonone@comcast.net
CL: Bill Norman
624 19th Street
South Pittsburg , TN 37380
(423)837-6693
FAX: (423)837-8903
billnorman@catcore.com

_____

Silverdale   (4MEWC)SETG2106
7407 Bonny Oaks Drive
Chattanooga, TN 37421
(423)892-8710   <Hamilton>
FAX: (423)892-7751
silverdalechurch@comcast.net
PA: Christian Smith   <M1>
7401 Bonny Oaks Drive
Chattanooga, TN 37421
(423)508-2490
csmith2490@gmail.com
CL: Dotty Manis
7939 Clara Chase Drive
Ooltewah, TN 37363
(423)238-4021
dottmae@centurylink.net

_____

South Pittsburg   (4MWC)SETG2123
PO Box 327 (mailing)
400 Elm Avenue (physical)
South Pittsburg, TN 37380

(423)837-6488   <Marion>
spcpc1@yahoo.com
PA: Kriss McGowan   <M1>
900 Alvin York Highway
Whitwell, TN 37397
(423)463-8609
krissmcg658@gmail.com
CL: George Holland
214 Dixie Avenue
South Pittsburg, TN 37380
(423)837-7113
georgehollandsp@att.net

_____

Sumach   (4MWC)SETG2124
PO Box 804 (mailing)
9203 Highway 225 N (physical)
Chatsworth, GA 30705
(706)695-4773   <Murray>
FAX: (706)695-4773
sumachcpchurch@windstream.net
PA: Glenn Brister   <M1>
2089 Sumach Church Road
Chatsworth, GA 30705
(706)934-8629
bearmountainpenworks@gmail.com
CL: Carolyn Luffman
926 Long Avenue
Chatsworth, GA 30705
(706)695-4346
cizzle44@hotmail.com

_____

Whitwell   (4C)SETG2122
7390 Highway 108
Whitwell, TN 37397
(423)658-5849   <Marion>
PA: Phillip Layne   <M1>
10699 Griffith Highway
Whitwell, TN 37397
(423)658-5849
cprevinsv@bellsouth.net
CL: Odus Caldwell
7390 Highway 108
Whitwell, TN 37397
(423)658-6463

_____

OTHERS ON MINISTERIAL ROLL:
Bertsch, Michael   <M1 RT>
115 Leatherwood Creek Estates
Bedford, IN 47421
(423)763-8314
silkpie@gmail.com
Cho, Sangsook   <M1 WC>
7 Falmouth Court
Middletown, CT 06457
(860)830-6808
lovejcamen@yahoo.com
Ferguson, E Blant   <M1 RT>
704 Bear Run
Hiawassee, GA 30546
(706)896-9296
blantferg@yahoo.com
Griffin, Justin   <M1 WC>
205 E Livingston Street
San Augustine, TX 75972
(936)275-2546
jjjgriff@gmail.com
Han, Seung Chon   <M0>
3075 Landington Way
Duluth, GA 30096
kpc0191@gmail.com
(678)469-5015
Jackson, Lamar   <M1 RT>

TENNESSEE-GEORGIA PRESBYTERY CONTINUED

280 Deer Ridge Drive Apt D
Dayton, TN 37321
(423)570-9348
hljaxn@charter.net

Kang, Jin Koo   \<M1 OM\>
2310 Hisway
Lawrenceville, GA 30044
(678)462-7526
agatopia@hanmail.net

Kelso, James H   \<M1 RT\>
131 Lords Way
Dawsonville, GA 30534
(706)216-7513
elgato@alltel.net

Kim, Kio Seob   \<M1 OM\>
14430 35th Avenue Apt A62
Flushing, NY 11354
(718)539-3476

Kim, Mi Young   \<M1 WC\>
IN KOREA

Kim, Min Soo   \<M1 OM\>
1050 Grace Drive
Lawrenceville, GA 30043
(404)518-0205

Lee, Sarah   \<M1 WC\>
(no address on file)

Ma, Choil   \<M1 WC\>
40 Conger Street #1404A
Bloomfield, NJ 07003

March, Kevin   \<M1 RT\>
1701 Ray Jo Circle
Chattanooga, TN 37421
(423)499-4180
kmadm1@aol.com

Martin, Theresa   \<M1 WC\>
116 Crisman Street
Chattanooga, TN 37415
(423)903-7260 (cell)
choochootm@usa.net

Martin, Tom   \<M1 WC\>
116 Crisman Street
Chattanooga, TN 37415
(423)903-7260 (cell)
choochootm@usa.net

McCarty, John   \<M1 M9\>
305 W Martindale Drive
Marshall, TX 75672
(423)650-8788
mtsjohn@gmail.com

McGowan, Rhonda   \<M1 WC\>
PO Box 869
Whitwell, TN 37379
(423)658-0590
rhondam658@gmail.com

Melton, Samuel D   \<M1 RT\>
2249 Bucks Pocket Road SE
Oldfort, TN 37362
(423)472-8467

Oh, Taeho   \<M1 WC\>
42-40 2908th Street #1
Bayside, NY 11361

Prosser, Forest   \<M1 RT\>
1157 Mountain Creek Road
Chattanooga, TN 37405
(423)877-4114
forestprosser@comcast.net

Ryoo, Hwa Chang   \<M1 WC\>
450 Island Road Unit 146
Ramsey, NJ 07446

Song, Byung Seon   \<M1 WC\>
(MOVED TO CANADA)
(404)512-9147

Song, Nam Hun   \<M1 WC\>
(IN KOREA)

Sumrall, Philip (Phil)   \<M1 WC\>
107 Barnhardt Circle
Fort Oglethorpe, GA 30742
(423)903-1938
phil.sumrall@gmail.com

Tolley, Robert (Butch)   \<M1 WC\>
1445 New Murraytown Road NW
Cleveland, TN 37312
(423)837-6488

Wright, B J   \<M1 WC\>
301 25th Street
Phenix City, AL 36867
(334)298-2896
bojobo3@yahoo.com

Yi, Woo Young   \<M1 WC\>
(IN JAPAN)

Yoo, Paul   \<M1 WC\>
IN KOREA
sungyy@msn.com

OTHER LICENTIATES ON ROLL:

Chin, Kwang Sik   \<M2\>
1168 Palisade Avenue
Fort Lee, NJ 07024
(201)220-3390

Jones, Harold   \<M2\>
4123 Wilkesview Drive Apt A
Chattanooga, TN 37416
(478)320-4222
harold@personalcharacter.com

Kennedy, Jim   \<M2\>
3818 Peace Court Apt F
Aberdeen Proving Ground, MD 21005

Sung, John   \<M2\>
26 Old Orchard Road
Cherry Hill, NJ 08003
(856)751-0227

OTHER CANDIDATES ON ROLL:

Garcia, Lucas   \<M3\>
875 Scenic Highway
Lawrenceville, GA 30045
(678)698-7971

Hollingshed, Lee   \<M3 ST\>
3612 Harmony Church Grove Road
Dallas, GA 30132
(770)548-0152
leearmstrong@bellsouth.net

Humphries, Rick   \<M3\>
187 Wilson Heights Circle NE
Cleveland, TN 37312
(423)331-0340
lshumphries@juno.com

Kang, Eun Hee   \<M3\>
14715 46th Avenue
Flushing, NY 11355
(718)762-0778

Kollie, Moses   \<M3\>
760 Harbor Point Court
Lawrenceville, GA 30044
(770)990-2215
kolliemoses70@yahoo.com

Middleton, Frank, Jr   \<M3 ST\>
1200 Adele Circle
Slidell, LA 70461
(770)655-0406
fmiddle@bellsouth.net

Park, Young   \<M3 ST\>
3340 Bentbill Crossing
Cummings, GA 30041
(404)661-6117
barkmogun@gmail.com

Rapson, Tim   \<M3\>
176 East Valley Road
Whitwell, TN 37397
(423)949-8214
tim.rapson@yahoo.com

Scott, Joel   \<M3\>
1848 Sassafrass Lane
Soddy Daisy, TN 37379
(423)240-2724
saejoescott@gmail.com

Turner, Glyn   \<M3 ST\>
1660 Chattanooga Valley Road
Flintstone, GA 30725
(585)307-7715
glynturner@outlook.com

Varnell, William   \<M3 ST\>
6729 Old Dunlop Road
Whitwell, TN 37397
(423)658-0506

Trinity Presbytery
MISSION SYNOD

	GENERAL	MEMBERSHIP			CHANGES				FINANCES				
	1.Church Number	2.Active	3.Total	4.Church School	5.Prof. of Faith	6.Gains	7.Losses	8.Children Baptized	9. OUR UNITED OUT-REACH	10. Total Out-Reach Giving	11. All Other Expenses	12. Total Income Received	13. Value Church Prop. 1=1000
	1	2	3	4	5	6	7	8	9	10	11	12	13
Antioch	8101	18	20	10	0	0	1	0	1,100	13,994	37,622	31,794	325
Austin, First	8601	38	36	4	1	1	3	0	250	287	121,149	106,899	2,397
Bertram	8605	183	176	40	0	2	2	3	9,900	33,321	96,453	84,731	324
Bethany	8102	9	24	7	CLOSED 2013			0	0	0	0	0	178
Concord	8104	55	96	35	1	0	1	1	10,486	33,950	85,033	113,583	805
Daingerfield	8106	10	13	6	0	0	1	0	1,500	5,975	26,134	22,592	150
Elmira Chapel	8111	75	134	45	0	3	27	0	7,361	75,966	173,893	242,919	4,000
Faith	8107	6	35	0	CLOSED 2013			0	4,800	0	0	0	668
Freeport	8103	30	30	5	2	2	2	0	0	1,200	64,759	80,647	933
Houston, 1st	8606	126	288	41	0	4	2	1	51,876	129,852	313,375	525,996	2,322
Jefferson	8109	40	53	28	7	30	2	3	0	12,024	73,925	94,190	650
Longview, 1st	8112	56	165	29	0	0	2	0	9,805	29,463	80,538	98,367	660
Marshall	8115	175	328	93	0	6	6	3	31,708	106,802	370,450	470,211	3,037
Mt. Hope	8117	3	3	0	0	0	1	0	0	0	0	0	183
Northminster+	8610	266	282	31	3	19	2	0	0	9,831	276,486	313,497	3,600
Nueva Vida	8612	89	134	26	No Report Received			0	0	0	0	0	0
Oak Grove	8607	6	62	0	0	0	0	0	0	0	3,000	2,500	200
Pine Hill*	8122	26	59	14	0	4	0	0	650	6,983	39,776	42,558	85
Pine Tree*	8113	30	72	22	No Report Received			0	3,349	0	0	0	800
Progress*	8123	6	7	6	No Report Received			0	0	0	0	0	0
Round Rock+*	8611	117	117	45	6	0	52	2	0	0	153,544	164,716	853
Shepherd/Hills+	8604	281	279	100	2	14	6	5	0	43,766	348,903	363,325	1,100
Shiloh	8125	11	42	0	0	0	2	0	0	6,075	18,349	22,772	65
Stone Oak	8608	115	140	42	0	4	54	1	0	34,936	217,363	261,197	2,200
TOTALS	24	1,771	2,595	629	22	89	166	19	132,785	544,425	2,500,752	3,042,494	25,535

*Math error corrected. **Purged roll. +Union Church

CHURCHES, PASTORS, AND CLERKS:

Antioch (4MWC)MSTR8101
PO Box 42 (mailing)
518 N Antioch Road (physical)
Quitman, LA 71268
(318)259-7069 <Jackson>
PA: Joshua Murray <M1>
527 N Antioch Road
Quitman, LA 71268
(318)259-7828
jdm4428@yahoo.com
CL: Jerry L Hanes
5104 Beech Springs Road
Quitman, LA 71268
(318)259-4246
lindaameme@hotmail.com

Austin First (4WC)MSTR8601
6800 Woodrow Avenue
Austin, TX 78757
(512)453-8434 <Travis>
cpaustin@prodigy.net
CL: Mike Coyne
1003 Justin Lane Apt 1113
Austin, TX 78757
(512)535-4110
coynonia@gmail.com

Bertram (4MEWC)MSTR8605
PO Box 242 (mailing)
430 Highway 29 (physical)
Bertram, TX 78605
(512)355-2182 <Burnet>
PA: Daryl Johnson <M1>
425 W Vaughan Street
Bertram, TX 78605
(512)355-2182
djchurch@earthlink.net
CL: Tommy Griffis
1701 County Road 254
Georgetown, TX 78633
(512)496-8878
tbgriffis44@gmail.com

Bethany (4M C)MSTR8102
CLOSED 2013

Concord (4MWC)MSTR8104
212 County Road 4705
Troup, TX 75789
(903)842-4745 <Cherokee>
FAX: (903)842-4745
revdad.duane@gmail.com
PA: Duane A Dougherty Jr <M1>
212 County Road 4705
Troup, TX 75789
(903)842-4745
revdad.duane@gmail.com
CL: Sandy Mager
356 County Road 4629
Troup, TX 75789
(903)842-3844

stmager@yahoo.com

Daingerfield (4MC)MSTR8106
PO Box 645 (mailing)
307 Broadnak (physical)
Daingerfield, TX 75638
(903)645-2183 <Morris>
sharjohn@windstream.net
SS: John C Lawson <M2>
PO Box 645
Daingerfield, TX 75638
(903)645-2183
sharjohn@windstream.net
CL: John C Lawson
PO Box 645
Daingerfield, TX 75638
(903)645-2183
sharjohn@windstream.net

Elmira Chapel (4MWC)MSTR8111
3501 Elmira Drive
Longview, TX 75605
(903)759-2069 <Gregg>
elmirachapel@aol.com
PA: James M Cantey <M1>
3505 Elmira Drive
Longview, TX 75605
(903)452-6049
CL: Sherry Poteet
3501 Elmira Drive
Longview, TX 75605
(903)759-2069

TRINITY PRESBYTERY CONTINUED

spoteet1@aol.com

Faith   (4C)MSTR8107
  CLOSED 2/15/13

Freeport   (4C)MSTR8103
  1402 W Broad Street
  Freeport, TX 77541
PA: Lee Attema   <M1>
  930 W 8th Street
  Freeport, TX 77541
  (281)728-6263
  lattema@comcast.net
SC: Cathy Bettoney
  1149 Ash Street
  Clute, TX 77531
  (979)265-7630
  dbettoney@sbcglobal.net

Houston First   (4EWC)MSTR8606
  2119 Avalon Place
  Houston, TX 77019
  (713)522-7821   <Harris>
  FAX: (713)522-8869
  firstcp@cphouston.org
PA: J Geoffrey Knight   <M1>
  2119 Avalon Place
  Houston, TX 77019
  (713)522-7821
  FAX: (713)522-8869
  geoff@family.net
CL: Diane Dickson
  2119 Avalon Place
  Houston, TX 77019
  (713)522-7821
  FAX: (713)522-8869
  firstcp@cphouston.org

Jefferson   (4EC)MSTR8109
  501 E Jefferson Street
  Jefferson, TX 75657
  (903)665-9365   <Marion>
  jeffersoncpc@juno.com
PA: Robert (Toby) Davis   <M1>
  PO Box 5
  Trilla, IL 62469
  (901)826-5755
  pastortobydavis@gmail.com
CL: Eric S Thomas
  250 Berea 1
  Jefferson, TX 75657
  (903)601-1146
  ethomas@etbu.edu

Longview First   (4WC)MSTR8112
  2401 Alpine Street
  Longview, TX 75601
  (903)758-5184   <Gregg>
  FAX: (903)757-2572
  fcpclongview@sbcglobal.net
PA: Steven W Turner   <M1>
  7622 Snider Road
  Gilmer, TX 75645
  (903)758-5184
  FAX: (903)757-2572
  fcpclongview@sbcglobal.net
CL: Mollie Benson
  567 Hidden Forest
  Longview, TX 75601
  (903)663-0443
  FAX: (903)757-2572
  fcpclongview@sbcglobal.net

Marshall   (4EWC)MSTR8115
  PO Box 1303 (mailing)
  501 Indian Spring Road (physical)
  Marshall, TX 75671
  (903)935-3787   <Harrison>
  FAX: (903)935-3193
  info@cumberlandofmarshall.org
PA: William Rustenhaven III   <M1>
  PO Box 1303
  Marshall, TX 75671
  (903)935-7275
  FAX: (903)935-3193
  rusty@cumberlandofmarshall.org
AP: Mary Kathryn Kirkpatrick   <M1>
  401 1/2 Henley-Perry Drive
  Marshall, TX 75670
  (903)930-6236
  mkkirpartick@gmail.com
CL: Shirley Jones
  104 Hillcrest Terrace
  Marshall, TX 75672
  (903)938-3980
  shopfarm75672@yahoo.com

Mt Hope   (4MC)MSTR8117
  Box 66
  Joinerville, TX 75658
  (903)847-3451   <Rusk>
CL: Anna J Holman
  PO Box 115
  Joinerville, TX 75658
  (903)847-3801

Northminster   (4U)MSTR8610
  6800 Tezel Road
  San Antonio, TX 78250
  (210)680-4825   <Bexar>
  FAX: (210)680-4826
  npcoffice@npcsatx.org
PA: Robert E Weston   <M1>
  11 Summer Bluff
  San Antonio, TX 78254
  (210)347-0232
  FAX: (210)680-4826
  rjaweston@gmail.com
CL: Marsha Schendel
  8730 Prince Heights
  San Antonio, TX 78254
  (210)681-4231
  marshaschendel@hotmail.com

Nueva Vida   (F)MSTR8612
  4505 Highway 6 N
  Suite 700
  Houston, TX 77084
  (832)593-8355   <Harris>
PA: Ruben D Albarracin   <M1>
  7411 Magnolia Shadows Lane
  Houston, TX 77095
  (281)463-8617
  FAX: (281)463-8617
  confiaendios@hotmail.com
CL: Patricia Nunez
  7303 Hollow Field W
  Cypress, TX 77433
  (281)855-1881
  FAX: (713)533-9735

Oak Grove   (4C)MSTR8607
  12951 Ranch Road 2338
  Georgetown, TX 78633
  ( )   <Williamson>
PA: John Paul Kessie   <M1>
  225 Clear Springs Road
  Georgetown, TX 78628
  (512)585-1617
  oakgrovecpcpastor@verizon.net

CL: Wanda Shelton
  2355 County Road 226
  Florence, TX 76527
  (512)579-1325

Pine Hill   (4C)MSTR8122
  8236 Farm Road 3019 (mailing)
  FM 3019 County Road 3281 (physical)
  Winnsboro, TX 75494
  ( )   <Hopkins>
CL: Elizabeth Aden
  404 Yates Street
  Mount Vernon, TX 75457
  (903)537-7288
  libbya1@suddenlink.net

Pine Tree   (4MWC)MSTR8113
  PO Box 151009 (mailing)
  1805 Pine Tree Road (physical)
  Longview, TX 75615
  (903)759-2685   <Gregg>
  nunnh@earthlink.net
PA: Donald W Nunn   <M1>
  203 Bridgers Hill Road
  Longview, TX 75604
  (903)297-6074
  dwnunn@earthlink.net
CL: Darlynn Jones
  1819 Flagstone Drive
  Longview, TX 75605
  (903)236-7310
  darlynnj@att.net

Progress   (4C)MSTR8123
  722 Gewin Lane (mailing)
  3643 Progress Church Road (physical)
  Pleasant Hill, LA 71065
  (318)796-3725   <Sabine>
  mamacgewin@yahoo.com
CL: Carolyn W Gewin
  722 Gewin Lane
  Pleasant Hill, LA 71065
  (318)796-3703
  mamacgewin@yahoo.com

Round Rock   (4U)MSTR8611
  4010 Sam Bass Road
  Round Rock, TX 78681
  (512)544-2152   <Travis>
  rrpc_info@roundrockpresbyterian.org
OD: Catherine Craley   <M5>
  4010 Sam Bass Road
  Round Rock, TX 78681
CL: Elaine B Dodd
  1805 Castleguard Way
  Cedar Park, TX 78613
  (512)260-0310
  doddeb@sbcglobal.net

Shepherd of the Hills   (4U)MSTR8604
  5226 W William Cannon Drive
  Austin, TX 78749
  (512)892-3580   <Travis>
  FAX: (512)892-6307
  church@shpc.org
OD: Laurance W Coulter   <M5>
  5226 W William Cannon Drive
  Austin, TX 78749
  (512)892-3580
  FAX: (512)358-0879
  larry@shpc.org
AP: Michael Killeen   <M1>
  5226 W William Cannon Drive
  Austin, TX 78749
  (512)560-0423

TRINITY PRESBYTERY CONTINUED

FAX: (512)358-0879
mike@shpc.org
AP: Britta Dukes   <M1>
  5226 W William Cannon Drive
  Austin, TX 78749
  (512)892-3580
  FAX: (512)358-0879
  britta@shpc.org
CL: Clift Bowman
  5226 W William Cannon Drive
  Austin, TX 78749
  (512)288-5839
  FAX: (512)358-0879
  cbowman24@austin.rr.com

Shiloh   (4C)MSTR8125
  4928 County Road 3275 (mailing)
  2467 County Road 3205 (physical)
  Clarksville, TX 75426
  (903)427-3785   <Red River>
  shiloh.presbyterian@yahoo.com
PA: Billy Jack Holt   <M1>
  5039 Highway 37 N
  Clarksville, TX 75426
  (903)428-9909
  jackdora@windstream.net
CL: Mary Jo McGill
  4928 County Road 3275
  Clarksville, TX 75426
  (903)427-3785
  hoopnmj@yahoo.com

Stone Oak   (4C)MSTR8608
  20024 Crescent Oaks
  San Antonio, TX 78258
  (210)497-7974   <Bexar>
  FAX: (210)497-8724
  officemanager@satx.rr.com
PA: Kevin Colvard   <M1>
  27027 Harmony Hills
  San Antonio, TX 78260
  (205)267-9372
  FAX: (210)497-8724
  rev_kev@satx.rr.com
CL: Barry Elliott
  2204 Sunderidge
  San Antonio, TX 78260
  (210)884-1749
  FAX: (210)497-8724
  barrydeanelliott@gmail.com

OTHERS ON MINISTERIAL ROLL:

Bone, W Harold   <M1 WC>
  3405 Stillman Loop
  Bryant, AR 72022
  (501)847-9473
  ruaha1@sbcglobal.net
Bowers, Sharon G   <M1 M9>
  1800 Post Road Apt 612
  San Marcos, TX 78666
  (512)230-7078
  sharon.bowers@gmail.com
Bozeman, Robert   <M1 WC>
  582 Bozeman Loop
  Belmont, LA 71406
  (318)256-5781
  bo@bozemanengineering.com
Brasher, Karen   <M1 WC>
  1640 King James Drive
  Alabaster, AL 35007
Chancellor, Hilton   <M1 WC>
  PO Box 341717
  Austin, TX 78734
  (941)907-0577
  FAX: (915)570-0866

hiltontex@aol.com
Diaz, Freddy   <M1 WC>
  2425 Holly Hall Apt B42
  Houston, TX 77054
  (832)305-2379
  fredglobeus@yahoo.com
Diaz, Gloria Villa   <M1 WC>
  2425 Holly Hall Apt B42
  Houston, TX 77054
  (832)305-2379
  fredglobeus@yahoo.com
Gonzalez, Nora   <M1 WC>
  2515 Blueberry Lane
  Pasadena, TX 77502
  (832)202-5572
Hamilton, Lynn   <M1 WC>
  4511 Lucksinger Lane Trailer 1
  Austin, TX 78745
  (512)443-6813
  lhamilton@minister.com
Hannah, Hugh   <M1 WC>
  217 Mitchell Road SE
  Cleveland, TN 37323
  (318)395-8729
Harris, Ernest   <M1 RT>
  PO Box 1403
  Clarksville, TX 75426
  (903)966-2481
  ernieandjeri@wmconnect.com
Hewitt, Gary   <M1 RT>
  521 Easy Street Unit 17
  Cleveland, TX 77327
  (281)592-3425
Hoke, Walter   <M1 WC>
  215 Navajo Trail
  Georgetown, TX 78633
  (512)869-1948
Insley, Michael   <M1 WC>
  8046 Manderly Place
  Converse, TX 78109
  (210)490-0817
  chapmdi@yahoo.com
Jarnagin, Mary   <M1 ST>
  1003 Justin Lane Apt 1017
  Austin, TX 78757
  (512)367-9922
  marjar27@yahoo.com
Magrill Jr, J Richard   <M1 WC>
  500 Miller Drive
  Marshall, TX 75672
  (901)685-9454
  FAX: (901)272-3913
  jrm@cumberland.org
McNeese, Mark   <M1 WC>
  6800 Woodrow Avenue
  Austin, TX 78757
  (512)453-8434
  FAX: (512)453-2911
  mam53@prodigy.net
McNeese, Michael C   <M1 WC>
  16410 Wesley Evans Road
  Prairieville, LA 70769
  (520)722-1350
  mcneesemc@cox.net
Mills, David M   <M1 M9 RT>
  528 County Road 322
  Bertram, TX 78605
  (512)355-3511
Mitchum, Mark   <M1 WC>
  21102 La Pena
  San Antonio, TX 78258
  (210)497-7974
  FAX: (210)497-8724
  mitchum@gmail.com
Park, Sung In   <M1 WC>

10109 Loxley Lane
Austin, TX 78717
Parsons, Hugh L   <M1 RT>
  1526 Welch
  Houston, TX 77006
  (713)522-6126
  p-h-parsons@comcast.net
Peters, David J   <M1 WC>
  4010 Sam Bass Road
  Round Rock, TX 78681
  (512)244-2152
Pic, Paul   <M1 WC>
  2425 Jefferson Avenue
  New Orleans, LA 70115
  (504)488-9000
Rush, Robert D   <M1 WC>
  17822 Deep Brook Drive
  Spring, TX 77379
  (901)213-4879
  rushrd74@comcast.net
Rustenhaven, William, Jr   <M1 WC>
  703 W Burleson Street
  Marshall, TX 75670
  (903)935-7056
  rustenhavendolores@yahoo.com
Santillano, Ray Paul   <M1 RT>
  8800 Starcrest Drive Apt 110
  San Antonio, TX 78217
  (808)349-3308
  ray.santillano@us.army.mil
Smith, Charles D   <M1 WC>
  12320 Moss Square
  St Francesville , LA 70775
  (225)635-4432
  cdsmith46@gmail.com
Smith, David R   <M1 WC>
  PO Box 892
  Rosepine, LA 70659
  (903)297-6074
  ogreyfox@att.net
Suenram, Timothy   <M1 WC>
  5704 Tyler Street
  Pearland, TX 77581
  (832)217-6367
  tsuenram@aol.com
Wayman, Sam   <M1 RT>
  707 High Hill Creek Road
  LaGrange, TX 78945
  (979)968-3734
  samdonnawayman@gmail.com
Winslett, Don   <M1 M9>
  Baptist Hospital/Pastoral Care
  1000 W Moreno Street
  Pensacola, FL 32521

OTHER LICENTIATES ON ROLL

Lawson, John   <M2>
  PO Box 142
  Lone Star, TX 75668
  (903)656-2986
  johnnyknocker@earthlink.net

OTHER CANDIDATES ON ROLL

Williams, James A   <M3 ST>
  1475 Kings Road
  Marshall, TX 75672
  (903)938-7345

West Tennessee Presbytery
GREAT RIVERS SYNOD

GENERAL		MEMBERSHIP		CHANGES				FINANCES				
1.Church Number	2.Active	3.Total	4.Church School	5.Prof. of Faith	6.Gains	7.Losses	8.Children Baptized	9. OUR UNITED OUTREACH	10. Total Out-Reach Giving	11. All Other Expenses	12. Total Income Received	13. Value Church Prop. 1=1000
1	2	3	4	5	6	7	8	9	10	11	12	13
Antioch Union 9401	21	31	30	No Report Received			0	1,237	0	0	0	343
Atwood 9101	7	7	5	0	0	0	0	298	582	9,167	10,271	200
Barren Springs 9102	5	37	4	No Report Received			0	0	0	0	0	25
Beech 9402	60	72	22	3	5	3	0	2,680	8,234	51,145	71,281	360
Bells Chapel 9403	23	63	16	0	2	0	0	800	1,400	21,588	34,544	500
Bethel (TC) 9301	23	34	15	No Report Received			0	0	0	0	0	300
Bethesda 9404	20	20	15	0	0	1	0	200	200	25,331	27,607	300
Bethlehem 9405	11	25	8	No Report Received			0	0	0	0	0	70
Bolivar 9202	30	47	6	No Report Received			0	2,881	0	0	0	350
Bradford 9104	49	131	31	No Report Received			0	2,375	0	0	0	175
Brunswick 9302	33	63	12	0	1	0	0	1,938	4,094	30,349	37,772	418
Camden 9105	55	117	40	No Report Received			0	312	0	0	0	900
Camp Ground 9204	16	29	30	No Report Received			0	1,000	0	0	0	175
Claybrook* 9205	8	8	6	No Report Received			0	150	0	0	0	10
Cloverdale 9407	3	6	5	No Report Received			0	0	0	0	0	5
Colonial 9305	40	139	28	4	10	3	3	7,054	11,434	128,423	135,476	2,000
Concord 9106	49	56	20	0	0	0	0	0	4,121	47,069	51,509	450
Cool Springs CC 9107	57	67	35	7	10	1	1	897	7,625	35,401	54,622	150
Cool Springs GC 9408	55	59	40	0	0	11	1	4,521	11,001	50,543	65,716	300
Davidson Chapel 9108	49	157	49	0	0	0	0	480	6,414	28,317	53,915	450
Double Springs 9109	52	64	43	0	2	27	2	4,902	8,680	47,293	55,863	565
Dresden 9110	30	57	18	0	0	2	0	3,356	4,810	24,121	31,647	315
Dyer 9409	118	219	74	7	8	5	0	10,177	19,521	138,713	101,773	1,085
Dyersburg, 1st 9410	373	638	147	3	9	16	2	46,924	137,230	569,850	722,662	5,711
Ebenezer (MC) 9206	6	6	7	No Report Received			0	0	0	0	0	50
Ebenezer (TC) 9303	128	128	60	No Report Received			0	3,000	0	0	0	380
Faith 9308	190	338	112	2	4	5	4	19,250	31,903	310,654	335,521	2,575
Fulton 9412	100	180	50	1	6	3	0	0	21,323	105,152	129,362	850
Germantown 9310	124	336	103	1	2	0	0	17,798	32,622	213,298	249,654	1,000
Gleason 9111	24	31	15	0	4	1	0	0	0	22,996	25,685	400
Good Springs 9112	19	54	12	No Report Received			0	0	0	0	0	296
Holly Grove 9304	735	735	260	6	8	5	2	0	20,939	301,365	324,979	1,300
Hopewell (BC) 9207	29	39	33	1	1	1	0	1,612	3,162	17,841	20,442	30
Hopewell (WC) 9115	18	14	18	0	0	0	0	2,348	4,169	16,231	25,567	90
Humboldt 9116	65	112	35	0	0	1	1	8,612	25,378	0	91,954	1,000
Hurricane Hill 9413	25	52	12	No Report Received			0	0	0	0	0	130
Jackson, 1st 9208	286	466	178	0	8	18	0	11,266	25,022	327,778	384,963	3,000
Kenton 9414	21	46	23	0	0	4	0	4,436	8,888	38,465	47,887	475
Korean 9322	50	50	12	0	5	5	0	0	850	1,657	49,744	1,000
Lexington First* 9209	65	115	25	1	0	2	1	4,297	6,053	37,817	46,314	700
Maple Springs 9210	79	145	18	0	4	2	0	0	4,473	85,241	93,163	485
Martin* 9117	25	55	20	No Report Received			0	3,236	0	0	0	435
Mason Hall 9415	7	20	4	No Report Received			0	0	0	0	0	100
McKenzie 9118	282	355	178	3	7	2	1	30,685	50,883	258,080	307,051	3,000
Medina 9119	13	34	13	0	0	3	0	1,268	3,163	18,687	18,817	75
Meridian 9120	65	141	35	No Report Received			0	0	0	0	0	175
Milan 9121	224	325	80	5	12	8	1	3,750	43,416	302,227	386,471	2,500
Mill Creek 9122	20	20	9	0	0	0	0	1,300	6,000	15,635	23,152	50
Morella 9416	6	26	6	No Report Received			0	0	0	0	0	125
Morning Sun 9314	60	84	32	0	0	1	1	3,770	11,727	82,848	99,324	750
Mt. Ararat 9417	93	295	65	0	1	7	0	4,800	25,268	69,207	94,142	500
Mt. Carmel* 9315	27	44	18	0	0	2	0	2,234	5,703	16,364	22,336	80
Mt. Olive* 9418	12	31	10	No Report Received			0	811	0	0	0	205
Mt. Vernon 9213	40	52	22	2	2	0	0	4,619	9,344	34,222	46,188	380
Mt. Zion 9214	97	192	66	2	2	0	0	19,500	42,207	165,800	196,000	2,000
New Beginnings 9306	138	198	39	No Report Received			0	300	0	0	0	170
New Bethel 9215	46	112	26	1	0	0	1	0	500	24,235	21,134	90
New Bethlehem 9420	5	5	5	No Report Received			0	802	0	0	0	0
New Ebenezer 9422	67	67	39	3	5	1	1	2,934	9,306	61,996	71,331	45
New Salem (MC)*9216	9	9	0	No Report Received			0	0	0	0	0	100

West Tennessee Presbytery   (Continued)
GREAT RIVERS SYNOD

	GENERAL	MEMBERSHIP			CHANGES				FINANCES				
	1.Church Number	2.Active	3.Total	4.Church School	5.Prof. of Faith	6.Gains	7.Losses	8.Children Baptized	9. OUR UNITED OUT-REACH	10. Total Out-Reach Giving	11. All Other Expenses	12. Total Income Received	13. Value Church Prop. 1=1000
	1	2	3	4	5	6	7	8	9	10	11	12	13
New Salem (SC)	9316	50	70	17	0	2	4	1	0	1,544	66,180	72,530	693
New Salem (WC)	9124	15	15	28	No Report Received			0	7,206	0	0	0	75
Newbern	9419	27	39	6	0	0	0	2	4,125	11,770	33,644	47,985	497
Nuevo Empezar	9324	20	25	22	6	6	3	0	2,763	2,673	31,510	36,875	0
North Union	9423	68	75	40	2	7	4	0	3,148	11,070	52,500	63,500	360
Oak Grove	9217	32	108	22	No Report Received			0	1,840	0	0	0	300
Oak Hill	9125	14	14	11	0	0	0	0	517	1,738	5,096	7,677	0
Olive Branch	9312	501	501	158	0	13	0	1	1,441	6,842	266,191	227,248	1,950
Oliver's Chapel	9127	30	69	25	0	0	1	0	3,036	4,706	40,224	32,963	478
Olivet	9220	216	346	110	5	6	11	4	7,425	26,495	277,288	303,784	2,000
Palestine (DC)	9424	5	5	7	No Report Received			0	250	0	0	0	50
Palestine (HC)	9221	56	116	40	No Report Received			0	5,038	0	0	0	150
Parsons, First	9222	40	113	20	0	0	0	0	1,920	3,600	33,653	34,039	500
Pleasant Green	9129	10	20	8	No Report Received			0	0	0	0	0	100
Pleasant Grove	9317	10	22		No Report Received			0	451	0	0	0	32
Pleasant Union	9318	120	150	40	1	1	1	2	0	7,601	95,198	105,983	300
Poplar Grove	9425	42	72	16	0	1	1	0	4,307	10,073	41,817	46,349	325
Protemus*	9426	30	37	43	0	1	0	3	6,540	18,913	37,861	65,401	125
Ramer	9223	16	16	12	No Report Received			0	409	0	0	0	100
Roellen	9428	7	7	7	0	0	0	0	600	1,847	4,584	7,897	60
Rutherford	9429	22	28	21	0	0	0	0	4,188	11,862	37,695	54,462	300
Salem	9430	8	17	16	No Report Received			0	0	0	0	0	135
Savannah, 1st**	9224	98	125	60	3	3	4	0	0	1,320	156,430	142,600	1,195
Selmer, Ct. Ave.**	9225	60	77	15	1	0	18	1	3,006	6,077	54,772	60,293	550
Sharon	9130	18	32	13	0	0	0	0	1,000	5,285	36,995	30,801	559
Shiloh (AC)	9226	35	35	32	1	3	0	0	5,243	26,888	36,013	36,375	95
Shiloh (CC)	9131	36	51	0	1	1	4	1	3,578	5,576	28,178	35,778	175
Trezevant	9132	17	27	17	No Report Received			0	0	0	0	0	150
Trimble	9431	4	4	4	No Report Received			0	1,161	0	0	0	125
Troy	9432	17	24	15	No Report Received			0	994	0	0	0	100
Union City*	9433	105	203	69	No Report Received			0	0	0	0	0	2,000
Walnut Grove	9320	14	28	18	No Report Received			0	75	0	0	0	300
West Union	9321	104	227	60	4	4	4	1	2,400	4,800	119,619	124,191	1,500
Woodward's Ch	9434	12	12	20	No Report Received			0	0	0	0	0	30
Yorkville	9435	26	59	22	No Report Received			0	0	0	0	0	575
Zion*	9133	6	11	5	No Report Received			0	200	0	0	0	95
TOTALS	96	6,278	9,838	3,358	76	166	195	38	317,671	788,325	5,190,554	6,102,570	55,677

*Math Correction*Math error corrected. **Purged roll.

CHURCHES, PASTORS, AND CLERKS:

Antioch Union   (4C)GRWT9401
6765 Mount Olive Road (mailing)
486 W Newman Glover Road (physical)
Union City, TN 38261
(731)885-6435   \<Obion>
PA: Mitch Boulton   \<M1>
1606 Ebenezer Road
Troy, TN 38260
(731)487-2318
steelermitch@gmail.com
CL: Sharon Barnes
5765 Mount Olive Road
Union City, TN 38261
(731)885-2521

Atwood   (4MWC)GRWT9101

PO Box 203 (mailing)
14010 Church Street (physical)
Atwood, TN 38220
(731)662-7692   \<Carroll>
rickylong@tennesseetel.net
SS: Richard Reed   \<M2>
236 Madison Street
Dyer, TN 38330
(731)692-3604
CL: Ricky Long
230 Brooks Road
Atwood, TN 38220
(731)662-7692
rickylong@tennesseetel.net

Barren Springs   (4C)GRWT9102
Box 14 (mailing)
1860 Barren Spring Church Road (physical)
Hollow Rock, TN 38342

( )   \<Carroll>
CL: Cassie Cooper
Box 14
Hollow Rock, TN 38342
(731)586-2167

Beech   (4MEC)GRWT9402
PO Box 553 (mailing)
880 Beech Chapel Road (physical)
Union City, TN 38261
(731)885-1710   \<Obion>
beth.williams@nwtdd.org
PA: Bobby D Williams   \<M1>
844 W Highway 22
Union City, TN 38261
(731)885-1710
CL: Beth Williams
844 W Highway 22
Union City, TN 38281

WEST TENNESSEE PRESBYTERY CONTINUED

(731)885-1710
beth.williams@nwtdd.org

_____

Bells Chapel　　　(2WC)GRWT9403
309 Bells Chapel Road
Dyer, TN 38330
(731)643-6729　　　<Gibson>
LS: Dennis Emerson　　　<M6>
137 Midway Road Apt 25
Dyer, TN 38330
(731)643-6539
dennied53@hotmail.com
CL: Dennis Emerson
137 Midway Road Apt 25
Dyer, TN 38330
(731)643-6539
dennied53@hotmail.com

_____

Bethel (TC)　　　(1WC)GRWT9301
PO Box 114 (mailing)
Tipton, TN 38071
3406 Tracy Road (physical)
Atoka, TN 38004
(901)837-0343　　　<Tipton>
SS: Kenneth L McCoy　　　<M1>
1422 Walton Road
Memphis, TN 38117
(901)682-0891
CL: Cindy Rhodes
PO Box 114
Tipton, TN 38071
(901)837-7793

_____

Bethesda　　　(4MWC)GRWT9404
10755 State Highway 188 (mailing)
9651 State Highway 188 (physical)
Friendship, TN 38034
(　)　　　<Crockett>
jirvin527@yahoo.com
CL: Jim Irvin
10755 State Highway 188
Friendship, TN 38034
(731)414-7180
jirvin527@yahoo.com

_____

Bethlehem　　　(4C)GRWT9405
711 Whirmantler Street (mailing)
1469 Bethlehem Road (physical)
Union City, TN 38261
(　)　　　<Obion>
CL: Charlotte Thomas
711 Whirmantler Street
Union City, TN 38261
(731)885-1672

_____

Bolivar　　　(4MWC)GRWT9202
PO Box 413 (mailing)
448 Nuckolls Road (physical)
Bolivar, TN 38008
(731)658-5459　　　<Hardeman>
CL: Faye Cromwell
2995 Naylor Road
Toone, TN 38381
(731)658-5329
cromwellr@bellsouth.net

_____

Bradford　　　(4MWC)GRWT9104
PO Box 186 (mailing)
117 Highway 45 S (physical)
Bradford, TN 38316
(731)742-3397　　　<Gibson>

PA: Keith Harwell　　　<M1>
13132 Stinson Street
Milan, TN 38358
(731)613-3780
CL: Don Lannom
PO Box 85
Bradford, TN 38316
(731)742-3838

_____

Brunswick　　　(4MWC)GRWT9302
PO Box 67 (mailing)
4976 Brunswick Road (physical)
Brunswick, TN 38014
(901)386-0105　　　<Shelby>
PA: Cory Williams　　　<M1>
3148 Long Bridge Lane
Arlington, TN 38002
(901)486-5981
coromis@hotmail.com
CL: Mary Ellen Starks
PO Box 142
Brunswick, TN 38014
(901)388-9862

_____

Camden　　　(4MWC)GRWT9105
239 W Main Street
Camden, TN 38320
(731)584-7598　　　<Benton>
FAX: (731)584-7598
camdencpoffice@bellsouth.net
SS: Carey Womack　　　<M1>
114 Doris Street
Camden, TN 38320
(731)220-3900
FAX: (731)584-7598
camdencppastor@bellsouth.net
CL: Nancy D Arnold
PO Box 214
Camden, TN 38320
(731)441-2778
FAX: (731)584-7598
arnldnnc@aol.com

_____

Camp Ground　　　(4C)GRWT9204
2535 Middleburg Road
Decaturville, TN 38329
(　)　　　<Decatur>
SS: David Hawley　　　<M1>
127 John Holt Road
Beech Bluff, TN 38313
(731)427-7284
dhpreach@aol.com
CL: Fred Brasher
771 Middleburg Road
Decaturville, TN 38329
(731)852-4400
fredhelen@tds.net

_____

Claybrook　　　(C)GRWT9205
1300 US Highway 412 E (mailing)
1364 US Highway 412 E (physical)
Jackson, TN 38305
(　)　　　<Madison>
SS: Jerald D Smith　　　<M1>
2625 Beech Bluff Road
Beech Bluff, TN 38313
(731)427-9316
jergensmith@aol.com
CL: Martha Wolfe
1300 US Highway 412 E
Jackson, TN 38305

(731)424-4979
jergensmith@aol.com

_____

Cloverdale　　　(2C)GRWT9407
3891 S Sellers Road (mailing)
3541 Cloverdale Road (physical)
Obion, TN 38240
(　)　　　<Obion>
FAX: (731)538-2383
CL: Billy J Sellers
3891 S Sellers Road
Obion, TN 38240
(731)538-2986
FAX: (731)538-2383
bsellers@ken-tennwireless.com

_____

Colonial　　　(4MWC)GRWT9305
1500 S Perkins Road
Memphis, TN 38117
(901)682-4747　　　<Shelby>
SS: Lisa Anderson　　　<M1 M9>
1790 Faxon Avenue
Memphis, TN 38112
(901)725-0924
anderli@aol.com
CL: George R Marston
1042 LaRue Place
Memphis, TN 38122
(901)685-1488
put11599@bellsouth.net

_____

Concord　　　(3MWC)GRWT9106
153 Herd Law Road
Trenton, TN 38382
(　)　　　<Gibson>
PA: Don McCurley　　　<M1>
4036 McAllister Street
Milan, TN 38358
(731)723-3623
dcmccurley@hotmail.com
CL: Don Gibson
4225 Christmasville Road
Medina, TN 38355
(731)783-0992

_____

Cool Springs CC　　　(4C)GRWT9107
240 Little Grove Road
Lavinia, TN 38348
(　)　　　<Carroll>
LS: Robert Barger　　　<M6>
7127 Highway 104 W
Lavinia, TN 38348
(731)987-2477
rbarger104@att.net
CL: Ann Hammett
8725 US Highway 70
Cedar Grove, TN 38321
(731)987-2516

_____

Cool Springs GC　　　(4MWC)GRWT9408
37 Cool Spring Road
Trimble, TN 38259
(731)643-6153　　　<Gibson>
SS: Steve Rogers　　　<M3>
37 Cool Spring Road
Trimble, TN 38259
(731)882-2229
CL: Mike Pruett
119 Heritage Drive
Rutherford, TN 38369
(731)665-6348

WEST TENNESSEE PRESBYTERY CONTINUED

mdpruett@tennesseetel.net

Davidson Chapel (4MWC)GRWT9108
399 Laneview Concord Road
Trenton, TN 38382
(731)618-1521
FAX: (731)664-3735
dale.cavaness@horne-llp.com <Gibson>
CL: Dale Cavaness
2093 Brentwood Drive
Milan, TN 38358
(731)618-1521
FAX: (731)664-3735
dale.cavaness@horne-llp.com

Double Springs (4WC)GRWT9109
18 Double Springs Road
Humboldt, TN 38343
(731)787-6422 <Gibson>
PA: Russell Little <M1>
29 Cotton Row
Medina, TN 38355
(731)783-3565
russelllittle@bellsouth.net
CL: Linda Fisher
65 Spencer Drive
Medina, TN 38355
(731)613-8355
lfisher@eplus.net

Dresden (4MWC)GRWT9110
PO Box 131 (mailing)
121 S Wilson Street (physical)
Dresden, TN 38225
( ) <Weakley>
PA: H Walter McClanahan <M1>
215 White Bros Road
Humboldt, TN 38343
(731)784-1176
waltermac2@hughes.net
CL: Martha Killebrew
PO Box 131
Dresden, TN 38225
(731)364-3294
FAX: (731)364-3500
killebrewm@frontiernet.net

Dyer (4MEWC)GRWT9409
PO Box 181 (mailing)
256 E College Street (physical)
Dyer, TN 38330
(731)692-2594 <Gibson>
dcpchurch@bellsouth.net
PA: Johnny E Watson <M1>
272 Madison Street
Dyer, TN 38330
(731)692-3555
rev.jwatson@bellsouth.net
CL: Johnny Ward
46 Old Dyer Trenton Road
Dyer, TN 38330
(731)692-2594
ward3363@bellsouth.net

Dyersburg First (4WC)GRWT9410
2280 Parr Avenue
Dyersburg, TN 38024
(731)285-5703 <Dyer>
FAX: (731)285-5792
cpoffice@cumberlandchurch.com
PA: Larry A Blakeburn <M1>

230 Heathridge Drive
Dyersburg, TN 38024
(731)286-2982
FAX: (731)285-5792
larry@cumberlandchurch.com
AP: Annetta Camp <M1>
2303 Mill Creek Road
Halls, TN 38040
(731)285-5703
FAX: (731)285-5792
annetta@cumberlandchurch.com
CL: William Mallard
198 Walnut Lane Ext
Dyersburg, TN 38024
(731)285-0837
FAX: (731)287-0873
wem1950@bellsouth.net

Ebenezer (MC) (2EWC)GRWT9206
Main Street
Mercer, TN 38392
(731)935-2391 <Madison>
CL: Pope Mulherin
8 Prestwick Drive
Jackson, TN 38305
(731)427-3113

Ebenezer (TC) (4WC)GRWT9303
70 Witherington Road
Mason, TN 38049
( ) <Tipton>
CL: Ann Burlison
564 Baskin Road
Burlison, TN 38015
(901)294-3614
aburlison@tipton-county.com

Faith (4WC)GRWT9308
3427 Appling Road
Bartlett, TN 38133
(901)377-0526 <Shelby>
FAX: (901)382-2600
faithcumberlandp@bellsouth.net
PA: Steven Shelton <M1>
7886 Farmhill Cove
Bartlett, TN 38135
(901)377-0526
faithcpcpastor@gmail.com
CL: Karen Patten
5728 North Street
Bartlett, TN 38134
(901)237-0535
mkpatten53@comcast.net

Fulton (4MWC)GRWT9412
PO Box 5343 (mailing)
1159 Parker Road (physical)
South Fulton, TN 38257
(731)479-9912 <Obion>
PA: David Bayer <M1>
3090 Tom Counce Road
South Fulton, TN 38257
(731)479-3060
dbayer9060@gmail.com
CL: Donald R Moore
155 Cox Road
Fulton, KY 42041
(270)436-2723
donaldmoore9@aol.com

Germantown (4EWC)GRWT9310

2385 Riverdale
Germantown, TN 38138
(901)755-3884 <Shelby>
FAX: (901)759-3653
cpcgww@aol.com
PA: William Warren <M1>
7139 Toro Cove
Germantown, TN 38138
(901)755-8058
cpcgww@aol.com
CL: Iva McCutchen
1240 Bristol Drive
Memphis, TN 38119
(901)761-0575
ivesmc@att.net

Gleason (4MC)GRWT9111
190 David Court (mailing)
McKenzie, TN 38201
171 Smyth Lane (physical)
Gleason, TN 38229
(731)648-5343 <Weakley>
PA: James (Jim) Pinnell <M1>
1525 Parks Well Road
Gleason, TN 38229
(731)648-5078
revpinnell@hotmail.com
CL: Donald Ray Stephens
190 David Court
McKenzie, TN 38201
(731)352-5852
tuvart@charter.net

Good Springs (4WC)GRWT9112
180 Barham Road (mailing)
Good Springs Road (physical)
Dukedom, TN 38226
( ) <Weakley>
SS: Dennis Weaver <M2 ST>
39 Cool Spring Road
Trimble, TN 38259
(731)643-6056
CL: Loretta Barham
180 Barham Road
Dukedom, TN 38226
(731)469-9555

Holly Grove (4MWC)GRWT9304
4538 Holly Grove Road
Brighton, TN 38011
(901)476-8379 <Tipton>
FAX: (901)476-3324
hollygrovecpchurch@att.net
PA: L Ronald McMillan <M1>
675 Kimberly Drive
Atoka, TN 38004
(901)837-1101
mcmillanron@bellsouth.net
CL: Donna E Lindley
4538 Holly Grove Road
Brighton, TN 38011
(901)476-8379
FAX: (901)476-3324
hollygrovecpchurch@att.net

Hopewell (BC) (2EWC)GRWT9207
2309 Saulsbury Road (mailing)
289 Hopewell Road (physical)
Walnut, MS 38683
( ) <Benton>
PA: Byron Forester <M1>

WEST TENNESSEE PRESBYTERY CONTINUED

2376 Eastwood Place
Memphis, TN 38112
(901)324-1707
bforester@bellsouth.net
CL: Kathy D Wilburn
2309 Saulsbury Road
Walnut, MS 38683
(662)223-6447
kwilburn@fareselaw.com

Hopewell (WC)   (2WC)GRWT9115
1061 Gaylord Road (mailing)
Route 1 Box 91 (physical)
Sharon, TN 38255
( )   <Weakley>
CL: Lonnie Hazlewood
1061 Gaylord Road
Sharon, TN 38255
(731)973-2426
lonminh@citlink.net

Humboldt   (4MEWC)GRWT9116
2375 E Mitchell Street
Humboldt, TN 38343
(731)784-2703   <Gibson>
pastor@humboldtcpc.org
PA: Robert Harris   <M1>
619 N 24th Avenue
Humboldt, TN 38343
(731)420-6067
pastor@humboldtcpc.org
CL: Carolyn Hunley
6 Clinton Road
Humboldt, TN 38343
(731)784-2031
carolynhunley16@yahoo.com

Hurricane Hill   (4C)GRWT9413
Newbern, TN 38059
( )   <Dyer>
CL: Robert C Lindley
1231 Lexie Cobb Road
Newbern, TN 38059
(731)627-3156

Jackson First   (4WC)GRWT9208
1730 US Highway 45 Bypass
Jackson, TN 38305
(731)664-1632   <Madison>
FAX: (731)664-1633
fcpc1730@bellsouth.net
PA: Terry M Hunley   <M1>
48 Charleston Square
Jackson, TN 38305
(731)660-5685
thunley1@charter.net
CL: Anne Austin
1730 US Highway 45 Bypass
Jackson, TN 38305
(731)660-2411
ama@eplus.net

Kenton   (4MEWC)GRWT9414
301 W College Street
Kenton, TN 38233
( )   <Obion>
LS: Charles McCall   <M6>
549 Mason Hall Road
Trimble, TN 38259
(731)297-3288
cmccall@ycinet.net

CL: Paul E Williams
206 Hillside Street
Kenton, TN 38233
(731)749-5656

Korean   (P)GRWT9322
7565 Macon Road
Cordova, TN 38018
(901)755-9101   <Shelby>
hjinlab@hotmail.com
SS: Ho-Jin Lee   <M2>
7565 Macon Road
Cordova, TN 38018
(901)754-7070
hjinlab@hotmail.com
CL: Gong Dickens
7565 Macon Road
Cordova, TN 38018
(901)758-1130

Lexington First   (4MWC)GRWT9209
PO Box 11 (mailing)
931 N Broad Street (physical)
Lexington, TN 38351
(731)968-7176   <Henderson>
patfreelandjones@yahoo.com
PA: C William Jones Jr   <M1>
109 Lakewood Drive
Lexington, TN 38351
(731)967-7618
patfreelandjones@yahoo.com
CL: Teresa Ferguson
7747 Middleburg Road
Scotts Hill, TN 38374
(731)968-9079

Maple Springs   (4MWC)GRWT9210
2625 Beech Bluff Road (mailing)
2005 Beech Bluff Road (physical)
Beech Bluff, TN 38313
(731)424-4065   <Henderson>
PA: Jerald D Smith   <M1>
2625 Beech Bluff Road
Beech Bluff, TN 38313
(731)427-9316
jergensmith@aol.com
CL: Tricia Fowler
37 Fowler Cut Off Road
Beech Bluff, TN 38313
(731)423-1255
tfowler@firstbankonline.com

Martin   (4MWC)GRWT9117
312 E Main Street
Martin, TN 38237
(731)587-3222   <Weakley>
FAX: (731)487-6484
cathyjahr@charter.net
PA: Michael T Lavender   (M1)
934 Church Street
Tiptonville, TN 38079
(731)431-9127
mike_lavender@yahoo.com
CL: Cathy Jahr
142 Rolling Meadows
Martin, TN 38237
(731)587-6484
cathyjahr@charter.net

Mason Hall   (2EWC)GRWT9415
549 Mason Hall Road (mailing)

Trimble, TN 38259
1861 CP Church Road (physical)
Kenton, TN 38233
( )   <Obion>
mccall.cmccall@gmail.com
CL: Charles McCall
549 Mason Hall Road
Trimble, TN 38259
(731)431-8195
mccall.cmccall@gmail.com

McKenzie   (4WC)GRWT9118
PO Box 133 (mailing)
16835 Highland Drive (physical)
McKenzie, TN 38201
(731)352-2440   <Carroll>
FAX: (731)352-3101
church@mckenziecpc.org
PA: R Tony Janner   <M1>
104 Northwood Drive
McKenzie, TN 38201
(731)352-8055
drtonyjanner@yahoo.com
CL: June Perritt
PO Box 133
McKenzie, TN 38201
(731)352-2440
FAX: (731)352-3101
church@mckenziecpc.org

Medina   (4EC)GRWT9119
104 Cumberland Street
Medina, TN 38355
(731)618-0192   <Gibson>
PA: Linda H Glenn   <M1>
49 Mason Road
Threeway, TN 38343
(731)618-0192
lindahglenn@click1.net
CL: Mark A Kee
67 Jim Jackson Road
Humboldt, TN 38343
(731)487-1088
markkee24@yahoo.com

Meridian   (4C)GRWT9120
1099 Adams Road (mailing)
2590 Meridian Road (physical)
Greenfield, TN 38230
( )   <Weakley>
CL: David McBride
1099 Adams Road
Greenfield, TN 38230
(731)235-3058

Milan   (4WC)GRWT9121
6083 S First Street
Milan, TN 38358
(731)686-1851   <Gibson>
office@milancp.org
PA: Doy L Daniels Jr   <M1>
1095 Crestview Drive
Milan, TN 38358
(731)686-1851
FAX: (731)723-9324
revdrdoy@gmail.com
AP: Corey Cummings   <M1>
1023 W Woodrow Street
Milan, TN 38358
(731)686-1851
corey@milancp.org

WEST TENNESSEE PRESBYTERY CONTINUED

CL: Ronnie Parks
62 Hughes Loop
Milan, TN 38358
(731)686-3065
ronnieparks@bellsouth.net

_____

Mill Creek   (4C)GRWT9122
239 Smith Street (mailing)
434 Mill Creek Road (physical)
Puryear, TN 38251
( )   <Henry>
vincent2@wk.net
CL: Richard E Vincent
239 Smith Street
Puryear, TN 38251
(731)247-5211
vincent2@wk.net

_____

Morella   (2EWC)GRWT9416
51 Morella Road
Kenton, TN 38233
( )   <Gibson>
CL: J C Reed
121 Tull Road
Kenton, TN 38233
(731)749-5545

_____

Morning Sun   (4MC)GRWT9314
2682 Morning Sun Road
Cordova, TN 38016
(901)382-3439   <Shelby>
mscpc13@gmail.com
PA: Joey Edwards   <M1>
5279 Ivy Creek Lane
Lakeland, TN 38002
(901)573-7579
edwardsjoey@bellsouth.net
CL: Gwen Hromada
4350 Thorpe Drive
Mason, TN 38049
(901)466-1154
gwen247@aceweb.com

_____

Mt Ararat   (4WC)GRWT9417
1465 Troy-Hickman Road
Union City, TN 38261
(731)536-5406   <Obion>
PA: Robert A Smith   <M1>
PO Box 501
Newbern, TN 38059
(731)627-3332
ras1957@bellsouth.net
CL: Bobby Hall
664 Mill Creek Road
Troy, TN 38260
(731)536-4798

_____

Mt Carmel   (4C)GRWT9315
106 E Marginal Street (mailing)
2355 Union Drive (physical)
Somerville, TN 38068
( )   <Fayette>
PA: Clinton Buck   <M1>
4986 Warwick Avenue
Memphis, TN 38117
(901)682-2358
clintonbuck@aol.com
CL: Harry N Wiles
106 E Marginal Street
Somerville, TN 38068
(901)465-9733

_____

Mt Olive   (4MEC)GRWT9418
76 Yorkville Highway (mailing)
42 Mt Olive Road (physical)
Dyer, TN 38330
( )   <Gibson>
PA: Charles Fike   <M1>
2070 N 1st Street
Milan, TN 38358
(731)686-0224
CL: Carolyn Martin
76 Yorkville Highway
Dyer, TN 38330
(731)692-2773

_____

Mt Vernon   (4MC)GRWT9213
3101 Mt Vernon Road
Ramer, TN 38367
(731)645-6420   <McNairy>
SS: Jeff DeWees   <M1>
3101 Mt Vernon Road
Ramer, TN 38367
(731)645-6420
shg_50@bellsouth.net
CL: Larry Gage
130 Shiloh Terrace Drive
Selmer, TN 38375
(731)645-6828
lgage6828@charter.net

_____

Mt Zion   (4MWC)GRWT9214
480 County Road 401
Falkner, MS 38629
(662)837-7013   <Tippah>
FAX: (662)837-7969
info@mtzioncpc.org
PA: Thomas Richie Lockhart   <M1>
700 County Road 343
Falkner, MS 38629
(662)837-4281
nmsdiamonddawgs@yahoo.com
CL: Jane H Childs
921 County Road 338
Falkner, MS 38629
(662)223-4285
jchilds@wgyates.com

_____

New Beginnings   (4C)GRWT9306
2300 Frayser Boulevard
Memphis, TN 38127
(901)353-4011
PA: Craig Wilson   <M1>
2300 Frayser Boulevard
Memphis, TN 38127
(901)277-4066
craigwilson2300@yahoo.com
SC: Elnora McKinzie
1111 Holmes Street
Memphis, TN 38122
(870)377-2174

_____

New Bethel   (4C)GRWT9215
3708 New Bethel Road
Selmer, TN 38375
( )   <McNairy>
CL: Preston King
3708 New Bethel Road
Selmer, TN 38375
(731)645-3150
kingpreston2828@yahoo.com

_____

New Bethlehem   (2EWC)GRWT9420
1585 Bethlehem Road (mailing)
825 Bethlehem Road (physical)
Newbern, TN 38059
( )   <Dyer>
CL: Mary Bell Murray
1585 Bethlehem Road
Newbern, TN 38059
(731)627-2332
murrayc2@juno.com

_____

New Ebenezer   (4MEWC)GRWT9422
PO Box 364 (mailing)
1606 Ebenezer Road (physical)
Troy, TN 38260
(731)536-4936   <Obion>
PA: Mitch Boulton   <M1>
1606 Ebenezer Road
Troy, TN 38260
(731)487-2318
steelermitch@gmail.com
CL: James R Kendall
2494 W State Route 21
Troy, TN 38260
(731)538-9933

_____

New Salem (MC)   (4C)GRWT9216
453 New Salem Road
Bethel Springs, TN 38315
( )   <McNairy>
SS: Earl Phelps   <M1>
172 Michie Pebble Hill Road
Stantonville, TN 38379
(731)632-5107
FAX: (901)632-9126
phelps.e@juno.com
CL: Malcolm Dickson
153 Harris Road
Bethel Springs, TN 38315
(731)934-7282
FAX: (731)934-0736
robert.dickson@aol.com

_____

New Salem (SC)   (4MWC)GRWT9316
6813 Salem Road
Lakeland, TN 38002
(901)829-3241   <Shelby>
FAX: (901)829-3241
ptcriss@hotmail.com
PA: Paul T Criss   <M1>
6831 Salem Road
Lakeland, TN 38002
(901)626-8462
ptcriss@hotmail.com
CL: Patty Butler Little
6909 Salem Road
Lakeland, TN 38002
(901)829-3218

_____

New Salem (WC)   (3C)GRWT9124
3220 Sharon Highway 89 (mailing)
Highway 89 (physical)
Sharon, TN 38255
( )   <Weakley>
SS: Kermit Travis   <M1>
3220 Sharon Highway 89
Dresden, TN 38225
(731)364-2315
CL: John C Clark
215 Rambo Road
Sharon, TN 38255

WEST TENNESSEE PRESBYTERY CONTINUED

(731)364-3921
jcjclark@frontiernet.net

Newbern   (4MWC)GRWT9419
310 E Main
Newbern, TN 38059
(731)627-3646   <Dyer>
CL: Jamie Kay Berkley
403 E Main Street
Newbern, TN 38059
(731)676-8626
jamiekayb@hotmail.com

North Union   (4EC)GRWT9423
15 Cardwell Road (mailing)
Dyer, TN 38330
78 Preacher Dowland Road (physical)
Kenton, TN 38233
(731)673-4122   <Gibson>
CL: Chad Murray
2067 Locust Grove Road
Newbern, TN 38059
(731)676-6027
chadgfc@gmail.com

Nuevo Empezar   (4EC)GRWT9324
3442 Tutwiler
Memphis, TN 38122
(901)644-0513
PA: Bertha Davis   <M1>
2242 Slocum Avenue
Memphis, TN 38127
(901)644-0513
CL: Session Clerk
3442 Tutwiler Avenue
Memphis, TN 38122
(901)644-0513

Oak Grove   (4MC)GRWT9217
3655 Talley Store Road
Henderson, TN 38340
(731)989-3825   <Chester>
marcus.hayes@att.net
SS: Marcus Hayes   <M1 OP>
3615 Talley School Road
Henderson, TN 38340
(270)841-7576
marcus.hayes@att.net
CL: Don Terry
1450 Braund Road
Henderson, TN 38340
(731)989-7982
FAX: (731)989-7982

Oak Hill   (1C)GRWT9125
5820 Highway 69 N (mailing)
8295 Highway 69 N (physical)
Paris, TN 38242
( )   <Henry>
PA: Francis Howe   <M1>
129 Manley Street
McKenzie, TN 38201
(731)352-5551
CL: Theresa Rushing
5820 Highway 69 N
Paris, TN 38242
(731)642-3499
trushing@utm.edu

Olive Branch   (4MWC)GRWT9312
8161 Germantown Road
Olive Branch, MS 38654

(662)893-7347   <Desoto>
FAX: (901)893-7347
officefcpc@yahoo.com
PA: James L Ratliff   <M1>
4027 Club View Drive
Memphis, TN 38125
(901)758-0125
pastorjimfcpc@yahoo.com
CL: Charlie Trapp
4750 Harvest Knoll Cove N
Memphis, TN 38125
(901)626-2952
charliebethtrapp@bellsouth.net

Oliver's Chapel   (4WC)GRWT9127
85 Olivers Chapel Road (mailing)
22 Olivers Chapel Road (physical)
Bradford, TN 38316
(731)742-3559   <Gibson>
FAX: (731)742-3994
mpybas@yahoo.com
PA: Sam Harwell   <M1>
23 Lake Hayes Estates Road
Trenton, TN 38382
(731)414-2153
sambharl@yahoo.com
CL: Marcy Tahmazian
85 Olivers Chapel Road
Bradford, TN 38316
(731)742-3097
FAX: (731)742-3994
mpybas@yahoo.com

Olivet   (4MWC)GRWT9220
6095 Highway 226
Savannah, TN 38372
(731)925-2685   <Hardin>
olivetcp@bellsouth.net
PA: James D Pounds   <M1>
40 Nellie Lane
Savannah, TN 38372
(731)925-2685
olivetcp@bellsouth.net
CL: Walton Williams
10875 Highway 64
Savannah, TN 38372
(731)412-7569

Palestine (DC)   (4C)GRWT9424
Route 2
Newbern, TN 38059
( )   <Dyer>
CL: Session Clerk Palestine CP Church
Route 2
Newbern, TN 38059
(731)627-9227

Palestine (HC)   (4MWC)GRWT9221
1010 Nobles Road (mailing)
6835 Highway 22A (physical)
Lexington, TN 38351
( )   <Henderson>
mcadamsjc@bellsouth.net
PA: Wayne Tompkins   <M1>
6835 Highway 22 A
Lexington, TN 38351
(731)968-4331
waynetompkinsministries@yahoo.com
CL: Cheri McAdams
1010 Nobles Road
Luray, TN 38352
(731)614-0433

mcadamsjc@bellsouth.net

Parsons First   (4MEWC)GRWT9222
PO Box 141 (mailing)
114 Virginia Avenue N (physical)
Parsons, TN 38363
(731)847-7148   <Decatur>
PA: David Hawley   <M1>
127 John Holt Road
Beech Bluff, TN 38313
(731)427-7284
haw177@aol.com
CL: Tony Collett
6636 Rockhouse Road
Linden, TN 37096
(931)589-5103
tacollett@tds.net

Pleasant Green   (4C)GRWT9129
c/o Helen Watkins (mailing)
2776 Highway 105
Trezevant, TN 38258
712 Idlewild-Holly Leaf (physical)
Atwood, TN 38220
( )   <Gibson>
OD: Keith Pence   <M5>
PO Box 703
Gleason, TN 38229
(731)819-2553
CL: Helen Watkins
2776 Highway 105
Trezevant, TN 38258
(731)669-1601
hjoy1@charter.net

Pleasant Grove   (2C)GRWT9317
2320 Pleasant Grove Road
Moscow, TN 38057
(901)877-3287   <Fayette>
CL: Jack Joyner
2320 Pleasant Grove Road
Moscow, TN 38057
(901)877-3287

Pleasant Union   (4MWC)GRWT9318
9251 Brunswick Road
Millington, TN 38053
(901)829-3262   <Shelby>
PA: Matthew Dean Cunningham   <M1>
1646 Brighton-Clopton Road
Brighton, TN 38011
(901)475-4252
mcunningham0528@comcast.net
CL: Patricia Parks
8995 Mulberry Road
Atoka, TN 38004
(901)829-3012
pittypat28@aol.com

Poplar Grove   (4C)GRWT9425
492 Church Road
Halls, TN 38040
(731)627-2445   <Lauderdale>
2Orrs.mn@charter.net
PA: Melvin Orr   <M1>
806 Washington Street
Newbern, TN 38059
(731)627-2445
2Orrs.mn@charter.net
CL: Larry Keen
323 Pennington Road
Halls, TN 38040

WEST TENNESSEE PRESBYTERY CONTINUED

(731)836-5546
lkeen@lctn.com

_____

Protemus (4EWC)GRWT9426
2372 W Shawtown Road (mailing)
2033 W Shawtown Road (physical)
Troy, TN 38260
( ) <Obion>
LS: James R Gunter <M6>
6997 Bud Barker Road
Obion, TN 38240
(731)538-9252
CL: Betty Rhamy
2372 W Shawtown Road
Troy, TN 38260
(731)538-9458

_____

Ramer (4MEWC)GRWT9223
4096 Highway 57 W
Ramer, TN 38367
( ) <McNairy>
OD: Albert Brown <M5>
1772 Buena Vista Road
Bethel Springs, TN 38315
(731)934-7349
CL: George Armstrong
216 Ballpark Road E
Ramer, TN 38367
(731)645-3987

_____

Roellen (2C)GRWT9428
6040 Highway 104 E (mailing)
Highway 104 E (physical)
Dyersburg, TN 38024
(731)285-0300 <Dyer>
krector@cableone.net
PA: Dennis Vance <M1>
1320 Valleywood Drive
Paris, TN 38242
(731)644-3627
rvdvance@hotmail.com
CL: Hal Rector
6040 Highway 104 E
Dyersburg, TN 38024
(731)285-0300
krector@cableone.net

_____

Rutherford (4MEWC)GRWT9429
945 S Trenton Street (mailing)
113 N Trenton Street (physical)
Rutherford, TN 38369
(731)665-6487 <Gibson>
PA: Hobert Walker <M1>
PO Box 66
Rutherford, TN 38369
(731)665-7236
rutherfordcpchurch@gmail.com
CL: Joe Bone
945 S Trenton Street
Rutherford, TN 38369
(731)665-7253
jobne@msn.com

_____

Salem (4MC)GRWT9430
174 Franklin Street (mailing)
184 Franklin Street(physical)
Gadsden, TN 38337
( ) <Crockett>
SS: Karl Schwarz <M1>
83 W Curtis Street
Bells, TN 38006
(731)663-3987

schw8651@bellsouth.net
CL: Ann Davis
174 Franklin Street
Gadsden, TN 38337
(731)784-4713
cloud31@bellsouth.net

_____

Savannah First (4WC)GRWT9224
300 Tennessee Street
Savannah, TN 38372
(731)925-4493 <Hardin>
savannah1stcp@hotmail.com
SS: Helen Hamilton <M3>
245 Elm Street
Savannah, TN 38372
(731)925-7338
helmackham@aol.com
CL: Levin Edwards
300 Tennessee Street
Savannah, TN 38372
(731)925-4493
levinedwards@gmail.com

_____

Selmer Court Ave (4MWC)GRWT9225
PO Box 741 (mailing)
234 Court Avenue (physical)
Selmer, TN 38375
(731)645-5257 <McNairy>
PA: Ben Luttrell <M1>
123 S 5th Street
Selmer, TN 38375
(731)645-5257
CL: Gwelda W Treece
299 Country Club Lane
Selmer, TN 38375
(731)645-5519
gweldat@bellsouth.net

_____

Sharon (4MEC)GRWT9130
PO Box 588 (mailing)
5414 US Highway 45 (physical)
Sharon, TN 38255
( ) <Weakley>
SS: David Lancaster <M1 PR>
426 Fugua Road
Martin, TN 38237
(731)588-5895
lancasterd@bethel-college.edu
CL: Patricia Elam
2275 Mount Vernon Road
Sharon, TN 38255
(731)456-2882
jimelam@frontiernet.net

_____

Shiloh (AC) (4WC)GRWT9226
164 County Road 634
Corinth, MS 38834
( ) <Alcorn>
PA: Brenda Laurence <M1>
2823 Nine Mile Road
Enville, TN 38332
(731)687-2022
southernmoma@hotmail.com
CL: LaWanda Burns
37 County Road 750
Corinth, MS 38834
(662)415-1038
ljmburns@gmail.com

_____

Shiloh (CC) (4C)GRWT9131
2880 Highway 423
McKenzie, TN 38201

( ) <Carroll>
church@shilohcp.org
PA: Melissa Reid Goodloe <M1>
225 Macedonia Road
McKenzie, TN 38201
(731)412-9657
rev.mgoodloe@shilohcp.org
CL: Vickie Summers
2880 Highway 423
McKenzie, TN 38201
(731)225-6714
vsum1956@gmail.com

_____

Trezevant (3EC)GRWT9132
PO Box 246 (mailing)
98 Church Street (physical)
Trezevant, TN 38258
(731)669-4525 <Carroll>
CL: James O Hinton
PO Box 246
Trezevant, TN 38258
(731)669-5277
johinton@charter.net

_____

Trimble (2MC)GRWT9431
PO Box 146 (mailing)
403 Pierce Street (physical)
Trimble, TN 38259
( ) <Dyer>
PA: George A Butler <M1>
306 Flora Circle
Newbern, TN 38059
(731)627-9416
CL: Hamilton Parks
PO Box 146
Trimble, TN 38259
(731)297-3691

_____

Troy (4WC)GRWT9432
PO Box 454 (mailing)
308 Main Street (physical)
Troy, TN 38260
( ) <Obion>
PA: Johnnie Welch <M1>
PO Box 1506
Dyersburg, TN 38025
(731)287-9008
johnniewelch@msn.com
CL: Alan Thompson
171 Country Valley Drive
Troy, TN 38260
(731)536-1107
atthompson2@netzero.com

_____

Union City (4MW C)GRWT9433
631 E Church Street
Union City, TN 38261
(731)885-9773 <Obion>
FAX: (731)885-9766
uccpc@bellsouth.net
PA: Drew Hayes <M1>
629 High Street
Union City, TN 38261
(731)796-7076
dhayes72@gmail.com
CL: Pat Wood
822 E Main Street
Union City, TN 38261
(731)885-4489
FAX: (731)885-6500
pat@woodcommunications.com

_____

WEST TENNESSEE PRESBYTERY CONTINUED

Walnut Grove   (4MWC)GRWT9320
1383 Walnut Grove Road
Burlison, TN 38015
(901)476-5533   <Tipton>
billyshires@bellsouth.net
PA: Lisa Peterson   <M1>
1770 Magnolia Tree Road
Memphis, TN 38138
(901)754-9316
petersonli@aol.com
CL: Denise Shires
681 Highway 179
Covington, TN 38019
(901)476-4590
billyshires@bellsouth.net

West Union   (4MWC)GRWT9321
3099 W Union Road
Millington, TN 38053
(901)876-5757   <Shelby>
westunionoffice@bigriver.net
PA: James R Hamblin   <M1>
60 Rolling Meadow Drive
Drummonds, TN 38023
(901)840-4747
brojim391@gmail.com
CL: W Judd Stafford
9281 Herring Hill Road
Millington, TN 38053
(901)876-3277
emcmwjs@aol.com

Woodward's Chapel   (2C)GRWT9434
1357 Webster Street (mailing)
Union City, TN 38261
3054 Bud O Yates Road (physical)
Obion, TN 38240
(731)431-9127   <Obion>
FAX: (731)623-4226
SS: Mike Lavender   <M3 ST>
934 Church Street
Tiptonville, TN 38079
(731)253-7308
FAX: (731)623-4226
mikelavender@alumni.vanderbilt.edu
CL: Alvin Minnick
1357 Webster Street
Union City, TN 38261
(731)442-1130
alviniraq2004@yahoo.com

Yorkville   (4MEC)GRWT9435
PO Box 156 (mailing)
17 Newbern Highway (physical)
Yorkville, TN 38389
(731)643-6594   <Gibson>
SS: Rian Puckett   <M2 ST>
42 Jesse Patterson Road
Trenton, TN 38382
(731)288-7743
rppuckett@memphisseminary.edu
CL: Mike Roberts
PO Box 213
Yorkville, TN 38389
(731)643-6237
roberts8@ycinet.net

Zion   (4C)GRWT9133
8670 Highway 436 (mailing)
3890 New Zion Road (physical)
McKenzie, TN 38201
(   )   <Carroll>

SS: Jon T Carlock   <M1>
248 Cherry Avenue
McKenzie, TN 38201
(731)693-0003
carlockj@bethelu.edu
SS: Richard Reed   <M2>
236 Madison Street
Dyer, TN 38330
(731)692-3604
CL: Stan Welch
3670 New Zion Road
McKenzie, TN 38201
(731)358-2238

OTHERS ON MINISTERIAL ROLL:

Akin, Hershel W   <M1 WC>
388 Mysen Drive
Cordova, TN 38018
(901)744-8980
Alexander, Merlyn A   <M1 HR>
80 N Hampton Lane
Jackson, TN 38305
m_j_alexander@eplus.net
(731)668-8185
Anderson, Barry L   <M1 DE>
1790 Faxon Avenue
Memphis, TN 38112
(901)725-0924
wa4mff@aol.com
Bagby, Larry   <M1 WC>
3189 Northwood Drive
Memphis, TN 38111
(901)452-1952
Barkley, Daniel   <M1 WC>
399 Laneview Concord Road
Trenton, TN 38382
(731)855-4162
dgbarkley@hotmail.com
Boatright, William R   <M1 WC>
513 S 6th Street
Murray, KY 42071
(270)761-5052
catfish.boat@gmail.com
Brown, Elinor   <M1 DE>
752 Hawthorne Street
Memphis, TN 38107
(901)274-1474
esb@cumberland.org
Brown, Mark   <M1 M9>
752 Hawthorne Street
Memphis, TN 38107
(901)274-1474
dmbrown@utmem.edu
Burns, J B, Jr   <M1 WC>
1020 Maud Road
Cherokee, AL 35616
(256)360-2252
Caperton, Donald   <M1 RT>
285 Britton Ford Road
Springville, TN 38256
(731)593-5096
dandjcaperton@vol.com
Coleman, Don L   <M1 WC>
85 Orchard Lane
Savannah, TN 38372
(731)925-9710
Condron, Dudley   <M1 RT>
1360 Harbert Avenue
Memphis, TN 38104
(901)726-1488
dudleywcondron@aol.com
Corbin, Eric   <M1 WC>
1629 Symington Road
Ranotul, IL 61866
(217)282-9702

eric@corbinzone.com
Crisp, Gregory W   <M1 WC>
635 Eden Brook Lane
Cordova, TN 38018
(901)266-0406
Drylie, James   <M1 M9>
512 JE Blaydes Parkway
Atoka, TN 38004
(901)837-1627
Dyer, Stuart   <M1 WC>
3574 Foxfield Trail
Bartlett, TN 38135
(901)388-0612
Eddleman, Keith   <M1 WC>
2787 Stage Park Drive
Memphis, TN 38134
(901)388-9885
Gam, John   <M1 WC>
1235 Sanders Street
Auburn, AL 36830
Gillock, Ed   <M1 WC>
PO Box 157
Savannah, TN 38372
(731)609-6744
Grimsley, Roger   <M1 WC>
215 N Oak Street
Springfield, TN 37172
Hames, Anne   <M1 M9>
118 Paris Street
McKenzie, TN 38201
(731)352-4066
FAX: (731)352-4069
hamesa@bethel-college.edu
Heflin, Donna S   <M1 WC>
4144 Meadow Court Drive
Bartlett, TN 38135
(901)382-8198
rdheflin@bellsouth.net
Hill, Jody   <M1 WC>
4030 St Andrew Circle
Corinth, MS 38834
(662)512-8226
jody.hill34@gmail.com
Holmes, Aaron G   <M1 WC>
PO Box 171
Atwood, TN 38220
(731)662-7595
agholmes@charter.net
Hubbard, Pratt   <M1 WC>
1565 Eli Brown Road
McKenzie, TN 38201
(731)352-9178
Jackson, Terry   <M1 M9>
1461 Mount Pleasant Road
Hernando, MS 38632
(662)429-9741
Jeong, Woo S   <M1 WC>
1205 Morganshire Drive
Collierville, TN 38017
(901)302-0558
FAX: (901)854-8185
Jett, Mace T Jr   <M1 WC>
109 Park Street
Martin, TN 38237
(731)587-0805
Kim, Yoong S   <M1 WC>
8601 Dogwood Road
Germantown, TN 38139
(901)490-8973
FAX: (901)756-7166
yoongkim1934@yahoo.com
Kleinjan, Lori   <M1 WC>
6516 Farnell Avenue
Memphis, TN 38134
(901)372-8413
lkleinj@prodigy.net
Latimer, James M   <M1 WC>

WEST TENNESSEE PRESBYTERY CONTINUED

7621 Richmond
Memphis, TN 38125
(901)787-7875
jimmylatimer@redeemerevangelical.com

Leslie, Eugene   <M1 WC>
13155 Center Hill Road
Olive Branch, MS 38654
(731)613-0425
eleslie1@bellsouth.net

Maynard, Geoffery   <M1 WC>
1356 Marcia Road
Memphis, TN 38117
(901)409-5269

McClung, Andy   <M1 WC>
919 Dickinson Street
Memphis, TN 38107
(901)606-6615
scubarev@att.net

McClung, Tiffany   <M1 M9>
919 Dickinson Street
Memphis, TN 38107
(901)606-6615
tmcclung@memphisseminary.edu

McKee, Margaret   <M1 RT M9>
774 Beasley Street
Memphis, TN 38111
(901)323-2339

Meeks, Brittany   <M1 WC>
2264 Morning Sun Road
Cordova, TN 38016
(901)336-9024

Minor, Mitzi   <M1 PR>
875 S Cox
Memphis, TN 38104
(901)278-6115

Mosley, Karen   <M1 WC>
PO Box 172154
Memphis, TN 38187

Nash, Zachary   <M1 M8>
1296 Hurst Drive
Enid, OK 73703
(580)213-7211
zachary.nash@vance.af.mil

Ndoro, Wonder   <M1 WC>
111 Roberta Avenue
Memphis, TN 38112
(901)334-5861
gusungo@yahoo.com

Norton, Thomas H   <M1 RT>
220 Evergreen Garden Drive
Elizabethtown, KY 42701
(353)584-4695
tnorton16@comcast.net

Perkins, Ed   <M1 RT>
721 E Paris Avenue
McKenzie, TN 38201
(731)352-2754

Pinion, Phillip   <M1 WC>
PO Box 87
Union City, TN 38281
(731)885-9175

Powell, Jeff   <M1 WC>
547B Fawn Drive
Henderson, TN 38340
(731)608-2040
jfpowell2003@yahoo.com

Prosser, Robert   <M1 DE>
1021 Old State Route 76
Henry, TN 38231
(731)243-4467

Qualls, Michael   <M1 DE>
3639 Tiffany Oaks Lane
Bartlett, TN 38135
(901)377-0526
FAX: (901)382-2600
mqualls1@yahoo.com

Ragsdale, Donnie   <M1 WC>

915 S Olive Street
Union City, TN 38261
(731)885-0014

Ridgely, Michael   <M1 WC>
5195 Broad Street S
Trezevant, TN 38258
(731)669-3767

Rietz, Allen   <M1 WC>
1239 Hopewell Church Road
Finger, TN 38334
(731)989-7872

Rose, Missy   <M1 DE>
5484 Peyton Randolph Street
Bartlett, TN 38134
(901)378-1133
missyrose3@yahoo.com

Scrivener, Carol   <M1 WC>
746 Willowsprings Boulevard
Franklin, TN 37064
(731)660-6469
csscriv@juno.com

Searcy, James M   <M1 WC>
1307 Lucy Way
Knoxville, TN 37912
(817)293-6132
gsearcy@earthlink.net

Smith, James A   <M1 WC>
8301 Poplar Pike
Germantown, TN 38138
(901)309-1992
james1493@att.net

Thomas, Don F   <M1 WC>
400 Park Hill Road
Collierville, TN 38017
(901)861-6398
thomas63981@comcast.net

Thompson, Tommy   <M1 WC>
9160 Tchulahoma Road
Southaven, MS 38671
(662)393-2552

Truax, Robert Lee, Jr   <M1 M9 RT>
2989 Champions Drive Apt 204
Lakeland, TN 38002
(901)266-5927

Turner, O Gene   <M1 WC>
5160 McSpadden Road
Rives, TN 38253
(731)536-0189

Walker, Michael C   <M1 WC>
1404 Wilshire Drive
Odessa, TX 79761
(731)643-6730
mworator@gmail.com

Ward, Frank   <M1 WC>
46 Henderson Cove
Atoka, TN 38004
(901)837-1972
bamaguy68@xipline.com

Westbrook, James   <M1 RT>
1717 Wedgewood Drive
Union City, TN 38261
(731)884-0918
westbrook731@bellsouth.net

Wheeler, Nathan   <M1 WC>
1255 Wedgewood Street
Memphis, TN 38111
(901)606-9535
nathantyac@gmail.com

White, Diann   <M1 WC>
9394 Alex Dickson Cove
Bartlett, TN 38133
(901)377-7776
diannwhite12@yahoo.com

Wilson, Thomas   <M1 WC>
4543 Lake Vista
Memphis, TN 38128
(901)382-6190

tomjw217@gmail.com

OTHER LICENTIATES ON ROLL:

Dalton, Frank   <M2>
1606 Ebenezer Road
Troy, TN 38260
(731)536-4553

Harwell, Jacob   <M2>
319 Joy Drive
McKenzie, TN 38201
(731)415-1457
rjharwell@student.memphisseminary.edu

Jett-Rand, Dana   <M2>
#78 Lester Lane
Martin, TN 38237
(731)587-0805

Magliolo, Sam   <M2 ST>
14352 Fairview
Byhalia, MS 38611
(662)838-7720
samagliolo@fedex.com

Marshall, Debbie   <M2>
1494 Bucksnort Road
Covington, TN 38019
(901)475-4055
dsmarshall05@att.net

McClanahan, Jo Ann   <M2>
215 White Brothers Road
Humboldt, TN 38343
(731)784-1176
jaw1940_1@bellsouth.net

Sims, Joyce   <M2>
6935 Highway 54
Paris, TN 38242
(731)364-3537

OTHER CANDIDATES ON ROLL:

Adams, Jamie   <M3 ST>
403 W Washington
Union City, TN 38261
(731)885-1217
adamsj2@k12tn.net

Dimo, Urelia   <M3>
171 Roberta Drive
Memphis, TN 38112

Gray, Brad   <M3>
6378 Highway 59 S
Mason, TN 38049
(901)475-6140
dgray@aol.com

Hernden, Matthew   <M3 ST>
206 Smith Lane
Brighton, TN 38011
(901)484-7661
mherndren023@gmail.com

Lannom, Pamela   <M3 ST>
220 Bradford Acres
Bradford, TN 38316
(731)742-3838
plannom@yahoo.com

Morris, Cary   <M3>
2167 W Shawtown Road
Troy, TN 38260
(731)538-9477
carey@cyberianwolf.net

Narowetz, Laura   <M3 ST>
129 Roberta Drive
Memphis, TN 38112
(662)213-7072
littlelaurarose@yahoo.com

Todd, Christopher   <M3 ST>
139 Roberta Drive
Memphis, TN 38112
(901)529-1072
ctodd2@msn.com

ALPHABETICAL ROLL OF MINISTERS

Symbols in this roll:

(M0) - Mentored Minister
(M1) - Ordained Minister
(M2) - Licentiate
(M3) - Candidate
(M4) - Minister of another denomination who through reciprocal agreement is enrolled as a member of presbytery and has temporarily the rights and privileges of such membership according to the Constitution, Article 5.3.

--==<< A >>==--

Acton, Donald W (M1)
1186 Jenkins Lane
Knoxville, TN 37922
(865)966-5132   SEET#2310

Acton, Donny (M1)
1413 Oak Ridge Drive
Birmingham, AL 35242
FAX: (205)991-5259
donny@newhopecpc.org
(205)991-3204   SEGR#0104

Acton, Mindy (M1)
1413 Oak Ridge Drive
Birmingham, AL 35242
FAX: (205)991-5259
mindy@newhopecpc.org
(205)991-3204   SEGR#0104

Acton, Wade (M1)
1615 Estes Drive
Glencoe, AL 35905
ginnyacton@juno.com
(256)492-8542   SEGR#0406

Acuff, David (M1)
4969 Quail Lane
Columbia, SC 29206
david.acuff@us.army.mil
(803)727-3910   TNNA#7300

Adams, Fred Michael (M1)
42 Julies Way
Somerset, KY 42503
fma46@twc.com
(606)451-9155   MICU#3314

Adams, Hunter (M3)
603 Red Fox Court
Burns, TN 37029
(615)943-7862   TNNA#7300

Adams, Jamie (M3)
403 W Washington
Union City, TN 38261
adamsj2@k12tn.net
(731)885-1217   GRWT#9100

Aden, Dare (M1)
1280 Kimber Road
Dongola, IL 62926
FAX: (618)827-4612
dare_aden@hotmail.com
(618)827-3625   MICO#3400

Aden, Marty (M1)
202 Bennington Place
Wilmington, NC 28412
maden@ec.rr.com
(910)795-1092   MSRR#8400

Agudelo, Gildardo (M1)
Cra 73C # 1A-54
Cali, COLOMBIA, SA
( )   MSCA#8223

Aguiar, Neil (M1)
405 E Moulton Street
Decatur, AL 35601
nlajap@yahoo.com

(256)616-1318   SEGR#0214

Ahn, Da-Wit (David) (M1)
1304 Kakyeng-Dong
Sangdang-Gu Cheongju-City
Choongbook, KOREA
(043)235-0219   SEET#2200

Akai, Anum (M1)
458 Dean Taylor Court
Simpsonville, KY 40067
(502)405-3120   MICU#3100

Akin, Hershel W (M1)
388 Mysen Drive
Cordova, TN 38018
(901)744-8980   GRWT#9100

Alas, William (M1)
612 King Valley Circle
Pelham, AL 35124
alas3542085@yahoo.es
(205)966-9411   SEGR#0115

Albarracin, Ruben D (M1)
7411 Magnolia Shadows Lane
Houston, TX 77095
FAX: (281)463-8617
confiaendios@hotmail.com
(281)463-8617   MSTR#8612

Alexander, Merlyn A (M1)
80 N Hampton Lane
Jackson, TN 38305
m_j_alexander@eplus.net
(731)668-8185   GRWT#9100

Alhart, Daryl (M1)
2187 Rutledge Ford Road
Decherd, TN 37324
dwalhart@aol.com
(931)349-7104   TNMU#7225

Allen, Gail (M1)
488 County Road 1650 N
Bethany, IL 61914
kallen1_61914@yahoo.com
(217)665-3387   MINC#5200

Alspaugh, Kevin (M1)
5102 Main Drive
New Hope, AL 35760
rev.alspaugh@gmail.com
(256)723-3808   SERD#0800

Alvarez, Samuel (M3)
3740 W Leland Avenue
Chicago, IL 60625
(773)509-9165   MINC#5200

Alverson, Elmer L (M1)
354 Roy Davis Road
New Market, AL 35761
budalv@bellsouth.net
(256)828-4503   SERD#0800

Anderson, Barry L (M1)
1790 Faxon Avenue
Memphis, TN 38112
wa4mff@aol.com
(901)725-0924   GRWT#9100

Anderson, Christopher (M3)
131 Roberta Drive

Memphis, TN 38112
csanderson@memphisseminary.edu
(870)805-0886   GRAR#1100

Anderson, Kyle (M3)
828 E Main Street
Batesville, AR 72501
kanderson@mempisseminary.edu
(870)834-5799

Anderson, Lisa (M1)
1790 Faxon Avenue
Memphis, TN 38112
anderli@aol.com
(901)725-0924   GRWT#9305

Ang, John (M1)
5843 S Farm Road 157
Springfield, MO 65810
pastorcares@yahoo.com
(417)886-3487   GRMI#4104

Appling, John (M1)
1722 S Fairway Avenue
Springfield, MO 65804
pegblessings@sbcglobal.net
(417)877-4643   GRMI#4100

Appling, Peggy (M1)
1722 S Fairway Avenue
Springfield, MO 65804
pegblessings@sbcglobal.net
(417)877-4643   GRMI#4100

Arase, Makihiko (M1)
3-355-4 Kamikitadai Higashi
Yamato-shi, Tokyo
207-0023, JAPAN
FAX: (042)567-2977
viator@cb3.so-net.ne.jp
(042)567-2977   MSJA#8309

Arias, John Jairo (M3)
Calle 144 Sur #496-08 / Apto 202
Caldas, Antioquia
COLOMBIA, SA
(57)317-693-1162   MSAN#8900

Ariza, Fabiola (M1)
COLOMBIA, SA
fatvioleta@hotmail.com
(316)419-8414   MSCA#8200

Aros, Jeremias (M1)
5649 W Roscoe Street
Chicago, IL 60634
jeremiasaros@sbcglobal.net
(773)685-4395   MINC#5200

Arteaga, Gilberto (M3)
Aereo 794
Buenaventura, COLOMBIA, SA
pastorgilbertoa@hotmail.com
( )256-4261   MSCA#8210

Asayama, Masaharu (M1)
6-3-2-308 Toyogaoka
Tama-shi, Tokyo
206-0031, JAPAN
asa@ipcc-21.com
(042)373-2710   MSJA#8300

Ashton, Christie (M1)

MINISTERS CONTINUED

10001 Bailey Cove Road SE
Huntsville, AL 35803
FAX: (256)881-0031
pastorhope@bellsouth.net
(256)881-4673 SERD#0800
Attema, Lee (M1)
930 W 8th Street
Freeport, TX 77541
lattema@comcast.net
(281)728-6263 MSTR#8103
Atwell, Keith G (M1)
7688 Hardyville Road
Hardyville, KY 42746
FAX: (270)524-9100
(270)528-3667 MICU#3102
Axton, Durant (M1)
2441 SE Browning Road
Evansville, IN 47725
(812)459-0089 MINC#5200

--==<< B >>==--

Babcock, Edward S, Jr (M1)
1007 San Ramone Avenue
Huntsville, AL 35802
ejsb1@aol.com
(256)882-9339 SERD#0800
Bagby, Larry (M1)
3189 Northwood Drive
Memphis, TN 38111
(901)452-1952 GRWT#9100
Ballow, Brent (M1)
140 Windmill Drive
Paducah, KY 42001
hcppastor@bellsouth.net
(270)564-8891 MICO#3414
Baltimore, Claud G (M1)
PO Box 1358
1430 Lakehurst Drive
Ada, OK 74821
baltimorejb@earthlink.net
(580)332-2679 MSRR#8400
Bane, Ted (M1)
903 W Old Hickory Boulevard
Madison, TN 37115
tedjan95@aol.com
(615)975-9343 TNNA#7300
Baranoski, Timothy (M1)
8040 Starz Loop
Killeen, TX 76544
(615)440-3499 TNNA#7300
Barkley, Daniel (M1)
2732 Rexford Street
Hokes Bluff, AL 35903
daniel@gadsdencp.com
(256)478-0397 SEGR#0402
Barnett, Rudolph (M1)
RR 5 Box 267
McLeansboro, IL 62859
(618)643-3253 MINC#5200
Barnhouse, Donald Grey, Jr (M1)
51 Harristown Road
Paradise, PA 17562
donaldbarnhouse@gmail.com
(610)337-4015 MICU#3131
Barrett, Geoff (M1)
155 Maude Lane
Harrodsburg, KY 40330
FAX: (256)881-0031
glbarrett@live.com
(859)748-8373 MICU#3111
Barron, Mark (M1)

836 McArthur Street
Manchester, TN 37355
FAX: (931)728-2975
mbarron@cafes.net
(931)728-2975 TNMU#7224
Barry, James (M1)
1405 Anna Street
Hixson, TN 37343
james_barry@bellsouth.net
(903)315-7998 SETG#2111
Barton, Cindy (M3)
83426 Argus Avenue
Trona, CA 93562
cbarton53@hotmail.com
(760)372-4033 MSDC#8700
Barton, Robert (M1)
22460 Klines Resort Road Lot #290
Three Rivers, MI 49093
csm2ndinfbde2002@yahoo.com
(859)613-2686 MICU#3100
Baugh, Roosevelt (M1)
4101 Hademan Street
Fort Worth, TX 76119
FAX: (817)534-1339
gmf1220@charter.net
(817)536-1315 MSRR#8408
Bautista, Juan (M1)
Tranv 30 No 17F-122
Cali
Colombia, South America
( )442-4562 MSCA#8217
Bayer, David (M1)
9060 Tom Counce Road
South Fulton, TN 38257
dbayer9060@gmail.com
(731)479-3060 GRWT#9412
Bell, Marc (M1)
811 Campbell Lane
Bowling Green, KY 42104
marcbell@insightbb.com
(270)846-4203 MICU#3503
Bell, Michelle (M3)
8643 Dry Creek Road Unit 1226
Centennial, CO 80112
mabbell@comcast.net
(720)344-4040 MSDC#870
Benadom, Dennis (M1)
13314 Sage Street
Trona, CA 93562
galerose91@msn.com
(760)372-4536 MSDC#8503
Bender, Richard J (M1)
5297 Normandy Place
Evansville, IN 47715
richardjbenderjr@yahoo.com
(812)983-9597 MINC#5200
Benedict, Mary McCaskey (M1)
69 Lennox Court
Richmond Hill, GA 31324
marykat_61@hotmail.com
(931)260-1422 TNMU#7200
Bennett, Alfred J (M1)
7286 Nolensville Road
Nolensville, TN 37135
(615)776-5181 TNNA#7300
Benson, William L (M1)
137 W Lowndes Drive
Columbus, MS 39701
willardb715@gmail.com
(662)386-3433 SEGR#0701
Bertsch, Michael (M1)
115 Leatherwood Creek Estates

Bedford, IN 47421
silkpie@gmail.com
(423)763-8314 SETG#2100
Betancur, Sergio (M1)
Iglesia El Rebano
Calle 128 sur #48-13
Caldas, Antioquia, COLOMBIA, SA
sergiobetancurposada@hotmail.com
(574)278-0787 MSCA#8208
Biggs, Jeff (M1)
1504 Cumberland Drive
Fairfield, IL 62837
jeffbiggsonline@gmail.com
(618)842-2219 MINC#5108
Black, Gary G (M1)
503 S Main Street
Piedmont, AL 36272
(205)447-7142 SEGR#0400
Blackburn, Samuel N (M1)
6706 S 6th Street
Fort Smith, AR 72908
(479)649-9436 GRAR#1100
Blair, Fonda (M1)
PO Box 11093
Murfreesboro, TN 37129
blairfonda2010@comcast.net
(615)491-2432 TNCO#7145
Blair, John (M1)
108 Cliff Drive
Lawrenceburg, TN 38464
jnbblair@charter.net
(931)766-2480 TNCO#7111
Blakeburn, Larry A (M1)
230 Heathridge Drive
Dyersburg, TN 38024
FAX: (731)285-5792
larry@cumberlandchurch.com
(731)286-2982 GRWT#9410
Blakeburn, Roy E (M1)
111 Park Place
Greeneville, TN 37743
FAX: (423)636-1017
(423)787-9609 SEET#2206
Blandon, Juan Esteban (M1)
Calle 51 #15-32
barrio Los Naranjos
Dosquebradas, Risaralda
COLOMBIA, SA
juanestebanblandon@yahoo.com
57(314)680-2246 MSAN#8907
Blanton, D B (M1)
ADDRESS UNKNOWN
( ) GRAR#1100
Blaum, Steve R (M1)
184 900 Street
Middletown, IL 62666
cumberland@frontier.com
(217)671-96226923 MINC#5405
Blevins, Ralph (M1)
1623 County Road 2375 E
Geff, IL 62842
pastorreblevins@gmail.com
(618)854-2494 MINC#5107
Blevins, Tom (M1)
50 Blevins Road
Center, KY 42214
(270)565-1792 MICU#3100
Board, N Ray (M1)
267 State Route 293 N
Princeton, KY 42445
rayboard@att.net
(270)365-0006 MICO#3609

MINISTERS CONTINUED

Boatright, William R (M1)
513 S 6th Street
Murray, KY 42071
catfish.boat@gmail.com
(270)761-5052   GRWT#9100

Boggs, Barry (M3)
1039 Johnnie Bud Lane
Cookeville, TN 38501
( )   TNMU#7200

Boggs, Robert (M1)
89 Maple Leaf Lane
Leitchfield, KY 42754
(270)259-5546   MICU#3100

Bond, Bill (M1)
205 Windmere Drive
Chattanooga, TN 37411
bill@wcbj.net
(423)316-0867   SETG#2102

Bond, Richard (M1)
2425 Fisk Road Lot 0
Cookeville, TN 38506
erbond@frontier.net
(931)854-0979   TNMU#7213

Bondurant, Lee (M1)
1453 Paseo Del Sur Court
El Paso, TX 79928
leebondurant@yahoo.com
(915)309-7269   MSDC#8700

Bone, Leslie (M1)
16504 George Franklyn Drive
Independence, MO 64055
lesliebone@comcast.net
(816)373-6625   GRMI#4100

Bone, W Harold (M1)
3405 Stillman Loop
Bryant, AR 72022
ruaha1@sbcglobal.net
(501)847-9473   MSTR#8100

Boulton, Mitch (M1)
1606 Ebenezer Road
Troy, TN 38260
steelermitch@gmail.com
(731)487-2318   GRWT#9422

Bower, Clay (M1)
221 Waterlemon Way
Monroe, NC 28110
cbower@lzbsoutheast.com
(704)575-9497   MSDC#8700

Bowers, Sharon G (M1)
1800 Post Road Apt 612
San Marcos, TX 78666
sharon.bowers@gmail.com
(512)230-7078   MSTR#8100

Bowling, Andrew (M1)
20945 Highway 16 E
Siloam Springs, AR 72761
(479)524-6576   GRAR#1100

Bozeman, Robert (M1)
582 Bozeman Loop
Belmont, LA 71406
bo@bozemanengineering.com
(318)256-5781   MSTR#8100

Bradberry, Jim (M3)
120 Hummingbird Lane
Searcy, AR 72143
(501)278-9750   GRAR#1205

Bradshaw, James (Jim) (M1)
415 S Red Street
Sheridan, AR 72150
(870)942-2525   GRAR#1105

Brantley, Kevin T (M1)
729 Old Hodgenville Road
Greensburg, KY 42743
kbrantley1971@windstream.net
(270)932-3780   MICU#3110

Brasher, Karen (M1)
1640 King James Drive
Alabaster, AL 35007
( )   MSTR#8100

Braswell, Jimmy (M1)
1514 E 10th
Odessa, TX 79761
jjcgbraz@cableone.net
(432)335-9346   MSDC#8703

Brewer, Barbara Jean (M1)
1360 White Oak Bluff Road
Rison, AR 71665
(870)325-6449   GRAR#1108

Brindley, Toy (M1)
PO Box 225
Gurley, AL 35748
(256)776-2331   SERD#0804

Brister, Glen (M1)
2089 Sumach Church Road
Chatsworth, GA 30705
bearmountainpenworks@gmail.com
(706)934-8629   SETG#2124

Brock, Dudley (M1)
490 County Road 1184
Cullman, AL 35057
preacherbrock@att.net
(256)734-0893   SEHO#0500

Brodbent, Josh (M3)
PO Box 587
Wynne, AR 72397-0587
( )   GRAR#1100

Brodeur, Evelyn (M1)
1005 Cleermont Drive SE
Huntsville, AL 35801
lifeandwater@aol.com
(256)536-1070   SERD#0800

Brooks, Wayne E (M1)
1505 Parkview Drive
Campbellsville, KY 42718
webrooks@windstream.net
(270)465-9235   MICU#3104

Brown, Amy (M2)
679 Freeze Bend Road
Newport, AR 72112
( )   GRAR#1100

Brown, Charles R (M1)
2908 Steve Drive
Hurst, TX 76054
cbrown@sttimothy-cpc.org
(817)915-2907   MSRR#8419

Brown, Dale M (M1)
HC 61 Box 4740
West Plains, MO 65775
pastorbrown44@yahoo.com
(417)257-0983   GRMI#4304

Brown, Elinor (M1)
752 Hawthorne Street
Memphis, TN 38107
esb@cumberland.org
(901)274-1474   GRWT#9100

Brown, Mark (M1)
752 Hawthorne Street
Memphis, TN 38107
dmbrown@utmem.edu
(901)274-1474   GRWT#9100

Brown, Philip (M3)
540 Mt Pisgah Road
Dongola, IL 62926
brownlp75@yahoo.com
(618)827-3516   MICO#5115

Brown, Rex (M1)
134 Everhart Drive
Greeneville, TN 37745
firstcumberland@gmail.com
(423)639-4298   SEET#2205

Brown, Stephanie S (M1)
1713 Arbor Mill Circle Apt 1424
Bedford, TX 76021
scrudderbrown7@yahoo.com
(901)729-3612   MSRR#8400

Brown, Whitney (M3)
137 Roberta Drive
Memphis, TN 38112
(865)387-0002   SEET#2200

Bruington, Don (M1)
PO Box 105
Falls of Rough, KY 40119
(270)257-2228   MICU#3202

Bryan, Hannah (M1)
32 Trenton Lane
Mead, OK 73449
hbryan@choctawnation.com
(580)775-4955   MSCH#6105

Buchanan, Larry (M1)
720 Shelby Road
Salem, KY 42078
(270)988-1880   MICO#3610

Buck, Clinton (M1)
4986 Warwick Avenue
Memphis, TN 38117
clintobuck@aol.com
(901)682-2358   GRWT#9315

Bunnell, Robert (Bob) (M1)
329 Lexington Drive
Glasgow, KY 42141
bob_bunnell@yahoo.com
(270)629-6209   MICU#3312

Bunting, Geoff (M1)
9229 Hedgewood Court
Evansville, IN 47725
geoff.bunting@yahoo.com
(812)925-6630   MINC#5200

Burgess, Ronald D (M1)
1208 Redwood Lane
Clarksville, TN 37042
revron4@bellsouth.net
(931)906-2868   TNNA#7315

Burns, Garrett (M2)
387 Forrest Avenue
McKenzie, TN 38201
gburns2888@gmail.com
(731)535-3126   GRAR#1100

Burns, J B, Jr (M1)
1020 Maud Road
Cherokee, AL 35616
(256)360-2252   GRWT#9100

Burrow, Vernon (M1)
707 Saratoga Drive
Murfreesboro, TN 37130
vernonburrow@comcast.net
(615)406-6385   TNMU#7233

Burrows, Arthur L, Jr (M1)
PO Box 511
Hopkinsville, KY 42241
(270)886-1301   MICU#3505

Butcher, Kenny (M1)
4608 Cather Court
Nashville, TN 37214
bhpastor@birch.net
(615)719-1887   TNNA#7325

Butler, Jim (M1)

MINISTERS CONTINUED

6322 Labor Lane
Louisville, KY 40291
jbutler54@insightbb.com
(502)635-8587　　　MICU#3222
Butler, John　　　(M1)
PO Box 257
Sacramento, KY 42372
butler8134@bellsouth.net
(270)736-2268　　　MICU#3512
Butler, Joseph H, Jr　　　(M1)
56 Cline Ridge Road
Winchester, TN 37398
jhbu737@bellsouth.net
(931)224-8423　　　TNMU#7205
Buttram, Jim　　　(M1)
103 Golfcrest Lane
Oak Ridge, TN 37830
FAX: (865)483-8445
littlejimb@gmail.com
(865)938-7418　　　SEET#2313
Byford, Ken　　　(M3)
58 Quincy Lane
Montevallo, AL 35115
kenabyford@gmail.com
(205)665-5753　　　SEGR#0100
Bynum, Ronald H　　　(M1)
121 Sycamore Road
Gurley, AL 35748
ronaldbynum@bellsouth.net
(256)776-9313　　　SERD#0800
Byrd, James F　　　(M1)
1158 Cornishville Road
Harrodsburg, KY 40330
jfbyrd@bluezoomwifi.com
(859)734-0534　　　MICU#3100
Byrd, Jimmy　　　(M1)
176 E Valley Road
Whitwell, TN 37397
FAX: (615)444-6671
revjimmybyrd@gmail.com
(615)289-3347　　　SETG#2115

--==<< C >>==--

Cadenbach, Mark　　　(M1)
PO Box 66
Westfield, IA 51062
cadenbm@nctc.net
( )　　　TNNA#7300
Caicedo, Efrain　　　(M3)
Aereo 6365
Cali, COLOMBIA, SA
( )　　　MSCA#8224
Cain, Greg　　　(M3)
155 Greggstown
Calvert City, KY 42029
(270)816-5259　　　MICO#3400
Calero, Aldrin　　　(M1)
Cattara 13 3-81
Guacari, COLOMBIA, SA
( )253-0453　　　MSCA#8212
Camp, Annetta　　　(M1)
2303 Mill Creek Road
Halls, TN 38040
FAX: (731)285-5792
annetta@cumberlandchurch.com
(731)285-5703　　　GRWT#9410
Campbell, Coyle　　　(M1)
186 Old Limestone Road
New Market, AL 35761
(256)379-4392　　　TNMU#7215
Campbell, Gordon C　　　(M1)

1469 E Wayland Street
Springfield, MO 65804
gofor12@gmail.com
(417)823-9567　　　GRMI#4100
Campbell, Thomas D　　　(M1)
PO Box 343
601 Park Street
Calico Rock, AR 72519
FAX: (870)297-3151
tdcampbellar@gmail.com
(870)297-2319　　　GRAR#1503
Campos, Eva　　　(M3)
PO Box 451405
Miami, FL 33245
(786)426-5997　　　SEGR#0100
Cantey, James M　　　(M1)
3505 Elmira Drive
Longview, TX 75605
(903)452-6049　　　MSTR#8111
Caperton, Donald　　　(M1)
285 Britton Ford Road
Springville, TN 38256.
dandjcaperton@vol.com
(731)593-5096　　　GRWT#9100
Cardona, Nancy　　　(M3)
Calle 51 #15-32
Dosquebradas, Risaralda
COLOMBIA, SA
nancycardona10@yahoo.com
(576)322-2938　　　MSAN#8900
Carlock, Jon T　　　(M1)
248 Cherry Avenue
McKenzie, TN 38201
carlockj@bethel-college.edu
(731)352-0800　　　GRWT#9133
Carlton, Gary　　　(M1)
108 Greenbrier Street
Dickson, TN 37055
gwcarlton@yahoo.com
(270)965-4358　　　TNNA#7313
Carpenter, David　　　(M1)
909 W Elm Street
Olney, TX 76374
olneycpc@brazosnet.com
(940)564-2339　　　MSRR#8416
Carr, Jill　　　(M3)
PO Box 1547
Lebanon, MO 65536
dig.micah.6.8@gmail.com
(417)532-6760　　　GRMI#4100
Carter, Billy Ray　　　(M1)
33 Mockingbird Drive
Leitchfield, KY 42754
cartercbc@windstream.net
(270)259-3897　　　MICU#3203
Carter, Gary　　　(M1)
806 Waverly Avenue
Muscle Shoals, AL 35661
garycarter51@gmail.com
(256)443-8389　　　SEHO#0202
Carter, James L　　　(M1)
6155 Hummingbird Lane
Whitesburg, TN 37891
jandjmt@comcast.net
(423)587-8423　　　SEET#2200
Carter, Patricia　　　(M1)
2509 Decatur Stratton Road
Decatur, MS 39327
revtree@yahoo.com
(601)604-3813　　　SEGR#0100
Carver, Gary　　　(M1)
2810 Cabin Road

Chattanooga, TN 37411
sandgatthecabin@epbfi.com
(423)698-2556　　　SETG#2104
Cassell, C J　　　(M3)
825 Aimes Court
Nashville, TN 37221
n4cjc@comcast.net
(615)594-2693　　　TNNA#7300
Castaneda, Ricardo　　　(M1)
Calle 65 #98-45 (Interior 174)
Altos de la Macarena-Robledo La Campina
Medellin, Antioquia, COLOMBIA, SA
rijcah@gmail.com
(574)577-0717　　　MSAN#8915
Castano, Juan Alexander　　　(M3)
Calle 127 sur #42-38 Apto 301
Caldas, Antioquia, COLOMBIA, SA
FAX: (574)278-0787
juanalexandercastano@hotmail.com
(574)306-4435　　　MSAN#8905
Chall-Hutchinson　　　(M3)
190 Ussery Road
Clarksville, TN 37043
challhut@gmail.com
(931)905-1671　　　TNNA#7300
Chamberlin, Edwin (Joey)　　　(M2)
7385 W Grant Ranch Boulevard Apt 1636
Littleton, CO 80123
ejcham@gmail.com
(817)929-9876　　　MSDC#8700
Chambers, Jason　　　(M1)
131 E Woods Street
Palestine, AR 72372
jmchambers@memphisseminary.edu
(870)807-1930　　　GRAR#1100
Chambers, Nicholas　　　(M1)
11300 Road 101
Union, MS 39365
nachambrs@hotmail.com
(870)231-4909　　　SEGR#0608
Chancellor, Hilton　　　(M1)
PO Box 341717
Austin, TX 78734
FAX: (915)570-0866
hiltontex@aol.com
(941)907-0577　　　MSTR#8100
Chang, John　　　(M1)
1753 Castro Drive
San Jose, CA 95130
FAX: (405)370-0643
(408)370-0643　　　MSDC#8700
Chang, Leo　　　(M1)
819 W Division SE
Springfield, MO 65803
(901)287-9901　　　GRAR#1100
Chapman, Harry W　　　(M1)
4908 El Picador Court
Rio Rancho, NM 87124
wrightrev@gmail.com
(505)620-2427　　　MSDC#8709
Chen, Steven　　　(M1)
865 Jackson Street
San Francisco, CA 94133
psalm1305@yahoo.com
(415)421-1624　　　MSDC#8501
Chesnut, Walter　　　(M1)
114 Cherrydale Drive
Greeneville, TN 37745
lc1916@yahoo.com
(270)259-4429　　　MICU#3100
Cheung, Kam Ho　　　(M3)
G/F 251 Tin Sam Village

MINISTERS CONTINUED

Shatin, NT, Hong Kong
FAX: (852)2607-2265
percycheung@hotmail.com
(852)2607-3414   MSHK#8807
Cheung, Luke   (M1)
A-D Flat 3/F 338-340 Castle Peak Road
Cheung Sha Wan
Kowloon HONG KONG
FAX: (852)2706-0114
luke.cheung@cgst.edu
(852)2794-6781   MSHK#8800
Cheung, Percy   (M2)
G/F & 1/F, 251, Tin Sam Village
Tai Wai, Shatin, NT, HONG KONG
FAX: (852)2607-2245
percycheung@hotmail.com
(852)2693-3444   MSHK#8800
Chin, Kwang Sik   (M2)
1168 Palisade Avenue
Fort Lee, NJ 07024
(201)220-3390   SETG#2100
Cho, Sangsook   (M1)
7 Falmouth Court
Middletown, CT
lovejcamen@yahoo.com
(860)830-6808   SETG#2100
Cho, Sung Wan   (M1)
1603 Coolhurst Avenue
Sherwood, AR 72120
swcho100491@gmail.com
(501)247-5953   GRAR#2135
Choe, Byung-Jae   (M1)
876-15 Dokok-1dong
Kangnam-Gu, Seoul, KOREA
(023)463-3939   SEET#2222
Choi, Ezra   (M3)
605 Arbor Hollow Circle #2103
Cordova, TN 38018
(901)236-8235   SEET#2200
Choi, Hyoung S   (M1)
32132 Huntly Circle
Salisbury, MD 21804
pastor0101@naver.com
(443)880-6776   SETG#2138
Choi, Justin   (M2)
605 Arbor Hollow Circle Apt 203
Cordova, TN 38016
flymetothemoon@hotmail.com
(901)605-4542   SEET#2200
Choi, Sean   (M2)
7565 Macon Road
Cordova, TN 38016
esloveh2@hotmail.com
(901)826-2993   SEET#2200
Cinco, Carlos   (M1)
611 Cheron Road
Madison, TN 37115
pastorcinco2020@gmail.com
(615)262-3134   TNNA#7314
Clark, Amber LaCroix   (M1)
338 Royal Oak Drive
Winchester, TN 37398
revamber@comcast.net
(931)967-2121   TNMU#7249
Clark, J Don   (M1)
1601 Lake Ridge Circle
Birmingham, AL 35216
jdsjcl@charter.net
(205)942-4054   SEGR#0100
Clark, Jeff   (M1)
327 Haynes Haven Lane
Murfreesboro, TN 37129
jclark7733@aol.com
(615)896-7733   TNMU#7250
Clark, Jonathan   (M1)

88 Woodcrest Drive
Winchester, TN 37398
FAX: (931)967-8444
clark3568@bellsouth.net
(931)967-9613   TNMU#7200
Clark, Michael   (M1)
134 Overlook Court
Winchester, TN 37398
michael.clark@winchestercp.org
(931)967-2121   TNMU#7249
Clark, Tom   (M1)
501 Cherokee Drive
Campbellsville, KY 42718
(270)469-5468   MICU#3100
Clark, Tommy   (M1)
124 Roberta Drive
Memphis, TN 37216
fattire77@gmail.com
(615)430-9158   TNCO#7100
Cleek, Phillip   (M3)
188 Cleek Lane
Estill Springs, TN 37330
(931)967-2354   TNMU#7200
Coati, DeAngelo   (M3)
11280 Pebble Hills Boulevard #165
El Paso, TX 79936
spccoatie@yahoo.com
(915)504-9032   MSDC#8700
Coker, Robert N   (M1)
721 Lakeview Drive
Loudon, TN 37774
FAX: (865)458-5360
nickcoker@bellsouth.net
(865)458-8791   SEET#2307
Cole, Dwayne   (M1)
3670 Herons Landing
Reno, NV 89502
tadpolejr@aol.com
(814)455-4983   TNCO#7100
Coleman, Bobby D   (M1)
704 E Webb Street
Mountain View, AR 72560
bobbycoleman@gmail.com
(870)213-5410   GRAR#1514
Coleman, Don L   (M1)
85 Orchard Lane
Savannah, TN 38372
(731)925-9710   GRWT#9100
Collins, Paul   (M1)
915 Warm Sands Drive SE
Albuquerque, NM 87123
FAX: (505)254-7707
chapp3@comcast.net
(505)294-3842   MSDC#8700
Colvard, Kevin   (M1)
20024 Crescent Oaks
San Antonio, TX 78258
FAX: (210)497-8724
rev_kev@satx.rr.com
(205)267-9372   MSTR#8608
Compton, Marcia   (M1)
218 N Kirk W
Indianapolis, IN 46234
mcomptonma@yahoo.com
(317)209-9798   MINC#5200
Condon, Thomas W, Jr   (M1)
6508 Victoria Avenue
N Richland Hills, TX 76180
(817)656-9334   MSRR#8400
Condron, Dudley   (M1)
1360 Harbert Avenue
Memphis, TN 38104
dudleywcondron@aol.com
(901)726-1488   GRWT#9100
Contini, John   (M1)
4344 Poor Ridge Pike

Lancaster, KY 40444
john@hillsidehritagefarm.com
(859)339-0747   MICU#3103
Cook, Carl   (M1)
475 Western Hills Loop
Mountain Home, AR 72653
carlc@suddenlink.net
(870)425-2570   GRAR#1100
Cook, Lisa   (M1)
4101 Dalemere Court
Nashville, TN 37207
tgoose@comcast.net
(615)868-4118   TNNA#7300
Corbin, Eric   (M1)
1629 Symington Road
Rantoul, IL 61866
eric@corbinzone.com
(217)282-9702   GRWT#9100
Corbin, William   (M1)
7300 N Lamar Road
Mount Juliet, TN 37122
raven.rest@comcast.net
(615)459-8998   TNNA#7300
Correa, John Jairo   (M1)
Calle 2 Norte #16-39
Armenia, Quindio, COLOMBIA, SA
FAX: (576)745-4860
jjcedp07@hotmail.com
(318)285-1209   MSAN#8903
Cottingim, Tom   (M1)
353 Atwood Drive
Lexington, KY 40515
FAX: (859)272-4315
t.cottingim@insightbb.com
(859)273-3800   MICU#3100
Coulter, Laurance W   (M1)
5226 W William Cannon Drive
Austin, TX 78749
FAX: (512)892-6307
larry@shpc.org
(512)892-3580   MSTR#8604
Cox, Jimmy R   (M1)
2250 County Road 156
Anderson, AL 35610
dcox01@msn.com
(256)710-1702   SEHO#0508
Craddock, Barry   (M3)
147 Moss Way
Glasgow, KY 42141
(   )   MICU#3100
Craig, Aaron   (M3)
325 Cherry Avenue
McKenzie, TN 38201
(731)352-6718   SEET#2200
Craig, Peggy Jean   (M1)
1659 Briar Cliff Road #2308
Atlanta, GA 30306
pjfpeggy@gmail.com
(256)277-1147   SEHO#0500
Craig, Robert A   (M1)
417 S Grove Avenue
Oak Park, IL 60302
v-craig@sbcglobal.net
(773)477-8249   MINC#5200
Cravens, Marvin L   (M1)
604 N Hovis Street
Mountain Grove, MO 65711
(417)926-5778   GRMI#4100
Crawford, Roger B   (M1)
541 Highway 25 N
Carthage, MS 39051
(601)298-1899   SEGR#0100
Crawshaw, Randy   (M1)
136 NE 1271 Road
Knob Noster, MO 65336
randy_crawshaw@yahoo.com

(660)563-5149 GRMI#4115
Crisp, Gregory W (M1)
635 Eden Brook Lane
Cordova, TN 38018
(901)266-0406 GRWT#9100
Criss, Paul T (M1)
6831 Salem Road
Lakeland, TN 38002
ptcriss@hotmail.com
(901)626-8462 GRWT#9316
Crosby, Ronald (M3)
407 N "A" Street
Calera, OK 74730
( ) MSCH#6100
Croslin, Dennis (M3)
165 Maple Street
Gordonsville, TN .38563
cro26110@hotmail.com
(615)934-2383 TNMU#7246
Cuartas, Joel (M0)
Calle 34 #24A-36
Cali, COLOMBIA, SA
(000)438-2512 MSCA#8211
Cummings, Corey (M1)
1023 W Woodrow Street
Milan, TN 38358
corey@milancp.org
(731)686-1851 GRWT#9121
Cunningham, Matthew Dean (M1)
1646 Brighton-Clopton Road
Brighton, TN 38011
mcunningham0528@comcast.net
(901)475-4252 GRWT#9318

--==<< D >>==--

Dallwig, Roger (M1)
1661 Hickory Lane
Corydon, IN 47112
rcd129@hotmail.com
(812)705-5071 MINC#5502
Dalton, Frank (M2)
1606 Ebenezer Road
Troy, TN 38260
(731)536-4553 GRWT#9100
Daniels, Doy L, Jr (M1)
1095 Crestview Drive
Milan, TN 38358
revdrdoy@gmail.com
(731)686-1851 GRWT#9121
Darland, Chris (M1)
582 Ada Drive
Harrodsburg, KY 40330
(859)734-2254 MICU#3303
Davenport, Donna (M1)
3539 State Route 339
Wingo, KY 42088
chamberdonna@yahoo.com
(270)376-5488 MICO#3403
Davenport, Mark A (M1)
8828 Highway 119
Alabaster, AL 35007
FAX: (205)663-8323
fpcapastor@bellsouth.net
(205)663-3152 SERD#0800
Davenport, Vondal (M1)
PO Box 823
Lavaca, AR 72941
(479)965-2036 GRAR#1408
Davis, C Timothy (M1)
8880 Childress Road
West Paducah, KY 42086
FAX: (904)994-6003
charles0828@earthlink.net
(850)995-8383 SEGR#0100
Davis, Robert (Toby) (M1)

502 S Alley Street
Jefferson, TX 75657
pastortobydavis@gmail.com
(901)826-5755 MSTR#8109
Daza, Edilberto (M1)
Cra 12 #8-47
Cartago, Valle
Colombia, South America
presbicartago@gmail.com
57(314)794-1905 MSAN#8906
Daza, Johan (M1)
1844 Eagle Shore Drive
Cordova, TN 38016
jdaza@cumberland.org
(330)703-2855 MSAN#8900
De Jimenez, Luciria Aguirre (M1)
AA6365
COLOMBIA, SA
pastorluciana50@yahoo.com.co
(300)686-9161 MSCA#8200
De Vries, Raymond (M1)
2080 Stanford Village Drive
Antioch, TN 37013
ray.devries@comcast.net
(615)332-3587 TNNA#7333
De Wees, Jeff (M1)
3101 Mt Vernon Road
Ramer, TN 38367
shg_50@bellsouth.net
(731)645-6420 TNNA#9213
Deaton, John (M1)
277 School Lanet
Springfield, PA 19064
deatonjr11@gmail.com
(215)906-7067 SEHO#0500
Deere, Thomas (Tom) (M1)
460 Yukon Drive
Russellville, AR 72802
tdeere@suddenlinkmail.com
(479)498-0318 GRAR#1212
Delashmit, Steve (M1)
2705 Garrett Drive
Bowling Green, KY 42104
steve.delashmit@twc.com
FAX: (270)781-2368
(270)796-8822 MICU#3304
Denton, Clyde M (M1)
(NO ADDRESS AVAILABLE)
Columbia, TN 38401
(931)388-7154 TNCO#7100
Dewhirst, Tim (M3)
3609 Oakbriar Lane
Colleyville, TX 76034
timdew@sbcglobal.net
(817)605-8147 MSRR#8415
Diamond, Cardelia Howell (M1)
1580 Jeff Road
Huntsville, AL 35806
clhdzmhd@hotmail.com
(256)837-6014 TNMU#7224
Diamond, James (M1)
PO Box 1220
Smyrna, TN 37167
FAX: (615)220-1077
james.diamond007@comcast.net
(615)220-2341 TNMU#7244
Diamond, Steven (M1)
1468 William Cove Road
Winchester, TN 37398
smdiam@hotmail.com
(931)636-7336 TNMU#7214
Diaz, Esperanza (M1)
Calle 2 Norte #16-19
Armenia, Quindio, COLOMBIA, SA
jjcedp07@hotmail.com
(576)745-0496 MSAN#8903

Diaz, Freddy (M1)
2425 Holly Hall Apt B42
Houston, TX 77054
fredglobeus@yahoo.com
(832)305-2379 MSTR#8100
Diaz, Gloria Villa (M1)
2425 Holly Hall Apt B42
Houston, TX 77054
fredglobeus@yahoo.com
(832)305-2379 MSTR#8100
Diaz, William (M1)
Calle 5 Con Cra 89
Cali, COLOMBIA, SA
nuevaesperanza1983@hotmail.com
( )332-5849 MSCA#8221
Dimo, Urelia (M3)
171 Roberta Drive
Memphis, TN 38112
( ) GRWT#9100
Dobson, H Wallis (M1)
150 Liberty Way
Greeneville, TN 37745
(423)798-8947 SEET#2200
Doles, Steve (M1)
7702 Indiana Avenue
Lubbock, TX 79423
steve@cpclubbock.com
(806)787-7551 MSDC#8702
Dougherty, Duane A, Jr (M1)
212 County Road 4705
Troup, TX 75789
revdad.duane@gmail.com
(903)842-474 MSTR#8104
Driskell, James P (M1)
154 Mountain Way
Anderson, AL 35610
FAX: (256)247-3339
patprespax@yahoo.com
(256)648-6758 SEHO#0517
Drylie, James (M1)
512 JE Blaydes Parkway
Atoka, TN 38004
(901)837-1627 GRWT#9100
Duke, Michael E (M1)
106 Friar Tuck Drive
Dickson, TN 37055
(615)446-6515 TNNA#7300
Dukes, Britta (M1)
5226 W William Cannon Drive
Austin, TX 78749
FAX: (512)892-6307
britta@shpc.org
(512)892-3580 MSTR#8604
Dumas, Byron (M1)
1775 Theresa Drive
Clarksville, TN 37043
bdumas7346@aol.com
(931)552-8772 TNNA#3302
Duncan, Ronnie (M1)
146 Deseree Broyles Road
Chuckey, TN 37641
ronkduncan@icloud.com
(423)552-0321 SEET#2204
Dyer, Stuart (M1)
3574 Foxfield Trail
Bartlett, TN 38135
(901)388-0612 GRWT#9100

--==<< E >>==--

Earheart-Brown, Daniel J (Jay) (M1)
866 N McLean
Memphis, TN 38107
jebrown@memphisseminary.edu
(901)278-0367 TNNA#7300
Eatherly, John (M1)

MINISTERS CONTINUED

1377 Moss Road
Chapel Hill, TN 37034
jrev@united.net
(931)364-2087   TNCO#7127
Eddleman, Keith   (M1)
2787 Stage Park Drive
Memphis, TN 38134
(901)388-9885   GRWT#9100
Edmonds, Wayne   (M1)
112 Dogwood Trail
Eclectic, AL 36024
sweetpea@comlinkinc.net
(334)857-2202   SEGR#0100
Edwards, James Scott   (M3)
226 Jasmine Drive
Alabaster, AL 35007
jedwards53163@bellsouth.net
(205)529-4507   SEGR#0101
Edwards, Joey   (M1)
5279 Ivy Creek Lane
Lakeland, TN 38002
edwardsjoey@bellsouth.net
(901)573-7579   GRWT#9314
Emsinger, Mike   (M3)
4910 Cox Cove
Helena, AL 35080
me0573@att.com
(205)620-4699   SEGR#0108
English, Don W   (M1)
4311 Guys Court
Bessemer, AL 35022
(205)428-4790   SEGR#0100
Eppard, Andrew   (M1)
1427 W McGee Street
Springfield, MO 65807
reformedminister@yahoo.com
(417)862-6434   GRMI#4314
Espinoza, Virginia   (M1)
PO Box 132
Boswell, OK 74727
vespinoza@choctawnation.com
(580)434-7971   MSCH#6109
Estep, William   (M1)
239 Skyline Drive
Harriman, TN 37748
(865)882-5114   TNMU#7200
Estes, George R   (M1)
7910 Cloverbrook Lane
Germantown, TN 38138
geoestes@gmail.com
(901)755-6673   MSDC#8700
Estes, Sam R, Jr   (M1)
3026 54th Street
Lubbock, TX 79413
(806)748-6116   MSDC#8700

--=<< F >>=--

Fackler, David   (M1)
3409 Benton Road
Paducah, KY 42003
woodlawnpastor@live.com
(270)442-7713   MICO#3417
Fahl, D Frederick (Fred)   (M1)
500 3rd Street
Fulton, KY 42041
dffahl@gmail.com
(270)432-3138   MICO#3419
Fajardo, Jose   (M1)
101 Vanderbilt
Waxahachie, TX 75165
(972)923-2955   MSRR#8400
Fancher, Michael E   (M3)
356 Breeding Road
Edmonton, KY 42129
princo1975@live.com

(270)579-3139   MICU#3101
Fell, Ron   (M2)
PO Box 285
Fairfield, IL 62837
r.fell@yahoo.com
(618)638-3744   MINC#5124
Ferguson, David   (M2)
1841 Pebble Lake Drive
Birmingham, AL 35232
fergusondavid15@yahoo.com
(205)200-9205   SEGR#0105
Ferguson, E Blant   (M1)
704 Bear Run
Hiawassee, GA 30546
blantferg@yahoo.com
(706)896-9296   SETG#2100
Ferguson, Elizabeth   (M1)
2251 Mansford Road
Winchester, TN 37398
ferguea9@gmail.com
(931)636-8076   TNMU#7235
Ferree, Carole   (M1)
2475 Fallen Timber Road
Campbellsville, KY 42718
ferree047@windstream.net
(270)789-4339   MICU#3100
Ferree, Ronald L   (M1)
2475 Fallen Timber Road
Campbellsville, KY 42718
ferree047@windstream.net
(270)465-1150   MICU#3129
Ferrell, Timothy W   (M1)
1850 Dunbar Road
Woodlawn, TN 37191
ferrelltw@aol.com
(931)920-2662   TNNA#7310
Ferrol, Ruben   (M1)
1823 Straford Court
Allentown, PA 18103
rubeferrol@msn.com
(610)966-7289   MSRR#8400
Ferry, Aaron   (M1)
PO Box 176
Winchester, TN 37398
amferry815@gmail.com
(615)946-3078   TNMU#7249
Fife, Patric   (M1)
73 Jordan Road
Lawrenceburg, TN 38464
pnlfifernak@gmail.com
(931)629-8146   TNCO#7130
Fike, Charles   (M1)
2070 N 1st Street
Milan, TN 38358
(731)686-0224   GRWT#9418
Fisk, James R   (M1)
311 Merril Drive
Benton, AR 72015
jimfisk95@yahoo.com
(870)367-3086   GRAR#1100
Fleming, Christopher   (M1)
133 Minerva Place
Paducah, KY 42001
holyday@vci.net
(615)424-8561   MICO#3415
Fleming, Patrick T   (M1)
616 N Border Street
Benton, AR 72015
ptfleming@live.com
(501)944-4678   GRAR#1100
Flores, Fabian   (M3)
Aereo 6365, Cali Valle
COLOMBIA, SA
(   )   MSCA#8222
Fly, William   (M1)
1146 Paradise Drive

Powell, TN 37849
(865)938-6273   SEET#2200
Fong, Danny   (M1)
1224 Fairfax Avenue
San Francisco, CA 94124
dfong@redeemersf.org
(415)671-2194   MSDC#8512
Fonseca, Roberto   (M1)
Cll 46 A No 4N 25
Colombia, South America
(   )446-3311   MSCA#8218
Foreman, Samuel L   (M1)
13700 Highway 488
Philadelphia, MS 39350
slfcpc@yahoo.com
(601)562-1415   SEGR#0708
Forester, Byron   (M1)
2376 Eastwood Place
Memphis, TN 38112
bforester@bellsouth.net
(901)324-1707   GRWT#9207
Fortner, Terry   (M1)
1079 Luzerne Depoy Road
Greenville, KY 42345
terryfortner@att.net
(270)821-6541   MICU#3508
Fossey, Donald, II   (M3)
328 Waterloo Road
Cookeville, TN 38506
dfossey@twlakes.net
(931)498-2149   TNMU#7223
Fowler, Scott   (M1)
1900 Alex Mill Road
Montevallo, AL 35115
springcreekcp@aol.com
(205)901-8478   SEGR#0113
Franco, Ricardo   (M1)
7 Hancock Street
Melrose, MA 02176
casadefericardo@verizon.net
(781)662-0267   SEET#2220
Franklin, Chris   (M1)
104 Delta Circle
Greeneville, TN 37743
chrisfranklin104@comcast.net
(423)972-3609   SEET#2208
Franklin, Curtis   (M1)
7620 Cross Mill Road
Paducah, KY 42001
brocurtis@fredonia.biz
(270)545-3481   MICO#3410
Frazier, Shawn   (M3)
459 Forrest Avenue
McKenzie, TN 38201
(865)414-8394   SEET#2200
Freeman, A Daniel   (M1)
210 Dogwood Drive
Greeneville, TN 37743
(423)638-5925   SEET#2200
Freeman, Jesse L, Jr   (M1)
270 Eastside Road
Burns, TN 37029
mptc@bellsouth.net
(615)441-6527   TNNA#7300
French, Jeff   (M1)
5 Rose Petal Lane
Dawson Springs, KY 42408
brojeff7@bellsouth.net
(270)993-0855   MICO#3615
Freund, Henry O   (M1)
913 Sam Houston Drive
Dyersburg, TN 38024
freundly@att.net
(731)285-1744   MSDC#8700
Frost, Sherrlyn   (M1)
5557 Surrey Lane

MINISTERS CONTINUED

Birmingham, AL 35242
FAX: (205)991-5259
sherrlyn@newhopecpc.org
(205)408-0729 SEGR#0104
Fulton, James (M1)
1520 Oak Grove Road
Benton, KY 42025
(270)437-4320 MICO#3619
Fung, David (M1)
1846 Gunston Way
San Jose, CA 95124
(408)266-3398 MSDC#8700
Fung, Lawrence (M1)
367 El Dorado Drive
Daly City, CA 94015
revfung@yahoo.com
(650)756-1702 MSHK#8800
Furr, Wayne (M1)
706 E 6th Street
Coal Valley, IL 61240
prespreacher@gmail.com
(309)791-1691 MINC#5200
Furuhata, Kazuhiko (M1)
#310, 9-41-15 Kamitsurumahoncho
Minamiku Sagamihara-shi
Kanagawa-ken
cpc.furuhata@gmail.com
252-0318, JAPAN
(501)430-8885 MSJA#8310

--==<< G >>==--

Gaither, Randy (M1)
No 3 Pacific Street
Belmopan City
BELIZE, CENTRAL AMERICA
rgaither@valuelinx.net
( ) SEGR#0100
Galvan, Melinda (M3)
205 Spring Creek Street
Chapel Hill, TN 37034
mgalvan@united.net
(931)364-3341 TNCO#7100
Galvis, Alexander (M3)
Calle 76 #87-14
Medellin, Antioquia, COLOMBIA, SA
alexgt7@hotmail.com
(300)778-4354 MSAN#8900
Gam, John (M1)
1235 Sanders Street
Auburn, AL 36830
( ) GRWT#9100
Garcia, Lucas (M3)
875 Scenic Highway
Lawrenceville, GA 30045
(678)698-7971 SETG#2100
Garcia, Maria (Mabe) (M1)
875 Scenic Highway
Lawrenceville, GA 30045
FAX: (678)225-0127
mabega@juno.com
(678)698-7971 SETG#2149
Garcia, Ramon (M1)
2714 Callista Court Apt 104
Naples, FL 34114
revga@hotmail.com
(239)200-5714 SEGR#0100
Gardner, Charles (M1)
124 Dawson Street
Penrose, CO 81240
(719)784-7744 MSRR#8400
Gary, Brian (M1)
105 Wilma Avenue
Radcliff, KY 40160
(502)351-6938 MICU#3100
Gaskill, Todd (M1)

430 Haysland Road
Petersburg, TN 37144
tgaskill@pens.com
(931)580-2708 TNCO#7121
Gaskin, Tony (M1)
479 County Road 1157
Cullman, AL 35057
tgaskin46@hotmail.com
(256)338-7893 SEHO#0507
Gates, J B (M1)
PO Box 289
Enfield, IL 62835
rjjbgate@hamiltoncom.net
(618)963-2306 MINC#5104
Gaviria, Mario (M1)
Cra 27 #7-48
Cali, COLOMBIA, SA
pastormariogaviria@hotmail.com
(314)773-2601 MSCA#8201
Gehle, Jeffrey A (M1)
PO Box 182
Burleson, TX 76097
FAX: (817)295-2576
jeff.gehle@stmattcpc.org
(817)295-5832 MSRR#8418
Gentry, Michele (M1)
Calle 3 Norte #12-87
Armenia, Quindio, COLOMBIA, SA
gentry.andes@yahoo.com
(576)745-1614 MSAN#8900
George, Thomas (M2)
908 N Brown Avenue
Casa Grande, AZ 85222
tgeorge@aerogram.net
(640)447-2676 MSDC#8700
Gerard, Eugene S (M1)
615 N 42nd Street
Paducah, KY 42001
(270)443-2889 MICO#3400
Gibbons, Jeannette (M3)
6204 S Haynes Avenue
Ozark, MO 65721
(417)889-9862 GRMI#4100
Gibson, Rachel (M3)
2520 Cairo Bend Road
Lebanon, TN 37087
(615)453-2724 TNMU#7200
Gillis, Aubrey Thomas (M1)
PO Box 869
Silverhill, AL 36576
FAX: (205)664-8323
tomgillis63@hotmail.com
(251)947-1638 SERD#0800
Gillis, Ernest H (M1)
3273 Bruckner Boulevard
Snellville, GA 30078
professorgil64@hotmail.com
(770)982-6587 SEET#2200
Gillock, Ed (M1)
PO Box 157
Savannah, TN 38372
(731)609-6744 GRWT#9100
Giraldo, Andres (M2)
Calle 76 #87-14 Apto 202
Medellin, Antioquia, COLOMBIA, SA
andresgiraldo@une.net.co
(574)422-6669 MSAN#8911
Giraldo, Marcela (M3)
Calle 68 D #40-15
Manizales, Caldas, COLOMBIA, SA
(576)878-5412 MSAN#8900
Giraldo, William (M1)
CLL 62 No 18 11
Cali, COLOMBIA, SA
( )439-5436 MSCA#8200
Giron, Francisco (M1)

3451 Los Mochis Way
Oceanside, CA 92056
FAX: (760)414-1236
thegirons@cox.net
(760)203-0381 MSDC#8700
Glenn, Linda H (M1)
49 Mason Road
Threeway, TN 38343
lindahglenn@click1.net
(731)618-0192 GRWT#9119
Goehring, Marty (M1)
8600 Academy NE
Albuquerque, NM 87111
FAX: (505)797-8599
mgoehring@heightscpc.org
(505)821-3628 MSDC#8701
Gonzales, Homer (M1)
8924 Armistice NE
Albuquerque, NM 87109
FAX: (505)841-4267
hgabq1985@gmail.com
(505)821-4376 MSDC#8700
Gonzales, Miguel (M3)
200 Bethel Drive
Lenoir City, TN 37772
(865)988-4238 SEET#2200
Gonzalez, Nora (M1)
2515 Blueberry Lane
Pasadena, TX 77052
(832)202-5572 MSTR#8100
Goodloe, Melissa Reid (M1)
225 Macedonia Road
McKenzie, TN 38201
rev.mgoodloe@shilohcp.org
(731)412-9657 GRWT#9131
Goodman, Robert (M1)
604 N Fourth Street
Marlow, OK 73055
rgoodman4gvn@hotmail.com
(580)756-4726 MSRR#6305
Goodwill, James L (M1)
205 S English Hill Lane
Hillsborough, NC 27278
jim@jimgoodwill.com
(704)526-8729 TNNA#7300
Goodwin, Earl (M1)
1012 Windsor Parkway
Moody, AL 35004
FAX: (205)664-8323
earlgoodwin@yahoo.com
(205)222-1741 SERD#0800
Gough, Ernest E (M1)
8366 Highway 70
Nashville, TN 37221
eegough@bellsouth.net
(615)646-4372 TNNA#7300
Graham, Steve (M1)
2223 US Highway 641
Marion, KY 42064
(270)825-4700 MICO#3400
Gray, Brad (M3)
6378 Highway 59 S
Mason, TN 38049
dgray@aol.com
(901)475-6140 GRWT#9100
Gray, Drew (M1)
5610 Country Drive #210
Nashville, TN 37211
(615)332-8360 TNMU#7220
Gray, Isaac (M1)
1211 AR 233 Highway
Pineville, AR 72566
revgray08@gmail.com
(870)373-4731 GRAR#1512
Gray, Randall (M1)
1230 New Liberty Big Meadow Road

MINISTERS CONTINUED

Knob Lick, KY 42154
(270)432-5322 MICU#3128
Green, Harry N (M1)
45 Wood Way
McMinnville, TN 37110
(931)815-9190 TNMU#7200
Green, Larry (M1)
525 Dearman Street
Smithville, TN 37166
larrylgreen24@aol.com
(615)597-5832 TNMU#7243
Green, Odis G (M1)
18 Oakwood Street NW
Rome, GA 30165
( ) TNCO#7100
Green, Paul (M1)
5228 Anchorage Avenue
El Paso, TX 79924
(915)751-7960 MSDC#8700
Green, Troy (M1)
105 Cobb Hollow Lane
Petersburg, TN 37144
thegreens101@att.net
(931)659-6627 TNCO#7135
Greene, Tammy L (M1)
109 Armitage Drive
Greeneville, TN 37745
tg6386@aol.com
(423)972-5525 SEET#2217
Greenwell, James C (M1)
7165 Wind Whisper Boulevard
Knoxville, TN 37924
FAX: (865)742-1653
greenwelljc@comcast.net
(865)742-1653 SEET#2200
Griffin, Adam (M3)
23502 Clinton Road
Lebanon, MO 65536
plowboy3500@hotmail.com
(417)588-2522 GRMI#4100
Griffin, Justin (M1)
205 E Livingston Street
San Augustine, TX 75972
jjjjgriff@gmail.com
(936)275-2546 TNGA#2100
Grimsley, Roger (M1)
215 N Oak Street
Springfield, TN 37172
( ) GRWT#9100
Gross, Ronald (M1)
2436 N 420th Street
Oblong, IL 62449
juneg@eiis.net
(217)932-2788 MINC#5200
Grounds, Clint (M3)
918 Stonewall Apt C
McKenzie, TN 38201
(731)415-1422 GRMI#4100
Guarneros, Stephen H (M1)
506 Clifton Court
Hopkinsville, KY 42240
pastorsteve88@yahoo.com
(270)869-7544 MICO#3606
Guasaquillo, Samuel (M3)
Aereo 10701, Cali
COLOMBIA, SA
FAX: (408)255-5938
( ) MSCA#8204
Guerrero, Cruzana (M2)
Calle 83 #74-179
Medellin, Antioguia, COLOMBIA, SA
(574)257-0613 MSAN#8900
Guerrero, Josue (M2)
Calle 76 #88-65
Medellin, Antioquia, COLOMBIA, SA
josueggutierrez@yahoo.es

(574)412-3504 MSAN#8900
Guerrero, Luz Dary (M1)
Calle 22 #25-33
Manizales, Caldas, COLOMBIA, SA
clementinajacobo7@hotmail.com
(576)888-4203 MSAN#8900
Guin, Larry (M1)
125 Glider Loop
Eagleville, TN 37060
lguin43@hotmail.com
(615)668-5236 TNCO#7123
Guthrie, William (M1)
11130 Frenchmen Loop Apt B
Maumelle, AR 72113
billybarloe@yahoo.com
(501)584-0019 GRAR#1100
Gutierrez, Libardo (M2)
Calle 83 #74-179
Medellin, Antioquia, COLOMBIA, SA
guzlibar@yahoo.es
57(314)600-2020 MSAN#8900
Guye, Dean (M1)
2759 Highway 70 E
Dickson, TN 37055
deanjoy@att.net
(615)446-7687 TNNA#7303

--==<< **H** >>==--

Ha, Ting Bong (M2)
3/F 338-340 Castle Peak Road
Kowloon, HONG KONG
FAX: (852)3020-0365
tingbongha@yahoo.com.hk
(852)2386-6563 MSHK#8803
Hackman-Truhan, Deborah (M1)
7314 N Miramar Drive
Peoria, IL 61614
cprevdeb@hotmail.com
(931)537-9040 MINC#5200
Hagelin, Gerald (M1)
10851 E Old Spanish Trail
Tucson, AZ 85712
azcef@cs.com
(520)275-8110 MSDC#8705
Haire, Shelby O (M1)
3179 Meeting Creek Road
Eastview, KY 42732
(270)862-3887 MICU#3219
Halford, Angela (M1)
PO Box 191466
Little Rock, AR 72219
(501)407-0065 GRAR#1100
Hall, Brad (M1)
1602 Toll Gate Road SE
Huntsville, AL 35801
(256)533-4845 SERD#0800
Hall, John D (M1)
109 Oddo Lane SE
Huntsville, AL 35802
johnhall33@comcast.net
(256)880-5129 SERD#0800
Hall, Roy W (M1)
87 Lee Hall Street
Scottsboro, AL 35769
royhall@scottsboro.org
(256)259-9340 SERD#0809
Hamazaki, Takashi (M1)
1551-1-202 Inokuchi Nakai-cho
Ashigarakami-gun
Kanagawa-ken
259-0151, JAPAN
gen22-14@qf7.so-net.ne.jp
(046)543-8550 MSJA#8300
Hamblin, James R (M1)
60 Rolling Meadow Drive

Drummonds, TN 38023
brojim391@gmail.com
(901)840-4747 GRWT#9321
Hamby, Gary (M3)
700 W 6th Avenue
Lenoir City, TN 37771
(731)986-2635 SEET#2200
Hames, Anne (M1)
118 Paris Street
McKenzie, TN 38201
hamesa@bethel-college.edu
(731)352-4066 GRWT#9100
Hamilton, Helen (M3)
300 Tennessee Street
Savannah, TN 38372
helmackham@aol.com
(731)925-4493 GRWT#9224
Hamilton, Lynn (M1)
4511 Lucksinger Lane Trailer 1
Austin, TX 78745
lhamilton@minister.com
(512)443-6813 MSTR#8100
Hamlink, Ronald L (M1)
PO Box 923
Fairacres, NM 88033
hamronelink@yahoo.com
(505)525-9867 GRAR#1100
Han, Seung Chon (M0)
3075 Landington Way
Duluth, GA 30096
kpc0191@gmail.com
(678)469-5015 SETG#2100
Hancock, B J (M1)
103 W Cowan Street
Cowan, TN 37318
(931)967-8491 TNMU#7228
Hannah, Hugh (M1)
217 Mitchell Road SE
Cleveland, TN 37323
(318)395-8729 MSTR#8100
Hansen, Terry (M1)
16549 Highway 5
Lebanon, MO 65536
(417)533-8106 GRMI#4315
Harbour, Ethan (M3)
1044 Alta Vista Road
Louisville, KY 40205
ethanharbour@hotmail.com
(479)849-6329 GRAR#1100
Hardisty, Randy (M1)
4908 Redondo Street
Fort Worth, TX 76180
rhardisty@sbcglobal.net
(817)428-3513 MSRR#8409
Harper, Carlton (M1)
8764 Cody Dan Court
Ooltewah, TN 37363
carltonone@comcast.net
(423)237-9257 SETG#2118
Harris, Anthony (M2)
1604 Parkview Drive
Campbellsville, KY 42718
aharris044@gmail.com
(270)403-1126 MICU#3214
Harris, Edward (M1)
517 Terrace Drive
Warrensburg, MO 64093
ed517@earthlink.net
(660)747-7447 GRMI#4111
Harris, Ernest (M1)
PO Box 1403
Clarksville, TX 75426
ernieandjeri@wmconnect.com
(903)966-2481 MSTR#8100
Harris, Robert (M1)
619 N 24th Avenue

MINISTERS CONTINUED

Humboldt, TN 38343
pastor@humboldtcpc.org
(731)420-6067   GRWT#9116

Harris, Rodney E   (M1)
7420 Conjar Court
Louisville, KY 40214
rodneypat@insightbb.com
(502)368-5501   MICU#3212

Harris, Wendell   (M1)
329 N Louis Tittle Avenue
Mangum, OK 73554
wendellharris@itlnet.net
(580)782-2142   MSRR#8400

Hartman, Gary   (M1)
3001 Hines Valley Road
Lenoir City, TN 37771
g37771@att.net
(865)986-4949   SEET#2304

Hartung, J Thomas   (M1)
2291 Americus Boulevard W Apt 1
Clearwater, FL 33763
revtom6@aol.com
(727)797-2882   SEGR#0100

Harwell, Jacob   (M2)
319 Joy Drive
McKenzie, TN 38201
rjharwell@student.memphisseminary.edu
(731)415-1457   GRWT#9100

Harwell, Keith   (M1)
13132 Stinson Street
Milan, TN 38358
(731)613-3780   GRWT#9104

Harwell, Sam   (M1)
23 Lake Hayes Estates Road
Trenton, TN 38382
sambharl@yahoo.com
(731)414-2153   GRWT#9127

Hassell, Victor   (M1)
510 N Main Street
Sturgis, KY 42459
FAX: (270)333-3118
hassellvictor@hotmail.com
(270)333-9170   MICO#3625

Hatcher, Carlton   (M1)
2111 Robin Road
Bowling Green, KY 42101
(270)842-8488   MICU#3310

Hawley, David R   (M1)
127 John Holt Road
Beech Bluff, TN 38313
haw177@aol.com
(731)427-7284   GRWT#9204

Hayes, Brian   (M1)
69 Cactus Drive
Benton, KY 42025
cprevbhayes@gmail.com
(270)210-8165   MICO#3422

Hayes, Drew   (M1)
629 High Street
Union City, TN 38261
dhayes72@gmail.com
(731)796-7076   GRWT#9433

Hayes, Jennifer   (M1)
3615 Talley Store Road
Henderson, TN 38340
(731)989-3825   TNMU#7200

Hayes, Marcus   (M1)
102 River Drive
McMinnville, TN 37110
marcus.hayes@att.net
(270)841-7576   TNMU#7222

Headrick, Anthony   (M1)
3327 N Eagle Road Ste 110-132
Meridian, ID 83646
chaps2a@yahoo.com
(619)524-8821   SEGR#0100

Headrick, Christopher   (M1)
1913 Vestavia Court Apt B
Vestavia Hills, AL 35216
bravespop@gmail.com
(205)240-0979   SEGR#0100

Headrick, Jerry   (M1)
9950 Old Stage Road
Stockton, AL 36579
willjheadrick@gmail.com
(251)377-9744   SEGR#0100

Heard, Robert   (M3)
527 Jack Thomas Drive
Manchester, TN 37355
(931)273-9687   TNMU#7200

Heflin, Donna S   (M1)
4144 Meadow Court Drive
Bartlett, TN 38135
rdheflin@bellsouth.net
(901)382-8198   GRWT#9100

Heflin, Robert   (M1)
4144 Meadow Court Drive
Bartlett, TN 38135
rdheflin@bellsouth.net
(901)382-8198   TNCO#7100

Heidel, Jason   (M1)
218 Morningside Drive
Hopkinsville, KY 42240
heidelj@hotmail.com
(270)498-7380   MICO#3611

Heilbron, Luz Maria   (M1)
Cra 12 bis #11-51
Pereira, Risaralda, COLOMBIA, SA
pastorapresbi@hotmail.com
(576)333-9295   MSAN#8916

Hendershot, Charles A   (M1)
122 Tree Shadow
Whitney, TX 76692
(254)694-3852   MSRR#8424

Henson, Kevin R   (M1)
1121 Raleigh Path
Denton, TX 76208
khenson@cpch.org
(817)354-1182   MSRR#8400

Heo, Mu Sak   (M1)
170 Applewood Drive #210
Lawrenceville, GA 30046
drhou@hanmail.net
(404)644-6514   SETG#2100

Hernden, Matthew   (M3)
206 Smith Lane
Brighton, TN 38011
mhernden023@gmail.com
(901)484-7661   GRWT#9100

Herring, C E (Ed), Jr   (M1)
969 Campground Circle
Scottsboro, AL 35769
edherring@scottsboro.org
(256)259-2721   SERD#0803

Herston, Terry   (M1)
390 County Road 95
Rogersville, AL 35652
tpaw51@gmail.com
(256)247-3004   SEHO#0513

Hess, Jean   (M1)
2200 E Dartmouth Circle
Englewood, CO 80113
jeanhess@316denver.com
(303)504-0275   MSDC#8700

Hess, Rick   (M1)
2200 E Dartmouth Circle
Englewood, CO 80113
rick@densem.edu
(303)504-0275   MSDC#8700

Hester, J David   (M1)
1212 Woodbury Court
Knoxville, TN 37922

FAX: (865)769-0540
jdavebar@icx.net
(865)769-0540   SEET#2200

Hester, Mark S   (M1)
763 Finn Long Road
Friendsville, TN 37737
markshester@att.net
(865)995-1541   SEET#2200

Hewitt, Gary   (M1)
521 Easy Street Unit 17
Cleveland, TX 77327
(281)592-3425   MSTR#8100

Hill, Jody   (M1)
4030 St Andrew Circle
Corinth, MS 38834
jody.hill34@gmail.com
(662)512-8226   GRWT#9100

Ho, Kelvin   (M2)
11 On Wing Centre, 2/F
Pak She Back Street
Cheung Chau, HONG KONG
kelvinskho@gmail.com
(852)2981-4933   MSHK#8801

Hocker, David   (M3)
309 N Taylor Street
Morgantown, KY 42261
davidhocker@hockerins.com
(270)526-6027   MICU#3311

Hoke, Walter   (M1)
215 Navajo Trail
Georgetown, TX 78633
(512)869-1948   MSTR#8100

Holley, Ann   (M1)
PO Box 345
Lockesburg, AR 71846
FAX: (870)289-2914
ladyrev1115@yahoo.com
(870)289-3421   GRAR#1100

Hollingshed, Lee   (M3)
3612 Harmony Church Grove Road
Dallas, GA 30132
leearmstrong@bellsouth.net
(770)548-0152   SETG#2100

Holmes, Aaron G   (M1)
PO Box 171
Atwood, TN 38220
agholmes@charter.net
(731)662-7595   GRWT#9100

Holt, Billy Jack   (M1)
5039 Highway 37 N
Clarksville, TX 75426
jackdora@windstream.net
(903)428-9909   MSTR#8125

Hom, Paul   (M1)
722 24th Avenue
San Francisco, CA 94121
FAX: (415)386-8423
(415)751-9766   MSDC#8700

Hong, Soon Gab   (M1)
13600 Doty Avenue Apt 4
Hawthorne, CA 90250
lemuelhong@hotmail.com
(972)446-0350   MSRR#8400

Hood, Charles   (M1)
6535 Bailey Road
Anderson, AL 35610
hooddad11@gmail.com
(256)229-6251   SEHO#0516

Hooper, David   (M3)
115 County Road 682
Holly Pond, AL 35083
davidhoop165@yahoo.com
(256)775-2419   SERD#0211

Hopkins, Daniel   (M3)
887 Penny Road
Hardin, KY 42048

MINISTERS CONTINUED

(270)205-1847   MICO#3620
Hopkins, Wayne (M3)
   1413 E Unity Church Road
   Hardin, KY 42048
   (270)437-4481   MICO#3400
Horst, Gail F, Jr (M3)
   14624 Lonepine Road
   N Little Rock, AR 72118
   gail_horst@yahoo.com
   (501)240-4034   GRAR#1100
Howe, Francis (M1)
   129 Manley Street
   McKenzie, TN 38201
   (731)352-5551   GRWT#9125
Howell, Linda (M1)
   PO Box 278
   Sebastopol, MS 39359
   lshowell1000@yahoo.com
   (601)942-2015   SEGR#0607
Howton, Orvie Ray (M1)
   4928 Montauk Trail SE
   Owens Cross Road, AL 35763
   arhowton@bellsouth.net
   (256)533-9224   SERD#0800
Hoyos, Amparo (M2)
   Cra 43 #20D-26
   Zamora, Antioquia, COLOMBIA, SA
   chilalu1147@hotmail.com
   (574)278-0784   MSAN#8900
Hoyos, Javier (M3)
   Calle 34 24A-36
   Cali, COLOMBIA, SA
   ( )445-5556   MSCA#8200
Hubbard, Donald (M1)
   2128 N Campbell Station Road
   Knoxville, TN 37932
   djhubbard@mindspring.com
   (865)693-0264   SEET#2200
Hubbard, Pratt (M1)
   1565 Eli Brown Road
   McKenzie, TN 38201
   (731)352-9178   GRWT#9100
Hudson, Barney (M1)
   10541 Fossil Hill Drive
   Fort Worth, TX 76131
   barneyrev@gmail.com
   (817)851-2960   MSRR#8425
Hudson, George Cliff (M1)
   4782 Waverly Court
   Ooltewah, TN 37363
   FAX: (423)476-6423
   gchudson3@gmail.com
   (423)238-6333   SETG#2108
Huey, Sharon (M1)
   3265 16th Street
   San Francisco, CA 94103
   sharon_huey@yahoo.com
   (415)703-6090   MSDC#8510
Hughes, Charles (M1)
   114 Gaul Street
   Estill Springs, TN 37330
   cphugs@cafes.net
   (931)649-5189   SERD#0800
Hughes, Douglas (M1)
   5545 Hocker Road
   Paducah, KY 42001
   milburnchapel@gmail.com
   (270)488-2588   MICO#3416
Hughes, Richard W (M1)
   2954 Bob Wade Lane
   Harvest, AL 35749
   hughesrichard23@gmail.com
   (256)859-3178   SERD#0806
Hullander, Jerry (Butch) (M1)
   767 Rifle Range Road
   Greeneville, TN 37743

jerryihs@catt.com
   (706)935-4878   SETG#2107
Humphries, Rick (M3)
   187 Wilson Heights Circle NE
   Cleveland, TN 37312
   lshumphries@juno.com
   (423)331-0340   SETG#2100
Hung, Ella Siu Kei (M2)
   2/F Welland Plaza
   188 Nam Cheong Street
   Sham Shui Po, Kowloon, HONG KONG
   FAX: (852)2771-2726
   siukee@taohsien.org.hk
   (852)2794-2382   MSHK#8800
Hunley, Jearl (M1)
   2618 Canterbury Road
   Columbus, MS 39705
   jdhunley@cableone.net
   (662)329-1516   SEGR#0100
Hunley, Terry M (M1)
   48 Charleston Square
   Jackson, TN 38305
   thunley1@charter.net
   (731)660-5685   GRWT#9208
Hunt, Shelley (M3)
   6035 State Route 506
   Marion, KY 42064
   sheljean@kynet.biz
   (270)704-2189   MICO#3400
Hurley, E C (M1)
   704 Rainswood Court
   Clarksville, TN 37043
   FAX: (931)645-7772
   hurleyec@gmail.com
   (931)802-2250   TNNA#7300
Hyden, John (M1)
   6525 Peytonsville Arno Road
   College Grove, TN 37046
   cp1876@hotmail.com
   (615)975-9584   TNCO#7116

--==<< I >>==--

Ikushima, Michinobu (M1)
   2074 Nakashinden
   Ebina-Shi Kanagawa-Ken
   243-0422 JAPAN
   m.ikushima@tbz.t-com.ne.jp
   (046)232-9888   MSJA#8300
Impastato, Paulino (M3)
   1547 Mt Zion Church Road
   Marion, KY 42064
   (270)965-9528   MICO#3400
Inoh, Yuki (M3)
   Tokyo Christian University
   3-301-5 Uchino Inzai-shi, Chiba
   270-1347 JAPAN
   yuki_inoh0615@yahoo.co.jp
   (047)646-1141   MSJA#8300
Insley, Michael (M1)
   8046 Manderly Place
   Converse, TX 78109
   chapmdi@yahoo.com
   (210)490-0817   MSTR#8100
Ishitsuka, Keishi (M1)
   Nucleo Colonial JK
   Lote 56 Mata De Sao Joao
   48280-000, Bahia, BRAZIL
   FAX: (5571)3664-1019
   kishitsuka@hotmail.com
   (5571)3664-1019   MSJA#8313
Ivey, Billy F (M1)
   409 Rodeo Drive
   Knoxville, TN 37922
   iveybe@tds.net
   (865)966-5946   SEET#2200

--==<< J >>==--

Jacks, Mathew Derek (M1)
   341 Shadeswood Drive
   Hoover, AL 35226
   pastorderek@homewoodcpc.com
   (205)903-8469   SEGR#0111
Jackson, Lamar (M1)
   280 Deer Ridge Drive Apt D
   Dayton, TN 37321
   hljaxn@charter.net
   (423)570-9348   SETG#2100
Jackson, Terry (M1)
   1461 Mount Pleasant Road
   Hernando, MS 38632
   (662)429-9741   GRWT#9100
Jacob, Randy (M1)
   PO Box 158
   Broken Bow, OK 74728
   FAX: (580)584-2099
   chocpres@pine-net.com
   (580)584-2099   MSCH#6106
James, William F (M1)
   2937 Arthur Drive
   Murfreesboro, TN 37127
   wimjim19@gmail.com
   (615)653-1396   TNMU#7227
Jang, Won Jeon (M1)
   Lot2-C Teresa Subdivision
   Tabucan Mandurriao
   Iloilo City 5000, Phillipine
   ( )   SEET#2200
Janner, R Tony (M1)
   104 Northwood Drive
   McKenzie, TN 38201
   FAX: (731)352-3101
   drtonyjanner@yahoo.com
   (731)352-8055   GRWT#9118
Jaramillo, Luciano (M1)
   6248 SW 14th Street
   West Miami, FL 33144
   ljara@aol.com
   (305)264-1074   SEGR#0310
Jarnagin, Mary L (M1)
   1003 Justin Lane Apt 1017
   Austin, TX 78757
   marjar27@yahoo.com
   (512)367-9922   MSTR#8100
Jeffrey, Peter (M1)
   61 Northwood Drive
   McKenzie, TN 38201
   jeffreyp@bethelu.edu
   (731)352-0792   TNMU#7200
Jeffrey, Sarah Ann (M1)
   5271 Highway 202 E
   Yellville, AR 72687
   FAX: (870)715-9229
   annjeffrey2001@yahoo.com
   (870)453-7076   GRAR#1100
Jenkins, Henry (M1)
   PO Box 148
   Magazine, AR 72943
   henryj@magtel.com
   (479)969-8352   GRAR#1401
Jenkins, William E (M1)
   1836 S Ridge Drive
   Valrico, FL 33594
   hopechurch4@aol.com
   (813)651-3802   SEGR#0308
Jeong, Woo S (M1)
   1205 Morganshire Drive
   Collierville, TN 38017
   (901)302-0558   GRWT#9100
Jett, Mace, Jr (M1)
   109 Park Street
   Martin, TN 38237

MINISTERS CONTINUED

(731)587-0805   GRWT#9117
Jett-Rand, Dana   (M2)
#78 Lester Lane
Martin, TN 38237
(731)587-0805   GRWT#9100

Jimenez, Jorge Enrique   (M3)
Urb Manantiales MzC Casa 6
Armenia, Quindio, COLOMBIA, SA
joenjimu@yahoo.es
(576)749-1166   MSAN#8900

Jobe, J Tommy   (M1)
PO Box 8
Eagleville, TN 37060
cppreacher@united.net
(615)776-7755   TNMU#7240

Johnson, Alan F   (M3)
10809 State Route 593
Owensboro, KY 42301
ajatlantic@yahoo.com
(386)-9340   MICU#3100

Johnson, Beverly B   (M1)
801 Riverhill Drive Apt 308
Athens, GA 30606
bevloujohnson@aol.com
(865)977-0405   SEET#2200

Johnson, Daryl   (M1)
425 W Vaughan Street
Bertram, TX 78605
djchurch@earthlink.net
(512)355-2182   MSTR#8605

Johnson, Ken   (M1)
122 Ridge Lane
Clinton, TN 37716
kenjoxav122@bellsouth.net
(865)463-7090   SEET#2314

Johnson, Lanny   (M1)
120 S Mill Street
Morrison, TN 37357
ljohnson37357@gmail.com
(931)212-1658   TNMU#7200

Johnson, Leslie A   (M1)
11716 Price Drive
Oklahoma City, OK 73170
ljohnson275@cox.net
(405)759-3189   MSRR#6205

Johnson, Roberta Smith   (M1)
397 Ouachita 54
Camden, AR 71701
(870)231-5827   GRAR#1309

Johnson, Rocky L   (M1)
321 Hope Road
Greeneville, TN 37745
(423)638-2771
kcor_98@yahoo.com

Johnson, Thomas C   (M1)
PO Box 566
Helena, AL 35080
revtomjohnson@aol.com
(205)936-1350   SEGR#0100

Johnson, Wesley H   (M1)
6222 Crestmoor Lane
Sachse, TX 75048
wjohnson@transitionconsulting.com
(972)270-6923   MSRR#8412

Jones, Gregory   (M1)
4808 Shiloh Canaan Road
Palmyra, TN 37142
greg1013@aol.com
(931)249-9512   TNNA#7338

Jones, Harold   (M2)
4123 Wilkesview Drive Apt A
Chattanooga, TN 37416
harold@personalcharacter.com
(478)320-4222   SETG#2100

Jones, Joseph M   (M1)
405 Lakeview Drive

Campbellsville, KY 42718
joepegjones@windstream.net
( )   MICU#3100

Jones, Michael   (M1)
120 Jennifer Lane
Branson, MO 65616
(417)334-2058   GRAR#1100

Jones, Steve   (M2)
PO Box 368
Burns, TN 37029
(615)441-6159   TNNA#7300

Jones, Victor   (M1)
7017 Highway 177 S
Jordan, AR 72519
mommom@centurytel.net
(870)499-5882   GRAR#1100

Jones, C William, Jr   (M1)
109 Lakewood Drive
Lexington, TN 38351
patfreelandjones@yahoo.com
(731)967-7618   GRWT#9209

Justice, Michael   (M1)
112B Vance Lane
Russellville, KY 42276
(270)726-6673   MICU#3501

--==<< K >>==--

Kang, Eun Hee   (M3)
147-15 46th Avenue
Flushing, NY 11355
(718)762-0778   SETG#2100

Kang, Jin Koo   (M1)
2310 Hisway
Lawrenceville, GA 30044
agatopia@hanmail.net
(678)462-7526   SETG#2100

Karasawa, Kenta   (M1)
3-15-10 Higashi
Kunitachi-shi, Tokyo
186-0002 JAPAN
FAX: (042)575-5549
k-kenta@roy.hi-ho.ne.jp
(042)575-5549   MSJA#8306

Katsuki, Shigeru   (M1)
2-14-16 Higashi-cho
Koganei-shi, Tokyo
184-0011 JAPAN
shigeru.katsuki@nifty.com
(042)231-1279   MSJA#8301

Kays, Michael   (M1)
2505 Canterbury Avenue
Muskogee, OK 74403
msppk@suddenlink.net
(918)577-6255   MSRR#8400

Keller, Abby Cole   (M1)
4415 Fieldstone Drive
Kingsport, TN 37664
colekeller@yahoo.com
(423)863-6565   SEET#2206

Kelly, Lawrence   (M1)
3471 Highway 41 A North Apt 5
Unionville, TN 37180
(615)934-1517   TNCO#7118

Kelly, Patrick L   (M1)
1449 Rainbow Road
Limestone, TN 37681
(423)727-4067   SEET#2200

Kelso, James H   (M1)
131 Lords Way
Dawsonville, GA 30534
elgato@alltel.net
(706)216-7513   SETG#2100

Kenedy, Don   (M3)
5335 Dizzy Dean Road
Booneville, AR 72927

donkennedy@centurytel.net
(479)675-4418   GRAR#1414

Kennedy, Jim   (M2)
3818 Peace Court Apt F
Aberdeen Proving Ground, MD 21005
( )   SETG#2100

Kennemer, Darren   (M1)
8828 Highway 119
Alabaster, AL 35007
darren.kennemer@va.gov
(205)663-3152   SERD#0107

Keown, Gale J   (M1)
2130 Cason Lane
Murfreesboro, TN 37128
galeesther@aol.com
(865)805-5451   SEET#2200

Kerner, Leanne   (M3)
156 State Route 348 W
Symsonia, KY 42082
cooldoll@bellsouth.net
(270)851-9709   MICO#3400

Kessie, John Paul   (M1)
225 Clear Springs Road
Georgetown, TX 78628
oakgrovecpcpastor@verizon.net
(512)585-1617   MSTR#8607

Keung Yung, Amos Chung   (M3)
28 Hong Yip Street
Yuen Long, NT, HONG KONG
FAX: (522)639-5620
amos@xilincpc.org.hk
(522)639-9176   MSHK#8809

Killeen, Michael   (M1)
5226 W William Cannon Drive
Austin, TX 78749
FAX: (512)892-6307
mike@shpc.org
(512)892-3580   MSTR#8604

Kim, Byong Sam   (M1)
6290 Dawnridge Court
Paradise, CA 95969
(530)877-4651   MSDC#8700

Kim, Kio Seob   (M1)
14430 35th Avenue Apt A62
Flushing, NY 11354
(718)539-3476   SETG#2100

Kim, Mi Young   (M1)
(IN KOREA)
( )   SETG#2100

Kim, Min Soo   (M1)
1050 Grace Drive
Lawrenceville, GA 30043
(404)518-0205   SETG#2100

Kim, Yoong S   (M1)
8601 Dogwood Road
Germantown, TN 38139
FAX: (901)756-7166
yoongkim1934@yahoo.com
(901)490-8973   GRWT#9100

Kim, YoungHo (Steve)   (M1)
B02 Hyundai I-Space 1608-2
Burim Dong, Dong An Gu
AnYang City, Kyunggi Do, S KOREA
paidion4377@naver.com
(231)348-8033   SEET#2200

King, Keith   (M2)
3341 S 137th E Avenue
Tulsa, OK 74134
(918)437-5464   MSRR#8400

Kinnaman, Richard T   (M1)
2018 Spring Meadow Circle
Spring Hill, TN 37174
kinnaman91@att.net
(615)302-3321   TNCO#7100

Kirkpatrick, Mary Kathryn   (M1)
401 1/2 Henley-Perry Drive

MINISTERS CONTINUED

Marshall, TX 75670
mkkirkpatrick@gmail.com
(903)930-6236   MSTR#8115
Kleinjan, Lori   (M1)
6516 Farnell Avenue
Memphis, TN 38134
lkleinj@prodigy.net
(901)372-8413   GRWT#9100
Knight, J Geoffrey   (M1)
2119 Avalon Place
Houston, TX 77019
geoff@cphouston.org
(713)522-7821   MSTR#8606
Knight, Melissa   (M1)
5730 Haley Road
Meridian, MS 39305
revlissa@gmail.com
(530)632-6472   MSDC#8700
Ko, John Jae   (M1)
13955 35th Avenue #5A
Flushing, NY 11354
spcko@hanmail.net
(718)762-4348   SECE#2141
Kollie, Moses   (M3)
760 Harbor Point Court
Lawrenceville, GA 30044
kolliemoses70@yahoo.com
(770)990-2215   SETG#2100
Koopman, David L   (M1)
5606 Brandon Park Drive
Maryville, TN 37804
racewthrev@aol.com
(865)660-2440   SEET#2311
Korb, Leon C   (M1)
15360 E 350 North Road
Ridge Farm, IL 61870
(217)662-8398   MINC#5200
Kurtz, David   (M1)
4709 Layla Road
Arlington, TX 76016
davidk36@yahoo.com
(817)683-4783   MSRR#8407

--==<< **L** >>==--

Labrada, Hector   (M1)
74 Cumberland Drive
McMinnville, TN 37110
( )   TNMU#7200
Ladd, Sherry   (M1)
4521 Turkey Creek Road
Williamsport, TN 38487
revsherryladd@gmail.com
(931)682-2263   TNCO#7138
Lain, Judy   (M1)
1928 Pine Ridge Drive
Bedford, TX 76021
judylane5@gmail.com
(817)660-8020   MSRR#8400
Lam, Janice   (M2)
G/F & 1/F 251 Tin Sum Village
Tai Wai, Shatin NT, HONG KONG
FAX: (852)2607-2245
janiceyeung929@gmail.com
(852)2693-3444   MSHK#8800
Lambert, James   (M1)
224 Peabody Road
Meridianville, AL 35759
(256)828-6850   SERD#0800
Lancaster, David   (M1)
426 Fugua Road
Martin, TN 38237
lancasterd@bethel-college.edu
(731)588-5895   GRWT#9130
Lannom, Pamela   (M3)
220 Bradford Acres

Bradford, TN 38316
plannom@yahoo.com
(731)742-3838   GRWT#9100
LaPerche, Michael   (M1)
3867 Evergreen Oaks Drive
Lutz, FL 33558
pastor-mike@earthlink.net
(727)859-3998   SEGR#0303
Lathem, W Ray   (M1)
452 County Road 1462
Cullman, AL 35055
lathemray@bellsouth.net
(256)734-7146   SEGR#0208
Latimer, James M   (M1)
7621 Richmond
Memphis, TN 38125
jimmylatimer@redeemerevangelical.com
(901)787-7875   GRWT#9100
Lau, Walter   (M1)
865 Jackson Street
San Francisco, CA 94133
FAX: (415)421-1874
walter@cumberlandsf.org
(650)583-7878   MSDC#8501
Laurence, Brenda   (M1)
2823 Nine Mile Road
Enville, TN 38332
southernmoma@hotmail.com
(731)687-2022   GRWT#9226
Lavender, Michael T   (M1)
934 Church Street
Tiptonville, TN 38079
mike_lavender@yahoo.com
(731)253-7308   GRWT#9117
Lawson, James   (M1)
1003 W 3rd Street
Fulton, KY 42041
(270)472-5272   MICO#3400
Lawson, Jerry L   (M1)
6039 MS Highway 415
Ackerman, MS 39735
lawson@dtcweb.net
(662)285-8295   SEGR#0707
Lawson, John C   (M2)
PO Box 645
Daingerfield, TX 75638
sharjohn@windstream.net
(903)645-2183   MSTR#8106
Lawson, Luke   (M1)
270 N Ridgeland Circle
Columbus, MS 39705
luke_lawson03@hotmail.com
(662)295-9322   SEGR#0706
Layne, Phillip   (M1)
10699 Griffith Highway
Whitwell, TN 37397
cprevinsv@bellsouth.net
(423)658-6421   SETG#2110
LeNeave, David   (M1)
8725 Hamletsburg Road
Brookport, IL 62910
leneavedavid@yahoo.com
(618)564-2437   MICO#5117
Lee, David   (M1)
hebrondavid@yahoo.com
(404)641-4359   SETG#2100
Lee, Douglas   (M1)
3265 16th Street
San Francisco, CA 94103
dlee@gum.org
(415)703-6090   MSDC#8510
Lee, George   (M1)
104 Parc Circle
Florence, AL 35630
butchleeautos@yahoo.com
(256)740-0809   SEHO#0514

Lee, Ho-Jin   (M2)
7565 Macon Road
Cordova, TN 38018
hjinlab@hotmail.com
(901)754-7070   GRWT#9322
Lee, Priscilla   (M3)
Tin Yuet Estate
Tin Shui Wai NT, HONG KONG
FAX: (852)2617-0287
wai_yung_lee@yahoo.com.hk
(852)2617-7872   MSHK#8800
Lee, Sang-Do   (M1)
1342 Seocho-2dong, Seocho-Gu
Seoul, KOREA
(023)474-8405   SEET#2200
Lee, Sarah   (M1)
( )   SETG#2100
Lee, Ted Shu Tak   (M2)
2/F Welland Plaza
188 Nam Cheong Street
Sham Shui Po, Kowloon, HONG KONG
FAX: (852)2771-2726
tedlee@taohsien.org.hk
(852)2783-8923   MSHK#8800
Lee, Timothy Daniel   (M1)
186 Blasingame Drive
Columbus, MS 39702
eelmit@bellsouth.net
(601)433-3714   SEGR#0702
Lefavor, David   (M1)
414 S Monroe Siding Road
Xenia, OH 45385
david.lefavor@med.va.gov
(813)613-4133   SEGR#0100
Leslie, Eugene   (M1)
13155 Center Hill Road
Olive Branch, MS 38654
eleslie1@bellsouth.net
(731)613-0425   GRWT#9100
Li, Chun Wai   (M2)
1/F Block B
14 Tsat Tsz Mui Road
North Point, Hong Kong
FAX: (852)2564-2898
cwli2000hk@yahoo.com.hk
(852)2562-2148   MSHK#8800
Liles, Dwight   (M1)
8467 Joy Road
Mount Pleasant, TN 38474
dwightliles@att.net
(931)379-0326   TNCO#7124
Lim, Abraham   (M2)
2/F Welland Plaza
188 Nam Cheong Street
Sham Shui Po, Kowloon, HONG KONG
FAX: (852)2771-2726
abraham@taohsien.org.hk
(852)2783-8923   MSHK#8800
Lim, Keum-Taek   (M1)
1342 Seocho-2dong, Seocho-Gu
Seoul, KOREA
limkt114@hanmail.net
(023)474-8405   SEET#2200
Lim, Min Young   (M3)
3480 Summit Ridge Parkway
Duluth, GA 30096
minyounglim63@gmail.com
(770)751-1148   SETG#2101
Lindsay, John V   (M1)
2004 Burning Tree Lane
Denton, TX 76209
(940)387-6811   MSRR#8404
Linski, David   (M3)
1060 Alpine Way
Indian Springs, AL 35124
david.linski@gmail.com

MINISTERS CONTINUED

(205)677-8163   SEGR#0100

Little, Russell (M1)
29 Cotton Row
Medina, TN 38355
russelllittle@bellsouth.net
(731)783-3565   GRWT#9109

Liu, Lai Yuet (M2)
2/F Fu Tung Shopping Center
Tung Chung
Lantau Island, HONG KONG
FAX: (852)2109-1737
(852)2109-1738   MSHK#8800

Lively, James W (M1)
906 Lyle Circle
Greeneville, TN 37745
FAX: (423)636-1017
jlively@gcpchurch.org
(423)798-1959   SEET#2206

Lively, Louella (M1)
196 Vicksburg Estate Road
Benton, KY 42025
(270)527-3776   MICO#3400

Livingston, Ronald L (M1)
5851 Quantrell Ave #201
Alexandria, VA 22312
( )   SERD#0800

Lockhart, Thomas Richie (M1)
700 County Road 343
Falkner, MS 38629
nmsdiamonddawgs@yahoo.com
(662)837-7281   GRWT#9214

Lockmiller, Lem Jr (M1)
5068 Louise Street
Hokes Bluff, AL 35903
(256)490-3021   SEGR#0403

Logan, Jason (M1)
4895 Diggins Drive
Fort Meade, ND 20755
jason.b.logan@dix.army.mil
(410)305-8494   TNMU#7200

Longmire, Ronald L (M1)
2041 Eckles Drive
Maryville, TN 37804
ronaldlongmire@charter.net
(865)984-1647   SEET#2309

Lopez, Wilson (M3)
Diag 26M #73A-69
Cali, COLOMBIA, SA
( )422-3940   MSCA#8225

Lorick, Keith (M1)
127 Chesapeake Boulevard
Madison, AL 35757
keithlorick@knology.net
(256)325-3865   SERD#0808

Louder, Paula (M1)
98 Gallant Court
Clarksville, TN 37043
paula.louder@cmcss.net
(615)804-4809   TNNA#7304

Louder, Stephen L (M1)
98 Gallant Court
Clarksville, TN 37043
pastorsteve@clarksvillecpc.com
(931)217-0369   TNNA#7304

Lounsbury-Lombard, Kristi (M1)
902 Clearview
Krum, TX 76249
kristilounsbury@gmail.com
(940)435-5077   MSRR#8400

Love, James R (M1)
14382 Sonora Hardin Springs Road
Eastview, KY 42732
(502)862-4119   MICU#3100

Lovelace, John G (M1)
814 Crestwood Drive
Evansville, IN 47715

jlove1234@aol.com
(812)476-5879   MINC#5200

Lowe, Randy (M1)
222 McDougal Drive
Murray, KY 42071
loweshodle@aol.com
(270)753-8255   MICO#3412

Lubo, Jaime (M3)
AA 6365
Montebello, COLOMBIA, SA
( )   MSCA#8223

Lui, Stephen (M1)
512 16th Avenue
San Francisco, CA 94118
FAX: (415)386-2302
(415)386-2302   MSDC#8700

Lumpee, Daniel (M3)
1200 Charles Court
College Station, TX 77840
dlumpee@gmail.com
(817)691-1945   MSRR#8400

Lunn, Calvin (M1)
859 Cranford Hollow Road
Columbia, TN 38401
pastor@fcpccolumbia.com
(931)381-2397   TNCO#7110

Luo, Tian-en (M1)
87 Berta Circle
Daly City, CA 94015
FAX: (650)754-9885
tianenyang555@gmail.com
(650)754-9885   MSDC#8700

Luttrell, Ben (M1)
123 S 5th Street
Selmer, TN 38375
(731)645-5257   GRWT#9225

--==<< **M** >>==--

Ma, Choil (M1)
300 Ringgold Road Apt 503
Clarksville, TN 37042
choilma@yahoo.com
(931)824-2443   TNNA#7342

Macy, William M (M1)
1358 Ephesus Church Road
Harned, KY 40144
(270)756-2775   MICU#3218

Madden, Judith Ellen (M1)
100 SW Brushy Mound
Burleson, TX 76028
jmadden@stmattcpc.org
FAX: (512)258-7325
(817)295-5832   MSRR#8400

Maddux, Cynthia (M1)
15042 Tinker Street
Houston, TX 77084
cmaddux1962@gmail.com
(823)343-8867   MSDC#8700

Magliolo, Sam (M2)
14352 Fairview
Byhalia, MS 38611
samagliolo@fedex.com
(662)838-7720   GRWT#9100

Magrill, J Richard, Jr (M1)
500 Miller Drive
Marshall, TX 75672
FAX: (901)272-3913
jrm@cumberland.org
(901)685-9454   MSTR#8100

Mak, Daphne Suet Chung (M2)
2/F Welland Plaza
188 Nam Cheong Street
Sham Shui Po, Kowloon, HONG KONG
FAX: (852)2771-2726
daphne@taohsien.org.hk

(852)2783-8923   MSHK#8800

Malinoski, Melissa (M1)
9087 Fenmore Cove
Cordova, TN 38016
FAX: (423)636-1017
mmalinoski@memphisseminary.edu
(420)620-0089   SEET#2206

Malinoski, T J (M1)
9087 Fenmore Cove
Cordova, TN 38016
mlmalinoski@comcast.net
(423)972-1239   SEET#2200

Malone, John W (M1)
3693 Highway 67 South
Sommerville, AL 35670
(256)778-8237   SEHO#0500

Malone, Michael (M1)
330 Holly Street
Johnson City, TN 37604
(865)692-2415   TNMU#7200

March, Kevin (M1)
1701 Ray Jo Circle
Chattanooga, TN 37421
kmadm1@aol.com
(423)499-4180   SETG#2100

Mariott, Keith L (M1)
155 Ridgewood Lane
Odenville, AL 35120
kjmariott@windstream.net
(205)903-5251   SEGR#0106

Marquez, Alfonso (M1)
389 Bethel Drive
Lenoir City, TN 37772
amarquez61@bellsouth.net
(865)660-7579   SEET#2320

Marquez, Martha (M1)
389 Bethel Drive
Lenoir City, TN 37772
(865)660-7579   SEET#2200

Mars, Stan (M2)
PO Box 274
Mt Pleasant, AR 72561
smars2@liberty.edu
(217)254-5120   GRAR#1517

Marshall, Debbie (M2)
1494 Bucksnort Road
Covington, TN 38019
dsmarshall05@att.net
(901)475-4055   GRWT#9100

Martin, James W (M1)
1922 Battleground Drive
Murfreesboro, TN 37129
(615)896-4442   TNMU#7200

Martin, Theresa (M1)
116 Crisman Street
Chattanooga, TN 37415
choochootm@usa.net
(423)903-7260   SETG#2100

Martin, Tom (M1)
116 Crisman Street
Chattanooga, TN 37415
choochootm@usa.net
(423)903-7260 (cell)   SETG#2100

Martin, William E, Jr (M1)
741 Chapel Hill Road
Marion, KY 42064
juniormartin@yahoo.com
(870)270-3344   GRAR#5110

Martinez, Dagoberto (M1)
Cra 62D #71-113
Bello, Antioquia
COLOMBIA, SA
(574)452-3466   MSAN#8900

Martinez, Rodrigo (M1)
Mz2 Casa 21 Urb Casas De Milan
Dosquebradas, Risaralda

MINISTERS CONTINUED

COLOMBIA, SA
oikoinonia@gmail.com
(576)322-2177   MSAN#8916
Martinez, Soledad   (M1)
5809 Calloway
Ft Worth, TX 761144
ismael3233@sbcglobal.net
(915)204-2449   MSDC#8700
Masuda, Yasuo   (M1)
1-11-20 Kokubu
Ichikawa-shi, Chiba-ken
272-0834 JAPAN
FAX: (047)369-7540
fwgc6854@mb.infoweb.ne.jp
(047)369-7540   MSJA#8314
Mata, Elizabeth   (M2)
PO Box 1040
San Elizario, TX 79849
hectoryliz@att.net
(915)851-5354   MSDC#8700
Mata, Hector   (M1)
PO Box 1040
San Elizario, TX 79849
hectoryliz@att.net
(915)851-5354   MSDC#8706
Mata, Isaac   (M1)
PO Box 1040
San Elizario, TX 79849
isaacmata96@yahoo.com
(915)851-5354   MSDC#8706
Mata, Jose   (M2)
230 Flor Blanca
Socorro, TX 79927
(915)694-8099   MSDC#8700
Mata, Pablo   (M1)
230 Flor Blanca
El Paso, TX 79927
pablomata@yahoo.com
(915)319-8407   MSDC#8700
Mathews, Nathaniel   (M3)
755 Cherokee Road
New Johnsonville, TN 37134
bro.nate-mathews@hotmail.com
(931)209-6645   TNNA#7300
Mathis, B J   (M2)
675 Newt McKnight Road
McMinnville, TN 37110
( )   TNMU#7200
Matlock, Joe   (M1)
5905 Hickory Grove Lane
Memphis, TN 38134
(731)689-3187   MSDC#8700
Matlock, Robert   (M1)
156 Dovenshire Drive
Fairfield Glade, TN 38558
revbobm@msn.com
(921)210-0614   TNMU#7200
Matsumoto, Masahiro   (M1)
2-14-1 Minami Rinkan
Yamato-shi, Kanagawa-ken
242-0006 JAPAN
matsumoto@koza-church.jp
(046)275-2767   MSJA#8313
Matsuya, Ryuzo   (M1)
72-2 Naka Kibogaoka Asahi-ku
Yokohama, Kanagawa-ken
241-0825 JAPAN
matsuya.r@woody.ocn.ne.jp
(045)364-8297   MSJA#8302
Matthews, James N   (M1)
241 Morning Star Drive
Huntsville, AL 35811
FAX: (256)828-0160
jamesnmatthews@bellsouth.net
(256)851-1694   SERD#0800
Mayfield, Randall   (M1)

12470 Daisywood Drive
Knoxville, TN 37932
FAX: (865)769-4756
mayfield07@comcast.net
(865)769-4756   SEET#2308
Maynard, Geoffery   (M1)
1356 Marcia Road
Memphis, TN 38117
(901)409-5269   GRWT#9100
Maynard, Terrell D   (M1)
639 Timber Creek Drive
Columbus, MS 39702
terrellmaynard@bellsouth.net
(662)244-0416   SEGR#0100
Mays, Ronald B   (M1)
1100 Cindy Lane
Mayfield, KY 42066
rbmays@wk.net
(270)247-0070   MICO#3400
McBeth, David L   (M1)
PSC Box 20085
Camp LeJeune, NC 28542
david.mcbeth@usmc.mil
(910)451-2375   SEET#2200
McCallum, Frank   (M1)
PO Box 56
Garfield, KY 40140
mccallum@bbtel.com
(270)580-4796   MICU#3208
McCarty, John   (M1)
305 W Martindale Drive
Marshall, TX 75672
mtsjohn@gmail.com
(423)650-8788   SETG#2100
McCaskey, Charles   (M1)
679 Canter Lane
Cookeville, TN 38501
charles@cookevillecpchurch.org
(931)526-4885   TNMU#7210
McClanahan, H Walter   (M1)
215 White Bros Road
Humboldt, TN 38343
waltermac2@hughes.net
(731)784-1176   GRWT#9110
McClanahan, Jo Ann   (M2)
215 White Bros Road
Humboldt, TN 38343
jaw1940_1@bellsouth.net
(731)784-1176   GRWT#9100
McClung, Andy   (M1)
919 Dickinson Street
Memphis, TN 38107
scubarev@att.net
(901)606-6615   GRWT#9100
McClung, Tiffany   (M1)
919 Dickinson Street
Memphis, TN 38107
tmcclung@memphisseminary.edu
(901)606-6615   GRWT#9100
McConnell, Donald R   (M1)
147 Confederacy Circle
Knoxville, TN 37934
donjoyce515@hotmail.com
(865)288-0230   SEET#2200
McCoy, Kenneth L   (M1)
1422 Walton Road
Memphis, TN 38117
(901)682-0891   GRWT#9301
McCurley, Don   (M1)
4036 McAllister Street
Milan, TN 38358
dcmccurley@hotmail.com
(731)723-3623   GRWT#9106
McDuff, Dwayne   (M1)
9770 County Road 5
Florence, AL 35633

fcpdmcduff@comcast.net
FAX: (256)766-0736
(256)764-6354   SEHO#0506
McDuffie, J C   (M1)
RR 3 Box 574
Fairfield, IL 62837
mactrapper4@frontier.com
(618)842-5624   MINC#5113
McGee, Charles Randall   (M1)
9037 Groveland Drive
Dallas, TX 75218
randallmcgee@sbcglobal.net
(214)328-2488   MSRR#8400
McGill, James A   (M1)
433 S Walnut Avenue
Cookeville, TN 38501
jam7235@frontiernet.net
(931)526-6936   TNMU#7234
McGowan, Kriss   (M1)
900 Alvin York Highway
Whitwell, TN 37397
krissmcg658@gmail.com
(423)463-8609   SETG#2119
McGowan, Rhonda   (M1)
PO Box 869
Whitwell, TN 37379
rhondam658@gmail.com
(423)658-0590   SETG#2100
McGuire, James D   (M1)
220 Southwind Circle #2
Greenville, TN 37745
jmcguire915@comcast.net
(423)638-6380   SEET#2200
McGuire, Timothy   (M1)
PO Box 42
Mt Sherman, KY 42764
brotim.cpc@gmail.com
(270)766-9027   MICU#3509
McInnis, Rodney   (M1)
280-B Coley Road
Glencoe, AL 35905
mcinnisrodneyand@bellsouth.net
(256)454-2399   SEGR#0404
McKee, Margaret   (M1)
774 Beasley Street
Memphis, TN 38111
(901)323-2339   GRWT#9100
McMichael, Jeff   (M1)
224 John Drane Lane
Harned, KY 40144
revmcmichael@outlook.com
(270)617-4016   MICU#3207
McMillan, L Ronald   (M1)
675 Kimberly Drive
Atoka, TN 38004
mcmillanron@bellsouth.net
(901)837-1101   GRWT#9304
McMillan, Lloyd Aaron   (M1)
8600 Academy Road NE
Albuquerque, NM 87111
FAX: (505)797-8599
amcmillan@heightscpc.org
(505)821-1993   MSDC#8701
McNeese, Mark   (M1)
6800 Woodrow Avenue
Austin, TX 78757
FAX: (512)453-2911
mam53@prodigy.net
(512)453-8434   MSTR#8100
McNeese, Michael C   (M1)
16410 Wesley Evans Road
Prairieville, LA 70769
mcneesemc@cox.net
(520)722-1350   MSTR#8100
McSpadden, Nancy   (M1)
2011 Woodridge Drive

MINISTERS CONTINUED

St Peters, MO 63376
revnancy77@gmail.com
(870)612-0067 GRAR#1100
Mearns, Duawn (M1)
107 Westoak Place
Hot Springs, AR 71913
lakehamiltonchurch@att.net
(501)276-1266 GRAR#1221
Medlin, Kevin (M1)
316 Dandelion Drive
Lebanon, TN 37087
FAX: (615)444-6671
kmedlin12@hotmail.com
(615)444-7453 TNMU#7220
Meeks, Brittany (M1)
2264 Morning Sun Road
Cordova, TN 38016
(901)336-9024 GRWT#9100
Meinzer, Alan (M1)
25 Rosewood Road
Batesville, AR 72501
natsdad@suddenlink.net
(870)793-8234 GRAR#1515
Mejia, Salvador (M3)
7618 S Highway 72
Loudon, TN 37774
(865)661-8267 SEET#2200
Melson, Glenda (M1)
634 W Fremont Road
Lebanon, MO 65536
gmelson@fidnet.com
(417)588-2758 GRMI#4100
Melton, Samuel D (M1)
2249 Bucks Pocket Road SE
Oldfort, TN 37362
(423)472-8467 SETG#2100
Meredith, Charles (M1)
144 Barbara Circle
Elizabethtown, KY 42701
(270)307-0607 MICU#3210
Merritt, Joyce (M1)
3929 Snail Shell Cave Road
Rockvale, TN 37153
(615)574-3047 TNMU#7239
Messer, James (M1)
3653 Old Madisonville Road
Henderson, KY 42420
jcmess@hotmail.com
(270)827-0711 MINC#5304
Middleton, Bill S (M1)
12826 Union Road
Knoxville, TN 37922
revbill@charter.net
(865)966-1706 SEET#2200
Middleton, Frank, Jr (M3)
1200 Adele Circle
Slidell, LA 70461
fmiddle@bellsouth.net
(770)655-0406 SETG#2100
Mikel, Jason (M1)
4630 Mt Sharon Road
Greenbrier, TN 37073
jasonemikel@gmail.com
(615)243-8938 TNNA#7321
Milby, Elizabeth L (M1)
207 Summersville Road
Greensburg, KY 42743
(270)932-5659 MICU#3100
Miller, Carol (M1)
1022 Cedar Creek Road
Vanleer, TN 37181
cmiller109@juno.com
(615)763-0742 TNNA#7300
Miller, James R (M1)
1214 Whitney Drive
Columbia, TN 38401

rev.james.miller@charter.net
(931)381-3367 TNCO#7101
Mills, David M (M1)
528 County Road 322
Bertram, TX 78605
(512)355-3511 MSTR#8100
Mink, R Allan (M2)
1113 Hidden Glen Court
Burleson, TX 76028
FAX: (817)295-2576
alan.mink@stmattcpc.org
(817)295-5832 MSRR#8418
Minor, Mitzi (M1)
875 S Cox
Memphis, TN 38104
(901)278-6115 GRWT#9100
Minton, Grant (M1)
PO Box 270
Auburn, KY 42206
FAX: (270)271-4603
gminton@logantele.com
(270)542-7991 MICU#3301
Mitchum, Mark (M1)
21102 La Pena
San Antonio, TX 78258
FAX: (210)497-8724
mitchum@gmail.com
(210)497-7974 MSTR#8100
Miyai, Takehiko (M1)
A-201 2-2-48 Higashihara Zama-shi
Kanagawa-ken
228-0004 JAPAN
FAX: (046)256-3212
(046)207-6558 MSJA#8304
Miyajima, Atsushi (M2)
Rua Araja
58 Paraiso Sao Joa
48280-000, Bahia, BRAZIL
ariel.atsushi@gmail.com
(5571)3664-1037 MSJA#8313
Montano, Jhony (M3)
Cra 9 No 6 6N 87 Bello Horizonte
Popayan
Colombia, South America
(092)823-8988 MSCA#8227
Montoya, David (M1)
Cra 12 bis #11-69
Pereira, Risaralda, COLOMBIA, SA
FAX: (576)324-4110
adamonva@gmail.com
(576)324-4109 MSAN#8916
Montoya, Eduardo (M1)
270 Windsor Drive
Roselle, IL 60172
edmontoya@hotmail.com
(630)980-1577 MINC#5203
Moore, Angela (M1)
3756 Douglass Avenue
Memphis, TN 38111
(870)581-2509 GRAR#1100
Moore, Hillman C (M1)
465 Russell Road
Jackson, TN 38301
hillmancm@att.net
(270)876-7163 MICO#3400
Moore, James R, Sr (M1)
2778 Marguerite Street S
Hokes Bluff, AL 35903
jmoore@microxl.com
(256)494-9030 SEGR#0100
Morgan, Jerome H (M1)
8420 Baumgarten Drive
Dallas, TX 75228
(214)323-7557 MSRR#8400
Morgan, Kenneth P (M1)
5400 Highway 101

Rogersville, AL 35652
FAX: (256)247-1424
kennymorgan330@hotmail.com
(256)247-3890 SEHO#0515
Morgan, Richard (M1)
191 Abby Lane
Baxter, TN 38544
icthuse@charter.net
(931)349-4474 TNMU#7210
Moro, Wilfredo (M2)
15292 SW 104th Street Apt 11-22
Miami, FL 33196
moraw@bellsouth.net
(786)554-1478 SEGR#0100
Morris, Carey (M3)
2167 W Shawtown Road
Troy, TN 38260
carey@cyberianwolf.net
(731)538-9477 GRWT#9100
Morrow, Charles (M1)
5032 Pine Grove Road
Union, MS 39365
morrowp7@yahoo.com
(601)479-0288 SEGR#0100
Mosley, Karen (M1)
PO Box 172154
Memphis, TN 38187
( ) GRWT#9100
Mosley, Steve (M1)
1200 N Arkansas Avenue
Russellville, AR 72801
FAX: (479)880-0071
stevemosley@hotmail.com
(479)968-1061 GRAR#1216
Moss, Larry (M1)
167 Bluegrass Drive
La Center, KY 42056
(270)292-2000 MICO#3400
Mullenix, Robert (M1)
1408 Azalee Lane
Chapel Hill, TN 37034
glonix@live.comt
(931)379-3617 TNCO#7133
Murphree, Hughlen (M1)
4298 County Road 1719
Holly Pond, AL 35083
hmurph@hiwaay.net
(256)796-5352 SERD#0800
Murray, Joshua (M1)
527 N Antioch Road
Quitman, LA 71268
jdm4428@yahoo.com
(318)259-7828 MSTR#8101
Murrie, Willard (M1)
506 11th Street
Vienna, IL 62995
(618)658-2430 MICO#3400

--==<< **N** >>==--

Narowetz, Laura (M3)
129 Roberta Drive
Memphis, TN 38112
littlelaurarose@yahoo.com
(662)213-7072 GRWT#9100
Nash, Zachary (M1)
1296 Hurst Drive
Enid, OK 73703
zachary.nash@vance.af.mil
(580)213-7211 GRWT#9100
Nave, Steve (M1)
5172 Fall River Road
Leoma, TN 38468
thenaves@wildblue.net
(931)424-0020 TNCO#7131
Ndoro, Wonder (M1)

MINISTERS CONTINUED

111 Roberta Avenue
Memphis, TN 38112
gusungo@yahoo.com
(901)334-5861   GRWT#9100

Neafus, Kenneth R   (M1)
237 Richland Church Road
Morgantown, KY 42261
(270)526-6835   MICU#3100

Nease, Dale   (M1)
500 S 30th Street
Clinton, OK 73601
(580)323-7557   MSRR#6302

Nelson, Charles E   (M1)
209 Classic Court
Springtown, TX 76082
dundeal10@aol.com
(903)641-5466   MSRR#8410

Newell, Jennifer   (M1)
2322 Maraco Circle
Chattanooga, TN 37421
newelljennifer3@gmail.com
(423)892-5834   SETG#2108

Nichols, Oscar Lee   (M1)
1035 N County Road 650E
Trilla, IL 62469
(217)234-6551   MINC#5200

Nicholson, Casey   (M1)
1020 Tusculum Boulevard
Greeneville, TN 37745
caseynicholson@mac.com
(423)638-4504   SEET#2202

Nickles, Philip   (M1)
5821 County Road 1114
Vinemont, AL 35179
nickles.phil@yahoo.com
(256)734-9847   SEHO#0213

Niswonger, Richard   (M1)
20941 Highway 16 E
Siloam Springs, AR 72761
rniswonger@cox.net
(479)524-4081   GRAR#1412

Niwa, Yoshimasa   (M1)
15-402 Narakita Danchi
2913 Naramachi Aoba-ku
Yokohama, Kanagawa-ken
227-0036 JAPAN
FAX: (042)725-9909
rsb09335@nifty.com
(045)961-1540   MSJA#8310

Norman, Maury A   (M1)
1750 Shipley Road
Cookeville, TN 38501
maurynorman@yahoo.com
(931)526-1644   TNNA#7229

Norris, Freddie   (M1)
330 Lexington Drive
Glasgow, KY 42141
(270)651-7932   MICU#3100

Norton, Austin   (M3)
1498 Bradshaw Boulevard
Cookeville, TN 38506
(931)261-3260   TNMU#7200

Norton, Kitty   (M1)
251 Westchase Drive
Nashville, TN 37205
kitty.a.norton@vanderbilt.edu
(615)584-1464   TNNA#7300

Norton, Thomas H   (M1)
220 Evergreen Garden Drive
Elizabethtown, KY 42701
tnorton16@comcast.net
(353)584-4695   GRWT#9100

Notley, Sharon   (M1)
16500 S Grey Wolf Apt 5
Odessa, TX 79766
sharon_standrewcp@sbcglobal.net

(432)210-9059   MSDC#8703

Nunn, Donald W   (M1)
203 Bridgers Hill Road
Longview, TX 75604
dwnunn@earthlink.net
(903)297-6074   MSTR#8113

Nye, John   (M1)
210 Crestview Drive
Mount Juliet, TN 37122
( )   TNMU#7200

--==<< O >>==--

O'Neal Danhof, Claire   (M1)
301 Whispering Hills Street
Hot Springs, AR 71901
acglenn@aol.com
( )   GRAR#1100

Oh, Taeho   (M1)
42-40 2908th Street #1
Bayside, NY 11361   SETG#2100

Ohi, Keitaro   (M1)
2-14-21 Minami Rinkan
Yamato-shi Kanagawa-ken
242-0006 JAPAN
keitaro_o@hotmail.com
(046)275-9616   MSJA#8303

Oliveira, Jose   (M1)
7310 Jasmine Drive
Hanover Park, IL 60133
valdirsoares@yahoo.com
(630)855-0870   MINC#5200

Oliver, Lisa   (M1)
110 Allen Drive
Hendersonville, TN 37075
( )   TNMU#7200

O'Mara, Shelia   (M1)
533 Loughton Lane
Arnold, MD 21012
chaplainshelia@aol.com
(410)757-5713   MSDC#8700

Ordway, Wendell   (M1)
4775 Calvert City Road
Calvert City, KY 42029
(270)395-7318   MICO#3423

Orozco, Joaquin   (M2)
Cra 3 #7-14
Aguadas, Caldas, COLOMBIA, SA
jeob40@hotmail.com
(576)851-4773   MSAN#8900

Orozeo Ariza, Juan Carlos   (M2)
Aereo 6365
Cali Vale, COLOMBIA, SA
( )   MSCA#8200

Orr, Melvin   (M1)
806 Washington Street
Newbern, TN 38059
2Orrs.mn@charter.net
(731)627-2445   GRWT#9425

Ortega, Juan   (M3)
COLOMBIA, SA
jortegaus@yahoo.com
(574)323-9305   MSAN#8900

Ortiz, Jaime   (M1)
Cra 50D #62-69
Medellin, Antioquia, COLOMBIA, SA
(574)421-6339   MSAN#8900

Ortiz, Milton   (M1)
817 Radiance Drive
Cordova, TN 38018
mortiz@cumberland.org
(901)276-4572   SEET#2200

Osorio, Fernando   (M3)
Aereo 329
Palmira, COLOMBIA, SA
( )272-7584   MSCA#8215

Overton, Janice M   (M1)
3320 Pipeline Road
Birmingham, AL 35243
FAX: (205)968-8105
jan@crestlinechurch.org
(205)281-6819   SEGR#0102

Overton, Twanda   (M2)
616 S Cox Street
Memphis, TN 38104
tdeeov@yahoo.com
(865)591-8881   SEET#2200

Owen, Rick   (M1)
3305 Wild Oaks Court
Burleson, TX 76028
FAX: (817)295-2576
rowen@stmattcpc.org
(817)295-5832   MSRR#8418

--==<< P >>==--

Page, Rickey   (M1)
736 Rodney Drive
Nashville, TN 37205
FAX: (615)352-2801
rickey.page@wncp.org
(615)353-7850   TNNA#7334

Paleak, Jock Tut   (M1)
614 N Water Street Apt #623
Gallatin, TN 37066
(615)585-2842   TNNA#7341

Palmer, Walter (Pete)   (M1)
1438 S 133rd East Avenue
Tulsa, OK 74108
peteangelblue@att.net
(918)438-0406   MSRR#8400

Paredes, Fabio   (M3)
Carerra 7 # 1-76
La Cruztala, Ipiales, COLOMBIA, SA
(092)773-1036   MSCA#8200

Park, Bo-Seong   (M1)
304-28 Sinlim-Dong, Kwanak-Gu
Seoul, KOREA
(002)884-3474   SEET#2200

Park, Jin Soo   (M1)
37 Arizona Avenue
Syosset, NY 11791
owcasa@hanmail.net
(516)558-7298   SECE#2137

Park, Sang Hoon   (M1)
3504 W Shawnee Drive
Springfield, MO 65810
hesed-park@hanmail.net
(417)888-0442   GRMI#4314

Park, Si Hoon   (M1)
511 4th Street #B
Palisades Park, NJ 07650
(201)944-7913   SECE#2137

Park, Sung In   (M1)
12320 Alameda Trace Circle #1309
Austin, TX 78727
( )   MSTR#8100

Park, Yang Rae   (M1)
4175 Buford Highway
Duluth, GA 30096
barkmoksa@hanmail.net
(770)912-7710   SETG#2130

Park, Young   (M3)
3340 Bentbill Crossing
Cummings, GA 30041
barkmogun@gmail.com
(404)661-6117   SETG#2100

Parker, Susan   (M1)
655 York Drive
Rogersville, AL 35652
park9301@bellsouth.net
(256)247-3877   SEHO#0500

MINISTERS CONTINUED

Parkhurst, L G, Jr   (M1)
    409 Woodhollow Trail
    Edmond, OK 73012
    (405)341-7477   MSRR#8400
Parks, Sam   (M1)
    138 Orchard Road Apt 16
    Kingston, TN 37763
    wsamparks@aol.com
    (423)949-3951   TNMU#7200
Parman, David   (M1)
    5034 S Monroe School Road
    Monroe City, IN 47557
    FAX: (812)743-5171
    (812)743-2646   MINC#5307
Parish, Johnny   (M1)
    102 Trousdale Court
    Hendersonville, TN 37075
    johnnyparish@bellsouth.net
    (615)824-5842   TNNA#7329
Parrish, Steven   (M1)
    4610 Dunn Avenue
    Memphis, TN 38117
    sparrish@memphisseminary.edu
    (901)743-9545   TNNA#7300
Parsons, Hugh L   (M1)
    1526 Welch
    Houston, TX 77006
    p-h-parsons@comcast.net
    (713)522-6126   MSTR#8100
Patterson, James H   (M1)
    1305 Falmouth Road
    Chattanooga, TN 37405
    FAX: (423)942-2188
    (423)267-8568   SETG#2113
Patterson, Jerry   (M1)
    7007 Whitaker Avenue
    Van Nuys, CA 91406
    (818)994-5828   MSDC#8700
Patton, Malcolm   (M1)
    921 Harris Drive
    Gallatin, TN 37066
    FAX: (615)824-6507
    bpatton11@comcast.net
    (615)452-5557   TNNA#7301
Patton, Roger, Jr   (M1)
    7217 Belle Chasse Drive
    Nashville, TN 37221
    rogerlpatton@att.net
    (615)673-8108   TNNA#7335
Payne, Robert (Bob)   (M1)
    1660 3rd Street NW
    Birmingham, AL 35215
    payne.bob.emmet@gmail.com
    (205)856-2427   SEGR#0100
Pedigo, Russell   (M1)
    1002 Haney Avenue
    El Dorado, AR 71730
    russell_pedigo@hotmail.com
    (870)862-4689   GRAR#1100
Peery, Terry   (M1)
    1431 Spainwood Street
    Columbia, TN 38401
    coppreacher@gmail.com
    (931)381-6871   TNCO#7143
Pejendino, Fhanor   (M1)
    Cra 26 #36-40
    Tulua, COLOMBIA, SA
    (317)654-5750   MSCA#8226
Perez, Jose   (M1)
    3512 Chesnut Ridge Lane
    Birmingham, AL 35216
    (205)663-3110   TNMU#7200
Perkins, Ed   (M1)
    721 E Paris Avenue
    McKenzie, TN 38201
    (731)352-2754   GRWT#9100

Perkins, William H   (M1)
    PO Box 632
    Central City, KY 42330
    (270)754-5333   MICU#3100
Peters, David J   (M1)
    4010 Sam Bass Road
    Round Rock, TX 78681
    (512)244-2152   MSTR#8100
Peterson, Lisa   (M1)
    1770 Magnolia Tree Road
    Memphis, TN 38138
    petersonli@aol.com
    (901)754-9316   GRWT#9320
Petty, Linda Lee   (M3)
    4401 W Elgin Street
    Broken Arrow, OK 74012
    (918)252-4741   MSRR#8400
Peyton, James L   (M1)
    1455 County Road 643
    Cullman, AL 35055
    jakjpeyton@att.net
    (256)734-6001   SEHO#0212
Peyton, Kevin   (M1)
    580 S Timothy Lane
    Galatia, IL 62935
    kevinp21@frontier.com
    (618)841-0076   MICO#5123
Phelps, Earl   (M1)
    172 Michie Pebble Hill Road
    Stanntonville, TN 38379
    FAX: (901)632-9126
    phelps.e@juno.com
    (731)632-5107   GRWT#9216
Phillips, Kenneth P   (M1)
    6419 Town Creek Road East
    Lenoir City, TN 37772
    (865)986-7344   SEET#2306
Phillips-Burk, Pam   (M1)
    1065 Legacy Lake Circle 104
    Collierville, TN 38017
    pam@cumberland.org
    (256)684-5247   SERD#0800
Piamba, Juan Carlos   (M3)
    Cra 7 #21N-35
    Popayan, COLOMBIA, SA
    (092)838-5761   MSCA#8200
Pic, Paul   (M1)
    2425 Jefferson Avenue
    New Orleans, LA 70115
    (504)488-9000   MSTR#8100
Pickard, Ronald   (M1)
    6292 Golden Drive
    Morristown, TN 37814
    (423)587-9735   SEET#2200
Pickett, Darrell   (M1)
    113 Woods Drive
    Glasgow, KY 42141
    dpickett@glasgow-ky.com
    (270)834-6102   MICU#3107
Pickett, Pat   (M1)
    1460 Cheatham Dam Road
    Ashland City, TN 37015
    tovahtoo@aol.com
    (615)792-4973   TNNA#7309
Pinion, Phillip   (M1)
    PO Box 87
    Union City, TN 38281
    (731)885-9175   GRWT#9432
Pinnell, James (Jim)   (M1)
    1525 Parks Well Road
    Gleason, TN 38229
    revpinnell@hotmail.com
    (731)648-5078   GRWT#9111
Pittenger, Ronnie M   (M1)
    547 Southcrest Drive
    Nashville, TN 37211

    (615)832-8832   TNMU#7200
Plachte, Richard   (M1)
    615 Grover Street
    Warrensburg, MO 64093
    rap@aerobiz.org
    (660)441-4427   GRMI#4100
Polacek, Fred E   (M1)
    907 Graham Drive
    Old Hickory, TN 37138
    nashvillepresb.sc.treasurer@gmail.com
    (615)754-5328   TNNA#7300
Pope, Charles (Buddy)   (M1)
    2391 Fairfield Pike
    Shelbyville, TN 37160
    pope6897@yahoo.com
    (931)205-6897   TNCO#7137
Porras, Rene Wilgen   (M3)
    Cra 4 bis #10-51
    La Virginia, Risaralda
    COLOMBIA, SA
    renewilgen@hotmail.com
    (576)367-9529   MSAN#8900
Potts, Danny   (M1)
    418 Eddings Street Apt 2
    Fulton , KY 42041
    (270)355-2264   MICO#3400
Pounds, James D   (M1)
    40 Nellie Lane
    Savannah, TN 38372
    olivetcp@bellsouth.net
    (731)925-2685   GRWT#9220
Powell, Jeff   (M1)
    547B Fawn Drive
    Henderson, TN 38340
    jfpowell2003@yahoo.com
    (731)608-2040   GRWT#9100
Powell, Omer T   (M1)
    11856 Sonora Hardin Springs Road
    Eastview, KY 42732
    (270)862-4720   MICU#3100
Preston, Dennis   (M1)
    7447 Knottsville Mount Zion Road
    Philpot, KY 42366
    dennis.preston@daviess.kyschools.us
    (270)925-8144   MICU#3507
Prevost, Abigail   (M3)
    4731 Lafayette Road
    Hopkinsville, KY 42240
    abbyprevost@gmail.com
    (731)343-5386   SEGR#0100
Prewitt, Curtis   (M1)
    3712 Carmel Lane
    Paducah, KY 42003
    prewitt@apex.net
    (270)554-9779   MICO#3400
Prosser, Forest   (M1)
    1157 Mountain Creek Road
    Chattanooga, TN 37405
    forestprosser@comcast.net
    (423)877-4114   SETG#2100
Prosser, Robert   (M1)
    1021 Old State Route 76
    Henry, TN 38231
    (731)243-4467   GRWT#9100
Puckett, Rian   (M3)
    42 Jesse Patterson Road
    Trenton, TN 38382
    rpuckett@dscc.edu
    (731)288-7742   GRWT#9435
Pursley, Andrew   (M3)
    1608 Pearl Street
    Owensboro, KY 42303
    (   )   MICU#3100

--==<< Q >>==--

MINISTERS CONTINUED

Qualls, Michael (M1)
3639 Tiffany Oaks Lane
Bartlett, TN 38135
mqualls1@yahoo.com
(901)377-0526 GRWT#9100

Quevedo, Mariano (M3)
289 Golf Club Lane
McMinnville, TN 37110
( ) TNMU#7200

Quinonez, Wilfrido (M1)
Cra 3 No 36-29, Juan XXIII
BuenaventurValle, COLOMBIA, SA
ipc.divinoredentor@gmail.com
(310)412-1711 MSCA#8206

Quintero, Alexander (M3)
Carrera 13 #3-81
Guacari, COLOMBIA, SA
( ) MSCA#8212

Quinton, Noah (M2)
2912 Waller Omer Road
Sturgis, KY 42459
noah.quinton@gmail.com
(270)952-3875 MICO#3400

--==<< R >>==--

Racines, Jairo (M1)
CLL 39 No 13-40
Cali, COLOMBIA, SA
(311)385-6546 MSCA#8200

Rackley, Mark (M1)
3060 Highway 140 NE
Rydal, GA 30171
pastormarkbcpcga@gmail.com
(770)382-3790 SETG#2101

Ragsdale, Donnie (M1)
915 S Olive Street
Union City, TN 38261
(731)885-0014 GRWT#9100

Ranson, Doris (M1)
9440 Fenwick Road
Owensboro, KY 42301
dorisranson@bellsouth.net
(270)229-2875 MICU#3100

Rapson, Tim (M3)
176 East Valley Road
Whitwell, TN 37397
tim.rapson@yahoo.com
(423)949-8214 SETG#2100

Ratliff, James L (M1)
4027 Club View Drive
Memphis, TN 38125
pastorjimfcpc@yahoo.com
(901)758-0125 GRWT#9312

Reed, Charles (M1)
10235 Highway 301
Dade City, FL 33525
instchuck12@embarqmail.com
(352)567-7427 SEGR#0311

Reed, Richard (M2)
236 Madison Street
Dyer, TN 38330
richardcplist@hotmail.com
(731)692-3604 GRWT#9101

Reese, Michael (M1)
404 Five Oaks Boulevard
Lebanon, TN 37087
michaelhreese@bellsouth.net
(615)443-0457 TNMU#7208

Reeves, Donald (M1)
PO Box 528
Rainsville, AL 35986
reevesd@nacc.edu
(256)228-4057 SERD#0800

Reid, Richard (M1)
1211 Provost Drive

Jefferson City, TN 37760
rjreid1964@msn.com
(865)475-3452 SEET#2100

Reid, Roger (M1)
1505 Experiment Farm Road
Lewisburg, TN 37091
drrtr@yahoo.com
(931)422-5257 TNCO#7125

Renner, Wallace (M1)
1648 Griffith Avenue
Owensboro, KY 42303
pwrenner@adelphia.net
(270)685-4359 MICU#3100

Rice, Keith (M1)
PO Box 582
Itasca, TX 76055
rsvkeith@yahoo.com
(254)087-2418 MSRR#8400

Rice, Perryn (M1)
537 Edgerowe Court
Cookeville, TN 38506
perryn@cookevillecpchurch.org
(931)526-6585 TNMU#7210

Richards, Carroll R (M1)
210 Allison Drive
Lincoln, IL 62656
FAX: (217)732-7894
dr_cr@comcast.net
(217)732-7894 MINC#5200

Richards, Kenneth (M1)
2 Kingston Road
Water Valley, KY 42085
kenrich111443@hotmail.com
(270)355-2089 MICO#3401

Richardson, W Jean (M1)
7533 Lancashire Boulevard
Powell, TN 37849
jeanandregena@frontier.com
(865)947-3111 SEET#2200

Richter, Justin (M1)
8600 Academy Road NE
Albuquerque, NM 87111
richteryp@gmail.com
(505)363-8738 MSDC#8701

Ricketts, Roger (M1)
205 Contantz Drive
Canton, MO 63435 MICU#3100

Ridgely, Michael (M1)
5195 Broad Street S
Trezevant, TN 38258
(731)669-3767 GRWT#9100

Rietz, Allen (M1)
1239 Hopewell Church Road
Finger, TN 38334
(731)989-7872 GRWT#9100

Rincon, Alfredo (M1)
12008 Fred Carter
El Paso, TX 79936
yaanaivitaly@yahoo.com
(915)857-1343 MSDC#8704

Rincon, Lyvia (M1)
12008 Fred Carter
El Paso, TX 79936
yaanaivitaly@yahoo.com
(915)857-1343 MSDC#8706

Rippy, James G (M1)
442 Trina Street
Gallatin, TN 37066
lgrippy@live.com
(615)681-7086 TNNA#7300

Rivera, Carlos A (M1)
Calle Tokio 610, Departmento 6
Colonia Portales Norte
Delegacion Benito
Juarez, C.P. 03300
caralrifra@une.net.co

(52)1-55-31058377 MSRR#8400

Rivera, Cenobia (M1)
Cra 12 #8-47
Cartago, Valle, COLOMBIA, SA
zenobiadedaza@yahoo.com.mx
(572)214-5060 MSAN#8906

Rodden, Linda (M1)
363 Cornelison Street
Lebanon, MO 65536
linda.rodden@mercy.net
(417)588-2207 GRMI#4306

Roddy, Lowell G (M1)
2583 Hedgerow Lane
Clarksville, TN 37043
lgroddy@yahoo.com
(931)368-1081 TNNA#7300

Rodgers, Howard (M1)
336 County Road 1216
Vinemont, AL 35179
djbr421@yahoo.com
(256)739-6296 SEHO#0202

Rodriguez, Jairo Hernan (M1)
Cll 42 No 80B 64
Barrio Versalles
Cali-Valle, COLOMBIA, SA
jairo.hrodriguez@hotmail.com
(572)377-8741 MSCA#8200

Rogers, Steve (M3)
37 Cool Spring Road
Trimble, TN 38259
(731)882-2229 GRWT#9408

Rojas, Antonio Mena (M2)
1421 1st Street NW
Cullman, AL 35055
antonio.mena.7@facebook.com
(256)531-8193 SEGR#0100

Rolman, William L, Jr (M1)
602 Canyon Drive
Columbia, TN 38401
wmrolmanjr@att.net
(931)388-2611 TNCO#7136

Roman, Julio (M3)
1714 S 4th Avenue
Maywood, IL 60153
pastorccc@clear.net
(312)714-6960 MINC#5212

Romines, Sam (M1)
PO Box 127
Lewisburg, KY 42256
sam60romines@hotmail.com
(270)755-4282 MICU#3307

Ros, Ramiro (M1)
107 Bracken Lane
Brandon, FL 33511
bethel@gte.net
(813)633-1548 SEGR#0100

Rose, Missy (M1)
5484 Peyton Randolph Street
Bartlett, TN 38134
missyrose3@yahoo.com
(901)378-1133 GRWT#9100

Rowlett, Ron (M1)
22 Diana Drive
Savannah, GA 31406
(912)351-0736 SEGR#0100

Rudolph, Allie D (M1)
855 Old Rosebower Church Road
Paducah, KY 42003
rallie307@aol.com
(270)898-4903 MICO#3400

Ruggia, Mario (Bud) (M1)
603 Rumsey Street
Kiowa, KS 67070
ruggia@aol.com
(620)825-4509 MSRR#8400

Rush, Kip John (M1)

513 Meadowlark Lane
Brentwood, TN 37027
pastor@brenthaven.org
(615)376-4563 TNNA#7331
Rush, Robert D (M1)
17822 Deep Brook Drive
Spring, TX 77379
rushrd74@comcast.net
(832)559-1500 MSTR#8100
Russell, Bud (M1)
9595 Wickliffe Road
Wickliffe, KY 42087
olen552@aol.com
(270)876-7272 MICO#3404
Rustenhaven, William, III (M1)
PO Box 1303
Marshall, TX 75671
FAX: (903)935-3193
rusty@cumberlandofmarshall.org
(903)935-6609 MSTR#8115
Rustenhaven, William, Jr (M1)
703 W Burleson Street
Marshall, TX 75670
rustenhavendolores@yahoo.com
(903)935-7056 MSTR#8100
Ryan, Jack (M1)
8806 Kennesaw Mountain Drive
Mabelvale, AR 72103
(501)749-8572 GRAR#1100
Ryoo, Hwa Chang (M1)
450 Island Road Unit 146
Ramsey, NJ 07446 SETG#2100

--==<< S >>==--

Saldana, Manuel (M2)
536 Telop
El Paso, TX 79927
campe13@yahoo.com
(915)317-9349 MSDC#8700
Salisbury, Rebecca (M1)
1033 Twin Oaks Drive
Murfreesboro, TN 37130
rebsalisbury@yahoo.com
(615)410-7801 TNMU#7200
Salyer, Stewart (M1)
2211 Foxfire Road
Clarksville, TN 37040
stewart.salyer@gmail.com
(931)980-2829 TNNA#7302
Sanchez, Josefina (M1)
7 Hancock Street
Melrose, MA 02176
fsfamily64@gmail.com
(479)970-8654 SEET#2220
Sanders, Thomas R (M1)
4201 W Kent Street
Broken Arrow, OK 74012
FAX: (918)437-2199
trsncf@msn.com
(918)269-0043 MSRR#6201
Sandiford, Holton (M3)
4227 E 300th Road
Casey, IL 62420
(217)259-3773 MINC#5200
Sansom, Vernon (M1)
7810 Shiloh Road
Midlothian, TX 76065
vernon@sansom.us
(972)825-6887 MSRR#8421
Santillano, Ray Paul (M1)
12313 Olga Mapula
El Paso, TX 79936
ramon.santillano@us.army.mil
(915)500-4928 MSTR#8100
Satoh, Iwao (M1)

9111 Cedarwood Drive
Pewee Valley, KY 40056
iwaosatoh@gmail.com
(502)210-0852 MSJA#8300
Schmoyer, Donna Marie (M1)
613 Mound Street
Monongahela, PA 15063
schmoyerdm@yahoo.com
(817)266-6572 MSRR#8400
Schott, Fred, Jr (M1)
606 Taylor Trail
Springfield, TN 37172
(615)384-8572 TNNA#7321
Schultz, Don (M1)
708 Gateway Lane
Tampa, FL 33613
(813)960-1473 SEGR#0100
Schwarz, Karl (M1)
83 W Curtis Street
Bells, TN 38006
schw8651@bellsouth.net
(731)663-3987 GRWT#9430
Scott, Jerry (M1)
2310 Sentell Drive
Maryville, TN 37803
dmjlscott@yahoo.com
(865)809-2621 SEET#2200
Scott, Joel (M3)
1848 Sassafrass Lane
Soddy Daisy, TN 37379
saejoescott@gmail.com
(423)240-2724 SETG#2100
Scott, Linda (M3)
960 S Katy Road
Atoka, OK 74525
(580)889-2292 MSCH#6100
Scott, Lisa (M1)
(On File in General Assembly Office)
lascott1979@att.net
(816)332-0604 GRMI#4100
Scott, Nathan (M1)
960 S Katy Road
Atoka, OK 74525
(580)364-6155 MSCH#6102
Scrivener, Carol (M1)
746 Willowsprings Boulevard
Franklin, TN 37064
csscriv@juno.com
(731)660-6469 GRWT#9100
Scrudder, Norlan (M1)
29688 S 534 Road
Park Hill, OK 74451
ndscrudder@gmail.com
(918)949-1326 MSRR#8400
Searcy, James M (M1)
1307 Lucy Way
Knoxville, TN 37912
gsearcy@earthlink.net
(817)293-6132 GRWT#9100
Seki, Nobuko (M1)
Yamato City
JAPAN MSJA#8300
Shanley, Dwight (M1)
16904 Old Mill Road
Little Rock, AR 72206
dwightshanley@att.net
(501)888-4190 GRAR#1100
Shannon, Randy (M1)
30282 Highway H
Marshall, MO 65340
pastor_randy_shannon@yahoo.com
(660)886-9545 GRMI#4210
Sharpe, Michael G (M1)
3423 Summerdale Drive
Bartlett, TN 38133
(901)276-4572 MSRR#8400

Shauf, Steve (M1)
3032 Monroe Street
Paducah, KY 42001
sshauf@hotmail.com
(870)291-2046 GRAR#1100
Shauf, Teresa (M1)
3032 Monroe Street
Paducah, KY 42001
theshaufs@hotmail.com
(870)291-2938 GRAR#1100
Shelton, Robert E (M1)
10508 Royalwood Drive
Dallas, TX 75238
bshelton67@yahoo.com
(214)349-7162 MSRR#8400
Shelton, Robert M (M1)
7128 Lakehurst Avenue
Dallas, TX 75230
(214)696-3237 MSRR#8400
Shelton, Steven (M1)
7886 Farmhill Cove
Bartlett, TN 38135
faithcpcpastor@gmail.com
(901)377-0526 GRWT#9308
Shepard, Denny C (M1)
8514 Newsom Station Road
Nashville, TN 37221
(615)662-1114 TNMU#7209
Shepherd, Sandra (M1)
525 Summitt Oaks Court
Nashville, TN 37221
woolywagon@gmail.com
(256)608-8701 TNNA#7300
Shin, Kyung I (M1)
1805 Gallinas Road NE
Rio Rancho, NM 87144
pastorkshin@gmail.com
(505)453-5461 MSDC#8700
Shipley, Howard E (M1)
3800 Dan Drive
Morristown, TN 37814
hshipley@charter.net
(423)581-1092 SEET#2207
Shirey, John (M1)
10181 State Route 56 W
Sturgis, KY 42459
amshirey7@ips.com
(270)389-3562 MICO#3400
Shirley, Betty L (M1)
811 Rotherham Drive
Ballwin, MO 63011
therevbls@prodigy.net
(636)386-3174 MINC#5200
Shoulta, John R (M1)
1154 Mount Carmel Road
White Plains, KY 42464
johnshoulta@bellsouth.net
(270)676-3563 MICO#3613
Shugert, Rich (M1)
5208 Bellis Drive
Fort Worth, TX 76244
shugertr@yahoo.com
(817)913-7211 MSRR#8413
Sides, Judy Taylor (M1)
534 Bethany Circle
Murfreesboro, TN 37128
(615)895-1627 TNMU#7231
Sims, Edward G (M1)
2161 N Meadow Drive
Clarksville, TN 37043
simseg@aol.com
(931)206-5759 TNNA#7300
Sims, Jacob (M1)
23716 Alabama Highway 9 N
Piedmont, AL 36272
jacobdsims@gmail.com

MINISTERS CONTINUED

(205)907-8273   SEGR#0406
Sims, Joyce   (M2)
  5935 Paris Highway 54
  Paris, TN 38242
  (731)364-3537   GRWT#9100
Sisco, Terra   (M1)
  6918 State Route 120
  Marion, KY 42064
  (270)965-0176   MICO#5119
Siu, Jonathan Chor K   (M1)
  251 Tin Sam Estate
  Shatin, HONG KONG
  FAX: (852)2607-2245
  cpccksiu@yahoo.com.hk
  (852)2693-3444   MSHK#8807
Skidmore, Garland   (M1)
  2083 US Highway 278 E
  Hampton, AR 71744
  (870)798-4634   GRAR#1101
Sledge, Jeff   (M1)
  241 Long Bow Road
  Knoxville, TN 37934
  pastorjeff@faithfellowshippcp.org
  (865)288-3375   SEET#2319
Small, Kevin   (M1)
  6492 E 400th Road
  Martinsville, IL 62442
  revkev61@gmail.com
  (618)569-4955   MINC#5211
Smith, Albert J   (M1)
  407 W Main Street Apt 131
  Wilkesboro, NC 28697
  ct_alsmith@casscomm.com
  (217)452-3408   MINC#5200
Smith, Billy T   (M1)
  49 Abby Lynn Circle
  Clarksville, TN 37043
  (931)368-0424   TNNA#7300
Smith, Charles D   (M1)
  12320 Moss Square
  St Francesville, LA 70775
  cdsmith46@gmail.com
  (225)635-4432   MSTR#8100
Smith, Christian   (M1)
  7407 Bonny Oaks Drive
  Chattanooga, TN 37421
  csmith2490@gmail.com
  (423)508-2490   SETG#2106
Smith, David R   (M1)
  PO Box 892
  Rosepine, LA 70659
  ogreyfox@att.net
  (903)297-6074   MSTR#8100
Smith, James A   (M1)
  8301 Poplar Pike
  Germantown, TN 38138
  james1493@att.net
  (901)309-1992   GRWT#9100
Smith, James   (M3)
  222 Southcrest Drive SW
  Huntsville, AL 35802
  dr.james.smith@netzero.com
  (256)655-6541   SERD#0800
Smith, Jerald D   (M1)
  2625 Beech Bluff Road
  Beech Bluff, TN 38313
  jergensmith@aol.com
  (731)427-9316   GRWT#9205
Smith, John Adam   (M1)
  916 Allen Road
  Nashville, TN 37214
  john.a.smith.81@gmail.com
  (573)453-8455   TNNA#7300
Smith, Kirk   (M1)
  813 1st Avenue
  Fayetteville, TN 37334

FAX: (931)438-8649
revkirk@fayettevilleelectric.net
(931)438-8649   TNCO#7122
Smith, Nicholas   (M3)
  101 Cumberland Street
  Glasgow, KY 42141
  pastornic@gcpchurch.tv
  (270)651-3308   MICU#3108
Smith, Robert A   (M1)
  PO Box 501
  Newbern, TN 38059
  ras1957@bellsouth.net
  (731)627-3332   GRWT#9417
Smith, Robert H   (M1)
  5055 S 76th East Avenue Apt D
  Tulsa, OK 74145
  rhsmith@sstelco.com
  (918)671-5520   MSRR#8400
Smith, Timothy   (M1)
  712 Morningside Drive
  Fayetteville, TN 37334
  FAX: (931)433-0056
  tims38@hotmail.com
  (931)438-2820   TNCO#7112
Smyrl, Jerry   (M1)
  3421 Montreal Street NE
  Albuquerque, NM 87111
  jwsmyrl@hotmail.com
  (505)293-0108   MSDC#8701
Snelling, Linda   (M1)
  15791 State Highway 1W
  Ada, OK 74820
  FAX: (580)332-9424
  lindasnelling@covenantcpc.org
  (580)332-0799   MSRR#6304
Snyder, Joel   (M1)
  224 Lord Lane
  Mountain View, AR 72560
  snyder.joel@ymail.com
  (870)269-9743   GRAR#1504
So, Lai Yuet   (M3)
  2/F Fu Tung Shopping Centre
  Tung Chung
  Lantau Island NT, HONG KONG
  FAX: (852)2109-1737
  laiyuet0914@gmail.com
  (852)2109-1738   MSHK#8800
So, Patrick   (M1)
  2/F Fu Tung Shopping Center
  Tung Chung
  Lantau Island, HONG KONG
  FAX: (852)2109-1737
  pattwso@gmail.com
  (852)2109-1738   MSHK#8810
Solis, Arcadio   (M1)
  Crr 42 D1 No 55-69
  Guapi, COLOMBIA, SA
  (   )328-5486   MSCA#8200
Solito, Carlos   (M3)
  106 Highway 63
  Calera, AL 35040
  fcg9700@gmail.com
  (205)329-8514   SEGR#0100
Song, Byung Seon   (M1)
  (MOVED TO CANADA)
  (404)512-9147   SETG#2100
Song, Nam Hun   (M1)
  (IN KOREA)
  (   )   SETG#2100
Sontowski, Marian   (M1)
  PO Box 3973
  Edmond, OK 73083
  marian.desk@gmail.com
  (405)340-7281   MSRR#6307
Sosa, Alexandri   (M1)
  8601 Huron Court

Tampa, FL 33614
FAX: (813)932-9700
sosapcus@gmail.com
(813)562-4289   SEGR#0307
Sotak, Max   (M3)
  7805 W 62nd Place
  Arvada, CO 80004
  msotak@regis.edu
  (303)423-5525   MSDC#8700
Spence, Thomas R   (M1)
  PO Box 809
  Burns Flat, OK 73624
  tomspence0302@gmail.com
  (580)562-4531   MSRR#6301
Spurling, Robert T, Jr   (M1)
  127 Wellington Circle
  Oak Ridge, TN 37830
  (865)803-8582   SEET#2316
Steeley, Tim   (M3)
  PO Box 281
  Mt Vernon, MO 65712
  tsteeley@swr5.k12.mo.us
  (417)466-4345   GRMI#4102
Stefan, Gregory   (M1)
  1153 Letort Road
  Conestoga, PA 17516
  pastorstefan@att.net
  (931)296-5291   GRWT#7300
Stephens, Blake   (M1)
  9980 Nashville Highway
  Mc Minnville, TN 37110
  blsteph@edge.net
  (931)939-2628   TNMU#7203
Stephenson, Joseph   (M3)
  PO Box 129
  Bethany, IL 61914
  (217)853-7819   MINC#5200
Stevens, Brittany   (M3
  606 Huntington Parkway
  Nashville, TN 37211
  bstevens5@my.apsu.edu
  (615)719-3362   TNNA#7300
Stone, Paul   (M1)
  3490 State Route 2837
  Clay, KY 42404
  stonepstc@aol.com
  (270)664-6244   MICO#3621
Stovall, Jeff   (M1)
  2829 Trelawny Drive
  Clarksville, TN 37043
  jeffstovall@juno.com
  (931)993-6104   TNNA#7300
Stowell, Andrew   (M2)
  2998 Trough Springs Road
  Clarksville, TN 37043
  andrewstowellcft@gmail.com
  (   )   TNNA#7300
Stutler, Tim   (M1)
  1044 Mansker Farm Boulevard
  Hendersonville, TN 37075
  gcpctim@bellsouth.net
  (615)859-5888   TNNA#7328
Suenram, Timothy   (M1)
  5704 Tyler Street
  Pearland, TX 77581
  tsuenram@aol.com
  (832)217-6367   MSTR#8100
Sumerlin, Larkin   (M2)
  174 Brookgreen Lane
  Indian Springs, AL 35124
  larkin_sumerlin72@hotmail.com
  (334)357-0007   SEGR#0100
Sumrall, Phil   (M1)
  107 Barnhardt Circle
  Fort Oglethorpe, GA 30742
  phil.sumrall@gmail.com

MINISTERS CONTINUED

(423)903-1938   SETG#2100
Sung, John   (M2)
26 Old Orchard Road
Cherry Hill, NJ 08003
(856)751-0227   SETG#2100
Suttle, Michael   (M1)
507 Ouachita 18
Camden, AR 71701
m_s_suttle@msn.com
(870)836-0008   GRAR#1317
Suzuki, Atsushi   (M1)
53-17 Higashi Kibogaoka
Asahi-ku Yokohama Kanagawa-ken
241-0826 JAPAN
asyuwa98@m10.alpha-net.ne.jp
FAX: (045)362-2603
(045)362-2603   MSJA#8315
Suzuki, Temote   (M2)
9-14-15-310 Honcho Kamitsuruma
Sagamihara-shi, Kanagawa-ken
228-0818 JAPAN
temo_suzuki@hotmail.com
( )   MSJA#8300
Sweet, Anna   (M3)
7225 Old Clinton Pike
Knoxville, TN 37921
(865)803-8582   SEET#2200
Sweet, Don   (M1)
3008 Shropshire Boulevard
Powell, TN 37849
marionondon77@netscape.com
(865)938-7435   SEET#2200
Sweet, Thomas   (M1)
2711 Windemere Lane
Powell, TN 37849
tsweet1@comcast.net
(865)938-0508   SEET#2301
Sweigart, John M   (M1)
PO Box 876
Dover, AL 72837
(479)229-4041   GRAR#1100
Sze, Joseph   (M1)
Rau Sao Joaquim, 382
Liberdale, Sao Paulo, SP
CEP 015068-000, BRAZIL
pastorsze@yahoo.com
( )   MSDC#8700

--==<< T >>==--

Tabor, Don M   (M1)
9611 Mitchell Place
Brentwood, TN 37027
FAX: (615)373-3356
dontabor@comcast.net
(615)776-7292   TNNA#7300
Taborda, Arturo   (M1)
Cra 43 #20D-46
Zamora, Medellin
Antioquia, COLOMBIA, SA
chilalu1147@hotmail.com
(574)267-1351   MSAN#8900
Talley, Edward   (M1)
404 Serenity Circle
Walland, TN 37886
vellate@att.net
(205)854-1886   SEGR#0405
Talley, James E   (M1)
203 Browning Place
Hopkinsville, KY 42240
(270)886-4184   MICU#3504
Tamai, Yukio   (M1)
3-17-57 Nakashinden
Ebina-shi Kanagawa-ken
243-0422 JAPAN
yukiotamai@me.com

(046)234-3426   MSJA#8311
Tan, Pek Hua   (M1)
7 Belhaven Avenue
Daly City, CA 94015
ptan27@yahoo.com
(415)515-0076   MSDC#8501
Tang, Po Kau   (M2)
2/F Welland Plaza
188 Nam Cheong Street
Sham Shui Po, Kowloon, HONG KONG
FAX: (852)2771-2726
cpc_pokau@yahoo.com.hk
(852)2794-2382   MSHK#8800
Terrell, Elizabeth   (M2)
2073 Vinton Avenue
Memphis, TN 38104
(901)647-2788   GRAR#1100
Thomas, Cassandra   (M1)
1920 Dancy Street
Fayetteville, NC 28301
chcothomas@yahoo.com
(910)488-4897   MSRR#8400
Thomas, Don F   (M1)
400 Park Hill Road
Collierville, TN 38017
thomas63981@comcast.net
(901)861-6398   GRWT#0501
Thomas, Don H   (M1)
4829 Caldwell Mill Road
Birmingham, AL 35242
dhtatn4ybc@cs.com
(205)742-0785   SEGR#0105
Thomas, Lynn   (M1)
4833 Caldwell Mill Lane
Birmingham, AL 35242
lynndont@gmail.com
(205)601-5770   SEGR#0100
Thomas, Micaiah   (M3)
PO Box 5204 SBN 499
Princeton, NJ 08543
micaiah.thomas@gmail.com
(205)478-5985   SEGR#0100
Thompson, Dee Ann   (M1)
226 W Bellville Street
Marion, KY 42064
deethomp5@hotmail.com
(270)445-0310   MICO#3207
Thompson, Eugene   (M1)
2825 Albatross Road
Del Ray Beach, FL 33444
( )   MICU#3100
Thompson, Tommy   (M1)
9160 Tchulahoma Road
Southaven, MS 38671
(662)393-2552   GRWT#9100
Thompson, W Fay   (M1)
210 Macbeth Lane
Glasgow, KY 42141
(270)646-2218   MICU#3100
Thornton, Jesse   (M1)
122 E Cherry Street
Chandler, IN 47610
jessthornton@msn.com
(812)925-6475   MINC#5302
Tobler, Garth   (M1)
136 Boat Landing Road
Oneonta, AL 35121
gatobler@gmail.com
(205)683-0298   SEGR#0100
Todd, Christopher   (M3)
139 Roberta Drive
Memphis, TN 38112
ctodd21@msn.com
(901)529-1072   GRWT#9100
Todd, Virgil H   (M1)
3095 E Glengarry Road

Memphis, TN 38128
(901)358-4336   TNNA#7300
Tolley, Robert (Butch)   (M1)
1445 New Murraytown Road NW
Cleveland, TN 37312
(423)837-6488   SETG#2100
Tompkins, Wayne   (M1)
6835 Highway 22 A
Lexington, TN 38351
waynetompkinsministries@yahoo.com
(731)968-4331   GRWT#9221
Topar, Shirley   (M1)
2233 Cambridge Drive SE
Grand Rapids, MI 49506
s_j_topar@yahoo.com
(616)245-0625   MINC#5200
Torres, Rodrigo   (M3)
Aereo 6365
Cali, COLOMBIA, SA
(011)882-8372   MSCA#8205
Travieso, Julio   (M1)
15910 Countrybrook Street
Tampa, FL 33624
jutra98@aol.com
(813)963-3727   SEGR#0100
Travis, Kermit   (M1)
3220 Sharon Highway 89
Dresden, TN 38225
(731)364-2315   GRWT#9124
Treadaway, Kenneth A   (M1)
172 Miller County 494
Texarkana, AR 71854
treadaways@ark.net
(870)574-1609   GRAR#1100
Trotter, Wendell   (M1)
1516 Fell Avenue NE
Huntsville, AL 35811
wendelltrotter@knology.net
(256)519-6571   TNCO#7100
Truax, Robert Lee, Jr   (M1)
2989 Champions Drive Apt 204
Lakeland, TN 38002
(901)266-5927   GRWT#9100
Truitt, Robert D   (M1)
1238 Old East Side Road
Burns, TN 37029
FAX: (615)446-7827
rdtjct@aol.com
(615)740-9180   TNNA#7308
Tsui, Jackson   (M2)
258 Carlos D'Assumpcao
Ed Kin Heng Long 4 Andar LMN
Macau
FAX: (852)2771-2726
(853)2892-1702   MSHK#8800
Tsujimoto, Mark   (M1)
88 S Broadway Unit 3210
Millbrae, CA 94030
mltsuijimoto@gmail.com
(650)697-6901   MSDC#8700
Tubb, Gary Robert   (M1)
103 Forest Drive
Mountain Home, AR 72653
grtubb@yahoo.com
(870)424-0603   GRAR#1505
Tucker, Greg   (M2)
PO Box 262
Coker, AL 35452
cokercpgreg@att.net
(205)541-7484   SEGR#0705
Tucker, James D   (M1)
PO Box 34
Mc Daniels, KY 40152
(270)257-8971   MICU#3100
Tucker, Paul   (M2)
3801 Brush Hill Pike

MINISTERS CONTINUED

Nashville, TN 37216
paultucker@gmail.com
(615)430-9158   TNCO#7100
Turner, Glyn
1660 Chattanooga Valley Road
Flintstone, GA 30725
glynturner@outlook.com
(585)307-7715   SETG#2100
Turner, O Gene   (M1)
5160 McSpadden Road
Rives, TN 38253
(731)536-0189   GRWT#9100
Turner, Leonard E, Jr   (M1)
12651 Wagon Wheel Circle
Knoxville, TN 37934
pastor@unioncpchurch.com
FAX: (865)675-3787
(865)966-8262   SEET#2315
Turner, Steven W   (M1)
7622 Snider Road
Gilmer, TX 75645
FAX: (903)757-2572
fcpclongview@sbcglobal.net
(903)758-5184   MSTR#8112
Turpen, R Brent   (M1)
PO Box 577
Locust Grove, OK 74352
mlturpen@hotmail.com
(918)479-5613   MSRR#6203
Tyus, Dwayne   (M1)
901 W Old Hickory Boulevard
Madison, TN 37115
dwayne.tyus@gmail.com
(615)862-0431   TNNA#7332

--==<< U >>==--

Underwood, Jerrell M   (M1)
PO Box 9
Garfield, KY 40140
(270)536-3706   MICU#3205
Ushioda, Kenji   (M1)
2-47-3 Akuwa-higashi Seya-ku
Yokohama, Kanagawa-ken
246-0023 JAPAN
ushioda@jc.ejnet.ne.jp
(046)361-4351   MSJA#8312

--==<< V >>==--

Valdez, Diana   (M1)
Cra 50 D#62-69
Medellin, Antioquia, COLOMBIA, SA
dianamariavaldezduque@gmail.com
(574)263-2154   MSAN#8915
Valencia, Jorge   (M1)
Aereo 4290
Cali, COLOMBIA, SA
( )332-5840   MSCA#8200
Valencia, Nulbel   (M1)
Diag 11D Casa 11 urbGemelas
Dosquebradas
Risaralda, COLOMBIA, SA
(576)330-7704   MSAN#8900
Van Meter, Bill   (M1)
10626 Highway 41
Charleston, AR 72933
revbill46@gmail.com
(479)965-2998   GRAR#1402
Vance, Dennis   (M1)
1320 Valleywood Drive
Paris, TN 38242
rvdvance@hotmail.com
(731)420-4261   GRWT#9428
Vanderlaan, D Kevin   (M1)
12 Willow Street

Bethany, IL 61914
pastorkevin2@gmail.com
(217)620-2723   MINC#5401
Varilla, Adan Manuel   (M3)
Calle 48 D E #96A-30
Medellin, Antioquia
COLOMBIA, SA   MSAN#8900
Varnell, William   (M3)
6729 Old Dunlop Road
Whitwell, TN 37397
billvatagts@hotmail.com
(423)658-0506   SETG#2100
Varner, Susan   (M1)
2766 N Rockcreek Parkway
Cordova, TN 38016
smvarner76@yahoo.com
(901)371-1249   TNNA#7300
Vasquez, Alejandro   (M1)
Cra 58 #32A-41 Apt 420
Bello, Antioquia, COLOMBIA, SA
almaesda@une.net.co
(574)451-4816   MSAN#8918
Vasseur, Terry   (M1)
121 Crossland Road
Murray, KY 42071
tvasseur@bellsouth.net
(270)876-8083   MICO#3400
Vaught, Joseph R   (M1)
7424 Highland Lick Road
Lewisburg, KY 42256
brojoe2@logantele.com
(270)726-8497   MICU#3308
Velez, Gabriel   (M1)
CL 8A #16A-26
Dosquebradas
Risaralda, COLOMBIA, SA
(576)330-1168   MSAN#8900
Velez, Gloria Patricia   (M3)
Cra 4 bis #10-51
LaVirginia, Risaralda
COLOMBIA, SA
renewilgen@hotmail.com
(576)385-4517   MSAN#8900
Vick, Joe   (M1)
6064 Old Hickory Boulevard
Whites Creek, TN 37189
joervick@gmail.com
(615)519-5249   TNNA#7318
Vickers, Fran   (M1)
7225 Old Clinton Pike
Knoxville, TN 37921
franv3@comcast.net
(865)859-0805   SEET#2301

--==<< W >>==--

Wada, Ichiro   (M3)
Tokyo Christian University
3-301-5 Uchino Inzai-shi, Chiba
270-1347 JAPAN
ichirowada@gmail.com
(047)646-1141   MSJA#8300
Wagner, Hugh   (M1)
12556 Timberline Drive
Garfield, AR 72732
hughawagner@gmail.com
(479)359-0021   MSRR#8400
Walker, Hobert   (M1)
PO Box 66
Rutherford, TN 38369
rutherfordcpchurch@gmail.com
(731)665-7236   GRWT#9429
Walker, Michael C   (M1)
1404 Wilshire Drive
Odessa, TX 79761
mworator@gmail.com

(731)643-6730   GRWT#9100
Walkup, Lyon   (M1)
225 Bertha Owen Road
Morrison, TN 37357
dirtroad@blomand.net
(931)604-3233   TNMU#7207
Wallace, Andrew   (M1)
816 Howard Avenue
Burlingame, CA 94010
( )   MINC#5200
Wallace, Boyce   (M1)
Cra 101 No 15-93
Cali, COLOMBIA, SA
hbwcali@yahoo.com
( )339-1579   MSCA#8200
Walsh, Devin   (M3)
801 East "M" Street
Russellville, AR 72801
(479)890-6716   GRAR#1100
Wan, Sonny   (M1)
13 Wexford Place
Aladema, CA 94502
sonny@cumberlandsf.org
(415)421-1874   MSDC#8501
Ward, Andrew   (M1)
407 Rose Hill Court
Goodlettsville, TN 37072
andrewbward@aol.com
(615)456-9136   TNNA#7319
Ward, Frank   (M1)
46 Henderson Cove
Atoka, TN 38004
bamaguy68@xipline.com
(901)837-1972   GRWT#9100
Warren, Christopher   (M1)
906 Prince Lane
Murfreesboro, TN 37129
chris@murfreesborocpc.org
(615)828-8719   TNMU#7232
Warren, Glenn   (M3)
116 Cedar Hill Drive
Waverly, TN 37185
gwarren224@gmail.com
(931)209-5431   TNNA#7339
Warren, Gordon   (M1)
811 Wall Street
Morrilton, AR 72110
jogordonwarren@suddenlink.net
(501)208-1120   GRAR#1219
Warren, Jo   (M1)
811 Wall Street
Morrilton, AR 72110
pastorjo47@ymail.com
(501)354-4139   GRAR#1211
Warren, Joy   (M1)
907 W Main Street
Murfreesboro, TN 37129
revjoywarren@gmail.com
(615)828-8719   TNMU#7200
Warren, William   (M1)
7139 Toro Cove
Germantown, TN 38138
FAX: (901)759-3653
cpcgww@aol.com
(901)755-8058   GRWT#9310
Washburn, Gloria   (M3)
PO Box 2484
Jordan, AR 72519
grwashburn07@gmail.com
(870)321-4596   GRAR#1100
Watkins, Robert B   (M1)
235 Misty Drive
Somerset, KY 42503
watkr@mac.com
(319)431-0990   MINC#5200
Watson, April   (M2)

MINISTERS CONTINUED

529 W Bellville
Marion, KY 42064
aprilwatson@hotmail.com
(270)965-2850 MICO#3418
Watson, Dale (M1)
1705 Lawnville Road
Kingston, TN 37763
revdwatson@comcast.net
(865)376-2192 SEET#2317
Watson, Johnny E (M1)
272 Madison Street
Dyer, TN 38330
rev.jwatson@bellsouth.net
(731)692-3555 GRWT#9409
Watson, Jonathan (M1)
PO Box 518
Nolensville, TN 37135
watsonjonathan@bellsouth.net
(615)630-9153 TNCO#7144
Watt, Eva (M3)
258 Carlos D'Assumpcao
Ed Kin Heng Long 4 Andar LMN
MACAU
FAX: (852)2892-1702
eva6@hotmail.com
(853)2892-1702 MSHK#8804
Watts, Glenn David (M2)
7400 Willowbend Drive
Crestwood, KY 40014
hongkongbrother@hotmail.com
(502)241-0436 MICU#3100
Wayman, Sam (M1)
707 High Hill Creek Road
LaGrange, TX 78945
samdonnawayman@gmail.com
(979)968-3734 MSTR#8100
Weaver, Dennis (M2)
39 Cool Spring Road
Trimble, TN 38259
(731)643-6056 GRWT#9112
Webb, William G (M1)
7926 S 78th E Avenue
Tulsa, OK 74133
(918)294-9117 MSRR#8400
Welch, Johnie (M1)
PO Box 1506
Dyersburg, TN 38025
johnniewelch@msn.com
(731)287-9008 GRWT#9100
Weldon, Mark (M1)
1515 Chambliss Drive
Birmingham, AL 35226
weldonm@bellsouth.net
(205)330-8580 SEGR#0100
West, David (M1)
2027 Lucille Street
Lebanon, TN 37087
(217)732-7568 TNNA#7340
West, Earl (M1)
246 Maple Avenue
Greensburg, KY 42743
west5010@windstream.net
(207)932-5010 MICU#3116
West, Fred E, Jr (M1)
510 Cedaredge Drive
New Smyrna, FL 32168
jwest616@earthlink.net
(206)409-8321 SEET#2200
Westbrook, James (M1)
1717 Wedgewood Drive
Union City, TN 38261
westbrook731@bellsouth.net
(731)884-0918 GRWT#9100
Westfall, Charles K (M1)
94 Honeysuckle Drive
Gilbertsville, KY 42044

(270)362-0816 MICO#3411
Weston, Robert E (M1)
11 Summer Bluff
San Antonio, TX 78254
rjaweston@gmail.com
(210)347-0232 MSTR#8610
Whaley, Greg (M3)
4970 Comstock Road
Chapel Hill, TN 37034
( ) TNMU#7200
Wheelbarger, J J (M2)
PO Box 504
Joelton, TN 37080
jjwheelbarger@aol.com
(615)876-6948 TNNA#7300
Wheeler, Nathan (M1)
1255 Wedgewood Street
Nashville, TN 38111
nathantyac@gmail.com
(901)606-9535 GRWT#9100
Whitaker, Perry Eugene (M1)
235 Sykes Road
Brush Creek, TN 38547
brotherperry@msn.com
(615)631-1844 TNMU#7246
White, Charles (M1)
PO Box 44
Galatia, IL 62935
(618)268-4562 MICO#3400
White, Diann (M1)
9394 Alex Dickson Cove
Bartlett, TN 38133
diannwhite12@yahoo.com
(901)377-7776 GRWT#9110
Whitworth, Gary W (M1)
1706 Old Hickory Boulevard
Brentwood, TN 37027
garywwhitworth@att.net
(270)525-6311 TNNA#7300
Whray, Richard "Rocky" (M1)
201 8th Avenue SE
Winchester, TN 37398
rocklex1017@att.net
(931)636-4844 TNMU#7211
Wieland, Jack G Jr (M1)
PO Box 116
Napoleon, MO 64074
jgwieland@hotmail.com
(217)823-4331 GRMI#4100
Wiggins, Joe (M1)
2734 US Highway 41A S
Eagleville, TN 37060
(615)274-2011 TNCO#7109
Wilborn, Kimberley (M3)
4743 Happy Hollow Road
Hawesville, KY 42348
(270)927-9577 MICU#3204
Wilkerson, Patrick (M1)
3419 Jaydens Nest Way Apt 202
Powell, TN 37849
patrickwilkerson3@gmail.com
(865)617-9126 MICO#3400
Wilkinson, Michael (M1)
3515 Highway 14
Millbrook, AL 36054
FAX: (334)285-4640
mwilkinson1@elmore.rr.com
(205)533-2001 SEET#2305
Williams, Bobby D (M1)
844 W Highway 22
Union City, TN 38261
(731)885-1710 GRWT#9402
Williams, Cory (M1)
3148 Long Bridge Lane
Arlington, TN 38002
coromis@hotmail.com

(901)486-5981 GRWT#9302
Williams, Dale (M1)
3156 State Route 2837
Clay, KY 42404
dalewilliams@roadrunner.com
(270)664-2044 MICO#3618
Williams, David J (M1)
20 Acorn Drive
Harrisburg, IL 629463790
(618)252-1851 MICO#3400
Williams, James A (M3)
1475 Kings Road
Marshall, TX 75672
(903)938-7345 MSTR#8100
Williamson, Dave (M1)
PO Box 67
Dolph, AR 72528
(870)499-7448 GRAR#1513
Wills, Brent (M1)
4607 E Richmond Shop Road
Lebanon, TN 37090
bwills9185@yahoo.com
(615)449-3258 TNMU#7218
Wilson, Brenda (M1)
35 Collins Drive
Elizabethtown, KY 42701
susieq2007@windstream.net
(270)249-3835 MICU#3211
Wilson, Craig (M1)
2300 Frayser Boulevard
Memphis, TN 38127
craigwilson2300@yahoo.com
(901)277-4066 GRWT#9306
Wilson, Don (M1)
7300 Calle Montana NE
Albuquerque, NM 87113
don-wilson07@comcast.net
(505)823-2594 MSDC#8700
Wilson, James (M1)
2449 Sardis Airport Road
Addison, AL 35540
(256)338-0095 SEGR#0100
Wilson, Kevin (M1)
2225 North East Road SE
Cleveland, TN 37311
revkev1000@hotmail.com
(423)284-6397 SETG#2112
Wilson, Melissa (M3)
107 Hillwood Drive
Dickson, TN 37055
milzwilz@comcast.net
(615)446-7523 TNNA#7300
Wilson, Thomas (M1)
4543 Lake Vista
Memphis, TN 38128
tomjw217@gmail.com
(901)382-6190 GRWT#9100
Wing So, Patrick Tat (M1)
2/F Fu Tung Shopping Centre
Tung Chung
Lantau Island, HONG KONG
FAX: (852)2109-1737
cpctwso@yahoo.com.hk
(522)109-1738 MSHK#8810
Winn, Don (M1)
3655 Highway 49 E
Charlotte, TN 37036
dwinn@davidsonacademy.com
(615)789-5916 TNNA#7320
Winslett, Don (M1)
Baptist Hosp/Pastoral Care
1000 W Moreno Street
Pensacola, FL 32521
( ) MSTR#8100
Womack, Carey (M1)
114 Doris Street

MINISTERS CONTINUED

Camden, TN 38320
camdencppastor@bellsouth.net
(731)220-3900   GRWT#9105
Wong, Apple   (M3)
G/F & 1/F 251 Tin Sum Village Tai Wai
Shatin NT, HONG KONG
FAX: (852)2607-2245
yunnan_apple@yahoo.com
(852)2693-3444   MSHK#8800
Wong, Bruce   (M1)
822 Sunnyarbor Court
Campbell, CA 95008
revbwong@gmail.com
(408)628-4643   MSDC#8700
Wong, Samson   (M2)
CPC Yao Dao Primary School
Tin Yuet Estate
Tin Shui Wai, NT, HONG KONG
FAX: (852)2617-0287
wongchishui@yahoo.com.hk
(852)2617-7872   MSHK#8800
Wong, So Li   (M2)
2/F Fu Tung Shopping Centre
Tung Chung, Lantau Island
HONG KONG
FAX: (852)2109-1737
soliwong@gmail.com
(852)2109-1738   MSHK#8800
Wong, Yim Ngar   (M2)
Wing B&C, G/F, Ming Wik House
Kin Ming Estate
Tseung Kwan O,NT, HONG KONG
FAX: (852)2706-0114
yimngar@yahoo.com.hk
(852)2706-0111   MSHK#8808
Wood, Bennie R   (M1)
3697 S Mount Juliet Road
Hermitage, TN 37076
(615)449-8651   TNMU#7200
Wood, Kevin L   (M1)
1116 Park Hill Circle
Knoxville, TN 37909
FAX: (865)588-8581
revkev7285@earthlink.net
(865)588-8581   SEET#2200
Wood, Wayne   (M1)
HC 61 Box 600
Calico Rock, AR 72519
FAX: (870)297-3151
bexarwood@centurytel.net
(870)297-2205   GRAR#1100
Woodliff, George   (M1)
310 W Cleveland Street Apt A3
Prairie Grove, AR 72956
mwoodliff@kih.net
(479)410-1933   GRAR#1412
Wooten, Wallace   (M1)
1152 Melrose Road
Lockesburg, AR 71846
(870)289-2224   GRAR#1100
Wright, B J   (M1)
301 25th Street
Phenix City, AL 36867
bojobo3@yahoo.com
(334)298-2896   SETG#2100
Wright, John   (M3)
( )   TNMU#7200
Wright, Tim   (M3)
165 Quaker Knob Road
Chuckey, TN 37641
tdwright1123@yahoo.com
(423)639-0634   SEET#2200

--==<< X >>==--

--==<< Y >>==--

Yang, Buhwan   (M1)
19 Taylors Run
Tinton Falls, NJ 07712
yangmoksa@gmail.com
(732)458-2203   SECE#2131
Yano, Fumitsuta   (M1)
424-4 Kamide, Fjinomiya-shi
Shuizuika-ken JAPAN
(054)454-0313   MSJA#8300
Yaple, George H   (M1)
2051 Lost Creek Road
Carbon Hill, AL 35549
(205)924-9921   SEHO#0500
Yarce, Janeth   (M1)
3019 W Calavar Road
Phoenix, AZ 85053
janethyarce@yahoo.com
(630)518-0295   MINC#5200
Yarce, Omar   (M1)
10925 Neptune Drive
Cooper City, FL 33026
alphavida@gmail.com
(205)919-9685   SEGR#0100
Yarce, Virginia   (M3)
10925 Neptune Drive
Cooper City, FL 33026
ginnyyarce@gmail.com
(205)919-9685   SEGR#0100
Yates, Scott   (M1)
8818 New Town Road
Rockvale, TN 37153
scott@scottyates.net
(615)274-3000   TNCO#7141
Yau, Chat Ming   (M2)
G/F 251 Tin Sam Village
Shatin, NT, HONG KONG
FAX: (852)2607-2245
summerycm@yahoo.com.hk
(852)2693-3444   MSHK#8800
Yau, Eliza Yuk Lan Chui   (M2)
14-16 TsatTsz Mui Road
1/Fl Block B North Point
HONG KONG
FAX: (852)2564-2898
elizaylyau@yahoo.com.hk
(852)2562-2148   MSHK#8805
Yeung, William Kin Keung   (M1)
28 Hong Yip Street
Yuen Long, HONG KONG
FAX: (852)263-9562
william@xilincpc.org.hk
(852)2639-9176   MSHK#8809
Yi, Woo Young   (M1)
(IN JAPAN)
( )   SETG#2100
Yoo, Paul   (M1)
(IN KOREA)
sungyy@msn.com
( )   SETG#2100
York, Danny   (M1)
5420 State Route 902
Fredonia, KY 42411
nonnieyork@yahoo.com
(270)350-7262   MICO#3413
Young, Taylor   (M3)
255 Willard Drive
Nashville, TN 37211
brandontayloryoung@yahoo.com
(615)319-8294   TNNA#7300
Youngman, Betty   (M1)
1471 Creekview Court
Fort Worth, TX 76112

bettyy@swbell.net
(817)492-4100   MSRR#8400
Yu, Alexis   (M1)
1761 Willow Way
San Bruno, CA 94066
alexis.yu.k@gmail.com
(415)421-1624   MSDC#8501
Yu, Carver Tat Sum   (M1)
2/F Welland Plaza
188 Nam Cheong Street
Sham Shui Po, Kowloon, HONG KONG
FAX: (852)2771-2726
carver.yu@cgst.edu
(852)2794-2382   MSHK#8800
Yu, Grace Siu Tim   (M1)
2/F Welland Plaza
188 Nam Cheong Street
Sham Shui Po, Kowloon, HONG KONG
FAX: (852)2771-2726
yuleungsiutim@netvigator.com
(852)2783-8923   MSHK#8800
Yu, Pyong San (Sonny)   (M1)
139 Silverado Drive
Santa Teresa, NM 88008
pyongsanyu@hotmail.com
(915)329-3451   MSDC#8700
Yu, Wn-yong   (M1)
325-1 DongHyen-Dong
Jecheon-city, Choongbuk, KOREA
lifeyu@hanmail.net
(043)652-0540   SEET#2200
Yuen, Amos Pui Chung   (M1)
2/F Welland Plaza
188 Nam Cheong Street
Sham Shui Po, Kowloon, HONG KONG
FAX: (852)2771-2726
revyuen@taohsien.org.hk
(852)2783-8923   MSHK#8806
Yuen, Susanna   (M3)
28 Hong Yip Street
28 Hong Yip Street
Yuen Long, NT, HONG KONG
FAX: (522)639-5620
susanna@yuenlongcpc.org
(522)639-9176   MSHK#8800
Yung, Karen   (M2)
Flat D, 2/F
338-340 Castle Peak Road
Kowloon, HONG KONG
FAX: (852)3020-0365
(852)2386-6563   MSHK#8803

--==<< Z >>==--

Zumbrunnen, Craig   (M1)
1210 Country Club Road Apt 3
Santa Teresa, NM 88008
craigzum1@yahoo.com
(580)471-0308   MSRR#8400

ALPHABETICAL INDEX OF CHURCHES

The four letter abbreviation indicates the synod and presbytery of which the congregation
is a member. The four digit number indicates the church number.
(See pages 10-12 for abbreviations of presbyteries.)

--==<<A>>==--

Alabaster
    AL Alabaster .... SERD#0107
Algood
    TN Algood.....................TNMU#7201
Allsboro
    AL Cherokee .... SEHO#0501
Antioch
    AL Reform .... .SEGR#0701
    KY Knob Lick................... MICU#3101
    LA Quitman .... MSTR#8101
Antioch Union
    TN Union City .... GRWT#9401
Appleton
    AR Atkins........................ .GRAR#1202
Arkansas Loving
    AR Little Rock .... GRAR#2135
Arlington
    TN Erin ....TNNA#7311
Armenia
    CO Quindio .... MSAN#8903
Asahi Mission Point
    JA 241-0021 .... MSJA#8315
Ash Hill
    TN Spring Hill ....TNCO#7101
Atwood
    TN Atwood.....................GRWT#9101
Auburn
    KY Auburn....................... .MICU#3301
Austin, First
    TX Austin..........................MSTR#8601

--==<<B>>==--

Bald Knob
    KY Russellville .... MICU#3302
Baldwin Chapel
    AL Cullman....................... SEHO#0202
Banks
    TN Smithville....................TNMU#7202
Barren Fork
    AR Mount Pleasant .... GRAR#1501
Barren Springs
    TN Hollow Rock...............GRWT#9102
Bartow
    GA Rydal.............................SETG#2101
Bates Hill
    TN McMinnville ....TNMU#7203
Bayou de Chien
    KY Water Valley .... MICO#3401
Beaver Creek
    TN Knoxville .... SEET#2301
Beech
    TN Hendersonville............ TNNA#7301
    TN Union City .... GRWT#9402
Beech Grove
    TN Beechgrove ....TNMU#7204
Beersheba
    MS Columbus .... SEGR#0702
Belleview
    TN Franklin.......................TNCO#7104
Bells Chapel
    TN Dyer ....GRWT#9403
Belvidere
    TN Belvidere....................TNMU#7205

Ben Lomond
    AR Ben Lomond .... GRAR#1301
Benton
    KY Benton .... .MICO#3403
Bertram
    TX Bertram ....MSTR#8605
Betania Mission
    CO Cali .... .MSCA#8204
Bethany
    IL Bethany........................ MINC#5401
Bethel
    CO Cali .... .MSCA#8205
    KY Center .... .MICU#3102
    KY Kevil .... MICO#3404
    MO Wentworth .... GRMI#4102
    TN Atoka........................GRWT#9301
    TN Clarksville.................. TNNA#7302
Bethel #1
    KY Harrodsburg............... MICU#3103
Bethesda
    AR Camden..................... .GRAR#1302
    TN Fall Branch................... SEET#2201
    TN Friendship ....GRWT#9404
Bethlehem
    TN Union City .... GRWT#9405
Beulah
    KY Hartford .... MICU#3501
Big Cove
    AL Brownsboro................. SERD#0801
Blues Hill
    TN McMinnville ....TNMU#7207
Boiling Springs
    TN Portland...................... MICU#3303
Bolivar
    TN Bolivar ....GRWT#9202
Booneville
    AR Booneville.................. GRAR#1401
Boonshill
    TN Boonshill....................TNCO#7106
Bowling Green
    KY Bowling Green .... MICU#3304
Bradford
    TN Bradford.....................GRWT#9104
Branchville
    AL Odenville..................... SEGR#0106
Brenthaven
    TN Brentwood.................. TNNA#7331
Bridgeport 1st
    PA Bridgeport.....................MICU#3131
Brier Creek
    KY Bremen .... .MICU#3503
Brunswick
    TN Brunswick.................. GRWT#9302
Brush Hill
    TN Nashville..................... TNNA#7325
Burns Flat
    OK Burns Flat.................. MSRR#6301
Burnt Prairie
    IL Burnt Prairie .... MINC#5102
Byron
    AR Calico Rock .... GRAR#1508

--==<<C>>==--

Cairo
    MS Cedarbluff.................. SEGR#0704

Caleb Mission
    CO Montebello.................. MSCA#8223
Calico Rock
    AR Calico Rock .... GRAR#1503
Calvary
    KY Mayfield .... MICO#3405
    TN Clarksville.................. TNNA#7342
Camden
    AR Camden..................... GRAR#1303
    TN Camden ....GRWT#9105
Camp Ground
    AR Hampton ....GRAR#1101
    IL Anna .... MICO#5103
    TN Decaturville.................GRWT#9204
    TN Erin .... TNNA#7312
Campbellsville
    KY Campbellsville............. MICU#3104
Campground
    IL Greenville .... MINC#5402
Cane Ridge
    TN Cane Ridge................. TNNA#7326
Caneyville
    KY Caneyville................... MICU#3201
Cartago
    CO Valle........................MSAN#8906
Casa De Fe
    MA Malden .... SEET#2220
Casey
    IL Casey .... MINC#5201
Casey's Fork
    KY Marrowbone .... MICU#3105
Caulksville
    AR Ratcliff...................... GRAR#1402
Cedar Flat
    KY Edmonton .... MICU#3106
Cedar Hill
    TN Greeneville.................. SEET#2202
Cedar Springs
    TN Whitwell ....SETG#2119
Central
    CO Cali .... MSCA#8208
Champ
    TN Mulberry ....TNCO#7108
Chandler
    IN Chandler...................... MICO#5302
Chapel Hill
    TN Chapel Hill...................TNCO#7109
Charleston
    TN Cleveland ....SETG#2102
Charlotte
    TN Charlotte .... TNNA#7303
Chattanooga 1st
    TN Chattanooga ....SETG#2104
Cheung Chau
    HO Cheung Chau.............. MSHK#8801
Chinese
    CA San Francisco.............. MSDC#8501
Christ
    FL Lutz............................. SEGR#0303
    IN Indianapolis.................. MINC#5305
Christ Church
    AL Huntsville.................... SERD#0814
Clark's Grove
    TN Maryville..................... SEET#2302
Clarksville
    TN Clarksville.................. TNNA#7304

ALPHABETICAL INDEX OF CHURCHES CONTINUED

Claybrook
  TN Jackson.........................GRWT#9205
Clear Point
  KY Horse Cave ....MICU#3107
Cleveland
  TN Cleveland.....................SETG#2108
Clifton Mills
  KY Irvington ....MICU#3202
Clinton
  OK Clinton.......................MSRR#6302
Cloverdale
  TN Obion ....GRWT#9407
Cloyd's
  TN Mt Juliet....................TNMU#7208
Coal Creek
  OK Coalgate.....................MSCH#6102
Coker
  AL Coker.........................SEGR#0705
Colonial
  TN Memphis ....GRWT#9305
Columbia 1st
  TN Columbia......................TNCO#7110
Columbus
  MS Columbus ....SEGR#0706
Commerce
  TN Watertown...................TNMU#7209
Comunidad Cristiana
  IL Dundee ....MINC#5212
Concord
  AL New Market ....SERD#0802
  TN Trenton........................GRWT#9106
  TN Waverly ....TNNA#7306
  TX Troup............................MSTR#8104
Cookeville 1st
  TN Cookeville...................TNMU#7210
Cool Springs CC
  TN Lavinia ....GRWT#9107
Cool Springs GC
  TN Trimble........................GRWT#9408
Cornerstone Community
  TN Chattanooga.................SETG#2107
Corntassel
  TN Madisonville ....SEET#2304
Covenant
  OK Ada ....MSRR#6304
Cowan
  TN Cowan.........................TNMU#7211
Coyle
  KY Hudson ....MICU#3203
Crestline
  AL Birmingham ....SEGR#0102
Cristo Vive
  TN Madison ....TNNA#7314
Cumberland Chapel
  IL Fairfield ....MINC#5104
Cumberland Valley
  TN McEwen......................TNNA#7307

--==<<D>>==--

Daingerfield
  TX Daingerfield ....MSTR#8106
Davidson Chapel
  TN Trenton........................GRWT#9108
Den-en Mission
  JA 228-0818 ....MSJA#8310
Denton
  TX Denton.........................MSRR#8404
Desert Gardens
  AZ Tucson.........................MSDC#8705
Dibrell
  TN McMinnville ....TNMU#7212

Dickson
  TN Dickson .... TNNA#7308
Dilworth
  AR Horatio .... GRAR#1304
Divino Redentor
  CO Buenaventura.............. MSCA#8206
Donelson
  TN Nashville .... TNNA#7327
Dosquebradas
  CO Risaralda..................... MSAN#8907
Double Springs
  TN Humboldt ....GRWT#9109
Dover
  AR Dover .... GRAR#1203
  TN Morristown ....SEET#2203
Dresden
  TN Dresden ....GRWT#9110
Dry Fork
  TN Bethpage .... TNNA#7309
Dry Valley
  TN Cookeville...................TNMU#7213
Dukes
  KY Hawesville.................. MICU#3204
Dyer
  TN Dyer ....GRWT#9409
Dyersburg 1st
  TN Dyersburg ....GRWT#9410

--==<<E>>==--

E T Allen
  AR Ashdown .... GRAR#1307
East Point
  AL Cullman....................... SERD#0206
Eastlake
  OK Oklahoma City .... MSRR#6205
Ebenezer
  IL Chicago.........................MINC#5203
  IL Thompsonville...............MICO#5105
  TN Mason ....GRWT#9303
  TN Mercer.........................GRWT#9206
  TN Whitwell ....SETG#2110
Ebenezer Hall
  IL Buncombe.....................MICO#5106
Ebina Shion No Oka
  JA 243-0422 ....MSJA#8311
Edgefield
  AL Stevenson .... SERD#0813
Eidson Chapel
  AL Holly Pond .... SERD#0207
El Camino
  FL Miami .... SEGR#0310
El Paso 1st
  TX El Paso ....MSDC#8704
El Rebano
  CO Antioquia ....MSAN#8905
El Redil
  GA Lawrenceville ....SETG#2149
Elk Creek
  MO West Plains .... GRMI#4304
Elm River
  IL Cisne............................MINC#5107
Elmira Chapel
  TX Longview ....MSTR#8111
Elora
  TN Elora............................TNCO#7111
Emaus
  CO Buenaventura.............. MSCA#8219
Enon
  MS Ackerman .... SEGR#0707
Ephesus
  KY Harned ....MICU#3205

Erin
  MS Union.......................... SEGR#0601
  TN Erin .... TNNA#7310

--==<<F>>==--

Fairfield
  IL Fairfield ....MINC#5108
Fairview
  KY Bremen .... MICU#3504
  TN Afton ....SEET#2204
Faith
  AL Cullman.......................SEHO#0213
  MI St Clair Shores ....MINC#5501
  OK Tulsa ....MSRR#6201
  TN Bartlett ....GRWT#9308
Faith Fellowship
  TN Lenoir City..................SEET#2319
Faith-Hopewell
  AR Batesville .... GRAR#1502
Falling Water
  TN Hixson.........................SETG#2111
Falls Chapel
  AR Lockesburg .... GRAR#1308
Fayetteville
  TN Fayetteville ....TNCO#7112
Fellowship
  AR Camden....................... GRAR#1309
  AR Mountain Home.......... GRAR#1505
Fiducia
  TN Prospect.......................TNCO#7113
Filipos
  CO Cali .... MSCA#8211
First Hispanic
  FL Tampa .... SEGR#0307
Flat Lick
  KY Herndon ....MICO#3606
Flint Springs
  TN Cleveland ....SETG#2112
Flintville
  TN Flintville.....................TNCO#7115
Florence 1st
  AL Florence.......................SEHO#0506
Fomby
  AR Ashdown .... GRAR#1310
Forrest Avenue
  AL Gadsden.......................SEGR#0403
Fort Smith
  AR Fort Smith................... GRAR#1406
Franklin
  TN Franklin.......................TNCO#7116
Fredonia
  KY Fredonia......................MICO#3608
Freeport
  TX Freeport.......................MSTR#8103
Freedom
  KY Harned ....MICU#3207
Fullerton
  IL Farmer City ....MINC#5404
Fulton
  TN South Fulton...............GRWT#9412

--==<<G>>==--

Gadsden
  AL Gadsden.......................SEGR#0402
Garfield
  KY Garfield.......................MICU#3208
Gasper River
  KY Auburn ....MICU#3306
Gass Memorial
  TN Greeneville...................SEET#2205

ALPHABETICAL INDEX OF CHURCHES CONTINUED

Georgetown
 IL Georgetown .... MINC#5204
Germantown
 TN Germantown .... GRWT#9310
Getsemani
 CO El Cerrito .... MSCA#8210
Gilead
 IL Simpson .... MICO#5110
Gill's Chapel
 KY Guthrie........................ MICU#3307
Glasgow
 KY Glasgow...................... MICU#3108
Gleason
 TN Gleason .... GRWT#9111
Glencoe
 AL Glencoe .... SEGR#0404
Glory Church of Jesus Christ
 GA Duluth............................ SETG#2144
Good Hope
 KY Campbellsville............. MICU#3109
Good Prospect
 IL Trilla .... MINC#5205
Good Spring
 KY Fredonia...................... MICO#3609
 TN Dukedom..................... GRWT#9112
Goodlettsville
 TN Goodlettsville.............. TNNA#7328
Goosepond
 AL Scottsboro .... SERD#0803
Goshen
 TN Winchester .... TNMU#7214
Grace
 AR Fayetteville .... GRAR#1405
 CA San Francisco.............. MSDC#8510
 MI Lincoln Park................ MINC#5502
 TN Franklin......................TNCO#7145
Grace Community
 AL Millbrook .... SEGR#0407
Green Hill
 TN Bell Buckle ....TNCO#7118
Green Ridge
 KY Lewisburg.................... MICU#3308
Greeneville
 TN Greeneville................... SEET#2206
Greenfield
 MO Greenfield .... GRMI#4104
Greens Chapel
 AL Cleveland .... SEGR#0208
Greensburg
 KY Greensburg .... MICU#3110
Greenville
 KY Greenville.................... MICU#3505
Groverton
 MS Morton........................ SEGR#0602
Gum Creek
 TN Winchester ....TNMU#7215
Gum Springs
 AR Dardanelle................... GRAR#1206
 AR Searcy .... GRAR#1205
Gurley
 AL Gurley .... SERD#0804

--==<<H>>==--

Halls Creek
 TN Waverly...................... TNNA#7313
Happy Home
 MO Conway...................... GRMI#4306
Harmony
 MO San Antonio .... GRMI#4203
 TN Winchester ....TNMU#7216
Harpeth Lick

TN College Grove............. TNCO#7119
Harrodsburg
 KY Harrodsburg............... MICU#3111
Heartland
 Lenoir City .... SEET#2306
Heartsong
 KY Louisville.................... MICU#3222
Hector
 AR Hector .... GRAR#1207
Heights
 NM Albuquerque .... MSDC#8701
Helena
 AL Helena .... SEGR#0108
Hendersonville
 TN Hendersonville............ TNNA#7340
Hickory Grove
 AL Moulton....................... SEHO#0507
Hickory Valley
 TN Sparta ....TNMU#7251
Higashi Koganei
 JA 184-0011 .... MSJA#8301
High Point Community
 KY West Somerset .... MICU#3314
Highland
 KY Paducah .... MICO#3414
Hillsboro
 TN Hillsboro ....TNMU#7217
Hohenwald
 TN Hohenwald...................TNCO#7120
Holly Grove
 AL Princeton .... SERD#0805
 TN Brighton .... GRWT#9304
Homewood
 AL Homewood...................SEGR#0111
Hope
 AL Huntsville.................... SERD#0812
 FL Valrico.......................... SEGR#0308
Hope Korean
 NJ Tinton Falls...................SECE#2131
Hopewell
 AL Bessemer...................... SEGR#0101
 KY Canmer .... MICU#3112
 KY Salem .... MICO#3610
 MS Walnut .... GRWT#9207
 MO Lamar......................... GRMI#4105
 TN Sharon .... GRWT#9115
Hopkinsville
 KY Hopkinsville .... MICU#3611
Horeb-Central
 CO Antioquia .... MSAN#8915
House of Prayer
 AL Cullman....................... SEGR#0214
Houston 1st
 TX Houston.......................MSTR#8606
Howell
 TN Fayetteville ....TNCO#7121
Hubbard
 TX Hubbard .... MSRR#8410
Hueytown 1st
 AL Hueytown..................... SEGR#0109
Humboldt
 TN Humboldt.................... GRWT#9116
Huntsville 1st
 AL Huntsville .... SERD#0806
Hurricane
 AL Rogersville .... SEHO#0508
Hurricane Hill
 TN Newburn .... GRWT#9413

--==<<I>>==--

Ichikawa Grace Mission Point

JA 272-0834 .... MSJA#8314
Immanuel
 FL Dade City..................... SEGR#0311
Irvington
 KY Irvington .... MICU#3210
Izumi Mission
 JA 245-0016 .... MSJA#8312

--==<<J>>==--

Jackson 1st
 TN Jackson....................... GRWT#9208
Jasper
 TN Jasper .... SETG#2113
Jefferson
 TX Jefferson......................MSTR#8109
Jenkins
 TN Nolensville...................TNCO#7144
Jerusalem
 TN Murfreesboro ....TNMU#7218
Joywood
 TN Murfreesboro ....TNMU#7250

--==<<K>>==--

Kelly's Chapel
 TN Whitwell .... SETG#2120
Kelso
 TN Kelso............................TNCO#7122
Kenton
 TN Kenton......................... GRWT#9414
Kibougaoka
 JA 241-0825 .... MSJA#8302
Kingdom
 TN Unionville ....TNCO#7123
Knights Chapel
 IN Petersburg .... MINC#5306
Knoxville
 TN Knoxville .... SEET#2305
Korea 1st
 KO South Korea................. SEET#2221
Korean
 TN Cordova....................... GRWT#9322
Korean Living Stone
 GA Duluth.......................... SETG#2130
Kowloon Chapel
 HO Kowloon..................... MSHK#8803
Koza
 JA 242-0006 .... MSJA#8303
Kunitachi Nozomi
 JA 186-0002...................... MSJA#8306

--==<<L>>==--

La Rosa De Saron
 CO Antioquia .... MSAN#8911
La Virginia
 CO Risaralda..................... MSAN#8913
LaGuardo
 TN Lebanon ....TNMU#7219
Lake Hamilton
 AR Hot Springs................. GRAR#1221
Lake Highlands
 TX Dallas ....MSRR#8411
Lawrenceburg
 TN Lawrenceburg ....TNCO#7124
Lebanon
 TN Jefferson City............... SEET#2207
 TN Lebanon ....TNMU#7220
Lebanon North
 IL Fairfield .... MINC#5113
Lebanon South

ALPHABETICAL INDEX OF CHURCHES CONTINUED

ALPHABETICAL INDEX OF CHURCHES CONTINUED

HO Landau Island .... MSHK#8810
Murfreesboro
   TN Murfreesboro .... TNMU#7232

--==<<N>>==--

Naruse
   JA 194-0041 .... MSJA#8305
Neal's Chapel
   KY Glasgow...................... MICU#3122
Nebo
   AL Lexington .... SEHO#0512
Needham
   KY Eastview .... MICU#3219
New Beginnings
   TN Memphis .... GRWT#9306
New Bethel
   TN Columbia.................... TNCO#7134
   TN Greeneville.................. SEET#2210
   TN Selmer....................... GRWT#9215
New Bethlehem
   TN Newbern..................... GRWT#9420
New Cypress
   KY Rumsey....................... MICU#3508
New Ebenezer
   TN Troy........................... GRWT#9422
New Hope
   AL Birmingham .... SEGR#0104
   AR Batesville .... GRAR#1510
   IL Yale............................. MINC#5208
   KY Paducah .... MICO#3410
   MO Salem .... GRMI#4309
   TN Lebanon .... TNMU#7233
   TN Madisonville .... SEET#2311
   TN Stewart .... TNNA#7337
   TN Whitwell .... SETG#2115
New Providence
   TN Clarksville.................. TNNA#7305
New Salem
   TN Bethel Springs............. GRWT#9216
   TN Lakeland .... GRWT#9316
   TN Sharon....................... GRWT#9124
Newbern
   TN Newbern..................... GRWT#9419
Newberry
   TX Millsap .... MSRR#8415
North Pleasant Grove
   KY Murray....................... MICO#3411
North Point Chapel
   HO North Point................. MSHK#8805
North Union
   TN Kenton....................... GRWT#9423
Northminster
   TX San Antonio .... MSTR#8610
Nueva Esperanza
   CO Cali .... MSCA#8221
Nueva Jerusalen
   CO Cali .... MSCA#8222
Nueva Vida
   TX Houston...................... MSTR#8612
Nuevo Empezar.................. GRWT#9324
   TN Memphis

--==<<O>>==--

Oak Forest
   KY Summersville............... MICU#3123
Oak Grove
   KY Benton .... MICO#3412
   MO Springfield .... GRMI#4310
   TN Henderson................... GRWT#9217
   TN Whitwell .... SETG#2121

TX Georgetown................... MSTR#8607
Oak Grove Union
   KY Clay .... MICO#3619
Oak Hill
   TN Paris .... GRWT#9125
Oak Ridge
   TN Oak Ridge .... SEET#2313
Oakland
   KY Calvert City .... MICO#3413
   TN Telford......................... SEET#2211
Old Mt Bethel
   AL Rogersville .... SEHO#0513
Old Union
   AR Magazine .... GRAR#1409
Old Zion
   TN Sparta .... TNMU#7234
Oldham Chapel
   AL Ashville .... SEGR#0405
Olive Branch
   MS Olive Branch .... GRWT#9312
Oliver Springs
   TN Oliver Springs............... SEET#2314
Oliver's Chapel
   TN Bradford..................... GRWT#9127
Olivet
   TN Savannah..................... GRWT#9220
Olney
   TX Olney.......................... MSRR#8416
One Way
   NY Flushing...................... SECE#2137
Orange
   MO Aurora .... GRMI#4108
Our Good
   MD Salisbury..................... SETG#2138
Owens Chapel
   TN Winchester .... TNMU#7235
Owensboro
   KY Owensboro .... MICU#3509
Oxford
   AR Oxford.......................... GRAR#1511

--==<<P>>==--

Palestine
   AR Palestine..................... GRAR#1103
   TN Lexington.................... GRWT#9221
   TN Newbern..................... GRWT#9424
Panki Bok
   OK Eagletown................... MSCH#6108
Park Terrace
   AL Sheffield .... SEHO#0514
Parsons 1st
   TN Parsons....................... GRWT#9222
Pereira
   CO Risaralda.................... MSAN#8916
Petersburg
   TN Petersburg .... TNCO#7135
Philadelphia
   TN Limestone .... SEET#2212
Phillipsburg
   MO Phillipsburg................. GRMI#4311
Piedmont
   AL Piedmont .... SEGR#0406
Pierson
   MO Martinville .... GRMI#4312
Pigeon Roost
   OK Atoka .... MSCH#6109
Pilot Knob
   TN Bulls Gap .... SEET#2213
Pilot Prairie
   AR Waldron....................... GRAR#1411
Pine Bluff 1st

AR Pine Bluff.................. GRAR#1104
Pine Hill
   TN McDonald .... SETG#2117
   TX Winnsboro.................... MSTR#8122
Pine Ridge
   AR Grapevine.................... GRAR#1105
Pine Tree
   TX Longview .... MSTR#8113
Pineville
   AR Pineville .... GRAR#1512
Piney Fork
   KY Marion .... MICO#3620
Pleasant Green
   TN Atwood....................... GRWT#9129
Pleasant Grove
   AR Searcy .... GRAR#1214
   IL Annapolis.................... MINC#5210
   MO Knob Noster.............. GRMI#4109
   TN Moscow...................... GRWT#9317
Pleasant Hill
   AL Bessember .... SEGR#0710
   KY Owensboro .... MICU#3510
   TN Chuckey .... SEET#2214
Pleasant Mount
   TN Columbia.................... TNCO#7136
Pleasant Union
   TN Millington .... GRWT#9318
Pleasant Vale
   TN Chuckey .... SEET#2215
Pleasant Valley
   KY Kevil .... MICO#3418
Po Lam
   HO Tseung Kwan O,NT.... MSHK#8808
Point Pleasant
   KY Beaver Dam................. MICU#3313
Popayan
   CO Popayan .... MSCA#8227
Poplar Grove
   KY Sacramento .... MICU#3511
   TN Halls.......................... GRWT#9425
Prairie Grove
   AR Prairie Grove.............. GRAR#1412
Principe De Paz
   CO Cali .... MSCA#8201
Progress
   LA Pleasant Hill................. MSTR#8123
Prospect United
   TN Cleveland.................... SETG#2116
Protemus
   TN Troy........................... GRWT#9426
Providence
   IL Carriers Mills................ MICO#5122
   TN Hartsville................... TNMU#7238
Providence 1st
   KY Providence .... MICO#3621
Provo
   AR Lockesburg .... GRAR#1314

--==<<Q>>==--

--==<<R>>==--

Radcliff
   KY Radcliff....................... MICU#3220
Ramer
   TN Ramer......................... GRWT#9223
Red Bank
   TN Chattanooga .... SETG#2105
Redeemer
   CA San Francisco............... MSDC#8512
Renacer
   CO Cali .... MSCA#8225

ALPHABETICAL INDEX OF CHURCHES CONTINUED

ALPHABETICAL INDEX OF CHURCHES CONTINUED

LOCATION INDEX OF CHURCHES

The four letter abbreviation indicates the synod and presbytery of which the congregation
is a member. The four digit number indicates the church number.
(See pages 10-13 for abbreviations of presbyteries.)

ALABAMA

AL Alabaster
  Alabaster .... SERD#0107
AL Anderson
  Union Hill .... SEHO#0516
AL Ashville
  Oldham Chapel .... SEGR#0405
AL Bessemer
  Hopewell .... SEGR#0101
  Pleasant Hill .... SEGR#0710
AL Birmingham
  Crestline .... SEGR#0102
  New Hope .... SEGR#0104
  Roca De Salvacion .... SEGR#0115
  Rocky Ridge .... SEGR#0105
AL Brownsboro
  Big Cove .... SERD#0801
AL Cherokee
  Allsboro .... SEHO#0501
  Maud .... SEHO#0509
  Mt. Hester .... SEHO#0510
AL Cleveland
  Greens Chapel .... SEGR#0208
AL Coker
  Coker .... SEGR#0705
AL Cullman
  Baldwin Chapel .... SEHO#0202
  East Point .... SERD#0206
  Faith .... SEHO#0213
  House of Prayer .... SEGR#0214
  Welti .... SEHO#0212
AL Florence
  Florence 1st .... SEHO#0506
AL Gadsden
  Gadsden .... SEGR#0402
  Forrest Avenue .... SEGR#0403
AL Glencoe
  Glencoe .... SEGR#0404
AL Gurley
  Gurley .... SERD#0804
AL Helena
  Helena .... SEGR#0108
AL Holly Pond
  Eidson Chapel .... SERD#0207
  Union Grove .... SERD#0211
AL Homewood
  Homewood .... SEGR#0111
AL Hueytown
  Hueytown 1st .... SEGR#0109
AL Huntsville
  Christ Church .... SERD#0814
  Hope .... SERD#0812
  Huntsville 1st .... SERD#0806
AL Lexington
  Nebo .... SEHO#0512
AL Meridianville
  Meridianville .... SERD#0808
AL Millbrook
  Grace Community .... SEGR#0407
AL Montevallo
  Spring Creek .... SEGR#0113
AL Moulton
  Hickory Grove .... SEHO#0507
AL Muscle Shoals
  Mt. Pleasant .... SEHO#0511
AL New Hope
  Walnut Grove .... SERD#0811

AL New Market
  Concord .... SERD#0802
AL Odenville
  Branchville .... SEGR#0106
AL Piedmont
  Piedmont .... SEGR#0406
AL Princeton
  Holly Grove .... SERD#0805
AL Reform
  Antioch .... SEGR#0701
AL Rogersville
  Hurricane .... SEHO#0508
  Old Mt Bethel .... SEHO#0513
  Rogersville 1st .... SEHO#0517
  Springfield .... SEHO#0515
AL Scottsboro
  Goosepond .... SERD#0803
  Scottsboro .... SERD#0809
AL Sheffield
  Park Terrace .... SEHO#0514
AL Stevenson
  Edgefield .... SERD#0813
  Stevenson .... SERD#0810
AL Vance
  Union .... SEGR#0114

ARIZONA

AZ Tucson
  Desert Gardens .... MIDC#8705

ARKANSAS

AR Ashdown
  E T Allen .... GRAR#1307
  Fomby .... GRAR#1310
AR Atkins
  Appleton .... GRAR#1202
AR Batesville
  Faith-Hopewell .... GRAR#1502
  New Hope .... GRAR#1510
  Sidney .... GRAR#1515
AR Ben Lomond
  Ben Lomond .... GRAR#1301
AR Booneville
  Booneville .... GRAR#1401
  Lucas Community .... GRAR#1407
AR Calico Rock
  Byron .... GRAR#1508
  Calico Rock .... GRAR#1503
AR Camden
  Bethesda .... GRAR#1302
  Camden .... GRAR#1303
  Fellowship .... GRAR#1309
AR Charleston
  Marietta .... GRAR#1408
AR Dardanelle
  Gum Springs .... GRAR#1206
AR Dolph
  Trimble Camp Ground .. GRAR#1504
AR Dover
  Dover .... GRAR#1203
AR Fayetteville
  Grace .... GRAR#1405
AR Fort Smith
  Fort Smith .... GRAR#1406
AR Grapevine
  Pine Ridge .... GRAR#1105

AR Hampton
  Camp Ground .... GRAR#1101
AR Hector
  Hector .... GRAR#1207
AR Horatio
  Dilworth .... GRAR#1304
AR Hot Springs
  Lake Hamilton .... GRAR#1221
AR Jordan
  Rodney .... GRAR#1513
AR Little Rock
  Arkansas Loving .... GRAR#2135
AR Lockesburg
  Falls Chapel .... GRAR#1308
  Lockesburg .... GRAR#1311
  Provo .... GRAR#1314
AR London
  Mt Carmel .... GRAR#1212
AR Louann
  Sulphur Springs .... GRAR#1315
AR Magazine
  Old Union .... GRAR#1409
  Walnut Grove .... GRAR#1414
AR Magnolia
  Walkerville .... GRAR#1317
AR Melbourne
  Mt Olive .... GRAR#1517
AR Monticello
  Rose Hill .... GRAR#1106
AR Morrilton
  Trinity .... GRAR#1219
AR Mount Pleasant
  Barren Fork .... GRAR#1501
AR Mountain Home
  Fellowship .... GRAR#1505
AR Oxford
  Oxford .... GRAR#1511
AR Palestine
  Palestine .... GRAR#1103
AR Paris
  Shaver .... GRAR#1413
AR Pine Bluff
  Pine Bluff 1st .... GRAR#1104
  Shell Chapel .... GRAR#1108
AR Pineville
  Pineville .... GRAR#1512
AR Pottsville
  Mars Hill .... GRAR#1211
AR Prairie Grove
  Prairie Grove .... GRAR#1412
AR Ratcliff
  Caulksville .... GRAR#1402
AR Russellville
  Russellville .... GRAR#1216
AR Salem
  Salem .... GRAR#1514
AR Searcy
  Gum Springs .... GRAR#1205
  Pleasant Grove .... GRAR#1214
  Searcy .... GRAR#1218
AR Sherwood
  Sherwood .... GRAR#1220
AR Strawberry
  Milligan Camp Ground GRAR#1516
AR Waldron
  Pilot Prairie .... GRAR#1411

BRAZIL

BR Bahia
    Mata de Sao Joao .... GRAR#8313

CALIFORNIA

CA San Francisco
    Chinese..........................MSDC#8501
    Grace .... MSDC#8510
    Redeemer .... MSDC#8512
CA Trona
    Trona .... MSDC#8503

COLOMBIA

CO Antioquia
    Horeb-Central .... MSAN#8915
    El Rebano..................... MSAN#8905
    La Rosa De Saron .... MSAN#8911
    Zamora .... MSAN#8918
CO Buenaventura
    Divino Redentor............ MSAN#8206
    Emaus........................... MSCA#8219
CO Caldas
    Manizales .... MSAN#8914
CO Cali
    Betania Mission .... MSAN#8204
    Bethel .... MSCA#8205
    Central.......................... MSCA#8208
    Filipos .... MSCA#8211
    Nueva Esperanza........... MSCA#8221
    Nueva Jerusalen .... MSCA#8222
    Principe De Paz............. MSCA#8201
    Renacer .... MSCA#8225
    Samaria .... MSCA#8217
    San Marcos................... MSCA#8218
CO El Cerrito
    Getsemani .... MSCA#8210
CO Guacari
    San Pablo .... MSCA#8212
CO Guapi
    Maranatha .... MSCA#8220
CO Montebello
    Caleb Mission .... MSCA#8223
CO Palmira
    San Lucas..................... MSCA#8215
CO Popayan
    Popayan........................ MSCA#8227
CO Quindio
    Armenia........................ MSAN#8903
CO Risaralda
    Dosquebradas............... MSAN#8907
    La Virginia .... MSCA#8913
    Pereira .... MSAN#8916
CO Tulua
    Tulua Mission............... MSCA#8226
CO Valle
    Cartago......................... MSAN#8906

FLORIDA

FL Dade City
    Immanuel .... SEGR#0311
FL Lutz
    Christ............................ SEGR#0303
FL Miami
    El Camino .... SEGR#0310
FL Tampa
    First Hispanic .... SEGR#0307
FL Valrico
    Hope............................. SEGR#0308
FL Wimauma

GEORGIA

GA Chatsworth
    Sumach...........................SETG#2124
GA Duluth
    Glory Church of Jesus.....SETG#2144
    Korean Living Stone.......SETG#2130
GA Lawrenceville
    El Redil ....SETG#2149
GA Rydal
    Bartow...........................SETG#2101

HONG KONG

HO Cheung Chau
    Cheung Chau................. MSHK#8801
HO Kowloon
    Kowloon Chapel .... MSHK#8803
    Tao Hsien .... MSHK#8806
HO Landau Island
    Mu Min .... MSHK#8810
HO NT
    Yao Dao........................ MSHK#8811
HO North Point
    North Point................... MSHK#8805
HO Shatin NT
    Shatin .... MSHK#8807
HO Tseung Kwan O NT
    Po Lam .... MSHK#8808
HO Yuen Long
    Xi Lin .... MSHK#8809

ILLINOIS

IL Anna
    Camp Ground.................. MICO#5103
IL Annapolis
    Pleasant Grove .... MICO#5210
IL Beecher City
    Spring Hill...................... MINC#5411
IL Bethany
    Bethany .... MINC#5401
IL Brookport
    Mt. Sterling .... MICO#5117
IL Buncombe
    Ebenezer Hall.................. MICO#5106
IL Burnt Prairie
    Burnt Prairie................... MINC#5102
IL Carriers Mills
    Providence...................... MICO#5122
IL Casey
    Casey............................ MINC#5201
IL Chicago
    Ebenezer....................... MINC#5203
IL Cisne
    Elm River .... MINC#5107
IL Dongola
    Mt Zion .... MICO#5118
IL Dundee
    Comunidad Cristiana ...... MINC#5212
IL Fairfield
    Cumberland Chapel .... MINC#5104
    Fairfield......................... MINC#5108
    Lebanon North .... MINC#5113
    Union North .... MINC#5124
IL Farmer City
    Fullerton....................... MINC#5404
IL Galatia
    Lebanon South .... MINC#5114
    Union Chapel .... MICO#5123
IL Georgetown
    Georgetown.................... MINC#5204

IL Greenville
    Campground................... MINC#5402
    Mt. Gilead .... MINC#5406
IL Lincoln
    Lincoln 1st .... MINC#5405
IL Martinsville
    Willow Creek .... MINC#5211
IL Norris City
    Mt Oval .... MINC#5116
    United........................... MINC#5119
    Village .... MICO#5125
IL Petersburg
    Petersburg...................... MINC#5408
IL Simpson
    Gilead............................ MICO#5110
IL Thompsonville
    Ebenezer......................... MICO#5105
IL Trilla
    Good Prospect................. MINC#5205
IL Virginia
    Shiloh........................... MINC#5409
IL Yale
    New Hope .... MINC#5208

INDIANA

IN Chandler
    Chandler........................ MICO#5302
IN Evansville
    Morningside .... MINC#5304
IN Indianapolis
    Christ............................ MINC#5305
IN Monroe City
    Monroe City .... MINC#5307
IN Petersburg
    Knights Chapel................ MINC#5306
IN Washington
    Mt Olivet....................... MINC#5308

IOWA

IA New London
    Shinar........................... MINC#5410

JAPAN

JA 184-0011
    Higashi Koganei.............. MSJA#8301
JA 186-0002
    Kunitachi Nozomi........... MSJA#8306
JA 194-0041
    Naruse .... MSJA#8305
JA 207-0023
    Megumi......................... MSJA#8309
JA 228-0004
    Sagamino....................... MSJA#8304
JA 228-0818
    Den-en Mission.............. MSJA#8310
JA 241-0021
    Asahi Mission Point........ MSJA#8315
JA 241-0825
    Kibougaoka.................... MSJA#8302
JA 242-0006
    Koza............................. MSJA#8303
JA 243-0422
    Ebina Shion No.............. MSJA#8311
JA 245-0016
    Izumi Mission .... MSJA#8312
JA 259-1321
    Sibusawa....................... MSJA#8307
JA 272-0834
    Ichikawa Grace Mission . MSJA#8314

LOCATION INDEX OF CHURCHES CONTINUED

KENTUCKY

KY Auburn
    Auburn...........................MICU#3301
    Gasper River ....MICU#3306
KY Beaver Dam
    Point Pleasant................MICU#3313
KY Benton
    Benton...........................MICO#3403
    Oak Grove.....................MICO#3412
KY Big Clifty
    Mt Olive........................MICU#3216
KY Bowling Green
    Bowling Green...............MICU#3304
    Mt Olivet......................MICU#3312
KY Bremen
    Brier Creek....................MICU#3503
    Fairview ....MICU#3504
KY Calvert City
    Oakland.........................MICO#3413
    Vaughn's Chapel............MICO#3423
KY Campbellsville
    Campbellsville ....MICO#3104
    Good Hope.....................MICU#3109
    Liberty...........................MICU#3116
    Shiloh ....MICU#3129
KY Caneyville
    Caneyville ....MICU#3201
    Mt Pleasant...................MICU#3217
KY Canmer
    Hopewell.......................MICU#3112
KY Center
    Bethel ....MICU#3102
    Seven Springs................MICU#3128
KY Clay
    Lisman...........................MICO#3613
    Oak Grove Union...........MICO#3619
KY Dalton
    Macedonia......................MICO#3614
KY Eastview
    Needham ....MICU#3219
KY Edmonton
    Cedar Flat......................MICU#3106
KY Falls of Rough
    Short Creek ....MICU#3221
KY Fredonia
    Fredonia ....MICO#3608
    Good Spring...................MICO#3609
KY Garfield
    Garfield ....MICU#3208
KY Glasgow
    Glasgow ....MICU#3108
    Lick Branch...................MICU#3117
    Neal's Chapel ....MICU#3122
KY Glens Fork
    Mt Zion ....MICU#3121
KY Greensburg
    Greensburg ....MICU#3110
    Salem............................MICU#3127
KY Greenville
    Greenville......................MICU#3505
KY Guthrie
    Gill's Chapel..................MICU#3307
KY Hardin
    Unity ....MICO#3422
KY Hardyville
    Monroe Chapel...............MICU#3119
KY Harned
    Ephesus ....MICU#3205
    Freedom ....MICU#3207
KY Harrodsburg

Bethel #1 ....MICU#3103
    Harrodsburg ....MICU#3111
KY Hartford
    Beulah ....MICU#3501
KY Hawesville
    Dukes ....MICU#3204
KY Herndon
    Flat Lick........................MICO#3606
KY Hopkinsville
    Hopkinsville...................MICO#3611
KY Horse Cave
    Clear Point ....MICU#3107
KY Hudson
    Coyle ....MICU#3203
KY Irvington
    Clifton Mills..................MICU#3202
    Irvington........................MICU#3210
KY Kevil
    Bethel ....MICO#3404
    Pleasant Valley ....MICU#3418
KY Knob Lick
    Antioch..........................MICU#3101
    Wisdom ....MICU#3130
KY Leitchfield
    Leitchfield ....MICU#3211
    Mt Vernon ....MICU#3218
KY Lewisburg
    Green Ridge ....MICU#3308
    Lewisburg......................MICU#3309
KY Louisville
    Heartsong ....MICU#3222
    Louisville 1st.................MICU#3212
KY Madisonville
    Madisonville ....MICO#3615
KY Magnolia
    Magnolia ....MICU#3214
KY Marion
    Marion First ....MICO#3616
    Piney Fork ....MICO#3620
    Sugar Grove ....MICO#3626
KY Marrowbone
    Casey's Fork ....MICU#3105
KY Mayfield
    Calvary..........................MICO#3405
    Rozzell Chapel...............MICO#3419
KY Morgantown
    Little Muddy ....MICU#3310
    Morgantown...................MICU#3311
KY Murray
    Liberty...........................MICO#3406
    North Pleasant Grove.....MICO#3411
KY Nebo
    Rose Creek ....MICO#3622
KY Owensboro
    Owensboro ....MICU#3509
    Pleasant Hill..................MICU#3510
KY Paducah
    Highland........................MICO#3414
    Margaret Hank ....MICO#3415
    New Hope ....MICO#3410
    Woodlawn ....MICO#3417
KY Philpot
    Mt Zion ....MICU#3507
KY Providence
    Providence 1st................MICU#3621
KY Radcliff
    Radcliff..........................MICU#3220
KY Rumsey
    New Cypress ....MICU#3508
KY Russellville
    Bald Knob......................MICU#3302
KY Sacramento

Poplar Grove ....MICU#3511
    Sacramento.....................MICU#3512
KY Salem
    Hopewell.......................MICO#3610
KY Sturgis
    Sturgis ....MICO#3625
KY Sullivan
    Mt. Pleasant...................MICO#3618
KY Summer Shade
    Mt Moriah ....MICU#3120
KY Summersville
    Oak Forest.....................MICU#3123
KY Water Valley
    Bayou de Chien.............MICU#3401
KY West Paducah
    Milburn Chapel ....MICU#3416
KY West Somerset
    High Point ....MICU#3314
KY Wheatcroft
    Wheatcroft.....................MICO#3627
KY White Plains
    Mt Carmel ....MICO#3617

KOREA

KO Seoul
    Korea 1st........................SEET#2221
    Sumkim Presby ....SEET#2222

LOUISANA

LA Pleasant Hill
    Progress.........................MSTR#8123
LA Quitman
    Antioch..........................MSTR#8101

MACAU, PORTUGUESE PROVINCE

MA Andar LMN
    Macau...........................MSHK#8804

MASSACHUSETTS

MA Malden
    Casa De Fe ....SEET#2220

MARYLAND

MD Salisbury
    Our Good ....SETG#2138

MICHIGAN

MI Lincoln Park
    Grace.............................MINC#5502
MI St Clair Shores
    Faith ....MINC#5501

MISSISSIPPI

MS Ackerman
    Enon ....SEGR#0707
MS Cedarbluff
    Cairo.............................SEGR#0704
MS Columbus
    Beersheba......................SEGR#0702
    Columbus ....SEGR#0706
    Mt Zion ....SEGR#0709
MS Corinth
    Shiloh ....GRWT#9226
MS Falkner
    Mt Zion ....GRWT#9214

LOCATION INDEX OF CHURCHES CONTINUED

LOCATION INDEX OF CHURCHES CONTINUED

INDEX

CUMBERLAND PRESBYTERIAN CHURCH IN AMERICA

Denominational Center
226 Church Street, NW, Huntsville, AL 35801
(256)536-7481 OR FAX (256)536-7482
cpcaga@aol.com

Moderator of the General Assembly:
    Rev. Elton Hall, 305 Tiffton Circle, Hewitt, TX 76643, (254)799-5975

Vice-Moderator of the General Assembly:
    Rev. William Robinson, 15817 Mooresville Road, Athens, AL 35613, (256)262-9128

Administrative Director of the Cumberland Presbyterian Church in America:
    Rev. Dr. G. Lynne Herring, 3244 Vicksburg SW, Decatur, AL 35603
    (256)536-7481(w), (256)355-7677(h)

Stated Clerk of the General Assembly:
    Rev. Theodis Acklin, 3415 Mason Lake Road, Huntsville, AL 35810, (256)852-3229

Engrossing Clerk of the General Assembly:
    Rev. Lela Fencher, 620 Live Oak Circle, Fairfield, AL 35064, (205)780-4913

Church Paper: *THE CUMBERLAND FLAG*
    Editor: Rev. Dr. G. Lynne Herring, 3244 Vicksburg SW, Decatur, AL 35603
    (256)536-7481(w), (256)355-7677(h)

SYNODS - PRESBYTERIES - STATED CLERKS

Alabama Synod - Elder Vanessa Midgett, 118 Thunderbird Drive, Harvest, AL 35749
1. Birmingham Presbytery - Rev. Teresa Paige, 1739 51st Street Ensley, Birmingham, AL 35203
2. Florence Presbytery - Rev. Dr. Laurentis Barnett, 220 Wedgewood Terrace Road, Madison, AL 35757
3. Huntsville Presbytery - Rev. Dr. Theodis Acklin, 3415 Mastin Lake Road, Huntsville, AL 35810
4. South Alabama Presbytery - Elder Minnie McMillian, 54 Riverview Avenue, Selma, AL 36701
5. Tennessee Valley Presbytery - Rev. Jacqueline Lang, 904-35th Avenue, Tuscaloosa, AL
6. Tuscaloosa Presbytery - Rev. Critis Fletcher, 68 Mattie Street, Russellville, AL 35654

Kentucky Synod - Elder Leon Cole, Jr., PO Box 335, Warren, MI 48090
1. Cleveland, Ohio Presbytery - Elder Leon Cole, PO Box 335, Warren, MI 48090
2. Kansouri Presbytery - Elder Diane Smith, 2025 North St. Louis Avenue, Tulsa, OK 74106
3. Ohio Valley Presbytery - Elder Mary Powell, PO Box 85, Providence, KY 42450
4. Purchase Presbytery - Elder James Stubblefield, 59 Circle Drive, Mayfield, KY 42066

Tennessee Synod - Rev. Anthony Hollis, 1100 Gateway Avenue, Apt 12-200, Chattanooga, TN 37402
1. Elk River Presbytery - Elder Jacquelyn Cooper, 4705 Indian Summer Drive, Nashville, TN 37207
2. Hiwassee Presbytery - Elder Demetrius Ramsey, 228 Wool Street, Charleston, TN 37310
3. New Hopewell Presbytery - Elder Cecelia Bowden, PO Box 661, Huntington, TN 38344

Texas Synod - Rev.Robert E Thomas, 1017 N Englewood, Tyler, TX 76643
1. Angelina Presbytery - Elder Tom Jones, 739 County Road 4720, Troup, TX 75789
2. Brazos Presbytery - Elder Toni Evans, 1200 Lake Air Drive, PMB 170, Waco, TX 76710
3. East Texas Presbytery - Elder Kay Ward Creer, 1723 County Road 421N., Henderson, TX 75652

CUMBERLAND PRESBYTERIAN CENTER OFFICES
8207 TRADITIONAL PLACE
CORDOVA, TENNESSEE 38016

Central Telephone for Center Offices: (901)276-4572, Historical Foundation Telephone: (901)276-8602

BOARD OF STEWARDSHIP, FOUNDATION AND BENEFITS
Phone (901)276-4572   FAX (901)272-3913
Robert Heflin, Executive Secretary
   rah@cumberland.org   Ext-207
Mark Duck, Coordinator of Benefits
   rmd@cumberland.org   Ext-204
Kathryn Gilbert Craig, Administrative Assistant
   kgc@cumberland.org   Ext-206

CENTRAL SERVICES
Phone (901)276-4572   FAX (901)272-3913
Dan Scherf, Accounting Supervisor
   dscherf@cumberland.org   Ext-233
Matthew Gore, Computer Services
   mhg@cumberland.org   Ext-252

GENERAL ASSEMBLY OFFICE
Phone (901)276-4572   FAX (901)272-3913
Michael Sharpe, Stated Clerk
   msharpe@cumberland.org   Ext-225
Elizabeth Vaughn, Assistant to the Stated Clerk
   eav@cumberland.org   Ext-226

HISTORICAL FOUNDATION OF THE CPC & CPCA
Phone (901)276-8602   FAX (901)272-3913
Susan Knight Gore, Archivist
   skg@cumberland.org
Lauren Gam Gilliland, Archival Assistant
   lgilliland@cumberland.org

MINISTRY COUNCIL
Phone (901)276-4572   FAX (901)276-4578
Edith Old, Director of Ministries
   eold@cumberland.org   Ext-228
Megan Warren, Executive Assistant to the Director of Ministries
   mwarren@cumberland.org   Ext-217

PASTORAL DEVELOPMENT MINISTRY TEAM
Phone (901)276-4572   FAX (901)276-4578
Team Leader -- Position Vacant

COMMUNICATIONS MINISTRY TEAM
Phone (901)276-4572   FAX (901)276-4578
Mark J. Davis, Team Leader/Editor
   mdavis@cumberland.org   Ext-216
Sowgand Sheikholeslami, Senior Art Director
   sowgand@cumberland.org   Ext-211

CP RESOURCES
resources@cumberland.org   (901)276-4581

DISCIPLESHIP MINISTRY TEAM
Phone (901)276-4572   FAX (901)276-4578
Elinor Brown, Team Leader
   esb@cumberland.org   Ext-205
Matthew Gore, Resources Development
   & Distribution
   mhg@cumberland.org   Ext-252
Susan Groce, Youth & Young Adult Ministry
   scg@cumberland.org   Ext-218
Cindy Martin, Adult & Third Age Ministry
   chm@cumberland.org   Ext-219
Jodi Rush, Children & Family Ministry
   jhr@cumberland.org   Ext-223

MISSIONS MINISTRY TEAM
Phone (901)276-4572   FAX (901)276-4578
Milton Ortiz, Team Leader
   mortiz@cumberland.org   Ext-234
Jinger Ellis, Administration/Finance
   jellis@cumberland.org   Ext-230
Pam Phillips-Burk, Congregational/Women's Ministry
   pam@cumberland.org   Ext-203
Johan Daza, Cross Culture Ministries USA
   jdaza@cumberland.org   Ext-202
T.J. Malinoski, Evangelism & New Church Development
   tmalinoski@cumberland.org   Ext-232
Lynn Thomas, Global Cross Culture Missions
   4833 Caldwell Mill Lane, Birmingham, AL 35242 Ext-261
   lynndont@gmail.com   (205)601-5770

OTHER CHURCH OFFICES

BETHEL UNIVERSITY
325 Cherry Avenue, McKenzie, TN 38201
Phone (731)352-4000   FAX (731)352-6387
Walter Butler, Interim President
Dale Henry, Vice President for Development
Steve Perryman, Vice President for Finance
Nancy Bean, Vice President for College of Arts & Sciences
Roland Colson, Vice President for College of Public Service
Joe Hames, Vice President for College of Health Sciences
Kelly Kelley, Vice President for College of Professional Studies

CHILDREN'S HOME
909 Greenlee Street, Denton, TX 76201
   Mail Address: Drawer G, Denton, TX 76202
Phone (940)382-5112   FAX (940)387-0821
   cpch@cpch.org   www.cpch.org
Richard Brown, President, CEO & General Counsel   (817)360-6874
   rbrown@cpch.org
Larry Brown, Vice President, Development   Ext-258
   lbrown@cpch.org   (817)341-1235
Stephanie Brown, Chaplain   Ext-222
   sbrown@cpch.org

MEMPHIS THEOLOGICAL SEMINARY
168 East Parkway South, Memphis, TN 38104-4395
Phone (901)458-8232   FAX (901)452-4051
        www.MemphisSeminary.edu
Daniel J. Earheart-Brown, President
Cassandra Price-Perry, Vice-President of Operations/CFO
Stan Wood, Interim Vice-President of Academic Affairs/Dean
Cathi Johnson, Vice-President of Advancement
Laurie Sharpe, Executive Assistant to the President

OUR UNITED OUTREACH
4782 Waverly Court, Ooltewah, TN 37363
Cliff Hudson, Development Director   Phone (901)276-4572 Ext-210

PROGRAM OF ALTERNATE STUDIES
168 East Parkway South, Memphis, TN 38104-4395
Phone (901)334-5853   FAX (901)452-4051
Michael Qualls, Director
   mqualls@memphisseminary.edu
Karen Patten, Administrative Assistant
   kpatten@memphisseminary.edu

www.ingramcontent.com/pod-product-compliance
Lightning Source LLC
LaVergne TN
LVHW081316060426

835509LV00015B/1540